Right-Wing Radicalism

This book highlights recent developments in the radical right providing comparative analysis of current extremist activity in Eastern and Western Europe and the US. It reveals the growing amount of connections and continuities of right-wing movements and ideologies across national borders. Subjects covered include:

- Who joins radical right parties and why?
- Recent developments in parties in Eastern and Western Europe
- The transatlantic cross-fertilization of ideological perspectives
- How the US extreme right has changed since the emergence of the Tea Party movement

This will be essential reading for all students and scholars with an interest in the contemporary radical right and extremism.

Sabine von Mering is Associate Professor of German and Women's and Gender Studies and Director of the Center for German and European Studies at Brandeis University in Waltham, Massachusetts, US.

Timothy Wyman McCarty is Visiting Assistant Professor of Government at Franklin & Marshall College in Lancaster, Pennsylvania, US. His research and teaching focuses on political theory, the history of ideas, and literature and politics.

Routledge Studies in Extremism and Democracy

Series Editors: Roger Eatwell, *University of Bath*, and Matthew Goodwin, *University of Nottingham*.
Founding Series Editors: Roger Eatwell, *University of Bath* and Cas Mudde, *University of Antwerp-UFSIA*.

This new series encompasses academic studies within the broad fields of 'extremism' and 'democracy'. These topics have traditionally been considered largely in isolation by academics. A key focus of the series, therefore, is the (inter-)relation between extremism and democracy. Works will seek to answer questions such as to what extent 'extremist' groups pose a major threat to democratic parties, or how democracy can respond to extremism without undermining its own democratic credentials.

The books encompass two strands:

Routledge Studies in Extremism and Democracy includes books with an introductory and broad focus which are aimed at students and teachers. These books will be available in hardback and paperback. Titles include:

Understanding Terrorism in America
From the Klan to al Qaeda
Christopher Hewitt

Fascism and the Extreme Right
Roger Eatwell

Racist Extremism in Central and Eastern Europe
Edited by Cas Mudde

Political Parties and Terrorist Groups (2nd Edition)
Leonard Weinberg, Ami Pedahzur and Arie Perliger

The New Extremism in 21st Century Britain
Edited by Roger Eatwell and Matthew Goodwin

New British Fascism: Rise of the British National Party
Matthew Goodwin

The End of Terrorism?
Leonard Weinberg

Mapping the Extreme Right in Contemporary Europe: From Local to Transnational
Edited by Andrea Mammone, Emmanuel Godin and Brian Jenkins

Varieties of Right-Wing Extremism in Europe
Edited by Andrea Mammone, Emmanuel Godin and Brian Jenkins

Right-Wing Radicalism Today
Perspectives from Europe and the US
*Edited by Sabine von Mering and
Timothy Wyman McCarty*

Routledge Research in Extremism and Democracy offers a forum for innovative new research intended for a more specialist readership. These books will be in hardback only. Titles include:

1. **Uncivil Society?**
   Contentious Politics in
   Post-Communist Europe
   *Edited by Petr Kopecky and
   Cas Mudde*

2. **Political Parties and
   Terrorist Groups**
   *Leonard Weinberg and
   Ami Pedahzur*

3. **Western Democracies and
   the New Extreme Right
   Challenge**
   *Edited by Roger Eatwell and
   Cas Mudde*

4. **Confronting Right Wing
   Extremism and Terrorism in
   the USA**
   George Michael

5. **Anti-Political Establishment
   Parties**
   A Comparative Analysis
   Amir Abedi

6. **American Extremism**
   History, Politics and the Militia
   D. J. Mulloy

7. **The Scope of Tolerance:**
   Studies on the Costs of Free
   Expression and Freedom of
   the Press
   Raphael Cohen-Almagor

8. **Extreme Right Activists
   in Europe**
   Through the magnifying glass
   *Bert Klandermans and
   Nonna Mayer*

9. **Ecological Politics and
   Democratic Theory**
   Mathew Humphrey

10. **Reinventing the Italian Right**
    Territorial Politics, Populism
    and 'Post-Fascism'
    *Carlo Ruzza and
    Stefano Fella*

11. **Political Extremes**
    An Investigation into the
    History of Terms and
    Concepts from Antiquity to
    the Present
    Uwe Backes

12. **The Populist Radical Right
    in Poland**
    The Patriots
    Rafal Pankowski

13. **Social and Political Thought of
    Julius Evola**
    Paul Furlong

14. **Radical Left Parties
    in Europe**
    Luke March

15. **Counterterrorism in Turkey**
    Policy Choices and Policy
    Effects toward the Kurdistan
    Workers' Party (PKK)
    Mustafa Coşar Ünal

16. **Class Politics and the
    Radical Right**
    Edited by Jens Rydgren

17. **Rethinking the French
    New Right**
    Alternatives to modernity
    Tamir Bar-On

18. **Ending Terrorism in Italy**
    Anna Bull and Philip Cooke

Right-Wing Radicalism Today
Perspectives from Europe and the US

Edited by
Sabine von Mering and
Timothy Wyman McCarty

Routledge
Taylor & Francis Group
LONDON AND NEW YORK

First published 2013
by Routledge
2 Park Square, Milton Park, Abingdon, Oxon OX14 4RN

Simultaneously published in the USA and Canada
by Routledge
711 Third Avenue, New York, NY 10017

Routledge is an imprint of the Taylor & Francis Group, an informa business

© 2013 Selection and editorial matter Sabine von Mering and Timothy Wyman McCarty; contributors, their contributions

The right of Sabine von Mering and Timothy Wyman McCarty to be identified as editors of this work has been asserted by them in accordance with the Copyright, Designs and Patent Act 1988.

All rights reserved. No part of this book may be reprinted or reproduced or utilised in any form or by any electronic, mechanical, or other means, now known or hereafter invented, including photocopying and recording, or in any information storage or retrieval system, without permission in writing from the publishers.

Trademark notice: Product or corporate names may be trademarks or registered trademarks, and are used only for identification and explanation without intent to infringe.

British Library Cataloguing in Publication Data
A catalogue record for this book is available from the British Library

Library of Congress Cataloging in Publication Data
Right-wing radicalism today : perspectives from Europe and the US /
Edited by Sabine von Mering and Timothy Wyman McCarty.
    p. cm. – (Routledge studies in extremism and democracy)
    Includes bibliographical references and index.
    Radicalism–Europe. 2. Radicalism–United States. 3. Right-wing extremists–Europe. 4. Right-wing extremists–United States. I. Von Mering, Sabine. II. McCarty, Timothy Wyman.
    JC573.2.E85R54 2013
    320.5–dc23
                        2012044264

ISBN: 978-0-415-62723-8 (hbk)
ISBN: 978-0-415-62728-3 (pbk)
ISBN: 978-0-203-38163-2 (ebk)

Typeset in Times New Roman
by Taylor & Francis Books

Printed and bound by CPI Group (UK) Ltd, Croydon, CR0 4YY

Contents

List of illustrations ix
List of contributors x

1 Introduction 1
SABINE VON MERING AND TIMOTHY WYMAN MCCARTY

2 Globalized anti-globalists: the ideological basis of the internationalization of right-wing extremism 13
THOMAS GRUMKE

3 Right-wing extremism and populism in contemporary Germany and Western Europe 22
HANS-GERD JASCHKE

4 "National solidarity—no to globalization": the economic and sociopolitical platform of the National Democratic Party of Germany (NPD) 37
GIDEON BOTSCH AND CHRISTOPH KOPKE

5 Extreme right activists: recruitment and experiences 60
BERT KLANDERMANS

6 A comparative look at right-wing extremism, anti-Semitism, and xenophobic hate crimes in Poland, Ukraine, and Russia 85
JOACHIM KERSTEN AND NATALIA HANKEL

7 Welfare chauvinism, ethnic heterogeneity and conditions for the electoral breakthrough of radical right parties: evidence from Eastern Europe 106
LENKA BUSTIKOVA

8	From Tea Parties to militias: between the Republican Party and the insurgent ultra-right in the US CHIP BERLET	124
9	Cycles of right-wing terror in the US PETE SIMI	144
10	Adolf Hitler's *Mein Kampf*: a book of the past in the present OTHMAR PLÖCKINGER	161
	Afterword KATHLEEN BLEE	172
	Bibliography *Index*	174 193

Illustrations

Figures

6.1	Social distance of Ukranians to other ethnicities 1994–2006	93
6.2	General indicators of national tolerance in Ukraine (% of population)	94
6.3	Number of xenophobic offenses 2004–09	99
6.4	Sentenced offenders: right-wing extremist violence 2004–09	100
7.1	Ideal types of mainstream parties configurations	111
7.2	Comprehensive configuration, no radical parties	115
7.3	Policy positions of the major parties and the radical party in targeted configurations	116
7.4	Targeted configuration with radical parties	117
7.5	Radicalized large major parties	118
10.1	Heinrich Himmler's personal copy of *Mein Kampf* Vol. 2 by Adolf Hitler, 1927	162
10.2	Gerhard Hauptmann's personal copy of *Mein Kampf*	163
10.3	Number of copies sold of *Mein Kampf* in Germany 1925–32	164
10.4	Number of copies sold of *Mein Kampf* in Germany 1925–44	165
10.5	Satirical proposal for comments on *Mein Kampf* in a scholarly edition	169

Tables

3.1	Crimes with a right-wing extremist background in Germany	29
3.2	Right-wing extremist organizations banned by the German Federal Ministry from January 1990 to March 2009	31
3.3	Right-wing extremist parties in Western Europe	32
5.1	Right-wing extremism: demand and supply	63
6.1	Survey of political and social values and attitudes	87
7.1	Party names	107

Contributors

Chip Berlet is a journalist and independent scholar studying right-wing social movements in the US. His writings on scapegoating, conspiracism, and apocalyptic aggression have appeared in popular and academic serials and books. Berlet coauthored (with Matthew N. Lyons) Right-Wing Populism in America (Guilford, 2000); his chapter on populist resentment appeared in Steep: The Precipitous Rise of the Tea Party (University of California Press, 2012). Berlet coordinated the revisions for the entry on "Neo-Nazism" for the second edition of the Encyclopaedia Judaica, and contributed a chapter to The Sacred in Twentieth Century Politics: Essays in Honour of Professor Stanley G. Payne (Palgrave Macmillan, 2008).

Kathleen Blee is Distinguished Professor of Sociology at the University of Pittsburgh, US. She has published widely on gender and the far right, especially the increasing role of women in right-wing extremist movements in the US and Europe. She is the author of many books, including Inside Organized Racism: Women in the Hate Movement (University of California Press, 2002), Women of The Klan: Racism and Gender in the 1920s (University of California Press, 2012), and Women of the Right: Comparisons and Interplay Across Borders (Penn State University Press, 2012), co-edited with Sandra McGee Deutsch.

Gideon Botsch, DrPhil, studied political sciences at the Free University Berlin, Germany. He is Research Assistant at Moses Mendelssohn Zentrum Potsdam, and Lecturer at the University of Potsdam, and teaches modern Jewish history and the Holocaust at Touro College Berlin. His research focuses on right-wing extremism, nationalism, racism and anti-Semitism past and present, and on National Socialism and its crimes against humanity. Recently he has published the first comprehensive history of post-war Germany's far-right and ultra-nationalist movement: Die extreme Rechte in der Bundesrepublik Deutschland: 1949 bis heute (Wissenschaftliche Buchgesellschaft, 2012).

Lenka Bustikova holds a PhD in political science from Duke University, US, and Master's degrees from Harvard University, Central European University in Budapest, Hungary, and Charles University in Prague, Czech Republic. She is currently a postdoctoral fellow at Arizona State University in the US. Her research interests consider radical right voting, ethnic politics, democratization and clientelism in post-communist democracies.

Thomas Grumke has been a Professor of Political Science at the University of Applied Sciences for Public Administration and Management of North Rhine-Westphalia, Germany, since September 2012. Before that Grumke worked for more than eight years as a specialist on right-wing extremism at the Ministry of Interior of that state. He has published and lectured widely on the topic of political extremism, most recently: "Sozialismus ist braun. Kampagnenthemen als strategisches Instrument des Rechtsextremismus," in *"Wir oder Scharia"? Islamfeindschaft als Kampagnenthema im Rechtsextremismus*, edited by Wolfgang Benz and Thomas Pfeiffer (Schwalbach/Ts.: Wochenschau-Verlag, 2011).

Natalia Hankel heads the "Basis/assessment of politically motivated crime" department and is deputy chief of the "Central state security/counter-terrorism" division in the state office for criminal investigation at the police headquarters of the German state of Brandenburg. She completed a diploma in mathematics at Donetsk National University, Ukraine; an MA in Criminology and Police Science at Ruhr University in Bochum, Germany; and an MA in Police Administration and Police Management at the German Police University in Münster, Germany.

Hans-Gerd Jaschke is Professor of Political Science at the Berlin School of Economics and Law, Department of Police and Security Management in Germany. He has published widely on right-wing extremism in Germany and Europe since his research activities at the University of Frankfurt during the 1980s. His most recent studies deal with different forms of political extremism and the reactions of society and institutions. A second current focus is research on police and security in Europe.

Joachim Kersten is Professor and Head of the Police Science Department at the German Police University in Münster. He holds an MA in Political Science from McMaster University in Hamilton, Ontario, Canada; a PhD in Educational Science from the University of Tübingen, Germany; and a Habilitation in Sociology from the University of Konstanz, Germany. He has taught at the University of Melbourne in Australia; as an Asahi Fellow at Rikkyo University in Tokyo, Japan; and as DAAD Professor at Northwestern University in Evanston, Illinois, US. For nearly 20 years he has been a professor at universities for middle and senior management police officers. His publications include books and journal articles on juvenile prisons, youth violence, and gendered violence across cultures. At present he runs a European Union research project on minorities, police and restorative justice.

Bert Klandermans is Professor of Applied Social Psychology at the VU-University, Amsterdam, the Netherlands. His *Social Psychology of Protest* appeared in

1997. He is the editor and co-author (with Suzanne Staggenborg) of Methods of Social Movement Research (University of Minnesota Press, 2002) and (with Nonna Mayer) of Extreme Right Activists in Europe (Routledge, 2006). With Conny Roggeband he edited the Handbook of Social Movements Across Disciplines (Springer, 2007). He is the editor of Social Movements, Protest, and Contention, the prestigious book series of the University of Minnesota Press, and of Sociopedia.isa a new online database of review articles published by Sage in collaboration with the International Sociological Association. He is co-editor of Blackwell/Wiley's Encyclopedia of Social Movements.

Christoph Kopke, DrPhil, studied Political Sciences at the Free University Berlin, Germany. He is a lecturer at the University of Potsdam, and teaches Political Science at the Berlin School of Economics and Law. His research focuses on right-wing extremism, nationalism and anti-Semitism past and present, and on the history of National Socialism (NS), especially concentration camps and medicine in the NS era. He is currently working on a project about the persecution of Jewish physicians in Berlin from 1933 to 1945.

Timothy Wyman McCarty is Visiting Assistant Professor of Government at Franklin & Marshall College in Lancaster, Pennsylvania, US. His research and teaching focus on political theory, the history of ideas, and literature and politics. He has written on theories of political revolt and on politics in the work of Vladimir Nabokov. He is currently at work on a project that focuses on the relationship between taxation and democratic citizenship.

Othmar Plöckinger is a teacher of German language, history and mathematics at an evening high school in Salzburg, Austria. He is the author of Geschichte eines Buches (Oldenbourg, 2006) about Adolf Hitler's book Mein Kampf, and of Soldaten und Agitatoren (Schöningh, 2012) about early National Socialism in 1919–20. He is a member of the team of historians at the Munich, Germany Institut für Zeitgeschichte (Institute of Contemporary History), which is working on the scholarly edition of Mein Kampf.

Pete Simi is Associate Professor in the School of Criminology & Criminal Justice at the University of Nebraska at Omaha, US. His areas of interest include the social psychology of extremist identities, violence, and adolescent development. For the past 15 years he has been using ethnographic methods to study various facets of right-wing extremism in the US. He is the co-author of the book American Swastika: Inside the White Power Movement's Hidden Spaces of Hate (Rowman & Littlefield, 2010).

Sabine von Mering is Associate Professor of German and Women's and Gender Studies and Director of the Center for German and European Studies at Brandeis University in Waltham, Massachusetts, US. She received her PhD from the University of California Davis in 1998. Her research has covered a wide range of interests, including German women's drama, Jewish–German dialogue, German cinema, and international green politics. She is currently working on a project about climate change as a challenge for the humanities.

1 Introduction

*Sabine von Mering and
Timothy Wyman McCarty*

In recent years scholars have begun to recognize the surprising growth of various forms of international cooperation and identification among radical right-wing movements, especially in Europe. This book aims to explore this phenomenon further by opening up new directions for scholarly inquiry following trajectories of radical or extremist right-wing activity and thought across the European continent and even across the Atlantic to the US.[1] Although right-wing groups have for the most part avoided formally organizing across borders, there is a surprisingly long tradition of international networking of texts, ideologies, and tactics going back at least to the widespread distribution of such anti-Semitic texts as *The Protocols of the Elders of Zion* and Henry Ford's *The International Jew*. Contemporary developments suggest that such international networking is on the rise, and formal international cooperation among right-wing extremists may indeed be on the horizon. Scholars rightly have been critical of journalistic accounts that tend to overestimate the internationalization of right-wing extremism. However, recent studies have demonstrated the existence of some troubling trends. In particular, globalization and the rise of Islamophobia have provided renewed motivation for transnational cooperation and an increase in populist movements, while the simultaneous introduction of the Internet has supplied the medium. The studies in this volume investigate various manifestations of such trends and show that these developments are not restricted to the European continent alone.

Almost 25 years have passed since the Berlin Wall fell, which the communist regime had called the "anti-fascist protection wall" (*Antifaschistischer Schutzwall*). At the time the fall was hailed as the end of decades of fierce antagonism between the two opposing political ideologies in East and West, and expected to usher in a period of peaceful unification (first in Germany, then in Europe, and finally around the globe). Contrary to these expectations, Europe and the US are confronted today with radicals and extremists on multiple fronts. A time of global financial and economic uncertainty likely goes hand in hand with political radicalization, as those who see parallels between the present developments and those of the late 1920s are eager to point out.[2] However, speculations about the exact role of the Internet, Islamophobia, and globalization also raise many new questions and require readdressing questions we may have thought previously settled. Who are the people who join radical right-wing parties and extremist movements? What makes them join? What unites extremists' perspectives across national boundaries? What are they hoping to accomplish? Where are the boundaries between radical right-wing thought and extremist violence? How much more dangerous is this extremism in an increasingly interconnected world? Understanding and responding to these explosive political fringes has become increasingly difficult with rapid changes in the mechanisms of activism, recruitment, and communication. In this book we will focus primarily on what is generally described as a radical right-wing phenomenon and its extremist forms, although we are aware that the distinction between radicals on the left and right has always been blurred, not only in former communist countries, but also among radical elements in the US.

In Europe the growing influence of such parties as the French *Front National*, the Austrian *Freiheitliche Partei Österreichs*, the Dutch *Partij voor de Vrijheid*, and the Belgian *Vlaams Blok* proves that right-wing extremist thought is becoming a mainstream phenomenon. As David Art, who studies recent successes and failures of right-wing parties in Europe, observes in his book *Inside the Radical Right: The Development of Anti-Immigrant Parties in Western Europe*, "it is now difficult to imagine West European politics without radical right parties" (Art 2011: xi). Political developments in Hungary and Serbia suggest that former communist territories in Eastern Europe are equally if not more likely to embrace radical right-wing ideology. Compared to Europe, the US has seen relatively few radical challenges to its dominant two-party political system. Instead, developments in the US follow a different pattern, where individual radical acts seem more likely than radical movements. Scholars warn, however, that such acts must be understood as parts of a larger context, as Pete Simi argues: "When small groups and even single individuals commit acts of violence on behalf of a larger cause, these incidents should be viewed as part of a larger strategy of violence and not simply as random acts of isolated violence by deranged individuals" (Chapter 9, this volume).

In response to these developments, this volume draws together the work of scholars from Europe and the US, each of whom investigates contemporary radical right-wing activity from a distinct geographic and methodological perspective. This volume seeks to begin a transatlantic conversation among scholars of extremism across disciplines with deep regional expertise in the hope that their specialized knowledge may be brought to bear on what appears to be an increasingly prevalent problem. Through this conversation, we hope our readers gain an understanding not only of the particular trends of right-wing radicalism in Europe and the US, but also of the broader global context for these trends and their potential future direction.

The internationalization of right-wing radicalism

Cross-border collaborations among left-wing radicals have been a familiar phenomenon at least since Karl Marx and Mikhail Bakunin worked together in the *First Internationale*. By contrast, given its traditional embrace of nationalism and antipathy toward any forms of globalism, right-wing radicalism has tended to stick closer to home. However, in recent years a growing number of right-wingers have fused an anti-globalist ideology with a highly internationalist approach to activism.

This paradoxical stance points to a phenomenon that we aim to address in this volume, called by Thomas Grumke the "internationalization of right-wing extremism" (Chapter 2, this volume). Indeed, one of the most striking ironies underlying right-wing movements today is their professed antipathy towards the notion of international collaboration, a position that contrasts sharply with their steadily increased sharing of information and methods across borders. That the elite among right-wing nationalists unabashedly embrace and celebrate their unity was evident when 3,000 international supporters congregated in Vienna on January 27, 2012 to waltz at the traditional ball of Austria's right-wing fraternities on the day traditionally reserved for Holocaust commemoration (Paterson 2012). Free Party of Austria (Freiheitliche Partei Österreichs—FPÖ) chairman Heinz-Christian Strache fanned the flames when he claimed that the assembled had become "the new Jews" in a world dominated by left-wing extremists (almost 5,000 demonstrators staged a protest outside Vienna's Hofburg palace where the ball was held).[3] The incident confirms what Bert Klandermans explains in Chapter 5, namely that the stigmatization of right-wing radicals contributes to forging unity among them. Other uniting factors that connect right-wingers on both sides of the Atlantic are their shared belief in traditional gender roles, exaggerated militarism, and an exclusionary form of Christianity.

Even on the violent extremist end of the far-right spectrum there are signs of international ties. Anders Behring Breivik, the Norwegian who was found guilty of detonating a bomb in front of government buildings in Oslo and then going on to shoot 69 young people at a summer camp on the small Norwegian island of Utøya on July 22, 2011, is an example. On the day of the attack Breivik released his manifesto on the Internet detailing his plans for a "conservative cultural revolution" against the European tendency toward "cultural Marxism, multiculturalism, globalism, feminism, emotionalism, suicidal humanism, [and] egalitarianism" (Breivik 2011). The document draws upon a wide array of international sources such as the manifesto of the American "Unabomber" Ted Kaczynski, and pairs calls for a shared "duty as Europeans to prevent the annihilation of our identities" (ibid.) with demands to dismantle the European Union (EU) and boycott the United Nations (UN).

Globalization

Globalization in general is an obvious explanation for the growing internationalization of radical right-wing movements. Within Europe, the increasing impact of the EU on people's lives over the past two decades has inspired the paradoxical emergence of transnational cooperation among those opposed to

European unification. Perhaps most surprising on this front is the cooperation of radical right parties in the European Parliament, leading to the emergence of a class of what Dimitri Almeida has called "Europeanized Eurosceptics" (Almeida 2010: 237–53) which is primarily represented by the Members of the European Parliament (MEPs) in the "European Alliance of Freedom" (EAF). The group is made up of MEPs from the UK, Belgium, Austria, and Sweden, among several others. Although such efforts at formal organization of right-wing radicals on the European level have for the most part failed, their existence suggests that we have only just begun to see the effects of such transnational cooperation.[4]

Recognizing these trends, sociologist Jens Rydgren has analyzed the "cross-national diffusion" of a newly emergent "master frame combining ethno-nationalism based on 'cultural racism' (the so-called 'ethno-pluralist' doctrine) and a populist (but not antidemocratic) anti-political establishment rhetoric," which has slowly contributed to the rise of the extreme right in Europe over the course of the last four decades (Rydgren 2005: 413–37). The result is a growing shift toward an embrace of transnational conceptions of pan-Aryan identity, or in somewhat less radical contexts, shared white Christian heritage.

Right-wing extremists in the US have been ahead of their European counterparts in constructing a conception of a more global right-wing identity. In the US conceptions of a shared European heritage and identity—typically associated with the concept of whiteness—are much more familiar than on the other side of the Atlantic. Following the successes of the Civil Rights Movement in the US, many right-wing extremists regrouped in the 1980s under the auspices of what has sometimes been called "new racism."[5] In this context, white supremacists sought broader legitimacy by presenting "a version of white supremacy that is intellectualized, sanitized, and distanced from images of ignorance and violence," leading to the development of a "pan-ethnic imperative" in which "white supremacists find themselves reluctantly arguing for inclusion in an ethnic/minority cultural framework because they see it as a pragmatic approach that will help them in achieving their goals" (Berbrier 1998: 498–516).

However, even this conception of transnational white or European identity is not uncomplicated. In the first place, right-wing extremists share with much of mainstream American political culture a deep ambivalence toward Europe, given the dynamic of a sense of shared European heritage against the backdrop of a state forged in large part by those who purposefully left Europe behind, both through immigration and revolution.[6] Further complicating matters is the right-wing antipathy to contemporary European politics, which are seen by Americans as irredeemably socialist and otherwise beholden to left-wing ideologies.[7]

Islamophobia

Opposition to European unification traditionally arose in Europe among those who perceived the continental union as a threat to sovereignty in general, and to their own national identity in particular. This has begun to change as the growing influence of Islamophobia is contributing to the development of a pan-European conception of identity that right-wingers perceive as threatened by growing Muslim populations.[8] The move toward a post-national nationalism inspired by both European unification and Islamophobia could already be seen in attempts by far-right parties to oppose Turkey's bid for full membership in the EU (Zuquete 2008: 331). Although the opposition itself is unsurprising, it is nonetheless striking to see nationalist activists across Europe uniting in common cause to uphold a conception of the purity of the EU.

Difficulties with immigration and the integration of predominantly Muslim immigrants have been the key sources of the rise in right-wing extremist activity, as recent revelations and the continuing scandal surrounding investigations into the infamously labeled "Döner-Murders" in Germany confirm.[9] Indeed, the devastating killings in Norway at the end of July 2011 were only the most bloody in a string of events that highlight the difficulty Western countries are facing in the process of integrating mostly Muslim minorities.[10] The growing number of clashes between Islamic extremists and neo-Nazis in Germany in 2012 further served to highlight this growing dilemma. In many cases, too, politicians are fanning the flames: in August 2010, economist and Social Democratic Party (SPD) member Thilo Sarrazin had to resign from the German Federal Bank after causing a major stir with the publication of his book *Deutschland schafft sich ab. Wie wir unser Land aufs Spiel setzen* (*Germany Does Away with Itself. How we are Gambling with Our Country*), in which he criticized what he saw as the failure of German efforts at integrating "stupid" Muslim immigrants. German Chancellor Angela Merkel received a standing ovation in October 2010 after saying that "of course, the approach [to build] a multicultural [society] and to live side by side and to enjoy each other ... has failed, utterly failed" (BBC News 2010). In February 2011 British Prime Minister David Cameron claimed at a joint Munich conference with Merkel that it was due to the decades-old policy of multiculturalism that Islamic extremism was thriving in Britain, causing a storm of protest from British Muslims. In June of 2011 Dutch right-wing politician Geert Wilders, leader of the Freedom Party (*Partij voor de Vrijheid*) was acquitted of charges of "incitement to hatred and discrimination" that had been brought against him in conjunction with his controversial 2008 anti-Muslim film *Fitna*.[11] French right-wing politician Marine Le Pen, then still a contender for the French presidency, decided to remain silent in July 2011 after fellow *Front National* party member Jacques Coutela had called Breivik an 'icon' in an online blog post. Coutela was later suspended from the party.

While many European countries are seeing anti-Muslim activity increase and reach a level of mainstream acceptance, conservatives are stoking fears of the implementation of Sharia law in the US—most prominent among them the former Speaker of the House of Representatives Newt Gingrich, a failed contender for the Republican presidential nomination (Shane 2011). Even more pointedly than the EU, the perceived threat of Muslim immigrants and so-called 'creeping Sharia' (Boorstein 2010) has inspired not only transnational cooperation, but also a surprising move toward redefining the terms of right-wing politics in such a way as to draw more clearly a contrast with conceptions of Muslims. As Jose Pedro Zuquete has argued, "the concept of 'Islam' galvanizes group action: as the group rallies in 'defense' against Islamization, new issues emerge, existent issues heighten or decline in prominence, party objectives become reconsidered and new alliances form against the 'threat' of this 'common enemy'" (Zuquete 2008: 321–44).

This is evident in the rhetoric of the infamous Dutch politician Geert Wilders, whose steadfast anti-Islam stances have made him a hero to right-wingers across Europe and the US. As Zuquete shows, Wilders's vision for Europe nonetheless represents a departure from traditional right-wing radicalism. In attempts to draw the most pointed contrasts between his idealized Europe and the perceived threat posed by conservative Muslims, Wilders has been willing not only to invoke Enlightenment principles and "Judeo-Christian civilization," but also such unlikely markers of Western civilization as "liberal values mostly achieved since the 1960s, such as gay rights and gender equality" (Buruma 2011).

Such deceptively progressive rhetoric is not universally accepted among right-wing radicals, many if not most of whom continue to harbor traditional conservative views about culture and sovereignty, but it cannot be denied that the effort to draw contrasts between Islam and the (European) West have contributed to shifts in both rhetoric and tactics. The perception of Islam as a threat to Western civilization in general represents a further incentive for transnational cooperation among extreme right-wing activists. As the notion of defending Europe and the West from the influence of Islam has become dominant among right-wing radicals, "the defense of the original communities by these groups has been increasingly extended to the international level, and does not limit itself to the borders or territories of the country" (Zuquete 2008: 329). Since Islamophobia is also one of the key factors uniting members of the radical right in Europe with those in the US, we will likely see transnational political action increase in this area in the years ahead.

The Internet

The political and institutional incentives for the internationalization of right-wing radicalism represented by globalization and Islamophobia have been undoubtedly spurred on by the advent of mass communication technologies—most notably the Internet—which simplify the coordination and diffusion of tactics and ideas. The notion of Internet-fueled political activism has become so familiar as to seem nearly unremarkable, but in the context of traditional right-wing technophobia and emphasis on privacy, the degree to which the radical right has embraced the Internet as a means of communication and organization is perhaps something of a surprise. Despite this, right-wing extremists have been active from the earliest days of the Internet. As early as the mid-1980s, beginning with unsophisticated bulletin board networks such as the *Aryan Nations Liberty Net*, and emerging as a formidable web presence with the creation of the white supremacist hub *Stormfront* in 1995, "the far right has enthusiastically taken advantage of the new medium, and sees it as a powerful vehicle through which to spread its message" (Michael 2003: 179). In this vein, American white supremacist David Duke has said that "internet proficiency is as important to our cause as was learning to use a sword in the Middle Ages or a long rifle in the American Revolution" (Duke 1998, in Michael 2003: 179).

Yet, where many followed Duke in seeing the Internet "as a way to bypass the mainstream media and as a primary recruiting tool, like all activists, right-wing extremists have seen their high hopes for the internet somewhat blunted by reality" (Potok 2004: 53). The Internet has not yielded the boom in radical right-wing activity by empowering and activating the 'silent majority' as envisioned by Duke and others, but it has had the effect of establishing more wide-ranging networks, as "formerly isolated radical racists discovered like-minded people all over the country, and came to feel that they were part of a real movement—not simply social outcasts" (ibid.). Whether or not it has been effective in recruitment, the Internet has strengthened existing networks and provided opportunities for greater cooperation and communication, connecting extremists from around the world. Such networking also allows extremists to take advantage of different legal systems: while the publication of materials that deny the Holocaust and glorify the Nazis is illegal in Germany, for example, German extremists can freely download such materials from US sites where they are protected by the First Amendment.[12]

Scholarship: new directions

As extremists have responded to contemporary developments by looking beyond their traditionally sacrosanct borders in order to cope better with political realities, scholars of extremism must seek knowledge and methodological tools about these movements outside of national and disciplinary bounds. Comparativists in both political science and sociology have led the way in this regard and their work is invaluable in confronting the growing internationalization of right-wing radicalism. We seek to further the comparative project by drawing scholars with regional expertise together in this volume with the hopes of inspiring conversation across the traditional divisions of Western and Eastern Europe and the US.

How do the enduring features of right-wing radicalism relate to our rapidly changing world? The interdisciplinary articles in this volume seek to answer this question by highlighting the complex mechanisms contemporary right-wing radicals in Europe and the US develop in response to globalization. The scholars bring a diversity of methodological, geographic, and disciplinary expertise to bear on the problem of right-wing social movements on both sides of the Atlantic. While social science scholarship about the radical and extreme right has focused primarily on national developments, the articles in this volume demonstrate the shared ideologies, common mechanisms, and cultural continuities of right-wing radicalism that link individuals, movements, and ideologies across nations.

Thomas Grumke opens the volume with a seemingly counterintuitive look at the rise of what he labels "globalized anti-globalists." Grumke demonstrates that despite their explicit dedication to nationalism and antipathy toward multiculturalism, immigration, capitalism, globalization and almost all forms of global cooperation, right-wing extremists have entered into strategic alliances across borders and have even begun to craft ideological justifications for the development of a kind of "*Internationale* of nationalists." Not only are global right-wing extremist information networks growing rapidly, Grumke argues, but also a form of pan-Aryanism threatens to emerge as a powerful basis for worldwide radical activism.

Drawing on historical data from the post-war era up to the most recent developments, Hans-Gerd Jaschke shows how the National Democratic Party (*Nationaldemokratische Partei Deutschlands*—NPD) in Germany has developed since World War II. His analysis not only outlines its historical lineage, but also explores its role as a force in contemporary politics and contextualizes the NPD within the totality of right-wing activity in Germany today. Expanding from his focus on the NPD, Jaschke examines the broader political and sociological factors in contemporary Europe with an eye toward determining the likely role of right-wing radicalism in German and European politics in the coming years.

Gideon Botsch and Christoph Kopke present a detailed analysis of the sources and goals of the current platform of Germany's most prominent far right-wing party, the NPD. Through a careful study of NPD documents and public statements, Botsch and Kopke explore the promises made by the NPD platform, the rhetoric employed to persuade potential supporters, and the often surprising diversity of sources for the ideas and tactics involved in crafting and promoting the platform.

Bert Klandermans uses in-depth interview data to understand how activists in five European countries got involved in right-wing extremism and how this involvement has affected their lives. Drawing from interviews with right-wing extremist activists in Germany, France, Italy, Flanders, and the Netherlands, Klandermans reveals three dominant trajectories that lead to right-wing extremist activity. Mapping these trajectories along with political and sociological data from each country, Klandermans reveals the matrix of personal, political, and cultural factors that lead to right-wing extremist activity in contemporary Europe. In addition, his analysis explores how the shared experience of stigmatization helps to forge connections among activists and reinforce dedication to right-wing extremism.

Moving beyond Western Europe, Joachim Kersten and Natalia Hankel focus on the long-neglected radical right of Eastern Europe since the fall of the Soviet Union, presenting a detailed overview of right-wing developments within the countries of the former Warsaw Pact. Comparing the varieties of right-wing extremist activity—from the electoral participation of fringe right-wing parties to the proliferation of xenophobic and anti-Semitic hate crimes—in Poland, Russia, and Ukraine, Kersten and Hankel reveal the social, economic, and political forces contributing to these developments.

Lenka Bustikova continues the exploration of right-wing extremism in Eastern Europe with a theoretically rich investigation of the structural factors conditioning the success of extremist parties throughout the former Soviet bloc. Her analysis is detailed in its focus on Eastern Europe while simultaneously providing widely generalizable insights into the role that position-taking by mainstream parties plays in structuring the political landscape in which radical right-wing parties compete for support. In opposition to scholarship that sees mainstream parties primarily affecting the success of extremist parties through containment or engagement, Bustikova demonstrates the degree to which "the variance in the success of radical parties is structurally determined by the redistributive policy configurations of the mainstream parties" (Chapter 7, this volume).

Across the Atlantic, the chapters by Chip Berlet and Pete Simi focus on right-wing extremism and radicalization in the US. Chip Berlet's chapter injects some much-needed clarity into the analysis of the varieties of right-wing activism in the US, drawing on decades of research in order to locate the Tea Party movement within the context of the American right. Berlet analyzes the rise of the Tea Party in order to contextualize it within the larger panoply of right-wing activism. Despite its reputation in some circles as a radical right-wing movement, Berlet demonstrates that although it draws upon the same font of right-wing populism as many of the most radical extremists, the Tea Party is in fact relatively moderate when compared to the wide variety of far-right extremist activity in the US.[13]

In order to gain perspective both on the place of right-wing violence as a form of terrorism and on the recent surge in far-right activity, Pete Simi investigates two previous episodes of right-wing extremism in the US. His analysis demonstrates that the familiar categorization of acts of right-wing extremist violence that casts perpetrators as "lone wolves" is based on a misunderstanding of the structures of right-wing extremist organizations and networks. Simi argues that in order to be considered in any way comprehensive, our conceptualization of terrorism must include right-wing extremist violence.

Bringing to the forefront a theme that is a strong undercurrent in nearly all of the earlier chapters, Othmar Plöckinger focuses on the role a radical text may play in the spread of extremist ideologies across both borders and generations. His chapter explores the influence of Hitler's *Mein Kampf* and the issues surrounding the debate over the proposed publication of a critical edition of the text. Plöckinger describes the history of Hitler's text and its progression from a well-read text in the 1930s and 1940s, to its contemporary status as a mostly totemic item of radical contraband. He concludes by outlining the case for a scholarly edition, which aims to undermine the possibility of neo-Nazi-sponsored reprints once the original copyright expires.

Finally, in a short concluding chapter Kathleen Blee brings together the various themes developed in the preceding chapters and suggests how scholars may build upon the transatlantic discourse on right-wing extremism inaugurated in this volume.

Clearly, a broad phenomenon such as this cannot be dealt with comprehensively in one volume. Many issues that deserve attention could not be included. Anders Breivik highlighted the "Christian Justification of the Struggle" in his texts, and is known to have a Christian fundamentalist background. Religious fundamentalism is a growing problem in all religious denominations worldwide and deserves a volume of its own.[14] In Europe there is also a growing right-wing youth culture—from soccer hooligans to summer camps and open-air music festivals, and recent examples such as the shooting at a Sikh temple in Milwaukee by a man affiliated with white power rock bands suggests that this is a US phenomenon as well (Edgers 2001; see also Miller-Idriss 2009). It will be important to observe how extremist youth culture will be further transformed by the explosion of global connectivity among youth through social networking sites. Finally, although women tend to be under-represented in right-wing organizations that embrace traditional gender roles, Kopke, Botsch, and Klandermans mention the specific motivation of the growing number of women who are getting involved in right-wing activities,[15] and Pete Simi and Robert Futrell have shown in *American Swastika: Inside the White Power Movement's Hidden Spaces of Hate* (2010) how women's contributions often help stabilize and legitimize extremist circles despite the 'hypermasculinity' that is a staple of right-wing ideology.[16] Indeed, some of the largest far-right parties in Europe – in Norway and France are currently led by women. Nevertheless, there is no question that the large majority of violent extremists continue to be men. The preliminary investigations into the Boston Marathon bombings of April 2013 confirm that this is not the only parallel between Islamist extremist and right-wing extremist activity on both sides of the Atlantic. These and many other issues deserve to be studied more fully and will continue to be explored as the conversation moves beyond this volume.

It is our hope that the present volume represents both a significant contribution to the scholarly discourse on right-wing radicalism and an incentive for further transatlantic study and debate. The studies in this volume demonstrate that the increasingly global character of right-wing extremist activity requires scholars to look beyond national borders in order to comprehend these phenomena. As scholars, we are acutely aware of the need to comprehend the complex mechanisms, changing dynamics, and enduring patterns at play in contemporary radicalism. As citizens, we see the necessity not only of more global discourse among scholars, but also of extending this conversation beyond the academy and into the political communities confronting the kinds of radicalization and extremism discussed herein.

Notes

1 Although some writers may intend and readers may perceive a meaningful distinction, our text employs the terms "radicalism" and "extremism" basically interchangeably, albeit with an awareness that "extremist" tends in some circumstances in the English-speaking world to carry a more negative connotation than "radical."
2 See for example James Kurth, "A Tale of Four Crises: The Politics of Great Depressions and Recessions," *Orbis* (Summer 2011): 500–23, www.fpri.org/orbis/5503/kurth.fourcrises.pdf.
3 See www.reuters.com/article/2012/02/06/us-europe-austria-strache-idUSTRE8150UD 20120206 (accessed August 12, 2012). For a general impression of the festivities visit www.youtube.com/watch?v=jpqknYfEQnM (accessed August 12, 2012).
4 The EAF became a European party in the fall of 2010 and was formally recognized by the European Parliament in February of 2011. It is led by the Austrian FPÖ member Franz Obermayr. Front National chairwoman Marine Le Pen is vicechair.
5 The use of this term is not without controversy, as many believe that there is little substantive distinction between the new and old racisms. Simo V. Virtanen and Leonie Huddy, "Old-Fashioned Racism and New Forms of Racial Prejudice," *The Journal of Politics* 60, no. 2 (May 1996): 311–32.
6 Obviously, it is a very different story with regard to Native Americans, the descendants of African slaves, and non-European immigrants generally.
7 This particular narrative has resulted in the curious attempt by some American conservatives to cast Fascism and Nazism as left-wing movements, largely on the assertion that the use of the word socialism in the term "National Socialism" necessarily connotes a leftist ideology. Although the most notable proponent of such an interpretation is former Fox News host Glenn Beck, the closest thing to a scholarly text is probably Jonah Goldberg's *Liberal Fascism: The Secret History of the American Left: From Mussolini to the Politics of Meaning*, New York: Doubleday, 2008.
8 Michelle Hale Williams has noted that such deeply embedded facets of right-wing extremist ideology such as anti-Semitism have in many cases been superceded by Islamophobia in recent years. See Michelle Hale Williams, *Nationalism and Ethnic Politics* 16 (2010): 111.
9 The label itself spurred an extensive public debate and underscores the racist undertones of the issue after the murder/suicide of two young men in the East German town of Zwickau and the surrender of their female accomplice led police to uncover a right-wing terrorist cell called "National Socialist Underground" (*Nationalsozialistischer Untergrund*). The group is held responsible for killing nine immigrant businessmen as well as a female police officer between 2000 and 2006. The civilian victims, eight of them with Turkish and one with Greek background, were shot in the head in broad daylight. The administration of the German *Verfassungsschutz* responsible for domestic security has come under intense scrutiny in recent months. See for example www.spiegel.de/thema/braune_zelle_zwickau (accessed August 29, 2012).
10 For a discussion of Muslim minorities in Europe see especially Jytte Klausen, *The Islamic Challenge: Politics and Religion in Western Europe*, Oxford University Press, 2008.
11 In yet another internationalist twist Wilders's film is said to have been inspired by the Canadian-Israeli Raphael Shore's 2005 documentary *Obsession: Radical Islam's War Against the West*.
12 At the same time the Internet also allows for effective counter-activity, as cyber-attacks by the hacker group Anonymous on German neo-Nazi websites clearly show (see, for example, www.forbes.com/sites/mobiledia/2012/01/09/hackers-attack-neo-nazi-groups, accessed January 10, 2012).
13 The decision to include the phenomenon of the Tea Party in this discussion caused controversy leading up to the conference "The New Radical Right—A Transatlantic

Perspective," held at Brandeis University on April 28, 2009, which inspired this volume.
14 For an introduction, see Gabriel A. Almond *et al.*, *Strong Religion: The Rise of Fundamentalisms Around the World*, University of Chicago Press, 2003.
15 For earlier work on this issue see also Kathleen Blee, *Women of the Klan: Racism and Gender in the 1920s*, University of California Press, 1992.
16 The issue of women's role as partners of right-wing extremists was highlighted when German Olympic rower Nadja Drygalla turned out to be dating a right-wing extremist and NPD member. Although the 23 year old voluntarily left the Olympic village in London, the issue continued to be hotly debated in Germany. See also the work of Renate Bitzan at the University of Göttingen, Germany, www.dw.de/dw/article/0,3097355,00.html (accessed August 12, 2012).

References

Almond, Gabriel A., R. Scott Appleby, and Emmanuel Sivan (2003) *Strong Religion: The Rise of Fundamentalisms Around the World*, University of Chicago Press.

BBC News (2010) "Merkel Says German Multicultural Society has Failed," October 17, www.bbc.co.uk/news/world-europe-11559451.

Blee, Kathleen (1992) *Women of the Klan: Racism and Gender in the 1920s*, University of California Press.

Breivik, Anders Behring (2011) publicintelligence.net/anders-behring-breiviks-complete-manifesto-2083-a-european-declaration-of-independence/.

Edgers, Geoff, "White Trash," *GQ*, September 2001, www.gq.com/entertainment/music/200109/definite-hate-wade-page?currentPage=1.

Goldberg, Jonah (2008) *Liberal Fascism: The Secret History of the American Left: From Mussolini to the Politics of Meaning*, New York: Doubleday.

Hale Williams, Michelle (2010) *Nationalism and Ethnic Politics* (16): 111–34.

Klausen, Jytte (2008) *The Islamic Challenge: Politics and Religion in Western Europe*, Oxford University Press.

Kurth, James (2011) "A Tale of Four Crises: The Politics of Great Depressions and Recessions," *Orbis* (Summer): 500–23, www.fpri.org/orbis/5503/kurth.fourcrises.pdf.

Paterson, Tony (2012) "Waltz and All: Far Right has Ball in Vienna. Austria's Famed Ballroom Season has Exploded in Acrimony Over an Event Hosted by the Freedom Party," *The Independent* February 1, www.independent.co.uk/news/world/europe/waltz-and-all-far-right-has-ball-in-vienna-6297659.html.

Shane, Scott (2011) "In Islamic Law Gingrich Sees a Mortal Threat to US," *The New York Times*, December 21, www.nytimes.com/2011/12/22/us/politics/in-shariah-gingrich-sees-mortal-threat-to-us.html?pagewanted=all&_r=0.

Virtanen, Simo V. and Leonie Huddy (1996) "Old-Fashioned Racism and New Forms of Racial Prejudice," *The Journal of Politics* 60, no. 2 (May): 311–32.

2 Globalized anti-globalists

The ideological basis of the internationalization of right-wing extremism

Thomas Grumke[1]

Ultranationalism (e.g. if in the construction of national belonging specific ethnic, cultural or religious criteria of exclusion are reinforced, condensed to collective ideas of homogeneity and linked with authoritarian political models) doubtlessly is one of the ideological characteristics of right-wing extremism. This could lead to the conclusion that right-wing extremists for this reason do not tend to cooperate on a long-term basis with right-wing extremists from other countries. Especially in the 21st century that is absolutely incorrect. On the contrary, extensive international and transnational networking is taking place on the extreme right, which is more and more interlinked organizationally and ideologically.

The conditions of context for right-wing extremists are favorable in the era of globalization. That globalization aids and abets the evolution and spread of right-wing extremism has been shown repeatedly (see Stöss 2004; Grumke 2006). Globalization processes simply frighten many people: "Thus the fear of the seemingly unmanageable is transformed into fear of something that is not quite as hopeless to fight against, in fear of crime, the antisocial, of minorities and the like, or—what often amounts to the same—a structure is seen behind the threat" (Welzk 1998: 38).[2] The processes and impositions of globalization act as a breeding ground of right-wing extremism nationally and internationally.

The 2010 electoral success of the right-wing extremist Jobbik party in Hungary may be seen as proof of the above. In a message of greetings, the leader of Germany's far-right *Nationaldemokratische Partei Deutschlands* (NPD, National Democratic Party) Udo Voigt wrote on April 11, 2010:

> Ideologically, there is much agreement between our countries and our two parties ... On this day the Hungarian people begins to defend itself effectively against the sell-out, the exploitation by globalization, imperialism, and against the "American Way of Life" with its planned multicultural fusion with strangers ... We stand by your side! For a free Hungary, Germany and Europe!
> (NPD, November 4, 2010)

Likewise, greetings were sent by the new leader of the NPD, Holger Apfel, after the Greek *Chrysi Avgi* (Golden Dawn) won almost 7 percent of the vote and 21 seats (NPD, May 7, 2012).

The central themes of contemporary right-wing extremism and even the central ideological foundation for their international cooperation are mentioned here. Right-wing extremists have established their own definitions and thoughts, which will be briefly presented below in order to increase the basis for understanding the international networking of the scene. Structure follows ideology. In other words, it cannot be assumed that right-wing extremists from different countries cooperate or organize meetings and only then start thinking about what their common goals and ideas would be. On the contrary, unless there are economic or other specific interests involved there will typically be cooperation only because of ideological consensus and/or common political goals.

Michael Kühnen, who like no other has influenced the German extreme right, coined the phrase, "The system does not have flaws, it is the flaw," as well as the demand for the "fight against foreign infiltration,"[3] the volkishly motivated "fight against environmental destruction," and for a "cultural revolution against Americanism" (Kühnen 1987). Here, Kühnen already formulated in the mid-1980s what are today central elements of internationally active right-wing extremists.

In his greetings for the book *Alles Große steht im Sturm* (*All Great Things are Exposed to Strong Resistance*), published for the 35th anniversary of the NPD and the 30th anniversary of *Junge Nationaldemokraten* (JN), the founder and then leader of the West Virginia-based National Alliance, Dr William L. Pierce,[4] set forth his ideological parameters for international cooperation:

> Nationalists in Germany, in Europe and also in America are facing the common enemy of all people, the international monopoly capital that wants to deal the death blow to all historically grown nations in favour of a multicultural "melting pot." Our fight against the attempts for world domination and economic imperialism by multinational corporations will be hard and full of privations—but the goal of *Volksgemeinschaft* finding back to its roots will be worth taking on this tough fight and all difficulties that come with it.
>
> (Apfel 1999: 23)

This statement, which can be seen as paradigmatic for internationally active right-wing extremists, shows clearly that the "fight" is no longer just for the defense of one's nation from outside enemies, but for more. Crucial internationally operating activists like Pierce define nationality not by citizenship or geography, but by race. Worth defending and protecting is not the nation as such, but rather the seriously endangered "white race" (by "infiltration" and "race-mixing"), that is under massive attack in their ancestral nations by the "international capital" that has no traditions, history, or scruples. Openly or thinly veiled, this "international capital" is portrayed as Jewish dominated. The result is a brew of longstanding anti-Semitic or volkish theories and arguments as well as alternative ingredients like "international (racial) solidarity," "anti-imperialism" and "foreigners out" that are hard to digest.

The result is a so-called pan-Aryan *Weltanschauung*, which—no longer slavophobic like Hitlerian National Socialist (NS) ideology—explicitly includes Eastern Europe and Russia as a part of the "white world." Only with this in mind can the description of World War II as a "fratricidal disaster" be understood (Apfel 1999: 23). David Duke even puts his hopes on Russia to prevent what he calls the "relentless and systematic destruction of the European genotype," because "our race faces a world-wide genetic catastrophe. There is only one word that can describe it: genocide" (Duke 2004: 18).

To repeat: internationally cooperating right-wing extremists are not flag-waving patriots, but markedly fundamental enemies of pluralism, free democracy and *all* its representatives. The idea of ZOG (Zionist occupied government) meanwhile dominates the right-wing extremist discourse and is universally accepted as the description of what is seen as puppet governments of global (Jewish-dominated) financial interests in Europe and North America. The principal goal is the preservation (or purity) of the "white race," which consequentially results in the total rejection of any form of immigration, understood as "foreign infiltration" in a racial and cultural sense.

This falls in line with a virulent anti-Americanism, which indeed has to be described more accurately as anti-"American system" thought. The influence of American-based investment and media firms, including "Wall Street" is criticized as imperialistic and degenerating for the race and all nations. In Germany the right-wing extremists view the country as weakened by the government's *Überfremdungspolitik* "inundation policy," as well as by the demoralizing and humiliating references to the crimes of the past.

Anti-Semitism acts as the vital, internationally compatible ideological glue. The word "Jew" does not even have to be mentioned openly; right-wing extremists from both sides of the Atlantic know exactly who the "One Worlders" are and what "New World Order" or "East Coast" mean. This ideology is transported through internationally recognized and established codes, symbols and writings. This includes among other things the "14 words" of American right-wing terrorist David Lane ("We must secure the existence of our people and a future for White children"), or William Pierce's "Turner Diaries" (published under the pseudonym Andrew McDonald) from 1978, about which the author gloated after a trip through Europe: "*Every* nationalist in Europe has heard about *The Turner Diaries*" (*National Alliance Bulletin*, November 1998). The book has been translated into many languages and is now also available in German under the title *Die Turner Tagebücher*, translated by "German enthusiasts" (*National Alliance Bulletin*, December 1998).

In this novel, which has rightfully been called a right-wing extremist bible, the "Aryan revolution" starts out with a bomb attack on the US Federal Bureau of Investigation (FBI) headquarters and climaxes in the so-called "Day of the Rope," on which tens of thousands are hanged in the streets with signs around their necks saying "I betrayed my race." After a nuclear civil war and a "mopping-up period" (i.e. the killing of all "non-whites"), the entire world at the end of the novel is "Aryan." It is designative that violence is portrayed here more as the cure than as the malady and deliberately promoted and defended. This all-out positive position on political violence—as the only solution to the problem of what is seen as fundamental oppression of the "Aryan race" by ZOG—is inherent in a growing number of internationally active right-wing extremists. Violence is seen as no less than the forced last resource in the fight for survival.

"In this fight, every opponent of today's America is objectively our ally, even if tomorrow he will become our enemy," writes the extremist Swiss veteran Gaston Armand Amaudruz in his preface to the NPD volume *Alles Große steht im Sturm* (Apfel 1999: 15). The former chairman of the British National Party (BNP), John Tyndall, writes in his preface in the name of his party: "The same enemies, the same political and social problems, the same method of resolution for these problems and definitely also a common future. All this interconnects the nationalist parties of Europe" (Apfel 1999: 22).

The above-mentioned central ideological elements of pan-Aryan racism, anti-Semitism and (revolutionary) enmity towards the system in a political, cultural, social, and economic sense led a growing number of top right-wing extremists to the conclusion that "Cooperation across borders will become increasingly important for progress—and perhaps survival—in the future" (*National Alliance Bulletin*, November 1998).

Globalization is a central theme of propaganda and agitation for right-wing extremists worldwide. In addition, extreme right critics of globalization intertwine social and cultural issues and in turn ethnicize them. Their counter-proposal is a re-nationalized, racial order—no less than the reconstruction of an ethnically defined national volkish community. Definitions from the *Little Dictionary of Basic Political Concepts* (Deutsche Stimme-Verlag 2006), which is widely circulated among right-wing extremists, can be used as examples. Under the entry "globalization" we read: "Globalization is the tendency of international capitalism, if possible to create uniform conditions for profit-enhancing production of labor forces, exploitation of raw materials, and the monopolistic marketing of goods." This development has "caused the destruction of independent regional and national life and business forms" (Deutsch Stimme-Verlag 2006).

"Internationalism" is in turn seen as "the counterpart of nationalism." It is the attempt to "dominate the world's peoples, their economy and their traditional ways of life, to transform and exploit them for profit's sake" (Deutsch Stimme-Verlag 2006). Globalization, as right-wing extremists understand it, is an instrument of domination of all nations with the goal to destroy their uniqueness and autonomy in the name of profit. A significant risk is seen as coming mainly from the US, which is seen as a kind of globalization center, for "internationalism and globalization, and the imperialism of the western 'values' in the wake of the U.S. threaten the sovereignty of nations to a great extent" (Deutsch Stimme-Verlag 2006).

To that extent, from an extreme right point of view, not only the national economy, but more importantly national culture, identity, and tradition, are threatened by the process of globalization. MTV, McDonald's and other "American pabulum" consumed by young people in the right-wing extremist thinking are instruments of a carefully planned, controlled culture destroying internationalist "globalism." This in turn is the opposite of the desired drive for self-sufficiency (Deutsch Stimme-Verlag 2006). In contemporary right-wing extremism, the term "globalism" plays a central role and stands for the power of ahistoric and faceless big business, for "American cultural imperialism" and a "multi-racial genocide," allegedly sought by Washington, Wall Street and Hollywood. At the same time the idea of a US monopoly "on the East Coast" is a well-known code for an ostensible Jewish hegemony.

In terms of concepts and content one has to distinguish between the process of globalization and "globalism." In the *12 Theses on Globalism* created by the *Nationaldemokratischer Hochschulbund* (NHB), the student association of the NPD, which is widely circulated in the right-wing movement, the differentiation is clear: "globalization is the process used by the globalists to achieve their goals." More specifically, "The migration flows deliberately caused by the globalists lead to the uniformity of the markets, their products and their communication as well as to the destruction of grown languages and cultures" (NPD 2006).

Right-wing extremists thus see the process of globalization as a deliberately controlled destruction of cultures, traditions and values (and, ultimately, of nations and peoples) by the above-described powerful "globalists." In internationally understood right-wing extremist codes "globalists" are also "East Coast," "globalism" is also "New World Order" (NWO), and governments and elites involved in this "globalization plan" are the ZOG. ZOG, it is firmly believed, is a hidden Jewish world conspiracy, in which all democratic governments, banks, media and much more are secretly controlled by Jews and must be fought at all costs. Against such a powerful enemy, "white patriots" can only fight together.

Another bogeyman is the "One World" (or NWO), which the *Little Dictionary of Basic Political Concepts* calls a "delusion" that is "fed by the belief in a homogeneous humanity without ties and traditions" (Deutsch Stimme-Verlag 2006). In this context, two more enemy provisions are made: the United Nations (UN) and human rights. "The tool of imperialism to create the 'One World' are the 'United Nations'. The ideological limed twig on the global enforcement of the 'Western values' are 'human rights'" (Deutsch Stimme-Verlag 2006).

According to right-wing extremist logic, "the individual stands above a specific group in the name of human rights, selfish self-interests trump the alleged interests of the ethnic community" (see Pfahl-Traughber 2006: 41ff.). "The need of the hour," says Karl Richter, since 2009 deputy NPD national chairman and member of the Council of the City of Munich, "is a sustained and resolute stance against everything that is currently praised by the big brothers: globalization, human rights, multiculturalism, the liberalization and atomization of all areas of life" (Richter 2002: 1).

Who these "big brothers" are remains unclear, of course. Much more informative on this are the submissions in the NPD brochure *Arguments for*

Candidates and Officials: A Handout for Public Debate, in which the question "Why does the NPD so strongly reject globalization?" is answered as follows: "Globalization is the planetary spread of the capitalist economic system under the leadership of Big Money. Despite by its very nature being Jewish-nomadic and homeless, it has its politically and militarily protected location mainly on the East Coast of the United States" (NPD 2006: 19). Moreover, "Encouraged by modern communication technologies and mass media, cultural Americanization attacks the organically grown identities of peoples and aims to create a consumerist and uniform people." (NPD 2006: 19).

Globalization in a right-wing extremist context, in sum, stands for the power of international big business, for American cultural imperialism and for a "multi-racial genocide" or a "race destroying debris field," sought by "Washington, Wall Street and Hollywood," as the chairman of the BNP, Member of the European Parliament (MEP) Nick Griffin put it in an interview with the NPD paper *Deutsche Stimme* in March 2002 (p.3).

In the 21st century, a transnational network of right-wing extremists is forming, which is supported by a collective identity and an internationally compatible ideology. The collective identity is, first, that of a white man in the sense of ethnicity, and second, in terms of culture belonging to a decidedly Western culture. The compatible ideological elements are the re-nationalization and re-ethnicizing of politics and the volkish opposition to a parliamentary democratic system (see above; in greater detail, see Grumke 2006).

If right-wing extremists want to be more than the sum of national rallying points of protest against social change, progressive discourse and multiculturalism, if they really want to achieve their fundamental objectives politically, then they must also think and act globally and appear as transnational actors. Richard Stöss rightfully notes: "The degree of interconnection of national right-wing extremists, the question in particular, whether they manage to overcome national and international conflicts, can be an important indicator of political viability, and thus the potential threat right-wing extremists actually pose" (Stöss 2001: 2). Although often marginalized in their own countries, at least on an ideological level something like a transnational extreme right has evolved—more to the point: an *international* of nationalists. Agreement about their common enemy, a more and more defined infrastructure with regular events, fixed communication platforms, and a lively exchange of goods and ideas have developed over recent years.

There is now an ideological foundation for a transnational cooperation of the extreme right. Irrespective of the different context structures, mobilization, and agitation strengths of each national right-wing scene, cross-border networking of the extreme right has even reached the European Parliament in recent years. On November 17, 2004 the NPD chairman Udo Voigt visited the European Parliament in Strasbourg at the invitation of then-MEP Alessandra Mussolini. He also came to other meetings and informal discussions with Chairman of the National Front Jean-Marie Le Pen, Forza Nuova and the Lega Nord (NPD 2004). Apart from the usual slogans, a press statement about these meetings included the strict rejection of European Union (EU) membership of Turkey and the summoning of an international solidarity of the nationalists:

> There was agreement on the political struggle against alienation, globalization and the mitigation of the American economic imperialism, as on the rejection of an accession of Turkey to the EU. After intensive discussions, we came to an agreement to cooperate more intensively in the future in particular in Europe. The MEP Alessandra Mussolini assured the party leader of the NPD of her support for national German concerns in the European Parliament.
>
> (NPD 2004)

What seemed at that time still the exception, has now become the rule. Today it has become routine that regular right-wing dates such as the *Rudolf Hess Memorial*, May 1, or the commemoration of the bombing of Dresden take place with massive international participation. German right-wing extremists have also become regular participants in events, demonstrations and concerts of their "comrades" abroad.

Today, all right-wing extremists in Western industrialized countries are facing almost identical challenges. Their "enemy" is not organized nationally, but globally. Accordingly, more and more right-wing extremists are looking to a transnational network to fight against what they view as the overwhelming (Jewish) conspiracy. In the course of this development networking has become tighter, contacts abroad have intensified, communication channels have improved, altogether making for a permanent exchange of information and a vital event tourism. The number of internationally attended right-wing meetings, events and demonstrations are on the rise. This results in a complex web of cooperation, which is illustrated in the examples highlighted in this paper.

Pan-Aryanism, the ideological basis for this network, is essentially a modern anti-modern ideology. Guided by the internationally famous "14 Words" of the American right-wing terrorist David Lane ("We must secure the existence of our people and a future for white children") and the fundamental opposition to ZOG, right-wing extremists globally have a common counter-myth, which overrides all other ideological differences. Transnationally co-operating right-wing extremists are not simply flag-waving patriots, but very fundamental enemies of pluralism, parliamentary democracy, and its representatives. This identity-oriented resistance is de facto the globalization of hatred, and not only in Europe is it a battle for the parliaments and civil society.

The re-nationalization and re-ethnicization propagated by the extreme right is both a fundamental alternative to the dominant neo-liberal globalization as well as to the social-ecological version ("global governance") and must be taken seriously. The increasing reflexive modernity, i.e. the quickening pace of social and political change, also benefits the mobilization of the extremist right. In the 21st century, a deeper internationalization—or better, transnationalization—

of right-wing extremism, especially in an ideological but also in a structural sense, is apparent. It may seem paradoxical, but the "nationalist resistance" is not necessarily from one's own country. Right-wing anti-globalists "globalize"—and to make it even more complicated, a unifying ideological element is the struggle against "globalism."

The extreme right responds to the danger of "globalism," as they define it, where "the trend towards liquefaction ... is met with a re-homogenization of identity and a reaffirmation of supposed certainties" (Scharenberg 2003: 663). "Globalism" and the related social question have become new campaign and propaganda issues for right-wing extremists. At the same time, right-wing extremists see themselves as executors of the will of the people, who are irritated by how quickly the processes of globalization progress.

It should be noted in conclusion:

- Today, right-wing extremism can be described as an international, modern and multifaceted phenomenon (see Minkenberg 1998; Greven and Grumke 2006).
- Opposition to globalization and the defense of social justice—however understood—per se is owned by neither the political left nor the right in the 21st century.
- Right-wing extremists react "to the loss of traditions and boundaries of identity, accelerated by globalization and de-nationalization" (Scharenberg 2003: 662).
- The right extremists are not just regular critics of globalization, but anti-globalists, their approach is not progressive-democratic, but volkish-extremist.
- The ideological arsenal of the People (the Volk) and the nation is extended by the extreme right by ideas such as globalization, (anti-)capitalism, imperialism and identity, and thus made compatible internationally (see Grumke 2006).
- Both because of their internal structural conditions as well as external factors—particularly a "cultural resonance" with parts of the population (see Grumke 2008: 488ff.)—the right-wing extremist movement cannot be marginalized simply by external repression or the hope that it will one day implode. Unlike suspected by some authors, the right-wing extremist movement in Germany is not a "painful episode" (Ohlemacher 1994), but rather a "normal pathology of Western industrial societies" (Scheuch and Klingemann 1967: 12ff.).

Right-wing extremists live, like all fundamentalists, in a hermetically sealed ideological counter-world. So the question is: how can a free society accept a declaration of absolute enmity without betraying its own liberal democratic ideals?

Notes

1 This article is a slightly amended version of an earlier article published in Uwe Backes (ed.), *The Extreme Right in Europe*, Göttingen: Vandenhoeck & Ruprecht GmbH & Co.KG, 2011.

2 All translations of quotes are mine, T.G.
3 The original phrase is "Kampf gegen die Überfremdung," which is to be understood both in a cultural and a biological/racial sense.
4 William Pierce died from cancer on July 23, 2002 at the age of 68.

References

Apfel, Holger (Hrsg.) (1999) *Alles Große steht im Sturm. Tradition und Zukunft einer nationalen Partei*, Stuttgart: Deutsche Stimme Verlag.

Deutsche Stimme (2002) "Freiheitsrechte der Völker zurückfordern. Interview mit Nick Griffin," March: 3.

Deutsche Stimme-Verlag (ed.) (2006) *Taschenkalender des Nationalen Widerstandes 2006* [*Little Dictionary of Basic Political Concepts*], Riesa: Deutsche Stimme-Verlag, www.ds-versand.de.

Duke, David (2004) "Is Russia the Key to White Survival?" www.davidduke.com/?p=18.

Greven, Thomas and Thomas Grumke (eds) (2006) *Globalisierter Rechtsextremismus? Die extremistische Rechte in der Ära der Globalisierung*, Wiesbaden.

Grumke, Thomas (2006) "Die transnationale Infrastruktur der extremistischen Rechten," in T. Greven and T. Grumke (eds) *Globalisierter Rechtsextremismus? Die extremistische Rechte in der Ära der Globalisierung*, Wiesbaden, 130–59.

——(2008) "Die rechtsextremistische Bewegung," in R. Roth and D. Rucht (eds) *Die Sozialen Bewegungen in Deutschland seit 1945. Ein Handbuch*, Frankfurt/M., 475–92.

Kühnen, Michael (1987) *Lexikon der Neuen Front*, www.nazi-lauck-nsdapao.com (accessed May 10, 2003).

Minkenberg, Michael (1998) *Die neue radikale Rechte im Vergleich*, USA, Frankreich, Deutschland: Opladen.

NPD (2004) "NPD-Parteivorsitzender zu Gast bei Alessandra Mussolini in Straßburg," press release, November 21, www.npd.de.

——(2006) *Argumente für Kandidaten & Funktionsträger: Eine Handreichung für die öffentliche Auseinandersetzung*, Berlin, www.npd-goettingen.de/Weltanschauung/12_Thesen_zum_Globalismus.html (accessed April 21, 2010).

Ohlemacher, Thomas (1994) "Schmerzhafte Episoden. Wider die Rede von einer rechten Bewegung im wiedervereinigten Deutschland," *Neue Soziale Bewegungen* 4(7): 16–25.

Pfahl-Traughber, Armin (2006) "Globalisierung als Agitationsthema des organisierten Rechtsextremismus in Deutschland," in T. Greven and T. Grumke (eds) *Globalisierter Rechtsextremismus? Die extremistische Rechte in der Ära der Globalisierung*, Wiesbaden, 30–51.

Richter, Karl (2002) "Der Chaoskanzler," *Opposition* 1(5): 1.

Scharenberg, Albert (2003) "Plädoyer für eine Mehrebenenanalyse des Rechtsextremismus," *Deutschland Archiv* 4: 659–72.

Scheuch, Erwin K. and Hans-Dieter Klingemann (1967) "Theorie des Rechtsradikalismus in westlichen Industriegesellschaften," *Hamburger Jahrbuch für Wirtschafts-und Gesellschaftspolitik* 12: 11–29.

Stöss, Richard (2001) *Zur Vernetzung der extremen Rechten in Europa*, Arbeitshefte aus dem Otto-Stammer-Zentrum, Nr.5. Berlin.

——(2004) "Globalisierung und rechtsextreme Einstellungen," in Bundesministerium des Innern (ed.) *Extremismus in Deutschland*, Berlin, 82–97.

Welzk, Stefan (1998) "Globalisierung und Neofaschismus," *Kursbuch* 134 (December): 37–47.

3 Right-wing extremism and populism in contemporary Germany and Western Europe

Hans-Gerd Jaschke

In the first half of the 20th century, right-wing extremists came to power in Germany through a gradual process and not, as sometimes suggested, more or less overnight. Extremist ideologies had slowly developed throughout the period of industrialization in the second half of the 19th century: anti-Semitism, racism, and the belief in Germany's superior role in the world were popular reactions to modernization leading all the way up to the Holocaust several decades later (Jaschke 2006: 59ff). Preventing the return of right-wing extremism was therefore regarded as a major political challenge in Germany after World War II. This was the main motivation behind the establishment of the *Grundgesetz* (basic law) as a democratic constitution in 1949, with its emphasis on human rights, civil rights, and the freedom of political parties. The law also provided right-wing-extremist movements, associations, and parties with the freedom for political action. In the process of rebuilding the German party system, far-right parties such as the *Deutsche Reichs-Partei* (DRP) and the *Sozialistische Reichspartei* (SRP) were founded, gathering former National Socialist Party members and voters. Although far-right parties have so far never been particularly successful in the federal republic or even in any of the 16 states, they do still exist, some of them have existed for decades, and they are increasingly successful at recruiting and attracting younger members. Germany is not alone in witnessing these developments. Other European countries have experienced the revival of right-wing parties as well. Experts explain the phenomenon with larger social developments: globalization, growing social inequality, and high unemployment rates may be the most important ones. These may be the causes for dissatisfaction and social fears, which have always been the breeding-ground for right-wing extremism. However, the specifics of German post-war history also provide a unique environment that differs significantly from developments in other European countries.

What united all German post-war right-wing organizations for decades were the exaggeration of national and ethnic identity, the belief in the positive aspects of National Socialism, and the conviction that Germany was unjustly humiliated by the allied victors. Myths of persecution and the deprivation of rights as well as other conspiracy theories were developed from this perspective, as was the common expectation that "better times" would eventually return. In Germany, mainstream culture is able to use the politically, culturally, and morally charged shadow of the National Socialist past to threaten with sanctions right-wing extremist parties that refuse to disassociate from that past. Therefore the relationship of present right-wing extremist groups to National Socialism is not only a question of the proximity of their ideology.

Most right-wing organizations share a similar worldview. They share a belief in "systems of leaders and vassals, in struggling as an existential form of life, the belief that peoples should be sharply separated and the identification with one's own." Those are the basic patterns of a political ideology which is legitimated "by the unquestionable axiomatic faith that these principles are a natural given" (Jaschke 1993: 126). However, right-wing extremism has created different forms of political action since 1945. This study will focus on current trends in Germany and Western Europe by following the process of democratization and its obstacles after the Holocaust. Part one will give a summary of recent developments, including populist movements. Comparative studies of the situation in Italy, Austria, the Netherlands, Switzerland, Scandinavia and Germany indicate that extremist parties are increasingly becoming a challenge for mainstream conservative and social-democratic parties (Decker 2006). In Germany violent protest from the right has become a reality since the debates about asylum seekers at the beginning of the 1990s. Part two will deal with right-wing militancy and society's reactions. Part three gives a brief overview of right-wing extremist tendencies in neighboring Western European countries to show that although their ideology condemns them, extremist movements are clearly benefiting from globalization and European integration. Other questions of interest will be: Who actually votes for and supports right-wing extremist parties? What parts of society do the voters come from?

Germany today: right-wing extremism in transformation

In the course of the post-war period until the beginning of the 1960s right-wing extremist organizations gathered a number of former Nazi activists, but they were hardly noticed by the public. This is not a surprise. German politics denied the existence of a xenophobic far-right movement for many years in order to be accepted by the international community and to silence any discussion of the continuity of Nazi elites in post-war Germany. The SRP had been banned by the constitutional court in 1952 after having had some successes in elections in Lower Saxony. This was a signal to the non-democratic right-wingers and society at large, but it also reflected the limits of democratic tolerance in a very young democracy. The right-wing camp then divided into cultural organizations and activities, away from political activism. They began to edit journals and books and continued to hold semi-private meetings, but avoided public political action that could draw attention to them. In 1964 the *Nationaldemokratische Partei Deutschlands* (NPD, National Democratic Party) was founded by former Nazis and conservative right-wingers. It was a success, as the splintered right-wing camp managed to agree that one party would be their political leader. The NPD tried, more or less successfully, to hide Nazi ideas behind a Prussian conservative platform. Between 1966 and 1969 they entered seven state parliaments. The party and the public expected them to reach the 5 percent minimum of the electorate required to enter the national parliament in 1969, but in the end they failed, capturing only 4.3 percent of the vote.

Still, for German politics and society the ghost of the Holocaust had suddenly returned, fueling a political awakening among the younger generation. The student movement put questions to their parents' generation: How deeply had they been involved in the Nazi system and its unthinkable crimes? What had they really learned from the country's horrific history? Thus, the NPD election results indirectly contributed to a democratization of society: what had been kept secret for decades was now discussed in public. Confronting the dark side of recent German history led to heightened awareness of the threats of racism and anti-Semitism.

Between 1966 and 1969 the NPD was supported by conservative voters who opposed the student movement in Germany. They saw their traditional values threatened by the students' claim for radical change. Moreover, it must not be forgotten that Germany experienced a major economic crisis in 1966/67. The unemployment rates were rising for the first time after World War II. Thus, both the economic and the cultural crisis gave support to the NPD, which was fighting against the radical change of social values and for a traditional way of life. However, at the beginning of the 1970s the NPD was itself opposed by a younger generation of right-wingers from within and outside its own spectrum. The young generation longed for a stronger political program of Nazi ideals, for more action on the streets. This confrontation led the NPD into its first serious crisis. Struggles between different groups within the NPD lasted until German reunification in 1989/90. Then they began to focus on East Germany. The period between the beginning of the NPD's crisis until re-unification saw the establishment of two new parties on the far-right spectrum between the centrist conservative Christian Democratic Union (CDU) and the insurgent ultra-right. In addition to the NPD, the populist *Die Republikaner* was established in 1983, and the *Deutsche Volks-Union* (DVU) in 1987. The three parties ended up paralyzing each other during election campaigns.

The lives of East Germans changed profoundly in the wake of the radical change of the political and economic system that took place after 1989/90. On the one hand they embraced basic rights like travelling abroad, the benefits of the welfare state, and the opportunities of the free market. On the other hand they had to face the risks of capitalist societies. Many lost their jobs or their socio-economic status. Rich Western corporations eagerly entered the new markets, overwhelming societies unfamiliar with capitalist market structures. As the communist German Democratic Republic became part of unified Germany its old industrial structures were transformed into modern, service-oriented companies that required skilled workers. Unemployment rates kept growing and left parts of the former working class behind. These transformations of economy and society had taken place over a period of several decades in West Germany and other European countries. In East Germany it took only a few years to transform the former communist system into a modern economy. The speed with which the transformation occurred led to a new urban and rural underclass: typically male unskilled youth for whom there was no space in the labor market. These developments provided the breeding ground for right-wing extremist groups and parties. Although anti-fascism had been an official doctrine of the East German regime, it had no deep roots in the everyday life of society and people's minds. At the same time xenophobic attitudes, anti-Semitism, and authoritarian beliefs had always been part of the so-called socialist society. Since the beginning of the 1980s, years before re-unification, the racist skinhead movement and right-wing football hooligans appeared in some regions of East Germany (Stöss 2010: 106ff.).

The NPD provided a political pressure group for the social losers of re-unification by giving political and ideological support for militant action. The party also offered social services in villages and small cities, infiltrated young people's local meeting spaces and focused its energies on election campaigns in East Germany. They were successful in state elections in Saxony, Mecklenburg-West-Pommerania, and on the communal level in East Berlin. Another right-wing extremist party, the DVU was voted into the state parliament of Brandenburg. Today, the NPD is an established part of political life in the former East Germany, attracting members of the working class, the unemployed, and people fighting for jobs. Its stated goal is to overcome the "system" with a "four-point-strategy": the "battle for the streets"—reminiscent of a fascist slogan from before 1933—concentrating on demonstrations and public action; the "battle for the minds" by recruiting adolescents; the "battle for the parliaments" focused on election campaigns; and the "battle for the organized will" aimed at pooling the "national forces" (Ministry of the Interior (Germany) 2009: 73ff.). In 2003 the federal government, the *Bundesrat* (representatives of the states—similar to the US Senate) and the federal parliament together sued in Germany's highest court to ban the NPD. The suit was thrown out when undercover agents of the secret service were found to be in leading positions of the party. Nevertheless, the threat of a ban casts a shadow over the party's future perspectives (Flemming 2005).[1] In January 2011 the DVU officially merged with the NPD. The unification of the two may strengthen right-wing political extremists by overcoming competition within the right-wing camp and by attracting new members to the NPD.

Of course, official party politics are only part of the strategy employed by right-wing extremists to attract followers. In recent years there has been an upsurge in youth cultures and sub-cultures with racist and right-wing extremist tendencies. Skinheads first appeared at the end of the 1970s. Founded in the UK as a working-class youth culture, their lifestyle and outfits swept over to the continent and infused the racist subcultures and merged to some extent with right-wing extremist movements in Germany. Representing the predominantly male and militant camp of the right-wing, they offered music, concerts, and other activities attractive to young people. When the Internet began to become part of everyday life in the 1990s skinheads made use of it as a political platform and a cultural marketplace for young people which contributed to a change of the political style of right-wing extremism in Germany. Pseudo-military structures like those of the Hitler youth had been the predominant structures for kids available among old-fashioned right-wing organizations, but the skinheads turned racism and right-wing extremism into a lifestyle, making it attractive with street action, noisy rock music, and camping adventures. The fact that right-wing extremism is "hip" among a certain segment of young people today is mostly due to the activities of skinheads. Realizing that potential, the NPD, extremely old-fashioned and conservative until the 1970s, opened its doors to skinheads and other neo-Nazi groups over the course of the 1990s. Thus, a strong right-wing subcultural milieu emerged during the 1990s, making use of new media, modern instruments of event culture, and various other forms of attracting young people. However, the popularity of the skinhead movement seems to be waning in recent years, as many stylistic elements of its culture were taken over (and in some cases subverted) by other youth subcultures (Menhorn 2010).

For a short term only, far right populism even became attractive among more mainstream voters. Between 1989 and 1994 *Die Republikaner* managed to get into several state parliaments. They had their best electoral result in 1992, when they captured 10.9 percent of the vote in Baden-Wuerttemberg. This support did not solely arise from within the right-wing extremist camp, but instead also reflected voters disaffected with the CSU, an established conservative party in Bavaria. *Die Republikaner* succeeded in attracting conservative protest voters dissatisfied with the established conservatism in Germany as well as far-right voters coming from the extremist parties. Their platform included anti-immigrant policies, a tough stance on crime, and a rejection of what was seen as failed government policies in general. Franz Schoenhuber, their leader, was a charismatic politician, who can be compared to other European right-wing populist leaders such as Jean-Marie Le Pen in France and Jörg Haider in Austria. Although right-wing populism continues to thrive in parts of Western Europe, *Die Republikaner* quickly became insignificant as a party after 1994. Oscillating between conservatism and extremism, suffering from conflicts within the party, it quickly lost its voters again. The fact that right-wing populist positions have become part of mainstream discussions and election campaigns (racist and anti-migrant slogans appear regularly on the public agenda of mainstream parties now) also contributed to their demise.

Small so-called "citizens' movements" from the far right were founded in 2005 (*Pro Deutschland*) and 2010 (*Die Freiheit*) in support of strong anti-Islam positions. *Pro Deutschland* supported the spectacular Swiss ban of the construction of minarets, a decision confirmed by a referendum of the Swiss people in November of 2009. They also supported protests against the founding of mosques in Cologne and Berlin (Häusler 2008). So far they have not won parliamentary seats in national and state elections for lack of well-known charismatic leaders. However, although they have been ignored by mainstream parties and the press so far, their anti-Muslim attitudes are shared by a large part of German society today.

In the summer of 2010, a new book occupied the public agenda in Germany for several weeks. Thilo Sarrazin, an executive with the central bank and former social democratic minister of finance of the state of Berlin, published his book *Deutschland schafft sich ab* (*Germany is Abolishing Itself*), which became a best-seller shortly after publication. *Der Spiegel*, Germany's leading political magazine, published a cover story "Volksheld Sarrazin" (folk hero Sarrazin) (*Der Spiegel* No. 36, 2010); *Focus*, the second largest weekly, followed with a cover story called "Staatsaffäre Sarrazin" (Sarrazin Affair). All relevant political talk shows on television gave the agitator the floor. In his highly inflammatory work, Sarrazin emphasized racist positions by comparing the IQ of Germans and other ethnic groups and by referring to genetic codes for explaining the failings of multicultural society. He attacked immigration policies, claiming that the German population is becoming "increasingly stupid" because of the lower intelligence of Turkish immigrants and their refusal to learn the German language. Although his views on immigration and the multi-ethnic society include racist positions, Sarrazin hit the bull's eye: supporters and opponents of his arguments dominated German public discourse for weeks. Sarrazin's arguments are in line with those espoused by right-wing populist movements like *Die Republikaner* 20 years ago. Considerable support for xenophobic attitudes in German society has repeatedly been documented (ENAR 2008: 20f.). The political establishment struggled to respond to Sarrazin's attacks: after a few weeks of heated discussions he was fired by the central bank as his activities were not deemed "in line with the principles" of executives' public behavior. The Social Democratic Party (SPD) initiated a formal procedure to exclude him as a member of the party, but after a long-lasting, controversial discussion it decided to allow him to retain his membership.

To complete the picture of contemporary right-wing extremism in Germany the intellectual far-right needs to be mentioned here as well. Since the 1970s several publishing houses (Nation Europa, Mut Verlag, etc.) and a few individual authors (Armin Mohler, Andreas Moelzer, etc.) have proudly referred to authors of the "conservative revolution" of the 1920s—Carl Schmitt, Moeller van den Bruck, Ernst Juenger, and others—as their inspiration. They share a rejection of the ideas of the French Revolution: freedom, equality, and solidarity. They blame those ideas for what they view as the decline of politics, society, values, and the traditional German ways of life. The New Right attacks democracy and liberalism, fighting for a strong state, rejecting immigration and multicultural societies. They use intellectual forums—meetings, congresses, and publications—to spread their ideology. The German New Right was influenced by the rise of the French *Nouvelle Droite* and their mastermind Alain de Benoit. The French organization is the most powerful intellectual circle among the New Right in Europe, with direct connections to the powerful Front National and their successful strategy in election campaigns. The

German New Right has little influence on the NPD and other political organizations, but the NPD seems to be learning to pay attention to intellectual trends in order to increase acceptance in academic circles (Virchow and Dornbusch 2008: 91ff.). The NPD has adopted some ideas of the French New Right, but this seems to be relevant mainly among party elites, not for the majority of party members. Recent efforts at professionalization within the NPD also include practical training for party leaders in rhetoric and management skills (Kriskofski 2010). For now, however, the NPD's main platform continues to be an ill-defined muddle of ideas, fantasies, and attitudes, including conspiracy theories about the terrorist attacks of 11 September 2001, Jewish capitalism, organic democracy, and a stylish new outfit, modeled to some extent on left wing organizations (Wagner and Borstel 2009).

Political violence: crimes, offenders, and reactions of society and state authorities

In the end of the 1950s Germany began to recruit foreign workers from Yugoslavia, Turkey, Italy, Greece, Spain and Portugal to work for its growing industries. The German economic miracle required more and more so-called "guest-workers." They were expected to stay for a few years and then leave again. At first the foreign workers themselves also planned to return to their home countries. In the early years of labor migration they did not enter into competition with Germans, because there were jobs enough in the expanding industries. In the course of time many migrants settled down, their families joined them, and Germany slowly became a country of immigration (even though Chancellor Helmut Kohl and other officials continued to assert the contrary even after German unification). Turkish communities in West Berlin, the Rhein-Main area, and other urban areas with low rent and low cost of living emerged without a transparent policy of immigration. Many immigrants remained in their separate communities, unwelcomed by the native population. Most immigrants came to West Germany. The few migrants who found themselves in East Germany were laborers from Vietnam and Africa. They, too, remained isolated and were not integrated into society. Though ethnic conflicts were a reality in both parts of the country, they were not considered a major political issue. There was certainly discrimination against immigrants, but political violence on the streets did not exist until the 1990s. Small West German militias like the "*Wehrsportgruppe Hoffmann*," which was banned in 1980, operated secretly and had no remarkable support among the public (Fromm 1998). Since the beginning of the 1980s, right-wing extremist groups occasionally initiated campaigns against migrants and foreign minorities, spurred by their racist belief system, the crisis of the labor market, and rising unemployment rates. Migrants were now viewed as competing with domestic workers. However, politicians and the general public paid little attention to the protesters.

Things changed at the beginning of the 1990s, when, in the wake of the war in Yugoslavia, a wave of asylum seekers swept into Germany. This ignited a heated debate about immigration and led to several years of racist violence. In some East German cities such as Rostock and Hoyerswerda, asylum seekers were attacked and injured by young male right-wingers. In many cases the local population applauded the extremists' actions. The juvenile offenders were inspired to continue their street action, scaring minorities with their fascist outfits and xenophobic slogans. Between 1990 and 2010, 137 persons were killed by militant racist offenders (see www.tagesspiegel.de/opferliste). Some East German locations were generally considered "no-go areas" for visitors from abroad and domestic, especially dark-skinned, minorities. The NPD enthusiastically called them *"national befreite Zonen"* (nationally liberated zones) (see Virchow and Dornbusch 2008: 94ff.). This concept had been developed and discussed in the far-right press since 1990 (Döring 2006). The idea behind it was that occupying local public places, meeting points for young people, school areas, and other locations could ultimately lead to political power. The NPD, originally a national-conservative, racist party, was opening itself up to the young militant people from the far right who were attracted by these concepts. "Nationally liberated zones" intensified crime rates from the far right, when militant individuals and small groups aggressively attacked their opponents. To this day, the rate of crimes from far-right militant activists remains high.

Table 3.1 Crimes with a right-wing extremist background in Germany

Violent Crimes	2007	2008
Homicide	0	2
Attempted homicide	1	4
Bodily injury	845	893
Arson	24	29
Causing an explosion with intent to injure or damage property	1	0
Disruption of public order	37	46
Dangerous disruption of rail, air, ship or road transport	7	4
Unlawful deprivation of liberty	0	1
Robbery	11	10
Extortion	4	6
Resisting public authority	50	47
Sexual offenses	0	0
Total	980	1,042
Other criminal offences		
Property damage	821	1,197
Coercion, threat	146	144
Illegal propaganda activities	11,935	14,262
Desecration of cemeteries	18	32
Other criminal offenses, esp. incitement to hatred	3,276	3,217
Total	16,196	18,852
Total number of criminal offenses	17,176	19,894

Source: Figures based on data from the Federal Criminal Police Office (BKA), see www.bka.de

Most right-wing extremist criminal acts fall into the category of illegal propaganda activities. For historical reasons freedom of political action is restricted in Germany. According to the constitutional principles of a self-defending democracy and the criminal law, it is illegal to show the Hitler greeting in public, to deny the Holocaust, or to show badges and signs of banned organizations like the *Nationalsozialistische Deutsche Arbeiterpartei* (NSDAP, National Socialist German Workers Party). It is also forbidden to disseminate them (section 86 criminal code, see Stegbauer 2007). Bodily injury also ranks high among right-wing offenses. According to empirical studies the offenders are male and between 16 and 30 years of age. They are at a low level of training and education, very often in insecure social positions. They are driven by prejudice and hostile attitudes towards migrants and minorities. Most of the crimes are committed by groups, not by individuals, accepted by parts of mainstream society, in the East more than in West Germany. Only a few of the attacks are planned. Crimes like bodily injury are often caused by circumstantial factors: offenders may be stimulated by alcohol or events like a skinhead rock concert, by victims who can easily be attacked, by the group dynamics, etc. (Gamper and Willems 2006).

State authorities and civil society were mobilized by the increasingly militant offenses since 1990. Liberals and the left, trade unions and churches organized different forms of public protests such as demonstrations, rock against the far right concerts, and long lines of candlelight demonstrations. Professional activities focused on long-lasting social work with young people. Consultant projects advised communities how to react to far-right violence. Round tables were created, involving social workers, community representatives, the police, and other local agencies. Exit programs support individuals who are willing to leave right-wing subcultures. All this is supported by a number of anti-Nazi websites offering information and advice.

State authorities subsidized some of the projects. Alongside these instruments the Ministry of the Interior set an old instrument in motion that seemed to be successful in fighting right-wing extremist organizations: if they attack substantial principles of the basic law (democracy, rule of law, separation of powers, etc.) they can be banned. The Ministry of the Interior has the right to ban an organization under certain conditions. If it is a party, the constitutional court may do so. In 1952 the neo-Nazi SRP was banned, in 1956 the communist party KPD.

However, the politics of banning practiced in the 1990s (see Table 3.2) did not really weaken right-wing-extremism. On the contrary, they learned from being kept under surveillance and under prosecution and adapted accordingly. "*Freie Kameradschaften*" (free comradeships) were founded. They built structures on a very low level only, and hardly kept connections with other groups in order to avoid being watched by state authorities. In so doing they strengthened right-wing-extremism as a social movement: bullying political enemies and ethnic minorities, taking part in right-wing demonstrations, organizing right-wing rock concerts and many more activities turned them into a mysterious attraction beyond fixed organizational structures. A group called "autonomous

Table 3.2 Right-wing extremist organizations banned by the German Federal Ministry from January 1990 to March 2009

Organization	Date of ban
Nationalistische Front (NF)	November 26, 1992
Deutsche Alternative (DA)	December 8, 1992
Nationale Offensive (NO)	December 21, 1992
Wiking-Jugend (WJ)	November 10, 1994
Freiheitliche Deutsche Arbeiterpartei (FAP)	February 22, 1995
Blood & Honour (B&H) with White Youth	September 12, 2000
Collegium Humanum (CH) with Bauernhilfe e.V	April 8, 2008
Heimattreue Deutsche Jugend (HDJ)	March 31, 2009

Source: Ministry of the Interior 2009: 20ff.; *Der Spiegel* online 31 March 2009

nationalists" took the habits and outfits of the left-wing autonomous groups to infiltrate demonstrations. The Federal Office for the Protection of the Constitution reports them to be operating in the Berlin area and western Germany; target groups of their militant action are not migrants but political enemies like left-wing radicals and the police.[2]

Right-wing extremist parties in Western Europe

After World War I (1914–18) fascist parties were founded in many European countries. Benito Mussolini's fascists supported German National Socialists for a long time. Sir Oswald Mosley's British Union of Fascists, the Hungarian Szeged fascism, the Romanian iron guards, and Spanish falangism were further manifestations of right-wing reactions to the modernization of society. There are good reasons to speak of an "age of extremes," as Hobsbawm did in his great study on 20th-century Europe (Hobsbawm 1994). It is no surprise to meet fascist elements in modern European societies (again), although democratization has been rather successful after World War II.

Skepticism about immigration in general and about Islamic minorities in particular, about political elites in charge, bureaucratic structures, and the plan to give "democracy back to the people" are elements of modern European right-wing extremist parties. Some of them have changed their platforms from Nazi-parties to populist programs and strategies, others have been founded in conservative political milieux (Mudde 2007) and remained there. Three different types of right-wing extremist parties can be identified today: fascist parties fighting the democratic system such as the Spanish *Fuerza Nueva* and the Italian *Movimento Sociale Italiano*; nationalist and racist parties such as the French *Front National* and the Belgian *Vlaams Belang*; and right-wing populist parties such as the Austrian *Bündnis Zukunft Österreich* and the Swiss *Schweizer Volkspartei* (Stöss 2010). Since the 1970s, there is a different development in European countries. In some countries like Northern Ireland and the UK, these parties did not have any success in national elections. For the first time in history, Sweden now has members of a right-wing populist party in the

Table 3.3 Right-wing extremist parties in Western Europe

Country	Party	Current election results
Norway	Progress Party	22.9% (national elections 2009)
Switzerland	Swiss People's Party	26.6% (national elections 2011)
Germany	NPD	6%, States of Mecklenburg-Vorpommern (2011), 5.6% Saxonia (2009)
Great Britain	BNP	8.3% (EU elections 2009) 33 deputies in local parliaments
Italy	Lega Nord	10.2% (EU elections 2009)
Austria	FPÖ	12.7% (EU elections 2009)
	Bündnis Zukunft Österreich	4.6% (EU elections 2009)
Denmark	Danish People's Party	14.8% (EU elections 2009)
The Netherlands	Party for Freedom	17.9% (EU elections 2009). Local elections 2010: Strongest party in Almere, second in The Hague. National elections 2010: 24 seats (third strongest party)
Sweden	Sweden Democrats	5.7% (national elections 2010)
France	Front National	17.8% (regional elections 2010), 118 deputies
Belgium	Vlaams Belang	7.7% (national elections 2010)
Finnland	The True Finns	19.0% (national elections 2011)

Source: Author's own compilation

national parliament. In the general elections of September 2010, the Swedish Democrats got 5.7 percent of the vote after conducting a strong anti-Islamic election campaign. In Italy, Denmark, Norway, Austria, Belgium and France right-wing extremist parties must be reckoned with. They do have influence on parliamentary politics and the administration (Arzheimer 2008). These differences between countries are due to the fact of different election systems and the capability of the conservatives to cover the orientations of right-wing-extremist voters.

Jean-Marie Le Pen (*Front National*), the late Jörg Haider (FPÖ/BZÖ), Geert Wilders (Party for Freedom) and Christoph Blocher (Swiss People's Party) are/were nationally and internationally well-known leaders of their far-right parties. They are charismatic personalities, able to attract new right-wing voters. Jimmie Akesson, 31-year-old leader of the anti-Islamic Sweden Democrats, represents a younger generation, performing a smooth version of right-wing extremism. In Germany there is no charismatic person within the NPD or DVU. This makes a big difference, because on the far right, political success depends very much on these charismatic persons representing strong leadership. All of them cover the populist political model, attracting and integrating different wings of the parties and the electorate.

The rise of the British extreme right is an example of how current modernization of right-wing extremism will move forward. After 2000 the British National Party (BNP) won many seats in local elections in the former industrial belt, as in Oldham, Blackburn, Stoke and Burnley, where they became the second largest party (Eatwell 2004). After membership increased since 2001 and some more good results in local elections (London-Barking, London-Dagenham), they won 8.3 percent in the elections to the European Parliament in 2009, sending two representatives to the parliament now. The success of the BNP started in 1999, when Nick Griffin, a 40-year-old Cambridge graduate, took over the leadership of the party from John Tyndall. Griffin had been known as a Holocaust denier and strong extremist in the 1990s, but he began to modernize the BNP. He emphasized a new party platform, addressing target groups like poorer farmers and truck drivers, concentrating on local issues, improving the organization and distancing himself from fascist positions. Influenced by the French New Right he claimed that no race is superior to any other, they are just different (Eatwell 2004).

The boundary between far-right populism and traditional right-wing extremism in Europe remains blurred. A look at individual European countries shows that both militant action and populist programs are driving the right-wing political field. European countries are growing closer and closer together, cooperating in the European Union (EU) without borders under the Schengen treaty, ensuring since 1995 the free flow of human beings, goods, traffic and ideas. What about cooperation of right-wing extremist and populist parties? Right-wing groups in Europe know each other. They have been building networks reaching back to the interwar period after 1918. Ideas of "Euro-Fascism" were rediscovered in the 1950s. From that point of view cooperation of the far right in Europe is an attractive proposition. The elections to the European Parliament in 2009 transformed these ideas into parliamentary practice, but all attempts to build strong right-wing alliances in the European Parliament have failed. In 2006 the right-wing alliance of seven parties in the European Parliament was founded in order to provide more efficiency to parliamentary duties as well as to the national level. After one year the fragile pooling attempts broke because of programmatic and personal differences. Although there seem to be many obstacles when trying to build European coalitions, there is an impact on conservative parties on the national level. The threat for them is to lose parts of their constituencies. If the conservative parties perform too moderately and cut some of their traditional conservative positions, then these parts could join their radical forces.

Concluding discussion

It is said that times of crisis are a boon for right-wingers. German history shows that the rise of right-wing parties is deeply linked with social and economic crisis. Exploiting social fears of voters is the main business of far-right parties and social movements. Unemployment, social fears of the middle classes, low levels of democratic and republican awareness, and the inability of politics to manage the crisis led to the rise of the National Socialist movement up to 1933 in Germany. Do modern macro-economic developments such as globalization, migration and the post-industrial decline of manufacture employment in

Western Europe have a direct impact on the right-wing electorate? Comparative studies tend to reject this explanation, because the national policies dealing with these issues vary. Analyzing national elections in 16 European countries from 1981 to 1998, Swank and Betz found out that welfare state policies directly depress the right-wing electorate (Swank and Betz 2003). Thus, national strategies and policies against racist movements clearly affect the outcome: national, and even regional and local state players and counter-movements are responsible for democratization and for fighting back the extreme right. Although right-wing populist movements are rising in many European countries, there won't be a common strategy to counter them, as national and local conditions are very different. This might be one reason why the EU monitors racist developments but does not get involved in developing national strategies to counter them.

Non-acceptance of immigration and prejudice toward immigrants are common values of right-wing voters in Europe. This electorate mainly consists of younger males on a low skill and education level. Most of them are laborers or unemployed (Arzheimer 2008: 385ff.). The target groups of hostility differ across Europe: in France the targets are immigrants from the Maghreb and Africa, in Britain those from Pakistan, in Germany primarily migrants from Turkey. More and more, people with an Islamic background are becoming targets of racist hostility in Western European countries. The emergence of right-wing populism in many European countries has to be answered by a clear and transparent immigration policy. So far, there is no common European policy. Even in Germany immigration and integration have been neglected for many years.

Recent public discourse in Germany highlights right-wing extremism as a social movement (Klärner and Kohlstruck 2006; Hartleb 2009). This is a new development, because until now the political operations of the far right had been considered to be part of a subculture, neglected more or less by the general public. It is being argued now that the intensity of networking, demonstration and provocation turned the far right into a modern working-class movement, based on stable milieux. Political and cultural modes of behavior are more embedded in adolescent lifestyles than ever before. Although they are still minorities, this is a change indeed. Hitler's NSDAP benefitted from the decline of the middle class at the end of the Weimar Republic. Now members of the working class who are suffering from the economic crisis become targets of far-right propaganda. Until recently the NPD and other far-right organizations did not succeed in turning their adherents into a social movement. In the future the main target group will be young people who lack education and training, unable to begin "normal" working biographies. One way to support a democratic future will mean to devote more attention to education and training, and to fighting unemployment.

Right-wing populist movements come and go. Their time frame seems to be limited to just a few years. As can be seen in history, most of them existed for a limited time. Does this mean they will soon disappear in Europe? It can be argued that they will not, because they focus on the immigration issue. As long as ethnic conflicts and competition for jobs continue to rise or at least stay high, right-wing populists may continue to be successful in elections and in shaping public opinion. The "populist moment" that Goodwyn (1978) identified when studying the farmer's movement in the US at the end of the 19th century seems to be intensive even now, because the underlying social circumstances take decades if not centuries to change.

Right-wing populist movements have an impact on governmental policies. The leading mainstream parties must not neglect the attitudes and expectations of the right-wing electorate. Both Nicolas Sarkozy's moderate right in France and Silvio Berlusconi's party in Italy are sharing their voters with their right-wing competitors. Both developments have existed for years. The policies and programs implemented by the moderate right in charge are influenced by the extreme right. In many European parliamentary systems, coalitions between two or even more parties are preconditions for building parliamentary majorities and stable governments. After 1945 Germany has never had a government ruled by one party alone. Today there is a five-party system including conservatives, social democrats, greens, liberals and the left. Thus, successful parties from the far right can greatly influence the balance of a coalition.

Right-wing extremism and populism try to put the wheel of history into reverse. Understanding these phenomena means learning about the trends in modern society. The far right always has been a reaction to the speed of modernization and democratization. The Weimar Republic (1918–33) is a good example: transitioning from an authoritarian monarchy to a republic in 1918/19, to a democratic constitution and a modern economy led to violent reactions on the part of traditionally anti-democratic forces. Right-wing extremism and populism in contemporary Germany and Western Europe is a challenge again for politics and society. Empirical research and recent studies in the social sciences confirm that a positive political framework for the future must include transparent policies of migration and more political, cultural, and social participation in order to confront the consequences of globalization.

Note

1 On December 6 2012 German state premiers agreed to pursue a ban of the NPD in court, but the CDU/FDP government under Chancellor Merkel defeated the opposition's proposal in parliament on April 25, 2013. Representatives from all parties spoke in support of such a ban in the German parliament on February 1 2013.
2 Bundesamt für Verfassungsschutz 2009. The Federal Office for the Protection of the Constitution is a domestic secret service, offering public information and reports on political extremism (see: www.verfassungsschutz.de, click English version).

References

Arzheimer, Kai (2008) *Die Wähler der extremen Rechten 1980–2002*, Wiesbaden.
Bundesamt für Verfassungsschutz (2009) "Autonome Nationalisten—Rechtsextremistische Militanz", www.verfassungsschutz.de.
Decker, Frank (ed.) (2006) *Populismus. Gefahr für die Demokratie oder nützliches Korrektiv?*, Wiesbaden.

Döring, Uta (2006) "'National befreite Zonen.' Zur Entstehung und Karriere eines Kampfbegriffs", in Andreas Klärner and Michael Kohlstruck (eds) *Moderner Rechtsextremisms in Deutschland*, Hamburg, 177–206.

Eatwell, Roger (2004) "The Extreme Right in Britain: The Long Road to 'Modernization'," in Roger Eatwell and Cas Mudde (eds) *Western Democracies and the New Extreme Right Challenge*, London and New York, 62–80.

ENAR (2008) *Shadow Report 2008: Racism in Germany*, cms.horus.be/files/99935/MediaArchive/national/Germany%20-%20SR%202008.pdf.

Flemming, Lars (2005) *Das NPD-Verbotsverfahren*, Baden-Baden.

Fromm, Rainer (1998) *Die "Wehrsportgruppe Hoffmann"*, Frankfurt.

Gamper, Markus and Helmut Willems (2006) "Rechtsextreme Gewalt—Hintergründe, Täter und Opfer," in Heitmeyer and Schröttle (eds) *Gewalt. Beschreibungen, Analysen, Prävention*, Bonn, 439–61.

Goodwyn, Laurence B. (1978) *The Populist Moment*, Oxford, London, New York.

Hartleb, Florian (2009) "Gegen Globalisierung und Demokratie. Die NPD als eine neue soziale Bewegung im europäischen Kontext?", *Zeitschrift für Parlamentsfragen* 1: 96–108.

Häusler, Alexander (ed.) (2008) *Rechtspopulismus als Bürgerbewegung. Kampagnen gegen Islam und Moscheebau und kommunale Gegenstrategien*, Wiesbaden.

Heitmeyer, Wilhelm and Monika Schröttle (eds) (2006) *Gewalt. Beschreibungen, Analysen, Prävention*, Bonn, 439–61.

Hobsbawm, Eric (1994) *The Age of Extremes. The Short Twentieth Century 1914–1991*, London.

Jaschke, Hans-Gerd (1993) "Sub-Cultural Aspects of Right-Wing Extremism," in Dirk Berg-Schlosser and Ralf Rytlewski (eds) *Political Culture in Germany*, Houndmills, Basingstoke and London, 126–36.

——(2006) *Politischer Extremismus*, Wiesbaden.

Klärner, Andreas and Kohlstruck, Michael (2006) *Moderner Rechtsextremismus in Deutschland*, Hamburg.

Kriskofski, Torsten (2010) "Intellektualisierungsbemühungen im Rechtsextremismus", in Armin Pfahl-Traughber (ed.) *Jahrbuch für Extremismus-und Terrorismusforschung*, Bonn, 125–50.

Menhorn, Christian (2010) "Die Erosion der Skinhead-Bewegung als eigenständiger Subkultur", in Armin Pfahl-Traughber (ed.) *Jahrbuch für Extremismus-und Terrorismusforschung*, Bonn, 125–50.

Ministry of the Interior (Germany) (ed.) (2009) *Annual Report on the Protection of the Constitution 2008*, Berlin.

Mudde, Cas (2007) *Populist Radical Right Parties in Europe*, Cambridge.

Stegbauer, Andreas (2007) "The Ban of Right-Wing Extremist Symbols According to Section 86a of the German Criminal Code," *German Law Journal* 8(2).

Stöss, Richard (2010) *Rechtsextremismus im Wandel*, Berlin, www.fes-gegen-rechtsextremismus.de.

Swank, Duane and Hans-Georg Betz (2003) "Globalization, the Welfare State and Right-wing Populism in Western Europe," *Socio-Economic Review* 1: 215–45.

Virchow, Fabian and Christian Dornbusch (eds) (2008) *88 Fragen und Antworten zur NPD*, Schwalbach.

Wagner, Bernd and Dierk Borstel (2009) "Der Rechtsextremismus und sein gesteigertes Bedrohungspotential", in Wilhelm Heitmeyer (ed.) *Deutsch-deutsche Zustände*, Bonn, 284–98.

4 "National solidarity—no to globalization"

The economic and sociopolitical platform of the National Democratic Party of Germany (NPD)

Gideon Botsch and Christoph Kopke[1]

In 2010, Germany's *Nationaldemokratische Partei Deutschlands* (NPD, National Democratic Party), the oldest party within the extreme right-wing spectrum of the Federal Republic of Germany,[2] was able to de-escalate the internal battles that had kept members preoccupied for years. Such progress was needed in order to achieve what had long been a stated party goal:[3] at the convention on June 4–5 of that year, an agreement was reached on a national party platform headlined with the slogan *Work—Family—Fatherland*.[4] Furthermore, at year's end they announced the merger with the Deutsche Volks-Union (DVU, German People's Union), which means that one of its most serious competitors among right-wing extremist parties has now been de facto absorbed into the NPD. Almost all other political parties of the German extreme right have become insignificant in recent years,[5] and the neo-Nazi spectrum has similarly been integrated into the NPD. Apart from the fact that the NPD may have to fear the competition of xenophobic right-wing populism by other parties seeking to woo voters, it really remains the only nationally relevant political power openly expressing anti-government, anti-constitutional right-wing extremism. While its significance within the overall political culture of the Federal Republic remains marginal, within the right-wing extremist spectrum it has become a hegemonic power.

This means that Udo Voigt, who functioned as chairman from mid-1996 to the end of 2011, can claim to have achieved three essential goals he had been working towards since taking over the party leadership: to change the NPD's internal structure to turn it again into a visible political power; to overcome the division of the "national opposition" among DVU, NPD, and neo-Nazis; and to achieve a more convincing party platform with which the NPD could go public.

The platform that was valid from the end of 1996 to 2010 remained largely true to traditional middle-class protectionism, but at the same time supported a social Darwinist performance-oriented agenda, as can be found in the oldest programmatic NPD documents.[6] There the systems of social security were anchored relatively weakly despite a fundamental acceptance of the German tradition of the welfare state.[7] The party platform polemicized against the "mirage of the total welfare state" and saw it as the task of social policies simply to "protect the individual in the happenstance of human life from becoming the innocent victim of misery."[8] A flyer to that effect which was circulated as the party platform for the federal election campaign of 1998 articulated the NPD's central socio-political demand very clearly in the slogan "welfare policy for our people alone."[9]

Thus at a time in which the NPD was trying to establish itself as a positive social power, its rather anti-social program remained in effect.[10] Still, Voigt had already declared that "the social question" would be "the focal point of future political developments."[11]

Volksgemeinschaft vs. globalization

In its 1996 platform the NPD had already agitated against what it understood as globalization. The term then moved to the center of NPD propaganda from 2001 onwards. The NPD youth organization *Junge Nationaldemokraten* (JN, Young National Democrats), for example, created a website explicitly targeting globalization.[12]

In January 2002 Udo Voigt wrote a political strategy paper for the party leadership in which he outlined the party's socio-political direction. In it he declared that globalism/globalization would be their central theme in the federal election year.[13] Voigt defined globalism as a certain aspect of "economic imperialism" characterized by the "pushback of governmental decision-making competencies in favor of the dominance of capital," its "method" the "reduction of government control mechanisms over domestic markets, euphemistically called free trade." For Voigt, globalization is the description of the process of globalism, its consequences "poverty, unemployment, dismantling of social services, and environmental destruction."[14]

Voigt explained that this political focus was mainly chosen for strategic reasons in 2002. Starting with the assumption that it would only be possible to build a core of voters with "authentic national democratic themes," he declared the potential electorate of the *Partei des demokratischen Sozialismus* (PDS, Party of Democratic Socialism, now transformed into *Die Linke*) in central Germany, i.e. in the states on the territory of the former German Democratic Republic (GDR), to be an interesting target group:

> PDS voters are primarily people who are dissatisfied with the current situation in the FRG [Federal Republic of Germany]. Opinion polls show that these people tend to reject *Überfremdungserscheinungen* [foreign infiltration], growing crime rates, the loss of *gemeinschaftliche Werte* [communitarian values], growing unemployment, and the dismantling of social services. Together these themes show that they should actually … tend to vote for national parties … Our efforts should aim to lead these potential voters to the NPD.[15]

For Voigt the theme of globalization fulfills all requirements of a political focus theme: authenticity, exclusivity, sustainability, novelty, and a personal relevance for the targeted group: "Since globalization is closely linked to the dissolution of national sovereignty, it can be made believable that the NPD's stance against globalization is a serious effort for the preservation of national autonomy and a territorial people's economy." Other thematic areas, such as domestic security, immigration or themes related to the past, he said, were at a comparative disadvantage. In his view this is true as well for the theme "social justice," since except in special cases like the exclusion of foreign migrants from social security it would be difficult to demonstrate authenticity, let alone exclusivity. However, he concluded that the explosive nature of the theme could also be integrated into a globalization campaign.

Voigt demonstrated a series of possible articulations that would enable them to bring the anti-globalization rhetoric in line with the NPD's radical-nationalistic worldview. Apart from unemployment, dismantling of social services, and environmental destruction, he also wanted to see questions of sovereignty, civil rights, and "anti-imperialism" articulated. These would enable them, at least conceptionally, to address a much larger potential constituency instead of only those "losers of modernization" affected by unemployment and the loss of their status.

Voigt also regarded a second thematic area as appropriate for the election year: the notion of *Volksgemeinschaft* (community of the people—a key term in historical National Socialist propaganda). Only the NPD, said Voigt, uses this notion in a positive way, what he called "a counter strategy to the growing isolation of individuals in a multicultural society defined by consumption." The idea of *Volksgemeinschaft* would only be realizable politically, he said, if "the welfare of the people and not the welfare of capital" marked the center of politics. This was why "family and social policies must be addressed more forcefully in this context." However, Voigt added again that "at present the NPD has no competency in the area of family politics. Even the identification of the NPD with the idea of community is only relatively small."

In terms of content Voigt's ideas complement the "action program for a better Germany" which was drafted around the same time.[16] The roughly 80-page document articulated a lot more extensively than before how the NPD could claim to represent a positive social power in the context of its fight for the German *Volksgemeinschaft*. The title picture, showing a cute blond girl on a healthy green meadow, was supposed to express the competency in family politics that Voigt advocated. In the first part about "social policy" the program proclaims: "Whoever wants the welfare state must declare allegiance to the *Volksgemeinschaft!*"[17] In addition to its notorious attacks against foreigners ("jobs for Germans first"), in the section about economic and social policy the NPD demands, among other things, the establishment of "the ability for the government to act" through the introduction of a series of special taxes, the unraveling of multinationals, the control of the flow of capital, a qualification offensive, a social tax reform, and the revitalization of national competition through a series of measures in support of the middle class, including lowering the cost of social benefits. Beyond that, economic and sociopolitical questions are also addressed in other sections, especially in the context of family and population policy, but also foreign and European policies, education and research policies, as well as environmental protection.

In the fall of 2003 the NPD added a Europa platform in preparation for the elections to the European Parliament.[18] In the section "spatially oriented national economy instead of Europe-wide dominance of capital" it advocated in favor of a return to the D-Mark as "establishment of national state currency sovereignty," rejected the European Union (EU) expansion to the East, and demanded a "national policy of agriculture."

This set of programmatic documents formed the basis for the NPD's economic and socio-political agitation which has become more visible in the public arena since around 2004. It undoubtedly served to capture new groups of voters, especially in the eastern German states, and it garnered the first fruits in the European elections as well as in the regional elections in Saxony in June, and the state elections in September of 2004.[19]

"National Socialism"

Functionally, the themes of *Volksgemeinschaft*, globalization, and the "social question" also targeted the right-wing spectrum itself, achieving significant integration of neo-national socialist organizations such as the *Kameradschaften* into the NPD. Although these groups were less significant as potential voters in the "battle for the parliaments," they had a significant role to play in protest actions in the "battle for the street."[20] The NPD tried to demonstrate its presence in the area of socio-political protest with its own activities as well as by participating jointly in demonstrations together with broader, local co-operations with neo-national socialist organizations against the sociopolitical "Agenda 2010" of the federal government at the time.[21] The *Nationale und soziale Aktivisten Mitteldeutschland* (NSAM, National and Social Activists of Central Germany) served as transmission for a coordination of East German *Kameradschaften* with close connections to the NPD youth organization (JN).

In the concrete realization of these strategic focal targets, slogans and political styles from the camp of the political opposition were adapted and imitated— from the reformulation of old anti-imperialist GDR slogans, to the former West German radical left, to the outfit of the subcultural political milieu that resembled the stylistic elements of the *Autonome* (radical left-wing anarchist youth organizations). Such purely superficial imitations of the left have received increasing attention with the arrival of so-called "autonomous nationalists" in the same period. At its core this tendency is merely a form of hyperactivism that reduces the content to mere collectivism.[22]

Although the party leadership regards the "autonomous nationalists" with great skepticism,[23] the activities of the neo-national socialist organizations of the *Kameradschaften* represent an important element in the political strategy.

For the practical realization of anti-globalization campaigns Voigt articulated a series of possible activities already in 2002, including vigils and information desks in front of employment agencies.[24] Voigt saw the extreme right demonstrations in May as culmination and highlight of the planned campaign. Already the *Freiheitliche Deutsche Arbeiterpartei* (FAP) had organized neo-Nazi demonstrations in celebration of May 1, and in competition to the traditional left-wing and union events until 1993, when the Federal Government filed for a ban of the party (which came into effect two years later). The JN and the *Kameradschaften* organized their first joint demonstration on May 1, 1996. They have been trying to organize similar events both centrally or more regionally together with the mother party ever since.[25] Both NPD and *Kameradschaften* can benefit from the planning and organization of these activities: the NPD contributes the organizational infrastructure and guarantees the legal framework if necessary; the *Kameradschaften* mobilize their activist followers, which is the only way to actually arrive at a significant number of participants.

Voigt preferred to realize such demonstrations in the context of political campaigns, as he explained in his strategy paper.[26] The neo-Nazi spectrum, too, desired an expansion and a more flexible planning of its activities while at the same time wanting to coordinate individual activities with larger campaigns. This is confirmed, for example, in a reprint of a fierce pamphlet from 1971, which has been circulating among *Kameradschaft* members and JN activists since 2004. It states: "It is important that sporadic isolated activities are now replaced by total synchronization. All activities must be coordinated in this manner."[27]

In 2006 the spectrum from NPD to open neo-Nazis began to refer to a common framework in its hitherto little-coordinated activities in the area of economic and social policy. In reference to the left-wing jargon they created the short-hand "Antikap-Kampagne" (for "anti-capitalist campaign"). In 2007 the activities were merged into a joint mobilization for the G8 summit in Heiligendamm, with a common logo (*"Gib 8—sozial statt global,"* "pay attention—socially, not globally"), and the motto "There is no just globalization."[28]

The NPD expected resonance on all relevant levels: inside the party from the G8 campaign, inside the entire "national resistance" and also beyond the spectrum. In their view this campaign had been aimed at orienting the individual party sections to the political focus of the NPD, i.e. the anti-capitalist social and economic policy. It also intended to increase the public perception of Nationalists as opponents of globalization, and finally to assess the party's ability with respect to campaigns.[29] Already in the preparation of the anti-cap campaign NPD, JN and *Kameradschaften* had been working in close cooperation at least since the spring of 2006. In coordination with the campaign goals the federal executive committee of the JN at the time resolved in June of 2006 that "Nationalism means critique of capitalism." It said further that their goal was not only a tactical but a fundamental rejection of capitalist conditions, which reduced the diversity of the human being to the economic, the utilitarian, and the instinctual levels. Instead of differentiating between a true and false capitalism it must be criticized in its totality as a reductive trade relationship among humans.[30]

The concentrated approach and close cooperation between *Kameradschaften* and NPD/JN was visible throughout the beginning phase of the anti-cap campaign. Some passages in the nine-page mobilization declaration are almost identical to passages from NPD publications. This declaration describes globalization in the form of a mythic conspiracy of targeted aggression against the identity and stability of individual nations, their traditional values and structures:

> With its attack on the territorial sovereignty and legality principle of the national state globalization destroys the only imaginable geo-political space of people's rule in favor of anonymous, supra-national power structures. It is practically a program of political incapacitation as well as economic exploitation of the peoples. Contrary to this the "boundary setting, *volk*- and *heimat*-focused domestic counter principle of nationalism" must be "the only effective socialist weapon."[31]

In this context the slogan "Nationaler Sozialismus jetzt!" ("National Socialism now!") became one of the most frequent formulations on right-wing extremist banners and in choruses of demonstrators.[32] This actual talk about "national socialism" occasionally touches on ideas of a "Prussian" or "German socialism," which refers to an authoritarian and "caring" government with strict control of the economy, as for example envisioned by Oswald Spengler or Werner Sombart.[33] Gregor Straßer, who had developed into a critic of Hitler inside the *Nationalsozialistische Deutsche Arbeiterpartei* (NSDAP, National Socialist German Workers Party) and been murdered in 1934 in the context of the "Röhm" Affair, had varied this motif in the 1930s as well.[34] Even though there are occasionally individual quotes from Straßer or paraphrases and portraits of ostensibly "socialist" *Sturmabteilung* (SA, or stormtroopers) leaders such as Ernst Röhm or Karl Ernst in the texts,[35] today, Strasserism does not represent a central reference point in the majority of the "national" camp, certainly not as an alternative to the mistaken developments under National Socialist rule. The *Kameradschaften* with NPD on the one side certainly do not reflect a "left" or "revolutionary" vs. a "reactionary" wing of the "national opposition." In the majority of cases the term *nationaler Sozialismus* (national Socialism) simply serves as a variant of the word *Nationalsozialismus* (National socialism): whoever calls himself a "national Socialist," generally wants to declare his allegiance to the historical "Hitler movement," without having to fear legal consequences. There are numerous examples of this synonymous use of "National socialism" and "national Socialism."[36]

"*Raumorientierte Volkswirtschaft*"

The NPD's economic and social program can be traced back to three origins that are themselves closely connected to the programmatic development of historical national socialism and can count on broad acceptance in the federal German neo-Nazi spectrum: the thought of a "national solidarism"; the declaration of hostilities vis-à-vis "interest slavery"; and the demand for a "*raumorientierte Volkswirtschaft*" (spatially oriented national economy).

For the latter Per Lennart Aae serves as an expert inside the NPD. The *Kameradschaften* referred back to this advisor to the Saxon State Parliament representative during the anti-cap campaign in 2006 whenever they wanted to articulate alternatives to the existing system. Aae was one of the main speakers at the joint launch and training event in the context of the campaign in the Thuringian town of Lichtenhain-Oberweißbach on March 18, 2006. When the *Freie Kräfte Südthüringen* (Free Forces of Southern Thuringia) asked on their website "So what actually is our alternative?" they left it to Aae to answer.[37]

A treatise mainly scripted by Aae and Arne Schimmer about the "Principles of a national democratic doctrine of macro economy" struggled to specify the concept.[38] It is not about a continuation of national socialist space planning, autarchy, and restructuring concepts of the 1930s and 1940s. Those were oriented on the interests of highly concentrated trusts and monopolies, and were conceptualized as continental imperialism: autarchy, albeit propagandistically exaggerated, remained a function of the military and war economy.[39] The "spacially oriented national economy" is instead based on the idea of smaller, middle-class units: "That means an economic system that enables a harmonious, balanced, and differentiated economy in the local and regional home of the people, that is in socially and culturally comprehensible territory."[40]

With this concept the NPD reconnects to right-wing radical positions of the interwar years. Under the title "German Ways," Aae and Schimmer refer, for example, to the theorist Othmar Spann,[41] to Walter Eucken, and above all to Werner Sombart, one of the most important macroeconomists of the "conservative revolution in their eyes."[42] Indeed, Sombart's positions can easily be conflated with contemporary NPD positions. The NPD, too, is advocating renunciation and autarchy instead of the strengthening of the capitalist dynamic, armament, and imperialism.[43]

A more important reference for the NPD even than Sombart's *Deutscher Sozialismus* of 1934 is Johann Gottlieb Fichte's treatise *Der geschloßne Handelsstaat* (*The Closed Trade State*) from the year 1800. Its central motif is the de-coupling of Germany from the world economy. By advocating this, the philosopher did not advocate catching up with modernization during a phase of development through protective tariffs and infrastructure measures—as Friedrich List did a few decades later in order to lay the groundwork for competitiveness on the world market. The *geschloßne Handelsstaat*, rather, is meant to last forever. In the pre- and proto-industrial phase Fichte argued for the establishment of a "rational state" that would direct the private enterprise initiative by regulating the market on the inside and completely shutting it off from the outside. Fichte sees the basis for this in the total restriction and state control of the subjects' foreign contacts:

The state is bound to ensure the condition resulting from the balance of this traffic to all citizens through law and enforcement. But it cannot do so if any person has influence on this balance that does not fall within its legal realm and control. It must therefore completely cut off the possibility of such influence—all foreign interactions must be forbidden.[44]

This concept is not only open to xenophobia, but also to Fichte's hatred of the Jews, which led the way to modern anti-Semitism.[45] Although anti-Jewish potential is only latent in the text of *Der geschloßne Handelsstaat* and not yet explicit, the nationalist Fichte revival of the 20th century very much viewed the ideas of *Der geschloßne Handelsstaat* in conjunction with Fichte's anti-Semitism. This is what the architects of the NPD's economic program are connecting to, emphasizing the political demand which has been reiterated since the first publication of the NPD's Manifesto in 1965, and which belongs to the program's historical continuities: a primacy of national politics before economy. The latter should serve the *Volksgemeinschaft* and must therefore also accept political control. Still, the NPD was always intent on the principal security of private property and entrepreneurship on a microeconomic basis. It oriented itself on the concept of a regulated, partly structured, small-scale domestic market, in which the existing export dominance of the large German corporations should be reduced, and domestic agriculture, regional artisans and small and medium-size businesses consciously promoted and preferred.

Against "interest slavery" and "loan capital"

The NPD's aggressive agitation against the "brutal interest-capitalism"[46] refers to classical and central motifs of right-wing extremist economic and social programs: it is against "financial," more precisely against "loan capital," and agitates to "break the bonds of Interest Slavery." A critique of capitalism from the right traditionally begins with the sphere of circulation and tends to systematically overestimate the role of financial capital. The admittedly increased influence of this sector throughout the 20th century, however, certainly spurs such forms of *Kapitalismuskritik*. Indeed, catastrophic consequences of individual financial transactions as well as the structural problems resulting from changes in global capital markets are easily absorbed and mobilized in the volkish version of *Kapitalismuskritik*. One should not conclude from this, however, that concern about these actual tendencies is the driving motivation, because beyond all thematic actuality a high level of programmatic continuity can be seen in this area as well. This is most likely a consequence of the anti-Semitic foundation of right-wing extremist *Kapitalismuskritik*.

Although anti-Semitism was only latently present in Fichte's *Der geschloßne Handelsstaat*, and in Silvio Gesell's *Freiwirtschaftslehre* (*Doctrine of Free Economy*), which also influenced the program of the "national camp," the system of interest was openly blamed on a "greedy Jewish financial capital" by Gesell's disciple Gottfried Feder, who co-authored the NSDAP party program with

Adolf Hitler in 1920. Just briefly, Feder had the opportunity to influence the practical economic policy of the National Socialist regime as state secretary in the *Reichswirtschaftsministerium* in 1933/34. Does the "national opposition" now hark back to this "anti-capitalist" national socialism of the early time of struggle? Only partially. For example, under the title "Why Gottfried Feder had to fail," its campaign platform presented a somewhat older text by Reiner Bischoff, a supporter of a right-wing extremist variety of the "free economy doctrine." The author admonishes Feder for not having started by attacking the basic evil of money, i.e. its ability to be accumulated. He counteracted that evil with the notion that money is forced to circulate and focused solely on interest, but as a price for scarcity interest must remain, because "financial capital is a good and can certainly gain a price if its availability decreases. In the financial sector, too, the microeconomic law of supply and demand must retain its validity!"[47]

The authors of the NPD party program seem less critical of Feder.[48] His criticism of "interest slavery" and the anti-capitalism of the NPD and the neo-Nazi spectrum share an identical anti-Semitic core, but such motivation is not made explicit in all texts by NPD authors. Thus the text about the "foundations of a national democratic macroeconomic doctrine" mentions the investment banker George Soros's speculative maneuvers and their consequences—perhaps exaggerating them, too—but it refrains from mentioning his Jewish origins.[49] In the programs and in some other parts the explicit mention of Jews is avoided, while the propaganda works with stereotypes, which are coded, sometimes weaker, sometimes stronger, but at least in the closer circle of addressees are easily decodable. In one paper originally meant for internal reference, but compiled for the conversation with interested citizens and political opponents, the NPD explains its position thus: "Globalization is a planetary expansion of the capitalist economic system under the leadership of big money. Although it is essentially Jewish-nomadic and homeless, it is housed primarily in politically and militarily protected headquarters on the East coast of the USA."[50]

"National solidarity"

In socio-political questions the quoted paper (dubbed *Argumentationshilfe*—argumentation help) limits itself notably to three anti-positions: against foreigners, against globalization, and against the EU. A certain degree of redistribution is suggested, through stronger taxation of property and inheritance.[51] The NPD repeatedly declared its allegiance to the classic German welfare system, partly due to national chauvinism and heroization of Bismarck's personality. In order to ease the burden on the middle class—the NPD's most important social reference point—the party demands that the parity of financing should be partially abandoned and the employer's contribution not be calculated based on wages, but on actual value added.[52]

Do the more recent programmatic developments inside the NPD represent a break from its traditional middle class-oriented, anti-social and anti-employee position? The vehement foregrounding of social policy under the code of a "national Socialism" certainly seems to suggest such a break. The intense preoccupation with economic and social-political themes in the course of the above-mentioned campaigns, in conjunction with elections and the parliamentary work in the state parliaments of Saxony (since 2004, by now in the second term) and Mecklenburg-Prepommerania (since 2006, by now also in the second term), as well as in numerous regional parliaments, has at least led to a quantitative growth of demands, position papers, and text passages in this area, and also to a certain amount of differentiation and further precision. This was joined with increasing activity by women in the NPD, which led in 2009 to the foundation of a first NPD women's organization, the *Ring Nationaler Frauen* (RNF). Intensive debates in this circle led to principles of family and education policy, which seem to address the lack of competency Udo Voigt had complained about in 2002.

During the second half of the decade the push for a new party platform grew stronger and stronger. It was spurred by the desire to be able to address the social and economic crisis more competently, and to push the rather anti-social fixation of the program into the background. In 2008/09 such programmatic renewal was promised repeatedly, but the heavy internal crises prevented a real attempt. Observers assumed that a programmatic debate would confront the party with a dilemma which it could not escape without damage: "The break between the wings also goes along the social question: Does the NPD want to agitate aggressively for a "national Socialism" or does it want to emphasize stronger national conservative positions?"[53]

The internal crisis did not prevent the party from presenting a federal election platform in 2009, which again paid great attention to the economic and social political field. This platform does not represent a radical break with the protectionist middle class-oriented program at all. This can be seen, for example, in the demand for tax reductions in favor of small and medium-size businesses,[54] in the renewed affirmation of entrepreneurial freedom combined with emphasis on the "social responsibility that comes with property,"[55] and the demand for special protection of domestic agriculture.[56] However, the social Darwinist and performance-oriented rhetoric of the 1996 platform was reduced. The party hopes to distinguish itself with the demand for minimum or combined wages as well as minimum pensions or the re-communalization of public services—all these demands are considered basic among the targeted East German electorate. They do not represent a rejection of the party's traditional social orientation at all. What is worth noting, however, is that the profile in the area of family policy was successfully strengthened, demanding marriage credits, wages for mothers, and a quantitative expansion of aid money to young families—although primarily for "biopolitical" reasons, and in general only for "German" families, in NPD language.[57] In terms of educational policy the NPD's goals remain highly anti-social, because they passionately support the "multi-level school system,"[58] which represents a major source of blatant social disparity in the Federal Republic.

The 2009 platform is the first result of the programmatic discussion inside the party. It led to the new party program the following year. In terms of content it mainly reiterated the economic and socio-political platform, as it had been developed over the eight years prior. Thus it states in the introduction to the section on "social policy as national solidarity": "National social policy combines social justice and economic sensibility. It has to secure the individual in the community, and promote the individual's efforts for the whole."[59] Here the NPD varies one of its oldest programmatic formulations. One sentence had remained unchanged from 1967 until now: "We need a social policy that conforms with social justice and economic sensibility. It has the task to strengthen the welfare of the entire people, to protect the individual in all happenstance of human life from innocently becoming a victim of misery to securing him a worry-free old age."[60] The attacks against the social welfare state have been removed, as has the following sentence that used to follow in the original program: "A social policy based on the mirage of a total welfare state whose responsibilities become a burden for all those who work fails its role and is anti-social."[61]

These corrections express the desire to show stronger social competency—a desire that does not only refer back to the influence of the neo-national socialist *Kameradschaften* but that also represents the party profile that Udo Voigt is determined to shape. That is why there are numerous specifications of economic and socio-political positions in the new party platform, which are in line with the platform of 2009, such as the demand for a general minimum wage, or a "people's pension," or the rejection of privatization in the area of the social security systems.[62] At the same time the program concludes: "Every German has the right and the duty to work."[63]

The unfailing commitment to the German state social insurance system does not also mean a break with the general social orientation of the NPD in its party platform, which continues to be directed at the middle class. For example, in the context of more concrete explanations of "spatially oriented national economy" the program demands:

> a micro economy that is based on the domestic *Lebensraum* [living space] and on the needs of the people, multifaceted and balanced. It does not see its emphasis in the unilateral export orientation, but in the strengthening of the domestic economy. Inside the spatially oriented national economy regional economic cycles are being promoted ... The basic needs must be met through the domestic economic spaces close to people's lives.[64]

This also conforms with the economic policy founded on "a free, but socially responsible entrepreneurship as the cornerstone of an economic system based on solidarity. The domestic small and medium-size businesses must be protected from the market power of globally active corporations."[65]

The *Grundgedanken* (basic ideas) that summarize the content of the party program, conclude: "National solidarity means: Social justice for all Germans. Property means responsibility. The economy has to serve the people and not the other way around. Without a nation state there can be no welfare state. Globalization destroys the nation state as a social protective space."[66] Although the demand for "national solidarity," which is built on the concept of *nationaler Solidarismus*, has to some extent always been anchored in the NPD, it probably became more rooted under the influence of the opening towards the neo-Nazi spectrum. The late attorney Jürgen Rieger who had been a major representative of the openly neo-National socialist spectrum, sketched in the party newspaper *Deutsche Stimme* in 2007 what he thought this meant. According to him, *Solidarismus* is founded on two pillars, the *Volksgemeinschaft* and the *Betriebsgemeinschaft*.[67] *Gemeinschaft* in this case stands in contrast to the concept of *Gesellschaft* (society), which the new party platform explicitly points out: "Western societies are material *Zweckverbände* [organizations with shared goals] without communal values. They don't develop any unifying culture ... The solidarity of an existing *Volksgemeinschaft* is substituted by the exaggerated representation of individual or group interests."[68]

In order to create *Gemeinschaft*, the idea of *Betriebsgemeinschaft* is introduced in the economic realm. This is done through the distribution of shares and options for employees, as they were already used in the Weimar era and later in the Federal Republic in the Erhard years as instruments for the integration of workers. The goal continues to be to break the power of unions and establish peace inside companies. The identification of the worker with his (middle-class) business is meant to be enhanced and thus a piece of concrete *Volksgemeinschaft* created. In the NPD program this basic idea of *Solidarismus* can be found in the section "Participation of the employee in the production of wealth."[69] Despite its basic orientation in social terms towards the middle class and in ideological terms towards the *Betriebsgemeinschaft*, the "national opposition" still reacts with aggression and hostility toward the idea of independent organizations of employee interests,[70] despite a significantly high potential of right-wing extremist tendencies among union members.[71] In its daily propaganda, in which the NPD presents itself as "protective power of the little people," only platitudes without content remain, including slogans such as "Modern Socialism is lived solidarism."[72]

In other respects, too, the concept of "national solidarity" is actually a code for anti-solidarity and social exclusion.[73] The entire NPD program—and there is no difference in this respect between 1996 and 2010—is dominated by the demand for a rejection of immigration, the return of foreigners living here, and until that can be completed, their radical exclusion from German society, which can only thus become a *Volksgemeinschaft*. After all, the NPD adheres strictly to a "sense of blood" and refers to naturalized foreigners and their descendents with contempt as "plastic Germans." This is applied to people who have been living in Germany for three or four generations. Jews are generally included in the group of foreigners by the NPD. Based on that, Steffen Kailitz calculates that the number of people who should be excluded from the German *Volksgemeinschaft* according to the NPD would add up to more than 11 million, or 14 percent of the population.[74]

In order to achieve a "just" social policy, the NPD counts on 100 percent employment, which it claims would follow automatically in the closed system of a "spatially oriented national economy with sustainable promotion of the middle class." On the other hand—and this is emphasized—it is based on the "exclusion of foreigners from the social insurance system." They should be dealt with through a "special social law for foreigners," and social welfare for foreigners should be financed by "the foreigners themselves and the businesses who employ them."[75] The NPD leaves no doubt that the goal is a reduction by which "foreigners" living in Germany are meant basically to be starved—as can be seen in the cynical flyer "This is What Happens When the NPD Rules."[76] The new party program remarks that the law governing this system of special social policies for foreigners should "in the explanation of its duties and entitlements ... also be supportive of the idea of return."[77]

Crash scenarios

In practice, the "return" of the foreigners would mean the forced deportation of millions of people.[78] Since such a project could hardly be realized without violence, it poses the question of how the NPD wants to achieve its goal. Even the NPD cannot think it likely that it will emerge from federal elections as the strongest party, as the above-mentioned flyer entitled "This Can Become Reality" suggests.

So what does the NPD hope to achieve? Its platform is neither a "concrete utopia," nor based on a real political possibility. Supported by cultural pessimist *angst* scenarios, the milieu of the NPD counts on the inevitable collapse of the existing "globalist" systems. In this scenario the German people will be given one last chance for self-determination: "The 21st century will determine the German people's existence or eradication. It is characterized by existential threats such as the negative birth rate, a rapidly escalating *Überfremdung*, the control by supranational organizations and globalization with its devastating consequences."[79]

With its reference to Werner Sombart, the economic policy paper refers back to his diagnosis of time, according to which:

> capitalism is past its peak and in a phase of paralysis and crippling that is defined by the end of technical innovation, a kind of re-feudalization of agrarian structures, and the collapse of the world market into closed macro economic spaces. Far from deploring this development, one saw in it on the contrary the beginning of a healing process, through which the human being was led back to himself.[80]

The NPD, too, sees the prerequisite for a nationalist policy in the collapse of capitalism as it understands it. After this "great crash" it would face the task of:

> preparing the "de-marketization" of economic life—and, as in earlier times, strengthen the individual economy that is for example still dominant in

all family relationships instead of the market economy. That would not mean to no longer use the mechanism of the market at all, however! But there are concrete economic levers beyond market coordination.[81]

Problems of the economy, too, can therefore only be posed as "questions of the system."[82] Only after the collapse of the "system" will the path be free for the de-coupling from the international financial markets, in order to push back foreign capital. From this perspective the "crash" is actually a desirable event: "The current crisis of the world financial systems offers the historical opportunity to leave the vicious cycle of debt, interest and interest's interest, and the crazy monopoly stock market capitalism, in order to reach independence, decentralization, and finally the reclaiming of our national freedom of action."[83]

In expectation of the "great crash" the NPD practices "principled opposition,"[84] a consciously obstructive political style that remains disinterested in constructive participation in order to address concrete societal problems. That's why the party cannot become the "protective power of the little people," as it repeatedly claimed, but only articulate and further fuel their resentments. In this way it is determined to pick up problems of societal significance through the irrational and apocalyptic mobilization of fear in order to emotionalize them and connect them to its own basic positions. In the deep economic and structural crisis of recent years the NPD was able to attach special hope to the mobilization of anti-capitalist affects, which it adapted to its anti-Semitic basic motif. However, so far the extreme right has been unable to achieve significant mobilization outside of its radical nationalist milieu. At its demonstrations the members of the "national opposition" remain among themselves, the hoped-for surge of those who have been disaffected by the "system" is not taking place. Christoph Butterwegge recently pointed out that endogenous factors are active here: "Personal, programmatic and organizational weaknesses of rightwing extremism hinder the party from exploiting the weakness of the capitalist economy that would seem to support its aims."[85]

The policy of obstruction corresponds, however, to a strategic approach that promotes the relatively independent "national milieu," the development of which is hoped for especially in the socially highly problematic territories of the East German provinces. In these regions the NPD, supported by its "solidaristic" socio-political statements and its anti-globalization demands for a "spatially oriented national economy," wants to be recognized as a "social domestic party."[86]

In its federal election campaign platform the NPD praises itself as "the only authentic opposition party for all Germans," and as "the only social and national opposition that remains faithful to our *Heimat*."[87]

Notes

1 Translated by Sabine von Mering.
2 See Horst W. Schmollinger, "Nationaldemokratische Partei Deutschlands," in Richard Stöss (ed.) *Parteien Handbuch. Die Parteien der Bundesrepublik Deutschland*

1945–80, Opladen 1986, Vol. 4: NDP-WAV, 1922–94; Peter Dudek and Hans-Gerd Jaschke, *Entstehung und Entwicklung des Rechtsextremismus in der Bundesrepublik. Zur Tradition einer besonderen politischen Kultur*, Opladen 1984, Vol. 1, 280–355; Uwe Hoffmann, *Die NPD. Entwicklung, Ideologie und Struktur*, Frankfurt, 1999; Oliver Gnad, "NPD—Nationaldemokratische Partei Deutschlands. Mitgliedschaft und Sozialstruktur," in *Handbuch zur Statistik der Parlamente und Parteien in den westlichen Besatzungszonen und in der Bundesrepublik Deutschland, Vol. III: FDP sowie kleinere bürgerliche und rechte Parteien. Mitgliedschaft und Sozialstruktur 1945–90*, Düsseldorf 2005, 591–702; Marc Brandstetter, *Die NPD im 21. Jahrhundert. Eine Analyse ihrer aktuellen Situation, ihrer Erfolgsbedingungen und Aussichten*, Marburg, 2006; Uwe Backes and Henrik Steglich (eds), *Die NPD. Erfolgsbedingungen einer rechtsextremistischen Partei*, Baden-Baden, 2007; Gideon Botsch, "Parteipolitische Kontinuitäten der 'Nationalen Opposition.' Von der Deutschen Reichspartei zur Nationaldemokratischen Partei Deutschlands," in *Zeitschrift für Geschichtswissenschaft (ZfG)* 59 (2011), S. 113–37; Gideon Botsch and Christoph Kopke, *Die NPD und ihr Milieu. Studien und Berichte*, Ulm/Münster, 2009; Gideon Botsch, *Die extreme Rechte in der Bundesrepublik 1949 bis heute*, Darmstadt, 2012.

3 Contrary to the assumption that the battles were about programmatic directions (comp. with respect to the question of "anti-capitalism," for example, Dominik Clemens, "Die NPD: Eine 'neue' Arbeiterpartei von rechts?" in Richard Gebhardt and Dominik Clemens (eds) *Volksgemeinschaft statt Kapitalismus? Zur sozialen Demagogie der Neonazis*, Köln, 2009, 41–65, 60f.), we see them primarily as power struggles among the various leaders, comp. Botsch and Kopke, *Die NPD*, 103ff.

4 Arbeit. Familie. Vaterland. Das Parteiprogramm der Nationaldemokratischen Partei Deutschlands (NPD). Beschlossen auf dem Bundesparteitag am 4./5.6.2010 in Bamberg, 1, Auflage, Berlin 2010.

5 The only exception may be the right-wing extremist PRO NRW party, which was partly successful on a local level with a single-issue anti-Islamic campaign in the 2012 elections in the state of North Rhine-Westphalia. Its off-shoot *PRO Deutschland* had previously failed to gain voter support in Berlin. See Alexander Häusler (ed.), *Rechtspopulismus als "Bürgerbewegung." Kampagnen gegen Islam und Moscheebau und kommunale Gegenstrategien*, Wiesbaden, 2008; Michael Lausberg, *Die PRO-Bewegung. Geschichte, Inhalte, Strategie der "Bürgerbewegung Pro Köln" und der "Bürgerbewegung Pro NRW,"* Münster, 2010.

6 See for example Hans Maier and Hermann Bott, *Die NPD. Struktur und Ideologie einer "nationalen Rechtspartei,"* München 1968; Reinhard Kühnl, Rainer Rilling and Christine Sager, *Die NPD. Struktur, Ideologie und Funktion einer neofaschistischen Partei*, Frankfurt a.M., 1969, 75ff.; Hoffmann, *Die NPD*, 274ff.

7 See Gideon Botsch and Christoph Kopke, "'Raumorientierte Volkswirtschaft' und 'Nationale Solidarität'. Zur wirtschafts-und sozialpolitischen Programmatik und Propaganda der NPD und ihres neo-nationalsozialistischen Umfeld," *Bulletin für Faschismus-und Weltkriegsforschung* No. 31/32 (2008): 50–71.

8 *Programm der Nationaldemokratischen Partei Deutschlands*, December 1996, 10. Ed. 2004 (in the following: *NPD-Parteiprogramm* 1996), Pt. 7.

9 *NPD – Wahlprogramm zur Bundestagswahl 1998* (flyer).

10 Comp. Clemens, *Die NPD*, 48ff.

11 Bundesamt für Verfassungsschutz, *Ein Jahrzehnt rechtsextremistischer Politik. Strukturdaten-Ideologie-Agitation—Perspektiven 1990–2001*, 5, www.extremismus.com/vs/rex9.htm (accessed April 18, 2008), 9. Comp.: Thomas Grumke and Andreas Klärner, *Rechtsextremismus, die soziale Frage und Globalisierungskritik. Eine vergleichende Studie zu Deutschland und Großbritannien seit 1990*, Berlin, 2006; Friedrich-Ebert-Stiftung (ed.), *Neue Entwicklungen des Rechtsextremismus. Internationalisierung und Entdeckung der sozialen Frage*, Berlin, 2006; Christina Kaindl, "Antikapitalismus und Globalisierungskritik von rechts—Erfolgskonzepte

für die extreme Rechte?" in Peter Bathke and Susanne Spindler (eds) *Neoliberalismus und Rechtsextremismus in Europa. Zusammenhänge—Widersprüche—Gegenstrategien*, Berlin, 2006, 60–75; Botsch and Kopke, "Raumorientierte Volkswirtschaft"; Botsch and Kopke (eds), *Die NPD*, 88ff.; Fabian Virchow, "Volks-statt Klassenbewegung. Weltanschauung und Praxeologie der extremen Rechten in der Bundesrepublik Deutschland seit 1990 am Beispiel der 'sozialen Frage'," in Jürgen Hofmann and Michael Schneider (eds) *ArbeiterInnenbewegung und Rechtsextremismus*, Wien, 2007, 165–85; Fabian Virchow, "Von der 'antikapitalistischen Sehnsucht des deutschen Volkes.' Zur Selbstinszenierung des Neofaschismus als Anwalt der 'kleinen Leute'," in *UTOPIE kreativ*, Heft 198/2007, 352–60; Backes and Steglich (eds), *Die NPD*; Gebhardt and Clemens (eds), *Volksgemeinschaft*; Thomas Grumke, "'Sozialismus ist braun': Rechtsextremismus, die soziale Frage und Globalisierungskritik," in Stephan Braun, Alexander Geisler and Martin Gerster (eds) *Strategien der extremen Rechten. Hintergründe—Analysen—Antworten*, Wiesbaden, 2009, 148–62.
12 Comp. Anton Maegerle, *Globalisierung aus Sicht der extremen Rechten*, Braunschweig, 2004, 68ff.
13 Comp. NPD-Parteivorstand, *Strategische Leitlinien zur politischen Arbeit der NPD. Positionspapier des Parteivorstandes* (= Profil. Nationaldemokratische Schriftenreihe, Folge 12), Berlin 2002.
14 Ibid.
15 Ibid.
16 NPD-Parteivorstand (ed.), *Aktionsprogramm für ein besseres Deutschland*, Berlin, 2002.
17 NPD-Parteivorstand (ed.), *Aktionsprogramm*, 14.
18 NPD (ed.), *Europa-Programm. Europa wählt national*, Deutschland wählt: NPD—Die Nationalen, 2003.
19 Comp. Henrik Steglich, *Die NPD in Sachsen. Organisatorische Voraussetzungen ihres Wahlerfolges 2004*, Göttingen, 2006 (about the significance of socio-political themes: 35f.); Sebastian Rehse, *Die Oppositionsrolle rechtsextremer Protestparteien. Zwischen Anpassung und Konfrontation in Brandenburg und Sachsen*, Baden-Baden, 2008; Robert Philippsberg, *Die Strategie der NPD. Regionale Umsetzung in Ost-und Westdeutschland*, Baden-Baden, 2009.
20 See a comprehensive analysis of these "pillars" of the NPD strategy in Christoph Schulze, "Das Viersäulenkonzept der NPD," in Braun, Geisler and Gerster (eds) *Strategien*, 92–108. To see our divergent interpretation, compare Botsch, *Parteipolitische Kontinuitäten*, 134f.
21 Grumke and Klärner, *Rechtsextremismus*, 88–96; Anton Maegerle, *Rechte und Rechtsextreme im Hartz IV-Protest*, Braunschweig, 2006; Fabian Virchow, "Dimensionen der "Demonstrationspolitik" der extremen Rechten in der Bundesrepublik Deutschland," in Andreas Klärner und Michael Kohlstruck (eds) *Moderner Rechtsextremismus in Deutschland*, Hamburg, 2006, 68–101; Clemens, *Die NPD*, 54f.
22 Jürgen Peters and Christoph Schulze (eds), *"Autonome Nationalisten." Die Modernisierung neofaschistischer Jugendkultur*, Münster, 2009, cit. 13 and 36; see Michael Klarmann, "Nationalsozialismus extrem modern: Die Autonomen Nationalisten," in Gebhardt and Clemens, *Volksgemeinschaft*, 90–113; Jan Schedler, "Übernahme von Ästhetik und Aktionsformen der radikalen Linken. Zur Verortung der 'Autonomen Nationalisten' im extrem rechten Strategiespektrum," in Braun, Geisler and Gerster (eds) *Strategien*, 332–57; Jan Schedler and Alexander Häusler (eds), *Autonome Nationalisten. Neonazismus in Bewegung*, Wiesbaden, 2011.
23 See Peters and Schulze (eds), *"Autonome Nationalisten,"* 43ff.
24 NPD-Parteivorstand, *Strategische Leitlinien*.
25 See Maegerle, *Globalisierung*, 165.
26 See NPD-Parteivorstand, *Strategische Leitlinien*.

27 Einhart Möller (Ps.), *Strategie & Taktik: Vom NATIONALEN WIDERSTAND zum NATIONALEN ANGRIFF*, 1st expanded new edn, Heilbronn, 2004 [1971], 24.
28 See Clemens, *Die NPD*, 55f.
29 "Kampagnenfähigkeit der Partei stärken." The DS in conversation with federal NPD organizer Jens Pühse, in *Deutsche Stimme* (DS), July 2007.
30 Nationalismus heißt Kapitalismuskritik. Eine notwendige Standortbestimmung. Beschluß des Bundesvorstandes der Jungen Nationaldemokraten am 25.-26. Juni (2006) in Magdeburg, www.jn-buvo.de/index.php?option=com_content&task=view&id=21&Itemid=32 (accessed April 18, 2006).
31 Aufruf zur antikapitalistischen und antiglobalistischen Kampagne, "Zukunft statt Globalisierung" (2006), www.antikap.de/?antikap=aufruf (accessed April 18, 2008), see also: Virchow, *Von der "antikapitalistischen Sehnsucht,"* 356.
32 See Botsch and Kopke, *Die NPD*, 88ff.
33 See Oswald Spengler, *Preußentum und Sozialismus*, München 1919; Werner Sombart, *Deutscher Sozialismus*, Berlin-Charlottenburg, 1934. For the reception in the NPD see, for example, *Grundlagen einer nationaldemokratischen Volkswirtschaftslehre. Raumorientierte Volkswirtschaft statt "Basar-Ökonomie,"* Positionspapier des Arbeitskreises Wirtschaftspolitik beim NPD-Parteivorstand, Berlin (= Profil. Nationaldemokratische Schriftenreihe, Series 13), 19 ff.; Angelika Willig, "'Frei, sozial und national.' Über die Wiederkehr des Sozialismus," in *Deutsche Stimme*, March 2007, also in: sozial-geht-nur-national.de/index.php?s=berichte&id=9 (accessed April 18, 2006).
34 Reinhard Kühnl, *Die nationalsozialistische Linke 1925–30*, Meisenheim/Gl. 1966; Udo Kissenkoetter, *Gregor Straßer und die NSDAP*, Stuttgart, 1978; Norbert Madloch, "Zur Rezeption der Strasser-Ideologie im deutschen Neonazismus," in Kurt Gossweiler, *Die Strasser-Legende. Auseinandersetzung mit einem Kapitel des deutschen Faschismus*, Berlin, 1994, 128–43; Kurt Heiler, "'Linke Leute von rechts.' Anmerkungen zur Karriere eines politischen Kampfbegriffs," in Gebhardt and Clemens (ed.) *Volksgemeinschaft*, 17–40.
35 AG Zukunft statt Globalisierung-Sachsen, *Antikapitalismus ... von "rechts,"* Dresden, 2006, 2; Jürgen Gansel, "Der Abschied der Linken von der sozialen Frage. Der Nationalismus wird die Schutzmacht der kleinen Leute," in *DS*, December 2006.
36 Vgl. Kailitz, Steffen, "Die nationalsozialistische Ideologie der NPD," in Backes and Steglich, *NPD*, 339–53, here 338–39.
37 Per Lennart Aae, *Was ist denn nun überhaupt unsere Alternative?* 2007, www.fkst.de/artikel9.html (accessed April 18, 2008).
38 See NPD-Parteivorstand (ed.), *Grundlagen einer nationaldemokratischen Volkswirtschaftslehre. Raumorientierte Volkswirtschaft statt "Basar-Ökonomie,"* Positionspapier des Arbeitskreises Wirtschaftspolitik beim NPD-Parteivorstand (= Profil. Nationaldemokratische Schriftenreihe Series 13), Berlin, 2006.
39 Hans-Erich Volkmann, "Die NS-Wirtschaft in Vorbereitung des Krieges," in Wilhelm Deist, Manfred Messerschmidt, Hans-Erich Volkmann and Wolfram Wette (ed.) *Ursachen und Voraussetzungen des Zweiten Weltkrieges*, Frankfurt/M., 1991, 211–437; Horst Kahrs, "Von der 'Großraumwirtschaft' zur 'Neuen Ordnung'," in Götz Aly (ed.) *Modelle für ein deutsches Europa. Ökonomie und Herrschaft im Großwirtschaftsraum*, Berlin, 1992, 9–28; Werner Röhr and Brigitte Berlekamp (ed.), *"Neuordnung Europas." Vorträge vor der Berliner Gesellschaft für Faschismus-und Weltkriegsforschung 1992–96*, Berlin, 1996.
40 Aae, *Alternative*.
41 Similar to the late Günther Schwemmer in the DS, comp. Regina Wamper, "Gefühlter Antikapitalismus. Der Globalisierungsdiskurs in der Deutschen Stimme," in Gebhardt and Clemens (eds) *Volksgemeinschaft*, 66–89, here: 80f.
42 NPD-Parteivorstand (ed.), *Grundlagen einer nationaldemokratischen Volkswirtschaftslehre*, 19.

43 Stefan Breuer, *Die radikale Rechte in Deutschland 1871–1945*, Stuttgart, 2010, 193.
44 Johann Gottlieb Fichte, *Der geschloßne Handelsstaat. Ein philosophischer Entwurf als Anhang zur Rechtslehre, und Probe einer künftig zu liefernden Politik, mit einem bisher unbekannten Manuskript Fichtes "Ueber StaatsWirthschaft." Auf der Grundlage der Ausgabe von Fritz Medicus hg. u. mit einer Einleitung versehen v. Hans Hirsch*, Hamburg, 1979, 33. Note that Fichte's text is now available in a translation by Anthony Curtis Adler, SUNY, 2012.
45 See Armin Pfahl-Traughber, "Aufklärung und Antisemitismus. Kants, Lessings und Fichtes Auffassungen zu den Juden," *Tribüne. Zeitschrift zum Verständnis des Judentums* 40 (2001): 168–81; Gudrun Hentges, "Das Janusgesicht der Aufklärung. Antijudaismus und Antisemitismus in der Philosophie von Kant, Fichte und Hegel," in Samuel Salzborn (ed.) *Antisemitismus—Geschichte und Gegenwart*, Giessen, 2004, 11–32.
46 See for example NPD flyer "Fischereihandwerk erhalten," www.npd-fraktion-mv.de/components/com_pdf/pdf/1257326426.pdf (accessed February 10, 2011).
47 Reiner Bischoff, *Weshalb Gottfried Feder scheitern musste* (1996), www.antikap.de/downloads/gottfried_feder.pdf (accessed April 18, 2008).
48 See Botsch and Kopke, "Raumorientierte Volkswirtschaft," 63.
49 NPD-Parteivorstand (ed.), *Grundlagen einer nationaldemokratischen Volkswirtschaftslehre*, 23.
50 NPD-Parteivorstand—Amt für Öffentlichkeitsarbeit (Hg.), *Argumente für Kandidaten & Funktionsträger. Eine Handreichung für die öffentliche Auseinandersetzung*, 2nd edn, 2006, 19; comp. the almost identical wording in Jürgen Gansel, "Die Nation als soziale Schutz-und Solidargemeinschaft. Über die Gleichzeitigkeit von De-Nationalisierung und Re-Nationalisierung im Globalisierungszeitalter," in *DS*, December 2005; as well as in: *Aufruf zur antikapitalistischen und antiglobalistischen Kampagne*.
51 NPD-Parteivorstand (ed.), *Argumente für Kandidaten & Funktionsträger*, 15ff.
52 NPD-Parteivorstand (ed.), *Grundlagen einer nationaldemokratischen Volkswirtschaftslehre*, 91.
53 Clemens, *Die NPD*, 61.
54 NPD-Parteivorstand (ed.), *Bundestags-Wahlprogramm 09. Deutschlands starke Rechte*, Berlin o.J., 2009, 10.
55 NPD-Parteivorstand (ed.), *Bundestags-Wahlprogramm 09*, 12.
56 Ibid., 16.
57 Ibid., 26ff.
58 Ibid., 32.
59 *Arbeit. Familie. Vaterland*, 10.
60 See *Programm der NPD. Grundlagen nationaldemokratischer Politik*, 1967. Nachdruck in Maier and Bott, *NPD*, 65–87, here: 80f., and *Parteiprogramm* 1996, Pt. 7 (there are no numbers in the program). Programmatic texts of the 1970s and 1980s are articulated differently in some parts.
61 See ibid.
62 See *Arbeit. Familie. Vaterland*, 11f.
63 Ibid., 8.
64 Ibid., 9.
65 Ibid., 8.
66 Ibid., 5.
67 Jürgen Rieger, *Solidarismus—ein Gebot unserer Zeit. Ein Diskussionsbeitrag*, in *DS*, April/May 2007.
68 *Arbeit. Familie. Vaterland*, 6.
69 See *Arbeit. Familie. Vaterland*, 8; see also Peter List, "Die nationale Volkswirtschaft als Alternative zu Kommunismus und Kapitalismus," in *Staatsbriefe* 2/1994, www.staatsbriefe.de/1994/1994/list.htm (accessed July 2, 1997; no longer available).

70 Virchow, *Volks-statt Klassenbewegung*, 179–82.
71 See Bodo Zeuner, Jochen Gester, Michael Fichter, Joachim Kreis and Richard Stöss, *Gewerkschaften und Rechtsextremismus*, Münster, 2007, esp. 27–57.
72 Gansel, *Abschied*.
73 See Klaus Ahlheim and Bardo Heger, *Nation und Exklusion. Der Stolz der Deutschen und seine Nebenwirkungen*, Schwalbach/Ts., 2008, esp. 51ff.
74 See Steffen Kailitz, "Das nationalsozialistische Vertreibungs-und Nationalisierungsprogramm der NPD," in *Politische Studien, Themenheft* 1/2007: 44–53, here: 46.
75 *Arbeit. Familie. Vaterland*, 11.
76 Das passiert, wenn die NPD regiert. Ein Maßnahmekatalog, Hg., NPD-Parteivorstand (ca. 2009). This is not actually an action plan, but a collection of fictional radio messages after an ostensible NPD government has taken over. Thus it states, for example, for "March 15" a significant reduction in the number of foreigners that is explained by the "lowered financial attractiveness of the FRG for foreigners."
77 *Arbeit. Familie. Vaterland*, 11.
78 Kailitz, *Das nationalsozialistische Vertreibungs-und Nationalisierungsprogramm*.
79 *Arbeit. Familie. Vaterland*, 5.
80 Breuer, *Die radikale Rechte*, 193.
81 NPD-Parteivorstand (ed.), *Grundlagen einer nationaldemokratischen Volkswirtschaftslehre*, 32.
82 See *Aufruf zur antikapitalistischen und antiglobalistischen Kampagne*; Jürgen Gansel, "Abgesänge auf das liberale Gesellschaftsmodell. Die sozialen Verwerfungen der Globalisierung werfen die Systemfrage auf," in *DS*, April 2007.
83 NPD-Parteivorstand (ed.), *Bundestags-Wahlprogramm 09*, 6f.
84 Otto Kirchheimer, "Wandlungen der politischen Opposition," in *Parlamentarismus, hg. von Kurt Kluxen*, Köln/Berlin, 1967, 410–24.
85 Christoph Butterwegge, "Finanzmarktkrise, Armut und rechtsextreme Politik," in Christoph Kopke (ed.) *Die Grenzen der Toleranz. Rechtsextremes Milieu und demokratische Gesellschaft in Brandenburg. Bilanz und Perspektiven*, Potsdam, 2011, 41–55, quote: 53.
86 See Gideon Botsch, "Die extreme Rechte als 'nationales Lager.' 'Versäulung' im lebensweltlichen Milieu oder Marsch in die Mitte der Gesellschaft?" in Kopke (Hg.), *Grenzen der Toleranz*, 57–81.
87 NPD-Parteivorstand (ed.), *Bundestags-Wahlprogramm 09*, 6f.

References

Primary sources

Aae, Per Lennart, *Was ist denn nun überhaupt unsere Alternative?* 2007, www.fkst.de/artikel9.html (accessed April 18, 2008).
AG Zukunft statt Globalisierung-Sachsen, *Antikapitalismus ... von "rechts,"* Dresden, 2006.
Bischoff, Reiner, *Weshalb Gottfried Feder scheitern musste*, 1996, www.antikap.de/downloads/gottfried_feder.pdf (accessed April 18, 2008).
Fichte, Johann Gottlieb, *Der geschloßne Handelsstaat. Ein philosophischer Entwurf als Anhang zur Rechtslehre, und Probe einer künftig zu liefernden Politik, mit einem bisher unbekannten Manuskript Fichtes "Ueber StaatsWirthschaft,"* Auf der Grundlage der Ausgabe von Fritz Medicus hg. u. mit einer Einleitung versehen v. Hans Hirsch, Hamburg, 1979, 33.
Fischereihandwerk erhalten, *NPD flyer*, www.npd-fraktion-mv.de/components/com_pdf/pdf/1257326426.pdf (accessed February 10, 2011).

Gansel, Jürgen, "Die Nation als soziale Schutz-und Solidargemeinschaft. Über die Gleichzeitigkeit von De-Nationalisierung und Re-Nationalisierung im Globalisierungszeitalter," *Deutsche Stimme* (December 2005).

——"Der Abschied der Linken von der sozialen Frage. Der Nationalismus wird die Schutzmacht der kleinen Leute," *Deutsche Stimme* (December 2006).

——"Absänge auf das liberale Gesellschaftsmodell. Die sozialen Verwerfungen der Globalisierung werfen die Systemfrage auf," *Deutsche Stimme* (April 2007).

Kampagnenfähigkeit der Partei stärken, "The DS in Conversation with Federal NPD-Organizer Jens Pühse," *Deutsche Stimme* (July 2007).

List, Peter, "Die nationale Volkswirtschaft als Alternative zu Kommunismus und Kapitalismus," *Staatsbriefe* 2 (1994), www.staatsbriefe.de/1994/1994/list.htm (accessed July 2, 1997; no longer available).

Möller, Einhart (Ps.), Strategie & Taktik, *Vom NATIONALEN WIDERSTAND zum NATIONALEN ANGRIFF*, first expanded new edn, Heilbronn, 2004 [1971].

n.a., *Nationalismus heißt Kapitalismuskritik*, Eine notwendige Standortbestimmung. Beschluß des Bundesvorstandes der Jungen Nationaldemokraten am 25.–26. Juni (2006), in Magdeburg, www.jn-buvo.de/index.php?option=com_content&task=view&id=21&Itemid=32 (accessed April 18, 2006).

n.a., *Aufruf zur antikapitalistischen und antiglobalistischen Kampagne "Zukunft statt Globalisierung,"* 2006, www.antikap.de/?antikap=aufruf (accessed April 18, 2008).

n.a., *Arbeit. Familie. Vaterland. Das Parteiprogramm der Nationaldemokratischen Partei Deutschlands (NPD)*, Beschlossen auf dem Bundesparteitag am 4./5. 6. 2010 in Bamberg, 1. Auflage, Berlin, 2010.

NPD (ed.) *Wahlprogramm zur Bundestagswahl* (flyer), 1998.

——*Europa-Programm. Europa wählt national*, Deutschland wählt: NPD—Die Nationalen, 2003.

NPD-Parteivorstand (ed.), *Programm der Nationaldemokratischen Partei Deutschlands*, December 1996, 10th edn 2004.

——*Strategische Leitlinien zur politischen Arbeit der NPD*, Positionspapier des Parteivorstandes (= Profil. Nationaldemokratische Schriftenreihe, Folge 12), Berlin 2002a.

——*Aktionsprogramm für ein besseres Deutschland*, Berlin, 2002b.

——*Grundlagen einer nationaldemokratischen Volkswirtschaftslehre. Raumorientierte Volkswirtschaft statt "Basar-Ökonomie,"* Positionspapier des Arbeitskreises Wirtschaftspolitik beim NPD-Parteivorstand, Berlin 2006 (= Profil. Nationaldemokratische Schriftenreihe, Series 13).

——*Bundestags-Wahlprogramm 09*, Deutschlands starke Rechte, Berlin o.J., 2009a.

——*Das passiert, wenn die NPD regiert*, Ein Maßnahmekatalog (flyer), ca. 2009b.

NPD-Parteivorstand—Amt für Öffentlichkeitsarbeit (ed.), *Argumente für Kandidaten & Funktionsträger*, Eine Handreichung für die öffentliche Auseinandersetzung, 2nd edn, 2006.

Rieger, Jürgen, "Solidarismus—ein Gebot unserer Zeit. Ein Diskussionsbeitrag," *Deutsche Stimme* (April/May 2007).

Spengler, Oswald, *Preußentum und Sozialismus*, München, 1919.

Werner Sombart, *Deutscher Sozialismus* [German Socialism], Berlin-Charlottenburg, 1934.

Willig, Angelika, "Frei, sozial und national," Über die Wiederkehr des Sozialismus, *Deutsche Stimme* (March 2007), sozial-geht-nur-national.de/index.php?s=berichte&id=9 (accessed April 18, 2006).

Secondary sources

Ahlheim, Klaus and Bardo Heger, *Nation und Exklusion. Der Stolz der Deutschen und seine Nebenwirkungen*, Schwalbach/Ts., 2008.

Backes, Uwe and Henrik Steglich (eds) *Die NPD. Erfolgsbedingungen einer rechtsextremistischen Partei*, Baden-Baden, 2007.

Botsch, Gideon, "Die extreme Rechte als 'nationales Lager.' 'Versäulung' im lebensweltlichen Milieu oder Marsch in die Mitte der Gesellschaft?" in Christoph Kopke (ed.) *Die Grenzen der Toleranz. Rechtsextremes Milieu und demokratische Gesellschaft in Brandenburg. Bilanz und Perspektiven*, Potsdam, 2011a, 57–81.

——"Parteipolitische Kontinuitäten der 'Nationalen Opposition.' Von der Deutschen Reichspartei zur Nationaldemokratischen Partei Deutschlands," *Zeitschrift für Geschichtswissenschaft (ZfG)* 59 (2011b): S. 113–37.

——*Die extreme Rechte in der Bundesrepublik 1949 bis heute*, Darmstadt, 2012.

Botsch, Gideon and Christoph Kopke, "'Raumorientierte Volkswirtschaft' und 'Nationale Solidarität'. Zur wirtschafts-und sozialpolitischen Programmatik und Propaganda der NPD und ihres neo-nationalsozialistischen Umfelds," *Bulletin für Faschismus-und Weltkriegsforschung* No. 31/32 (2008): 50–71.

——*Die NPD und ihr Milieu. Studien und Berichte*, Ulm/Münster, 2009.

Brandstetter, Marc, *Die NPD im 21. Jahrhundert. Eine Analyse ihrer aktuellen Situation, ihrer Erfolgsbedingungen und Aussichten*, Marburg, 2006.

Braun, Stephan, Alexander Geisler and Martin Gerster (eds), *Strategien der extremen Rechten. Hintergründe—Analysen—Antworten*, Wiesbaden, 2009.

Breuer, Stefan, *Die radikale Rechte in Deutschland 1871–1945*, Stuttgart, 2010.

Bundesamt für Verfassungsschutz (ed.), *Ein Jahrzehnt rechtsextremistischer Politik. Strukturdaten–Ideologie-Agitation—Perspektiven 1990–2001*, 2001, 5, www.extremismus.com/vs/rex9.htm (accessed April 18, 2008).

Butterwegge, Christoph, "Finanzmarktkrise, Armut und rechtsextreme Politik," in Christoph Kopke (ed.) *Die Grenzen der Toleranz. Rechtsextremes Milieu und demokratische Gesellschaft in Brandenburg. Bilanz und Perspektiven*, Potsdam, 2011, 41–55.

Clemens, Dominik, "Die NPD: Eine 'neue' Arbeiterpartei von rechts?" in Richard Gebhardt and Dominik Clemens (eds) *Volksgemeinschaft statt Kapitalismus? Zur sozialen Demagogie der Neonazis*, Köln, 2009.

Dudek, Peter and Hans-Gerd Jaschke, *Entstehung und Entwicklung des Rechtsextremismus in der Bundesrepublik. Zur Tradition einer besonderen politischen Kultur*, Opladen, 1984, 2 vols.

Friedrich-Ebert-Stiftung (ed.), *Neue Entwicklungen des Rechtsextremismus. Internationalisierung und Entdeckung der sozialen Frage*, Berlin, 2006.

Gnad, Oliver, "NPD—Nationaldemokratische Partei Deutschlands. Mitgliedschaft und Sozialstruktur," in *Handbuch zur Statistik der Parlamente und Parteien in den westlichen Besatzungszonen und in der Bundesrepublik Deutschland, Vol. III: FDP sowie kleinere bürgerliche und rechte Parteien. Mitgliedschaft und Sozialstruktur 1945–90*, Düsseldorf, 2005, 591–702.

Grumke, Thomas, "'Sozialismus ist braun': Rechtsextremismus, die soziale Frage und Globalisierungskritik," in Stephan Braun, Alexander Geisler and Martin Gerster (eds) *Strategien der extremen Rechten. Hintergründe—Analysen—Antworten*, Wiesbaden, 2009, 148–62.

Grumke, Thomas and Andreas Klärner, *Rechtsextremismus, die soziale Frage und Globalisierungskritik. Eine vergleichende Studie zu Deutschland und Großbritannien seit 1990*, Berlin, 2006.
Häusler, Alexander (ed.), *Rechtspopulismus als "Bürgerbewegung." Kampagnen gegen Islam und Moscheebau und kommunale Gegenstrategien*, Wiesbaden, 2008.
Heiler, Kurt, "'Linke Leute von rechts'. Anmerkungen zur Karriere eines politischen Kampfbegriffs," in Richard Gebhardt and Dominik Clemens (eds) *Volksgemeinschaft statt Kapitalismus? Zur sozialen Demagogie der Neonazis*, Köln, 2009, 17–40.
Hentges, Gudrun, "Das Janusgesicht der Aufklärung. Antijudaismus und Antisemitismus in der Philosophie von Kant, Fichte und Hegel," in Samuel Salzborn (ed.) *Antisemitismus—Geschichte und Gegenwart*, Giessen, 2004, 11–32.
Hoffmann, Uwe, *Die NPD. Entwicklung, Ideologie und Struktur*, Frankfurt, 1999.
Kahrs, Horst, "Von der 'Großraumwirtschaft' zur 'Neuen Ordnung'," in Götz Aly (ed.) *Modelle für ein deutsches Europa. Ökonomie und Herrschaft im Großwirtschaftsraum*, Berlin, 1992, 9–28.
Kailitz, Steffen, "Das nationalsozialistische Vertreibungs-und Nationalisierungsprogramm der NPD," in *Politische Studien, Themenheft* 1 (2007a), 44–53.
——"Die nationalsozialistische Ideologie der NPD," in Uwe Backes and Henrik Steglich (eds) *Die NPD. Erfolgsbedingungen einer rechtsextremistischen Partei*, Baden-Baden, 2007b, 339–53.
Kaindl, Christina, "Antikapitalismus und Globalisierungskritik von rechts—Erfolgskonzepte für die extreme Rechte?" in Peter Bathke and Susanne Spindler (eds) *Neoliberalismus und Rechtsextremismus in Europa. Zusammenhänge—Widersprüche—Gegenstrategien*, Berlin, 2006, 60–75.
Kirchheimer, Otto, "Wandlungen der politischen Opposition," in Parlamentarismus, hg. von Kurt Kluxen, Köln/Berlin, 1967, 410–24.
Kissenkoetter, Udo, *Gregor Straßer und die NSDAP*, Stuttgart, 1978.
Klarmann, Michael, "Nationalsozialismus extrem modern: Die Autonomen Nationalisten," in Richard Gebhardt and Dominik Clemens (eds) *Volksgemeinschaft statt Kapitalismus? Zur sozialen Demagogie der Neonazis*, Köln, 2009, 90–113.
Kopke, Christoph (ed.), *Die Grenzen der Toleranz. Rechtsextremes Milieu und demokratische Gesellschaft in Brandenburg. Bilanz und Perspektiven*, Potsdam, 2011.
Kühnl, Reinhard, *Die nationalsozialistische Linke. 1925–1930*, Meisenheim/Gl., 1966.
Kühnl, Reinhard, Rainer Rilling and Christine Sager, *Die NPD. Struktur, Ideologie und Funktion einer neofaschistischen Partei*, Frankfurt a.M., 1969.
Lausberg, Michael, *Die PRO-Bewegung. Geschichte, Inhalte, Strategie der "Bürgerbewegung Pro Köln" und der "Bürgerbewegung Pro NRW,"* Münster, 2010.
Madloch, Norbert, "Zur Rezeption der Strasser-Ideologie im deutschen Neonazismus," in Kurt Gossweiler, *Die Strasser-Legende. Auseinandersetzung mit einem Kapitel des deutschen Faschismus*, Berlin, 1994, 128–43.
Maegerle, Anton, *Globalisierung aus Sicht der extremen Rechten*, Braunschweig, 2004.
——*Rechte und Rechtsextreme im Hartz IV-Protest*, Braunschweig, 2006.
Maier, Hans and Hermann Bott, *Die NPD. Struktur und Ideologie einer "nationalen Rechtspartei,"* München, 1968.
Peters, Jürgen and Christoph Schulze (ed.), *"Autonome Nationalisten." Die Modernisierung neofaschistischer Jugendkultur*, Münster, 2009.
Pfahl-Traughber, Armin, "Aufklärung und Antisemitismus. Kants, Lessings und Fichtes Auffassungen zu den Juden," in *Tribüne. Zeitschrift zum Verständnis des Judentums* 40 (2001): 168–81.

Philippsberg, Robert, *Die Strategie der NPD. Regionale Umsetzung in Ost-und Westdeutschland*, Baden-Baden, 2009.
Rehse, Sebastian, *Die Oppositionsrolle rechtsextremer Protestparteien. Zwischen Anpassung und Konfrontation in Brandenburg und Sachsen*, Baden-Baden, 2008.
Röhr, Werner and Brigitte Berlekamp (eds), *"Neuordnung Europas." Vorträge vor der Berliner Gesellschaft für Faschismus-und Weltkriegsforschung 1992–96*, Berlin, 1996.
Schedler, Jan, "Übernahme von Ästhetik und Aktionsformen der radikalen Linken. Zur Verortung der "Autonomen Nationalisten" im extrem rechten Strategiespektrum," in Stephan Braun, Alexander Geisler and Martin Gerster (eds), *Strategien der extremen Rechten. Hintergründe—Analysen—Antworten*, Wiesbaden, 2009, 332–57.
Schedler, Jan and Alexander Häusler (eds), *Autonome Nationalisten. Neonazismus in Bewegung*, Wiesbaden, 2011.
Schmollinger, Horst W., "Nationaldemokratische Partei Deutschlands," in Richard Stöss (ed.) *Parteien Handbuch. Die Parteien der Bundesrepublik Deutschland 1945–80*, Opladen, 1986, Vol. 4: NDP-WAV, 1922–94.
Schulze, Christoph, "Das Viersäulenkonzept der NPD," in Stephan Braun, Alexander Geisler and Martin Gerster (eds) *Strategien der extremen Rechten. Hintergründe—Analysen—Antworten*, Wiesbaden, 2009, 92–108.
Steglich, Henrik, *Die NPD in Sachsen. Organisatorische Voraussetzungen ihres Wahlerfolges 2004*, Göttingen, 2006.
Virchow, Fabian, "Dimensionen der 'Demonstrationspolitik' der extremen Rechten in der Bundesrepublik Deutschland," in Andreas Klärner and Michael Kohlstruck (eds) *Moderner Rechtsextremismus in Deutschland*, Hamburg, 2006, 68–101.
——"Volks-statt Klassenbewegung. Weltanschauung und Praxeologie der extremen Rechten in der Bundesrepublik Deutschland seit 1990 am Beispiel der 'sozialen Frage'," in Jürgen Hofmann and Michael Schneider (eds) *ArbeiterInnenbewegung und Rechtsextremismus*, Wien, 2007a, 165–85.
——"Von der 'antikapitalistischen Sehnsucht des deutschen Volkes.' Zur Selbstinszenierung des Neofaschismus als Anwalt der 'kleinen Leute'," in *UTOPIE kreativ, Heft* 198 (2007b): 352–60.
Volkmann, Hans-Erich, "Die NS-Wirtschaft in Vorbereitung des Krieges," in Wilhelm Deist, Manfred Messerschmidt, Hans-Erich Volkmann and Wolfram Wette (eds) *Ursachen und Voraussetzungen des Zweiten Weltkrieges*, Frankfurt/M., 1991, 211–437.
Wamper, Regina, "Gefühlter Antikapitalismus. Der Globalisierungsdiskurs in der Deutschen Stimme," in Richard Gebhardt and Dominik Clemens (eds) *Volksgemeinschaft statt Kapitalismus? Zur sozialen Demagogie der Neonazis*, Köln, 2009, 66–89.
Zeuner, Bodo, Jochen Gester, Michael Fichter, Joachim Kreis and Richard Stöss, *Gewerkschaften und Rechtsextremismus*, Münster, 2007.

5 Extreme right activists
Recruitment and experiences

Bert Klandermans

Between 1995 and 1999 we conducted life-history interviews with 157 activists of extreme right organizations in Flanders (Belgium), France, Germany, Italy and the Netherlands. Based on these interviews I try to answer the following questions: How did these activists become involved in the extreme right and how did it change their lives?[1] During the 1990s, when we conducted our interviews, the shape of right-wing extremism (RWE) in the five countries differed: it was marginal and dispersed in Germany and the Netherlands, and sizeable and united in Flanders, France, and Italy. Moreover, in Germany and the Netherlands RWE was associated with the dark era of National Socialism, while in France, Flanders, and Italy it was rooted in a 'heroic' nationalist past. As a consequence, affiliating with RWE meant different trajectories and had different consequences in these countries. This chapter begins with a comparison of RWE in the five countries at the time of our interviews. In the sections that follow I will compare patterns of recruitment into activism and the experience of activism, respectively. Recruitment patterns appear to differ contingent on the state of RWE in the various countries. The same held for the experience of being an active member of an extreme right organization, as demonstrated by a discussion of stigmatization.

Five countries: five times extreme right

Legacies from the past

In each of the five countries, today's right-wing extremism is linked with the past, but the structures that support the extreme right in the various countries and shaped its trajectory are quite different. Links with the past appear to be an ambivalent asset. On the one side, abeyance structures provided contemporary RWE with connections to former movements, a reservoir of experienced activists, ready-made action repertoires, and ideological interpretation frames on which to lean. On the other hand, links with Nazism and fascism are essentially de-legitimizing. RWE movements are better off when they can rely on a more diversified set of abeyance structures, as is the case in Flanders, because of the pre-existing nationalist movement, and in France, with its two centuries-old tradition of reactionary and revolutionary right. Italy is yet another case. *Alleanza Nazionale* (AN) is the direct heir of fascism and has built on the existing networks ever since the war, but Italian fascism was perceived as a lesser evil than Nazism, especially in the south, its traditional strongholds. In northern Italy a two year-long bloody civil war (1943–45) opposing partisans to the fascist Republic of Salò strongly rooted anti-fascism in the region. In the south fascism had a better image, associated with public works and social integration. There was no civil war and the 'liberation war' ended two years earlier than in the north. Moreover, AN is now offering the image of a democratic 'post-fascist' right-wing party and has marginalized the nostalgia of the old *Movimento Sociale Italiana* (MSI).

Psychologically speaking, the differences discussed above between the five countries are significant differences. The history of a group is an important element of its members' social identity. A heroic past is something to be proud of and to identify with, but a dark history makes one feel ashamed and guilty (Doosje *et al.* 1998; Klandermans *et al.* 2008; Lagrou 2000). In Flanders, France, and Italy the extreme right has a history that can be framed independently from Nazism. Although in all three countries the RWE did collaborate with German Nazism during the war, it has more than that to refer to and thus in which to take pride. In Germany and the Netherlands such a possibility did not exist. There the extreme right has nothing but a dark past. Hence, individuals were recruited into different movements.

Demand for RWE movement activity

During the years that we conducted our interviews, a substantial reservoir of support for platforms advocated by the radical right existed in all five countries (Lubbers 2001). Such a reservoir can be defined as the movement's mobilization potential. Elsewhere I have characterized this as the demand side of protest (Klandermans 2004). The more support a movement finds in a society, the more demand there is for the movement's activities. Significant differences appeared from one country to another. In 1989, on a xenophobia scale combining 10 items about ethnic minorities, the highest proportion of agreement was found among Belgian respondents (56 percent) and the lowest (30 percent) in the Netherlands (Dekker and van Praag 1990). In the Euro-barometer of 1997, people were asked to position themselves on a 10-point scale ranging from "not at all racist" to "very racist." Belgians came first, 55 percent of the sample scoring between 6 and 10, compared with 48 percent of the French, 34 percent of the Germans, 31 percent of the Dutch and 30 percent of the Italians. Whatever the reasons for these differences, of our five cases, at the time of our interviews Belgian citizens were potentially the most receptive to the xenophobic appeals of extreme right-wing parties and Italian and Dutch citizens the least. In other words, demand for RWE activities was the highest in Belgium and the lowest in Italy and the Netherlands.

Supply of RWE movement activity

Even a strong demand would not generate a strong movement if strong and effective organizations do not supply opportunities to participate. This I called the supply side of protest. A strong supply in combination with a strong demand lays the groundwork for successful mobilization (Klandermans 2004). The supply of RWE politics appeared stronger and more effective in Flanders, France, and Italy, and therefore more attractive to potential supporters than in the two other countries. In the Netherlands, although the demand for an extreme right movement was relatively low, it was large enough for a viable movement to develop, had the supply been more attractive.[2] However, the *Centrumdemocraten* (CD) were weak, in an outspokenly hostile environment. In Germany the context of extreme right activism was even bleaker, despite an apparently stronger anti-immigrant sentiment than in the Netherlands. In view of public opinion, the objective of the *Republikaner* (REP) to create a political option to the right of the CDU/CSU (Christian Democratic Union of Germany/Christian Social Union of Bavaria) made sense. However, RWE in Germany was so much burdened by the past, and the political and legal opportunities were so limited that it was hardly possible to turn that potential demand into a viable movement.

Very different was the situation in the other three countries. In France there was a clear demand for a RWE movement and a strong supply. The French extreme right had a long history with which people could identify, but the political opportunities to turn organizational strength into political influence were limited. The *Front National* (FN) could turn this into an advantage by defining itself in opposition to the political establishment and the mainstream parties (the "gang of four" in the words of Jean-Marie Le Pen). Such a configuration helped create a politicized collective identity, uniting the militants against "the rest of the world" (Simon and Klandermans 2001; Bizeul 2003). In Flanders the situation was even more favorable for RWE mobilization. People could take pride in the past of the extreme right because of its link with Flemish nationalism, and most importantly there was both a strong demand and a strong supply, without many legal restrictions. On top of that entering the political arena was easy. The only difficulty was the counter-movement and the *cordon sanitaire* strategy of the other political parties that kept the extreme right in an isolated position. Though again, like in France, this could be turned into an advantage. Indeed, the *Vlaams Blok* (VB, Flemish Block) made use of the movement–counter-movement dynamic by developing into an anti-system party and creating among its members an oppositional identity. The friendliest environment existed in Italy. AN offered an attractive supply as a populist right-wing party with political influence and faced very little opposition or restriction. In fact, it had some powerful allies that made it even more influential. Nor was there much societal opposition expressing itself due to the absence of a strong counter-movement.

Mobilization

The presence of demand for and a supply of the extreme right is not a sufficient explanation for right-wing activism. Mobilization is the process that brings demand and supply together and makes people join the movement and become activists (Klandermans 1997, 2003). Such a process of mobilization may be initiated by the individual or a movement organization. We hold that often critical events play a crucial role in the process of mobilization. Such events may include an encounter with someone who already belongs to the movement, or some media event (a television or radio program; reading a newspaper article, magazine, or book), or being confronted with some dramatic situation which involves the movement directly or indirectly. Critical events are hard to predict. Obviously, many people who encounter these same events will never join a movement. It is the potentiality as it has developed before that gives the event its impact on a specific life course. This is not to say that the convergence of demand and supply in the event is completely accidental. Indeed, potential participants may have been seeking direction and signs that tell them what to do and where to go, and that may actually have brought them to the event (Teske 1997). Therefore we have chosen to conduct life-history interviews as a device to reconstruct the socialization and experiences that create potentialities and turn them into actual commitment to a RWE movement. Obviously, a life-history interview generates a social reconstruction of the interviewee's life course. Inevitably, it consists of facts *and* fiction. It is the world according to the interviewee.

In sum, the contexts in which these life histories evolve are significantly different; therefore we expect recruitment processes to be significantly different as well. Indeed, a strong demand and supply make for a movement that is visibly present in a society. Moreover, a strong supply and/or demand imply that relatively large numbers of people grow up in a RWE milieu. Under such circumstances it is less difficult to recruit activists.

This is what we observe in both Flanders and France. Italy, on the other hand, demonstrates that a strong supply with a relatively weak demand can still make for successful recruitment. A weak supply, however, makes effective recruitment difficult even in the context of a relatively strong demand, as the German case illustrates. Activist recruitment is the most difficult when both demand and supply are weak, as is the case in the Netherlands. What holds for the recruitment process similarly holds for processes of stigmatization: the strength of demand and supply will influence the experience of being an activist.

Table 5.1 Right-wing extremism: demand and supply

	Strong demand	*Weak demand*
Strong supply	Flanders, France	Italy
Weak supply	Germany	Netherlands

Recruitment

We encountered three types of life histories: continuity, conversion, and compliance. *Continuity* refers to life histories wherein movement membership and participation are a natural consequence of the preceding political socialization (Roth 2003; Andrews 1991; Teske 1997). *Conversion*, on the other hand, relates to those trajectories where movement participation implies a break with the past. Often critical events play a role in these life histories. Conversion rarely comes out of the blue. It is rooted in growing dissatisfaction with life as it is; usually the critical event is the last push toward change (Teske 1997). The third trajectory our interviews revealed was *compliance*, which refers to the situation where people enter activism more or less in spite of themselves. Compliance stories usually tell of friends or family members who persuaded someone to become actively involved in the extreme right.

Which trajectory recruitment into activism takes appears to be contingent on characteristics of the RWE movement in a country. In Flanders, France and Italy—with their viable RWE sectors—socialization, especially by the family, contributes most to the recruitment of activists. This holds for Germany as well. To be sure, in Germany the supply side was relatively weak, hence few were recruited into RWE activism, but those who were recruited grew up in an extreme right milieu. Thus in these four countries continuity was the dominant trajectory. In the Netherlands the weak demand and supply meant that very few people grew up in extreme right-wing families; consequently, only half of the Dutch interviewees told stories of continuity while the other half told stories of conversion or compliance. Moreover, the stories of continuity were stories of self-educated right-wing extremism rather than stories of socialization in the family.

Flanders

In Flanders almost all the respondents considered their present activism as the continuation of a commitment that originated a long time ago. In general, their activism followed a gradual and often "obvious" course. At the center is a family tradition of Flemish nationalism, which has sometimes developed over several generations. This is how Paul describes it: "In our house people were always very pro-Flemish. We talked a lot about Flemish politics ... We took it in with our mother's milk" (Paul, *Vlaams Blok*, male, 27). Or: "It has always been a part of me ... I was brought up on that ... I was raised as a Flemish nationalist" (Kris, *Vlaams Blok*, male, 50). The dominant role of the family was perhaps most strongly worded by Anton:

> To give you one small example: every time you used a French word in our house, for example, or an English word, it cost you half a frank or a quarter. We had to pay a fine for using a word which had a Dutch equivalent. No French was used in our house, English neither, nor German.

He continues:

> In the evenings there were discussions about the issues of Flanders, Flemish songs were sung in our house, we went on the IJzer pilgrimage,[3] we went to the "Flemish-National Song festival."[4] So you got the impulses at home. My parents were pro-Flemish.
>
> (Anton, *Vlaams Blok*, male, 59)

One-third of the Flemish activists come from a so-called "black family": their parents or grandparents were radically pro-Flemish before and during World War II, and were active in organizations collaborating with the German occupiers. There are frequent references to positions within the *Vlaams Nationaal Verbond* (VNV, National Flemish League),[5] and some fought with the Germans against communism on the Eastern front (Russia). After the war, many were convicted because of their involvement. Within radical Flemish circles, outspoken and uncompromising Flemish nationalism is linked to a right-wing world view (de Witte 1996). The convictions of these parents did not disappear after World War II, and were kept alive in the family circle. Many interviewees refer to discussions pertaining to "Flemish issues," to the presence of the radical Flemish-national weekly *'t Pallieterke* in their house, and to the participation in Flemish-national manifestations. When one considers the life histories of this group of interviewees, one is struck by the continuity in their evolution. The torch is lit at home and is passed on. Those involved thus become ever more integrated into the greater radical right-wing Flemish-national movement.

One-quarter of the interviewees grew up in families with a "moderate" Flemish-national orientation. The parents (mostly the father) are described as pro-Flemish, although they mostly do not participate actively in politics. In most cases they were pro-*Volksunie* (VU, People's Union).[6] Two interviewees in this group indicated more active involvement on their parents' side: they participated in Flemish-national manifestations and were active within the VU. Annemie (*Vlaams Blok*, female, 33) puts it as follows:

> My father was already involved in politics [the VU]. And from the time I was six or seven I went along to stick up posters with my older brothers and their friends. It's something that comes from childhood.

For most of them this was not the case, however. The interviewees often describe their parents as "modest" or "half-hearted" Flemish nationalists, in contrast to their own more radical involvement. Still, this does not mean that the parents did not play a socializing role. Marij (*Vlaams Blok*, female, 26) comments as follows:

> The thing about wanting to be Flemish actually comes from home. Being Flemish had its importance in our house. If my father crossed the street and someone asked him the way in French, he would refuse, or he would have to be sure that it was a Frenchman.

France

What makes the *Front National* different from the other parties looked at in this study is that it is the descendant of a literally centuries-old tradition, going back to the Revolution in 1789. Over such a long time the French extreme right has gradually absorbed contrasting ideological currents. This makes the FN more diverse and heterogeneous than its counterparts elsewhere. Indeed, many of the activists we interviewed grew up in one of those extreme, radical right milieux and many of them joined the movement before 1972 (the year when the FN was founded). The FN found its roots in the historical extreme right, in anti-communism, in the Algerian liberation war, and in the new right. Continuity was the dominant recruitment trajectory in France as well, as evidenced by the following two quotes, referring to a personal history in French nationalism and the French colonist's resistance against Algerian independence, to mention two currents.

> My grandfather was a member of Action Française ... I was eleven; we were sitting around the family table and I used to listen to them talking about it ... Once I was invited to an extreme right meeting held by a nationalist party ... There were about fifty of us, people my age who were speaking ... Some other people there, about 80 years old, and thus slightly older than me, who had lived at the time when the right wing, the real right, was well-established, recounted the whole story as told by Zeev Sternhell.[7] And there were young people in the room who were dumbfounded by the richness and abundance of ideas, and they were also slightly disappointed to discover they didn't know anything ... They drank in these people's words, these people who had lived all this. The right of Drumont etc. Drumont's "La France Juive," Charles Maurras, Léon Daudet, all that ... Look at this: this is my grandfather's [right-wing] library [a cupboard with seven shelves in it!]: Henri Dupont 1853–1931. And nowadays all this is not well known, and even though it is rightfully part of our history, it's regarded in a very biased way!
>
> (Hubert, FN, male, 78)

> Well, word got round that [Tixier-Vignancour] was organizing his first meeting ... Of course, friends of mine were in his entourage, and as they needed me, they phoned me ... After that, you know, things went quiet for a while—I kept campaigning with "X" and, then we were invited, for instance, to funerals of mutual friends when they died, and my friends and myself often met famous soldiers—Algerian War veterans—at these funerals, and that's how it began.
>
> (Jacques, FN, male, 65)

Anti-communism was another root of French RWE, as the following quote illustrates:

As a young man of 16, and from a farming and Gaullist family, I've always been deeply committed to the right wing, and so, anti-left-wing and above all, anti-communist. I was 17 when I saw the events of May 1968, and in a way, I was rather revolted by it all, and took a stand against it, which I suppose is normal, just reacting against something. At the time, the "against something" for us was to be standard bearers for the convictions of General De Gaulle: proud to be French. That's it, ... France first ... You made a commitment against something? Against the Communist Party, against anarchy, against the shit-mongers, against the person who said "it is forbidden to forbid" because that goes against being part of society ... [1968] was the point I became conscious, when everybody was saying "the Reds are here," well I'm anti-Red. That's all.

(Jean-Pierre, FN, *Mouvement National Republicain* (MNR), male, 46)

Italy

In Italy RWE is rooted in fascism as many of the interviewees acknowledged. Most of our interviewees when describing how they had become involved in politics made frequent reference to fascism, both as the ideology they wanted to follow in joining the party and as the reason why they suffered discrimination from the very beginning of their political involvement. This was true both for older interviewees, who had directly experienced the fascist era, and for younger interviewees, whose knowledge of fascism was only indirect, acquired through different sources. Many of our interviewees started their political activity within the MSI and they claimed that they had joined that party exactly because it defended the fascist worldview. This is consistent with Orfali's (2002) finding that in 1990 and 1994 MSI activists still preferred the label of "fascists" as self-description rather than the label of "right-wing extremists." For example, when Salvatore recalls the reason why he and other MSI supporters joined the party, he says:

We young MSI supporters had taken that side not simply because it was a right-wing party, rather because we had assimilated the fascist idea ... the original idea of fascism and ... the fascism of the Repubblica Sociale Italiana.

(Salvatore, *Movimento Sociale-Fiamma Tricolore* (MS-FT), male, 42)

Our analysis highlighted that most interviewees, both in northern and southern Italy, could find some kind of social support inside their own families. Many interviewees reconstructed commitment to fascist values and to membership in extreme right-wing parties as a heritage they took over from their parents, or from their larger families. The case of Vittorio is exemplary. His father was a true fascist who after the war was taken by US troops; his mother founded the post-fascist *Movimento Italiano Femminile* (Italian Movement of

Women), the aim of which was to look for fascists who had been arrested or who were missing after the war. Accordingly, Vittorio reconstructs his decision to get involved in active politics within the ranks of the MSI party as a natural consequence of his coming from a fascist family:

> In 1945 I was about thirteen, so I experienced, for example, even the civil war: I mean, I saw it, I absorbed it, I breathed it ... I, being the son of a fascist ... I absorbed it through my family; I breathed this political atmosphere of great and tragic events. So it was only natural for me, as a young boy, immediately to get involved in politics, you know, the usual route: enrolment in juvenile organizations, enrolment in the party, activism, militancy, it all came natural to me.
>
> (Vittorio, MS-FT, male, 65)

As these quotes demonstrate, most interviewees developed a feeling of belonging to an ideological position the distinctive feature of which was a positive interpretation of fascism in their families first. However, interviewees were not just passive receivers of ready-made positive images of fascism; rather, they carried out their own positive reconstruction of fascism, as it is well described in Davide's words:

> When you enter, since right-wing culture is very composite, you are not given a sacred text, you are not given a Bible that can make you know how to be a perfect right-wing guy. There are really many books you can read; you can approach right-wing culture through many different experiences ... construction of a strong identity is a long personal process, very long and complex, that keeps developing, and that cannot be reduced to a couple of books.
>
> (Davide, AN, male, 21)

Germany

Our German activists tell yet another story. More than any of the other activists they define themselves as nationalists rather than extreme right. To be sure, we found that in all five countries, but most among our German interviewees. This is made evident over and again in the interviews. It is mostly in their family that our interviewees developed the nation-centered worldview that made them potentially receptive to RWE ideas.

Many interviewees actually described their parents as "not politically interested." Only eight interviewees could clearly state their parents' impact on their worldview. The case of Hans (*Junge Freiheit* (JF), male, 36), whose father was an official in the *Nationaldemokratische Partei Deutschlands* (NPD, National Democratic Party), came as an exception: Though Hans's father disapproved of the political activities of his 15-year-old son, both Hans's political interest in politics and his choice of information were clearly determined by his father:

So principally, I was already interested maybe since when I was 14, 15 [years old]. So actually the most important things, for example, were TV newscasts and newspapers. So actually I started to read newspapers in a quite funny way, very early on. [Amused] Because my father always read several newspapers and he marked the very important articles. And I always cut these items out for him, and in this way, I started to read what he had marked or what else I found interesting ... So from that time on, I actually tried to get involved at a very early stage.

(Hans, JF, male, 36)

However, even for those who were not aware of a direct influence from their parents, the interviews reveal that parents provided fundamental elements of their current political viewpoint, mainly conservative ideas oriented to the "German question" which made them sensitive to the ideas of the REP later on. For instance, many interviewees refer to the difficult experience their parents went through as expellees, displaced after the end of the war. Michael's father was a member of the CDU (Christian conservatives) until the 1970s; later he voted for the FDP (free market oriented), while his mother voted for the SPD (social democrat). Yet what marked him is the fact his parents were, as he described them, "national conscious" and it made him interested in German history:

And we often talked about politics. But I was always interested in politics, because history was already my favorite past time in elementary school ... So I liked to read history books, historical novels, etc., etc.

(Michael, REP, male, 41)

Franz remembers his father as following the tradition of Prussian officers:

His attitude was: an officer doesn't join a political party ... So he completely condemned the idea that officers made a career due to their party membership book, just like the SPD-generals in the 70s. Because he said: "an officer is a government official representing the state, not a party." So from this viewpoint, I didn't have any political models.

(Michael, REP, male, 41)

However, during the interview there was a clearer indication of his father's influence on his political development:

INTERVIEWER: "But did you generally have political discussions?"
FRANZ: "Yes, with my father, that's clear. Well, of course he was conservative, also right-wing and nationally oriented. That's right. What's funny is, I never built up an anti-attitude as some people do, who want to obviously be the absolute opposite of their fathers. Although we didn't agree with each other in many things, in a funny way, we had the same political

opinion. But he didn't try to impose his ideas on me or to indoctrinate me, but it happened by itself."

(Franz, REP, male, 41)

Heinrich, after also describing his parents as people who held Prussian traditions and virtues, confirmed his mother's impact on his development:

> My mother was very nationalistic, ... but national-conservative, upright, without any extreme tendencies of course ... My father was a bit more reserved; I would say he was a liberal nationalist ... But it was always a dream of my mother that I should march here, through Berlin, as an officer of the guard.
>
> (Heinrich, REP, male, 78)

Silke describes her parents as very conservative. Silke explained:

> Principally I always had a conservative attitude, actually with an affinity to the CDU. I knew that from the magazines my parents received ... Our teachers didn't mould us differently, either ... We still grew up with classical ideals, [amused] which are no longer valid today.
>
> (Silke, REP, female, 56)

The Netherlands

Unlike the activists in the other countries in our study, those in the Netherlands were hardly influenced by their parents. Indeed, those who refer to an early interest in right-wing politics were rebelling against rather than following their parents and teachers. Two kinds of *continuity* stories are told by significantly different types of activists: educated angry young men who want to revolt versus much older political wanderers who end up in extreme right politics having traveled from one party to the other in search of a political home.

The involvement in extreme right politics of the "revolutionaries" (as we named them) started invariably as a manner of provocation at an early age. They are all involved in the radical sector of the extreme right.

> At age 13 I began to read creepy booklets about the Third Reich and the SS. Eh, hm, that was, of course, cool. My mother wasn't really happy with it I remember and god at school I was already a special case. The creepy booklets were about Hitler and the Third Reich and so on. I even brought such booklets to school, eh, that surprised the teachers a little bit, though ... Yeah, I did have problems at school ... I began to rebel, so to say. At some point, I was kicked out of school.
>
> (Michael, *Centrumpartij* '86 (CP '86), male, 34)

The "political wanderers" are not only much older, as a natural consequence of their rambling through the political landscape, but they entered the extreme right movement much later in their lives than the "revolutionaries." When he was 19 years old, Chris began his political career in the Social Democratic Party (PvdA), the party of his parents. He would have preferred a party with a more nationalistic platform, but couldn't find a proper political home. It took 15 years before he left the party, although the discrepancy between his political ideas and those of the PvdA grew over the years. After a period of detachment from politics, he started to look around again.

> In 1980 I read *Vrij Nederland* and the *Haagsche Courant* [two Dutch weeklies] and saw that Janmaat and Brookman [two founding members of an extreme right party] were involved in something that appealed to me. Somewhat with more national consciousness, but not extreme right. He [Janmaat] was immediately defined as "that goes in the wrong direction," and so on, but I did not think so at all. In my view it went precisely in the right direction. Janmaat's appeal to a more nationalistic attitude. "Netherlanders first" and obviously that related to frittering away Netherlands' interests to the multiculturalism or the capital or both.
> (Chris, CD, male, 56)

All but one of the activists who told a *conversion* story were men who joined the movement in the early 1990s when the extreme right peaked in the polls and the elections. Kathleen Blee (2002) describes how stories of conversion are built around events from the individual's past. Henk's story brings us to the city of Schiedam. Migrants had opened a coffeehouse and mosque which were both seen to be a nuisance to Henk's neighborhood. This came on top of a whole lot of other problems in the community.

> All of a sudden there were a coffeehouse and a mosque. The municipality knew nothing of it and the police had heard about it, that it was going to happen and that it happened without permission. But that nobody makes work of it, that it is winked at! Eventually we were left holding the baby. Look I won the lawsuit and I had the whole neighborhood behind me from the very beginning. I did that properly. But if you then see what you come across, how the municipality and the police are treating you, that is unreal ... As a matter of fact we are discriminated against.
> (Henk, CD, male, 38)

Interestingly, all but one of the women we interviewed told stories of *compliance*. This seems to contradict Blee's (2002) assertion that not all women in movements of the extreme right are compliant followers of the men in their lives. Our findings seem to confirm that stereotype. Stories of compliance may be more typical for the women we interviewed, but it does not necessarily mean that these women were just compliant followers. To be sure, it was friends, husbands or brothers who pulled them in, but as Maria's story illustrates, this does not make them necessarily marginal figures in the movement. This is confirmed by the example of Janneke:

> In fact, I became only active just before the city council elections in 1994. He [her husband] was already a member, I not yet, I also had my doubts, the same prejudices you hear everywhere until he came home with the platform and then you study it in more detail and in fact it wasn't that bad. Then, it was said we want women on the list [for the elections] would that be something for you? I said you can put me on the list but at the bottom. But as a matter of fact, he became number one and I number three, and thus we both were elected.
>
> (Janneke, CD, female, 36)

Indeed, RWE activists in Belgium, France, Germany and Italy predominantly tell continuity stories when it comes to their recruitment into activism. Half of the Dutch activists, on the other hand, tell compliance and conversion stories. As expected, a strong demand and/or supply ensures that comparatively many people grow up in RWE milieux, and therefore define their recruitment into RWE activism as a logical continuation of their socialization at home. The case of Germany, however, exemplifies that demand alone is not sufficient. The weak RWE supply in that country results in a weak movement. Obviously, movement strength is a self-perpetuating phenomenon. Strong movements easily attract many activists and employing many activists keeps the movement strong.

Stigmatization

RWE movements and organizations are not particularly well-liked in the countries where they are active. Indeed, activists experience varying degrees of stigmatization. We would expect most stigmatization in countries where both the demand and the supply side of right-wing extremism are weak. This seems indeed to be the case. More than anywhere else, RWE activists in the Netherlands were confronted with stigmatization. This is not to say that the Netherlands was the only country where we encountered stigmatization. On the contrary, in each country included in our study the interviewees reported that they suffered from discrimination by a hostile environment. Reprobation reaches its climax in the Netherlands and in Germany. In those countries, being an extreme right activist not only isolates from mainstream society but can jeopardize one's job, career, and sometimes life. It is at its lowest level in Italy where a party like *Alleanza Nazionale* has become part of the political establishment. This hierarchy is mirrored by the experts' judgment collected by van der Brug and van Spanje (2004) in their study of policies countering "anti-immigrant parties" in Europe. Germany and the Netherlands ranked highest among the 11 countries they studied. Lower in the rank order one finds Flanders and France where the Flemish *Vlaams Blok* and the French

Front National have succeeded on the partisan and electoral level, but were kept out of office. Italy ranks at the very bottom as the country where the AN not only attracted voters and militants but gained access to power. The hierarchy of ostracism reflects the political achievement of these movements. The more stigmatized they are, the more costly it is to join them, the more difficult is their electoral and partisan development. Yet stigmatization is at the same time a resource for the movement, helping it to hold together, as shown in the French interviews. These findings confirm the experience of the French journalist Anne Tristan who joined a local section of the FN, in the underprivileged northern housing projects of Marseille. She lived there for two months. She concludes the book she wrote on her experience by quoting Albert Cohen's comment about his experience of anti-Semitism in Marseille: they are "decent people who love each other from hating together" (Tristan 1987: 257).

Flanders

In Flanders, like in Italy (as we will see later) some of our interviewees refer to the stigmatization of their parents or grandparents because of their role during World War II. After the war, they were sentenced because of collaboration with the German occupier.

> And so I grew up in a Flemish-national family, with the consequences one can imagine, that is: my father and mother had problems after the war. Not because they were in league with the Germans, because I never thought that they really knew what was going on, but because they were Flemish nationalists, part of the VNV, that was the reason why they were convicted after the war.
>
> (Anton, *Vlaams Blok*, male, 59)

Of greater importance for our subject were the feelings of collective discrimination because of their membership in a political movement. Nearly all interviewees complained that their organization and their viewpoints were wrongly represented in the media. Maria (*Voorpost*, female, 39): "You're right-wing and you're put in people's black books and associated with violence." They also complained that they were being denied the right to express their opinions freely and have meetings. A few of them gave examples of discrimination. They were threatened with dismissal or persecuted because of their views. In conclusion, some pointed to the fact that they were in danger of being seized in a physical and violent manner. Rita (*Voorpost*, female, 46) explains: "The general climate in the country is against nationalists. Twenty years ago it was easier in that sense. Now it's becoming more and more difficult to defend our own ideas." Note that this unfair treatment was not what prompted them to become active in their organization, but rather *resulted* from it. It's *because* of their activism that the threats and negative treatment fell to their lot.

Through their strong involvement in ethnic nationalism, these extreme right-wing militants in fact stand a greater chance of experiencing discrimination, since they are being stigmatized by society for taking this radical political stand.

France

Interestingly, in France the stigmatization applied to the extreme right works to inspire militants of all ages: they collectively feel this negative sentiment of being pariahs, of being excluded from the political arena. This feeling of exclusion and injustice is the cement that binds these militant groups together despite their social and political incompatibilities: the shared experience of stigmatization is the common ground and the means to identify with one another. The cement is in fact skillfully wielded to this end by the FN party machine.

FN militants can identify with crusaders whose set task it is to defend the memory of forgotten martyrs, to re-establish for all future generations a social order that had all but disintegrated, and to be the sacrificial lambs of contemporary politics. For the militants the FN is like a family linked by the idea of exclusion. Working in the FN is like finding a family for Algerian veterans who reconstructed their old support networks in the party, rediscovering conviviality in the process, and for young recruits seeking strong social ties alike.

> We have evening get-togethers, we get together in groups for a pizza, at a friend's house or at home, I always end up cooking for seven or eight, it's always spontaneous, we never plan in advance, that's what's great, is that we're one big family ... Here it's very fraternal, they call me Miss, if you like I'm a sort of girlfriend, well not really, but the girlfriend of a boyfriend, a girlfriend to the group ... We are a large, not family exactly, but group, sort of.
>
> (Blanche, FN, MNR, female, 22)

The stigmatization of the FN deflects each individual back into their personal difficulties such as how to acquire a social role or a job, so they are in phase with contemporary social struggles. The FN becomes in this way a refuge where the face that cannot possibly be shown anywhere else can be developed with fervor: this is the face of one or several fictional heroes. Mobilizing with the FN is also for some a way of re-affirming a social domination that was outmoded and had become inoperative, but which was still going strong in a micro-society like the FN.

> We are knights in armor in the strongest sense of the word. Warriors, yes, I feel like a knight, just the fact of swimming against the tide, not going with the current trend, it almost seems aristocratic, it means refusing the present, it means refusing what we are presented with. So it's quite a chivalrous or noble spirit, because it's hard, you have to fight.
>
> (Philippe, FN, MNR, male, 25)

Italy

When we asked our Italian interviewees about stigmatization many began to tell stories about how they or their families were persecuted by "the other side." This was true both of interviewees who had witnessed World War II and interviewees who had not because they were born after the end of the war. For example, Vittorio was born in 1932 and both his parents were fascists. When asked whether there were any crucial events that drove him to political militancy, he answers:

> Actually, I was already convinced, consciously or unconsciously I do not know ... because it was a natural passage. My father was arrested; my father went to a concentration camp [that is, a US prisoner of war camp]; my father was the first person to be made a prisoner in the province of [XXX], so ... it was this.
>
> (Vittorio, MS-FT, male, 65)

Also younger interviewees reported episodes of discrimination because of their political ideas, which happened mainly during their adolescence or early adulthood, at high school or at the university. Many of these interviewees said that extreme left-wing students had assaulted them verbally or physically, exclusively because they supported fascist ideals. In fact, those episodes did not discourage them from professing fascist views. Rather, they fostered their decision to get involved in active politics and to join extreme right-wing parties. In this light, Davide's account of how he decided to go to the MSI party local office for the first time is exemplary:

> Well, I approached MSI juvenile movement, which was called *Fronte della Gioventù* [Youth Front], in December 1992, mainly as a consequence of an event I was involved in ... I was assaulted just in front of my high school, the Leonardo Da Vinci scientific lyceum, by a group of extreme left-wing students attending the Faculty of Political Science at the university of Milan ... When I came here [that is, the party local office in Milan] and said: "Look, I'm that guy who was beaten in front of the Leonardo School last month," they were very surprised and answered: "Yeah, we didn't know we had any supporters there, and we were wondering who the hell they were. So here you are. Great."
>
> (Davide, AN, male, 21)

The activists we interviewed described a host of material and social disadvantages they experienced due to prejudice towards extreme right-wing parties. With regard to material disadvantages, practically all interviewees said that there was nothing to gain from supporting their party. Rather, there was a lot to lose, and they made a long list of material costs they paid for their political membership: injuries suffered from public disturbances; time subtracted from study, leisure or other social activities; low grades at high school and/or at university; difficulties finding a job. With regard to social disadvantages, interviewees described a wide range of social costs they paid for their militancy. Other costs were closely related to membership in a group that was politically stigmatized. Actually, almost all interviewees recalled that MSI had been kept out of Italian social and political life for the entire time of its existence. For example, when asked to think about advantages and disadvantages of membership in that party, Bartolomeo answers:

> No advantages ... No advantages ... [Rather] disadvantages ... disadvantages could be many. For example, being discriminated against at school ... when one said that he supported MSI, he was discriminated against. In the 1960s, admitting to having right-wing views was bad enough, but if right-wing meant fascist, it was even worse ... there were slogans like "fascist berets go to hell," killing fascists was not considered a crime ... because the State allowed it ... the State did not intervene ... and it did not punish.
>
> (Bartolomeo, MS-FT, male, 51)

For many Italian extreme right-wing activists social isolation and political stigmatization improved after the AN party was founded. AN interviewees admitted that activities and recruitment of new members were much easier in AN than they had been in MSI; furthermore, in some municipalities the party could also exert real political power since it had got some seats in city councils. However, AN interviewees declared that they still happened to encounter some difficulties because the burden of their previous membership in an "embarrassing" party was often brought against them, and they were required to show that they had really changed.

Germany

Most German interviewees refer to some kind of stigmatization, friends whom they lost, difficulties at work, threats by opponents, threatening phone calls, and so on. While some complain about the media neglecting their party, others complain about the biased, prejudiced picture the news media are giving. For instance, Heinrich (REP, male, 78) remarks that "the reputation of the REP is so run down by media that you are often ashamed to stand for the party." As a consequence, his children didn't like his engagement with the REP. His wife didn't like it either but she agrees that REPs are treated unfairly by society. Klaus (REP, male, 48) takes a party meeting in Hannover (October 1996) as an example of the way the media treat the party. He himself was very impressed by the discussions and by the resulting platform, even if there was a "horrible time-pressure," but "The distortion in the press was really astonishing. Initially, you would think, you've visited a different meeting."

Klaus also refers to the many costs involved in his affiliation with the REP: he himself was physically attacked by a foreign ANTIFA (anti-fascist) activist, and he tells about how his children became targets at school by classmates who exclaimed: "Hi [name], how many Jews has your father gassed today?" Asked about perceived threats, Heinrich tells about threatening phone calls such as "You pig, we'll beat you to death," and about writings on his house like "REP = Nazis, Nazis raus, Nazis = pigs." To be engaged in the REP, in the words of Silke (REP, female, 56), always means "to swim against the tide," i.e. to defend against "propaganda" and "slander." In former times "we also had obscene phone calls, threats and so on." In addition, some time ago at a "left-wing meeting [point]" in Aschaffenburg—a "hashish-dump"—she was called names such as the "people's enemy number 1." Concerning professional disadvantages she has had some trouble with one of her superiors. Also, her husband was removed from his position due to his political stance. Once he confronted a Turkish woman (a client) with a Turkish flyer against Germany, and asked her "inconvenient questions" about it. As the woman had nothing to do with it, this became one of the reasons he was removed. In private life, too, there were negative consequences. For instance, when a former school friend and her husband visited Silke and her husband, they insisted on not talking about politics. Because Silke didn't want to talk only about cooking recipes she broke off the relationship.

Jakob's (REP, male, 63) family fears that he will be elected to the *Bundestag*, because of the trouble they expect. If he then were to go to Berlin, "father won't live very long anymore." Of course, Jakob doesn't agree, but he nonetheless brings it up. He often talks about stigma and taboos, i.e. the REP is blamed for bringing up taboo themes, which he says actually interest many people in Germany. In this context he also tells about repression against the REP. For example, in his hometown Tübingen party meetings were prevented by the police, because "the security of citizens would not be ... guaranteed." After a fire assault on his house and car it is not surprising that he perceives himself to be threatened, but on the other hand, it doesn't scare him too much. "Without being prepared to take risks, nobody would ever enter politics ... nobody would be able to live," he reasons, as every decision in life includes doubts and risks. He is disappointed, though, by former friends who turned their back on him because of his engagement with the REP. He calls them "the weak ones," and recollects how some of them, "even very Catholic, very serious, felt very sorry for it and then said good-bye." What disappointed him most was that nobody was willing to discuss things in a friendly, fair manner.

The Netherlands

All our Dutch interviewees explain how they have experienced stigmatization, be it in the form of repression, attacks from the counter-movement, or exclusion from their social environment. Organizations and individuals were repeatedly brought to court because of the leaflets or statements they issued. If not prohibited by authorities, events and meetings were interrupted by anti-fascist organizations or demonstrations. In the political arena proper representatives of the RWE were neglected or boycotted. In their personal life interviewees and their families were blackmailed and threatened; they lost their job or business, or experienced problems with their employer or colleagues. Many interviewees lost friends and were ousted from organizations or groups to which they belonged.

As far as repression is concerned, the authorities for a long time banned any demonstration by the RWE and tended to prohibit meetings. Leaflets and other written material were scrutinized and individuals or organizations were prosecuted if unlawful passages were found. One of the parties (CP '86) was prosecuted and eventually sentenced for being a criminal organization, which in fact meant the end of the organization. Frans remembers how he and the other members of CP '86 in his hometown were rounded up by the police because he stood for CP '86 in an election:

FRANS: Six o'clock in the morning the police stood at the door.
Q: At your door?
FRANS: Yeah, wanting me at my door. I had to come with them, suspected of membership in a criminal organization. Yeah, they can take everybody into custody for that in principle thus that, ehm ...
(Frans, VNN, Voorpost, male, 34)

In terms of attacks by the counter-movement, Cor remembers his swearing-in as a member of the city council:

Ehm ... the whole event, the whole, ehm, ehm ... the whole ceremony heh, that was ehm, you see that the whole hall is completely jammed with, ehm ... punkers and squatters heh, that are just your arch-enemies and then it takes an hour and a half for the police to bully everybody out that is just a great, great, great pity.
(Cor, CD, *Nederlands Blok* (NB), male, 47)

The archetypical attack by the counter-movement to which every interviewee referred is the hotel fire of Kedichem in 1986. The anti-fascist organizations in the country used to besiege meetings of the extreme right if they became aware of them, which often resulted in violent confrontations. As a consequence, most owners of meeting spaces tended to refuse to rent space to extreme right-wing organizations. In turn, these organizations reacted to the situation by attempts to rent meeting space secretly in disguise (as an organization and as individuals), or to go to places individually and set up a meeting on the spot rather than rent space collectively. Kedichem was one of those meetings set up in the late 1980s between representatives of the CD and CP '86 to discuss a possible merger. The anti-fascist movement got the information about the meeting and turned the place into a battlefield. Be it deliberately or by accident, the hotel was set on fire and several attendees of the meetings were seriously wounded—*inter alia* Cor, one of our interviewees.

In the political arena proper the representatives of the extreme right are neglected and excluded by their colleagues. Paula describes how representatives of other parties refuse to work with her or even talk to her. All this came to a climax with the death of her son Bart.

> Bart then passed away. I received a card from only two council members, I mean, that's not normal! I really think so ... I find that really ... Of course, they could have read it in the newspaper. They knew it all too well, because I sent a card to the mayor, to the aldermen who sent a letter of condolence, to be sure, but not a single personal gesture because you must not think that Opstelten [the then mayor] will shake hands with me, so sorry for the wife of [Bart], forget it ...
>
> (Paula, NB, female, 45)

Making public someone's affiliation to the extreme right is a common strategy of the counter-movement. First of all, every person who is known to be a member of an extreme right organization is listed on several websites of the counter-movement, including personal information about him or her the counter-movement can get hold of. Second, several of our interviewees found themselves confronted with information in the media meant to publicize their involvement in the extreme right. Willem is one of them. One day an anti-fascist magazine had an article titled "The Nationalistic Shopkeeper."

> The article with the name of the shop and the street has the title "The Nationalistic Shopkeeper" with statements like "the odd man, a wolf in sheep's clothing, the smartest and an erudite man." Well, that was flattering, of course, as such it made me smile. Thus far, my activism had not provoked any reaction. It was in that paper on Thursday. I [was] scared stiff, I had my heart in my throat. The day after I met some colleagues who pounded me on my shoulder saying don't let them put you down.
>
> (Willem, *Voorpost*, male, 34)

Eventually, Willem had to give up his business.

Almost every interviewee reports stories of exclusion. Be it friends or members of their family who do not want to meet them anymore, a job they lost or could not get, a business that was troubled. Maria, for instance, concludes a long story about how the reactions of her friends have shocked her by saying:

> They put me down ... I mean, ... I was always ready for everybody, also for the people who dropped me, for whom I really did everything. But they never gave me the chance to explain what my motives were. In fact, there should be no need to do so. For, if they were real friends then we would discuss a lot with them. Real friends must be able to do so. Indeed,

they should then know my motives. They could perhaps throw at me "Maria, this is not the way." That would have been fine, but it didn't happen, it left me embittered.

(Maria, CD, female, 56)

Johan had planned to finish his studies before he ran for the municipal elections, but then a car accident ruined his plans.

> I was still busy with my thesis when I was already running for the elections. When my supervisor got to know that, he withdrew. He didn't want to supervise my thesis anymore, because yeah initially he was very enthusiastic, because yeah it would be publishable, and yeah we could turn it into a book, because nobody had ever written about it. Thus he was very enthusiastic about it, because he thought, of course, that could be nice for him too, that his name would be on it as well, but yeah then he discovered who I was and then he didn't find it so nice anymore that his name would be on it.

(Johan, CP '86, male, 33)

He could not find anybody else willing to supervise him, and in fact never finished his studies.

Edwin lost his job after his boss saw him on television taking part in a right-wing demonstration. It was the first time that a mayor allowed a demonstration by the extreme right in his community. The first Monday after the weekend when Edwin went to work his boss said:

> I saw you on television. What were you doing there? I don't want you here anymore. Your future here is over ... And of course, quite a few members of my family did not know. Must be scary all those bald heads and then they think are you part of this? I have always seen you as a nice guy. Their whole ideal fell apart so to say.

(Edwin, *Voorpost*, male, 29)

Although we encountered different levels of stigmatization in the five countries—the Netherlands being the extreme—the most significant finding in this respect is perhaps that RWE activists in *all five* countries experience stigmatization. Many of them comment on the unfairness of being suppressed and stigmatized while other parties or political organizations are not. At the same time this does not make them quit. On the contrary, many of them respond with entrenchment. For our activists, as diverse as they are, one could well say: it's being hated together that makes them love each other all the more.

Conclusion

RWE parties and movements are on the rise in Europe. In this paper I have reported on the life histories of the activists who are the leaders of this expansion. So far, little is known about the organizers of the extreme right. In this paper we have tried to understand how organizers were recruited and how being visibly active in the RWE impacted their lives. I have argued that recruitment into activism and the experiences of activism are context dependent. Contextual differences can be characterized in terms of the demand and supply of RWE activities. In order to assess the impact of such contextual variation one needs to conduct comparative research. In this study we compared life histories of activists in Flanders, France, Italy, Germany, and the Netherlands. Compared to Germany and the Netherlands, Flanders, France and Italy have relatively strong RWE movement sectors. The latter three countries accommodate a relatively strong supply of RWE movement activity in combination with a relatively strong demand for such activities. As a consequence, the RWE movements in these countries are relatively strong. The Netherlands and Germany, on the other hand, have relatively weak RWE movements. Recruitment and the experience of stigmatization appear to depend on these contextual differences. Interestingly, differences in the supply side of the RWE movement seem to have more influence than differences in the demand side. In a way this is understandable. A modest mobilization potential can still turn into a mass movement if an appealing supply of movement activities is staged.

Appendix 1: methods

The objective of our study was to interview militants rather than mere supporters of extreme right organizations. It was agreed that in each country we would aim for people at different levels in the movement, with an emphasis on the lower echelons in the organizations rather than the leaders. As for the selection of the organizations, for each country we composed a list of organizations that indisputably were perceived as extreme right. Members of any of these organizations qualified as interviewees. We also agreed that we would try to interview activists from both political parties and other types of organizations. Furthermore, we decided to restrict ourselves to those organizations that, as far as we were able to see, stayed within the rules of the law. Finally, we attempted to diversify our interviews in terms of gender, age, region, and other background variables. In each country the study was introduced as a study on political engagement initiated by the Vrije Universiteit, Amsterdam. It was emphasized that we would treat the information provided in the interviews confidentially.

Within this framework the actual sampling strategies differed in the five countries, although a mixture of snowball sampling and approaching potential interviewees at meeting places was used everywhere. Indeed, options such as sampling from membership lists were not feasible, as such lists did not exist or were not made available to us.

In the course of the interview the interviewer and the interviewee try to reconstruct a specific part of the interviewee's life. As our study concerned the interviewee's career in a given RWE movement, the interview started with the question of when and how the interviewee became involved in this movement. Subsequently, it moved on to questions about what it is like to be actively involved in this field and whether the interviewee had considered occasionally quitting activism. Two important additional sections of the interview concerned social and political beliefs and attitudes, and what it meant to the interviewee personally to be involved in such an organization. Towards the end of the interview the interviewees were asked to answer a set of biographical queries about their age, education, profession, position in the organization, duration of their membership, etc.

The interviews were conducted by the junior members of our team, who took part in interview training sessions. After the first few interviews were conducted the team convened to discuss the experiences. On the basis of this discussion the interview scheme was finalized. In the course of the interview period the junior members of the team met to discuss progress and experiences.

The majority of the interviews were conducted in 1997 and 1998. Some interviews were conducted in 1999, as were some follow-up interviews. We left the interviewee the choice of the location for the interview. All interviews were audio taped. The interviews lasted from one hour to many hours, but the modal interview was approximately three hours long. In preparation for an interview, interviewers tried to deepen their understanding of the organization in which the interviewee participated and, if possible, the role of the interviewee in the organization. Much was done to gain the confidence of the interviewee. Many of these people have negative experiences with interviews and journalists and were initially very distrustful. On the whole, however, we believe that we succeeded in establishing the rapport needed for reliable and valid interviews.

Data processing took place in several steps. First, all 157 interviews were fully transcribed in their original language. Second, on the basis of our interview scheme and theoretical notions we developed a tentative coding scheme. This tentative coding scheme was tested on the first five interviews. The experiences with the coding were evaluated and used to improve the coding scheme. Third, on the basis of the key questions in the coding scheme the interviews were summarized and exemplary quotes were selected for each interview. The summaries and exemplary quotations were translated into English. Fourth, the actual coding and analyzing of the full interviews was undertaken by the individual country teams on the basis of the interviews in their original language.

Notes

1 See Appendix 1 for a description of the methods employed.
2 In the years following our study this was evidenced by the electoral successes of Pim Fortuyn's party (the Lijst Pim Fortuyn—LPF) first and Geert Wilders's party (the Partij voor de Vrijheid—PVV) later.
3 The 'IJzer pilgrimage' is a large-scale political manifestation of Flemish nationalism, held yearly in Diksmuide at the *IJzertoren* (a tower erected in memory of

fallen Flemish soldiers of World War I). Several thousand Flemish nationalists attend this manifestation, in which the Flemish movement expresses its demands and agenda. At the margins of this manifestation, extreme right-wing groups from all over Europe organize annual meetings and exchange ideas and texts.
4 The Flemish National Song Festival (*Vlaams Nationaal Zangfeest*) is a yearly mass gathering of Flemish people, who sing Flemish (ethnic) folk songs, watch Flemish folk dances, and listen to a choir singing Flemish songs. The first of these manifestations was held is 1933, so this festival has a long tradition.
5 The VNV is a Flemish-national political party, founded in 1933. Its ideology was closely related to authoritarianism and 'new order' ideas (e.g. extreme right-wing ideology). During World War II, the VNV collaborated with the German occupier.
6 *Volksunie* is a Flemish nationalist party.
7 Israeli historian and specialist of the French historical extreme right.

References

Andrews, M. (1991) *Lifetimes of Commitment. Aging, Politics, Psychology*, Cambridge: Cambridge University Press.

Bizeul, D. (2003) *Avec ceux de FN: Un sociologue au Front National*, Paris: La Découverte.

Blee, K. (2002) *Inside Organized Racism. Women in the Hate Movement*, Berkeley: University of California Press.

Dekker, P. and C. van Praag (1990) "Xenofobia in West Europa," *Migrantenstudies* 4: 37–57.

de Witte, H. (1996) "On the 'Two Faces' of Rightwing Extremism in Belgium. Confronting the Ideology of the Extreme Rightwing Parties in Belgium with the Attitudes and Motives of their Voters," *Res Publica. Belgian Journal of Political Science* 38: 397–411.

Doosje, B., N.R. Branscombe, R. Spears, and A.S.R. Manstead (1998) "Guilty by Association: When One's Group Has a Negative History," *Journal of Personality and Social Psychology* 75: 872–86.

Klandermans, B. (1997) *The Social Psychology of Protest*, Oxford: Blackwell.

——(2003) "Collective Political Action," in David O. Sears, Leonie Huddy and Robert Jervis (eds) *Oxford Handbook of Political Psychology*, Oxford: Oxford University Press, 670–709.

——(2004) "The Demand and Supply of Participation: Social Psychological Correlates of Participation in a Social Movement," in David A. Snow, Sarah Soule and Hanspeter Kriesi (eds) *Blackwell Companion to Social Movements*, Oxford: Blackwell, 360–79.

Klandermans, B. and N. Mayer (2006) *Extreme Right Activists in Europe. Through the Magnifying Glass*, London: Routledge.

Klandermans, B., M. Werner and M. van Doorn (2008) "Redeeming Apartheid's Legacy: Collective Guilt, Political Ideology, and Compensation," *Political Psychology* 29: 331–50.

Lagrou, P. (2000) *The Legacy of Nazi Occupation. Patriotic Memory and National Recovery in Western Europe, 1945–1965*, Cambridge: Cambridge University Press.

Lubbers, M. (2001) *Exclusionistic Electorates: Extreme Right-wing Voting in Western Europe*, PhD dissertation, Catholic University, Nijmegen.

Orfali, B. (2002) "La Droite de Coeur, ses dissension et ses consensus," *Les Cahiers Internationaux de Psychologie Sociale* 53: 10–19.

Roth, S. (2003) *Building Movement Bridges. The Coalition of Labor Union Women*, Westport: Praeger.

Simon, B. and B. Klandermans (2001) "Toward a Social Psychological Analysis of Politicized Collective Identity: Conceptualization, Antecedents, and Consequences," *American Psychologist* 56: 319–31.

Teske, N. (1997) *Activists America. The Identity Construction Model of Political Participation*, Cambridge: Cambridge University Press.

Tristan, A. (1987) *Au Front*, Paris: Gallimard.

van der Brug, W. and J. van Spanje (2004) "Consequences of the Strategy of a 'Cordon Sanitaire' Against Anti-immigrant Parties," paper presented at the ECPR joint sessions of workshops, April 13–18, Uppsala, Sweden.

6 A comparative look at right-wing extremism, anti-Semitism, and xenophobic hate crimes in Poland, Ukraine, and Russia

Joachim Kersten and Natalia Hankel

Introduction: Eastern Europe after 1989

With the breakdown of the Soviet Union, and with Mikhail Gorbachev's politics of glasnost and perestroika, suppressed religious and national movements emerged as visible elements of political conflict in what once constituted the Union of Soviet Socialist Republics (USSR). While in the former USSR this concerned the huge former "Turkestan" region with its religious roots in Islam, and the Orthodox denominations of Russia and the Ukraine, the post-USSR Eastern European satellite states saw an eruption of both nationalism and/or suppressed Catholicism. Mark Juergensmeyer (2008: 152) describes how in Russia, the Ukraine, and Poland "religion became the expression of a nationalist rejection of the secular socialist ideology."

Partly, the free expression of religion was a component of what could be termed a democratic "eruption," and at the same time it created strong links to "nationalist and transnationalist identities of a bygone era" (Juergensmeyer 2008: 156). The role of right-wing extremism, xenophobia, and anti-Semitism ought to be assessed in the context of the transformation of the post-Stalinist political cultures of Eastern Europe and Russia. As much as religion and its institutions were indispensable for the opposition to the Stalinist state, they helped to recreate the old nationalisms of the 19th century (and earlier) of which anti-Semitism was often an integral component. Religious zeal combined with nationalistic patriotism contains ideologies of purity for which "others," be they ethnic minorities or Jews, were the paramount danger and source of a feared "racial pollution" (cf. Douglas 1966/2007). In the early 1990s, after German re-unification, similar developments could be observed in parts of the former German Democratic Republic.

Minkenberg (2002) sees the rehabilitation of the nation state (*Nationalstaat*) in Eastern Europe in line with the spread of nationalistic rhetoric and the concept of a national ethnic identity. In the context of economic, and partly also cultural crisis, minorities are used as a scapegoat for the problems at hand. Combined with a rejection of internationalism, diversity, and European Union (EU) integration, such resentments seem like "natural" consequences of newly formed national identities (Thieme 2007a, 2007b). In the findings of the European Social Survey (2006), Polish, Hungarian, and Ukrainian populations frequently show more sympathy for conservative (right-wing) politics, gender inequality, and homophobia than Western European societies.[1]

The data for this chapter were collected from official governmental sources, police statistics, and data generated by non-governmental organization (NGO) research in the respective countries. Based on these findings, expert interviews were conducted in the three countries under comparison. The questions raised addressed the following discourses: nationalism, legal situation, hate crimes, related subcultures, "national identity," the party system, NGOs, and civil society. The sample of interview partners (n = 8) consisted of political scientists, political experts, and members of NGO staff. On average each interview lasted about one hour. They were recorded and transcribed and formed an important part of the research project.

The term "right-wing extremism/radicalism" is far from precise. For the purpose of our study Hans-Gerd Jaschke's (2001) definition proved the most applicable. Jaschke depicts the phenomena of right-wing extremism as:

> an entity of attitudes, behavior, and activities, whether in an organized form or not, that originate from ideologies of a racially or ethnically based inequality of human beings; a demand for the ethnic homogeneity of nations; a rejection of the norm of equality of human rights declarations; insistence on the primacy of *Gemeinschaft* over the interests/rights of individual members of society and on the overall subordination of citizens under the state (*raison d'état*); repudiation of pluralism in liberal democracies, and an intention to revoke the process of democratization of society.
> (Jaschke 2001: 30, trans. by the authors)

The core elements of right-wing ideologies/extremism include xenophobia, racism, anti-Semitism, authoritarianism, anti-parliamentarianism, and the ideology of a united, ethnically homogeneous nation, a *Volksgemeinschaft* (cf. Winkler 2006: 131f). These ideologies are frequently associated with a denial of the Shoah or other forms of minimization of genocide and mass murder under Hitler, National Socialism, and Nazi Germany's occupation of its neighboring countries and the Soviet Union.

A number of theoretical approaches can be looked at for an explanation of right-wing extremism as an outcome of the transformation process in the countries under comparison among which modernization theories and *anomie* theory in the classical tradition of Durkheim and Merton seem most suitable; i.e. the turn towards right-wing extremism is seen as compensation for anomie following the breakdown of the previous system of control through the state, its secret police and their support through informants. At the same time, extremism that remains unchallenged by state authorities or citizens indicates a lack of structures that constitute a civil society. We shall return to such theorems after the discussion of the data.

Comparative work on right-wing extremism in Eastern Europe is still rather scarce. However, opinion surveys regarding right-wing attitudes were carried out as early as 1991. The questions asked then were:

- Do you consider yourself on the political right?
- Do you feel you are a determined patriot?
- Should one fight for one's own country whether it is right or wrong?
- Do parts of your neighboring countries actually belong to your own nation?
- Should the country control who is coming in (migration)?
- Do you have a negative opinion about Jews?

A similar 2006 survey including 24 European countries (but no data on the attitudes of Russians) asked respondents to position their political standpoint on a scale from 0 (= political left) to 10 (= political right). On this scale Ukrainians scored close to 6, respondents from Poland nearly 5.5 (Germans 4.5). Asked about the rights of homosexuals, negative responses were led by Poland (61 percent against such rights) and Ukraine (70 percent against) (compared to 11 percent against such rights in the Netherlands, in Germany 27 percent against). Ranking the disadvantages (= 0) and advantages (= 10) of migration, Poland stood at 5.5, Ukraine 4.9 (Germany 4.7, Greece 3.4). Thus, the survey data on migration indicate more liberal attitudes in some Eastern European populations, while homophobia and right-wing orientations appear to be more pronounced in the Eastern than in the Western parts of the continent.

One is well advised to be cautious when adapting the concept of political right vs. left in Western democracies to the Eastern European party systems. Often there is a mix of populist "left" and "right" in one and the same party program. Also, due to the state socialist past, there is very little pronounced left-wing extremism in the range of political parties. Extremist parties gain support because of an "unprepossessed ... political mix of populist right-left" positions and because they can reject any responsibility whatsoever for the oppressive systems of the past (Thieme 2007b: 23f.).

Poland (population 38.1 million)

Until the early 17th century the kingdom of Poland was one of the great powers of Europe. Its territories included Lithuania, Latvia, Belarus, and substantial parts of Russia, Estonia, Romania, and the Ukraine. Since then continuous partitions have reduced the former empire. For 123 years there was no Poland. A strong belief in a Polish national identity supported by the Roman Catholic

Table 6.1 Survey of political and social values and attitudes

	Political right	Strong patriotism	Willingness to fight	Irredentist attitudes	Anti-migration	Anti-Semitism
Russia	9%	60%	42%	22%	45%	22%
Ukraine	n.a.	62%	36%	24%	31%	22%
Poland	20%	75%	47%	60%	58%	34%

Source: *Times Mirror*, 1991, published by Center for the People and Press, The Pulse of Europe; quoted in Falter *et al.* 1996: 438

Church led to the country's renewed independence. After the end of the occupation by Nazi Germans, who saw Polish people as *Untermenschen*, the country fell under the political control of the Soviet Union. Unlike in other satellite states of the Warsaw Pact, the communist government in Poland neither managed a collectivization of the agrarian industry, nor could they diminish the importance of the Roman Catholic Church among the population. In 1980 the *Solidarnosc* movement emerged after strikes at Baltic ports. The government responded with heavy-handed attempts to suppress the political opposition. Perestroika under Gorbachev led to a respite of communist hegemony, and *Solidarnosc* came to power. Poland was the first country to start open conflict with the Russians.

Since 2004, when Poland became a member state of the EU, the country has experienced considerable economic success. Some 75 percent of the population are pro-EU. Exports have become more diversified and the agrarian sector has been stabilized. Although this sector produces only 3 percent of Poland's gross domestic product (GDP), it offers employment to 15 percent of the workforce: 38 percent of citizens live in the countryside. More than half of Polish households live in very modest economic conditions, 15 percent suffer relative poverty and 10 percent have to live in extreme poverty. Some 26 percent of children are poor and 2 million citizens are counted as "working poor." Unemployment stands at 13 percent.

During the transformation from post-Stalinist state socialism to democracy the former privileges of the working class and of the employees of the state/civil service started to dwindle. This led to widespread disappointment and mistrust in the new political system. There was a continuation of a political climate that Kupferberg (1998) had observed in Eastern Europe and in the former Soviet Union: the state didn't trust the citizens, and the people had no confidence in the state. Although nearly 70 percent of the population in Poland are pro-democracy today, nearly half of the citizenry express dissatisfaction with the present democratic system because of its lack of transparency and too much corruption. Under the previous government a coalition of conservative, populist and right-wing parties led by Jaroslav and Lech Kacynski, caused considerable damage to the parliamentary and justice systems (Vetter 2010: 3–9).

> At the forefront [of this political climate] stands a cult of being a victim, the evocation of a permanent threat for Poland, the reinterpretation of defeats into "moral victories," the suppression of a critique of the nation that was seen as a looming historical revisionism, and the prevailing Polonocentrism in the face of historical events
>
> (Ruchniewicz 2005: 7; trans. by the authors)

Since the 2010 election more moderate political forces have gained power. It remains to be seen how this will affect the political climate.

Before World War II the country was a multi-ethnic society with one-third of the population Ukrainian, Lithuanian, Byelorussian, German, and Jewish.

At present, 97 percent speak Polish as a first language, and a mere 0.7 percent consider themselves as members of an ethnic minority. Other estimates see the minorities in Poland amounting to 2–3 percent, mostly Ukrainians, Byelorussians, Armenians and Vietnamese. As mentioned above, the general attitude towards migration is more positive than in parts of Western Europe. Some 3 million citizens of Poland have taken up work in EU countries, which has supported the internationalization of the Polish culture. Those who return bring language skills and a broader knowledge about European cultures to their homes and families.

The constitution of Poland contains principles of non-discrimination and equality of its citizens before the law. As in other former Eastern European socialist states that were part of the Soviet Warsaw Pact, Nazism, fascism, and communism are put into one and the same category. In theory political parties that promote any of these are prohibited. Equally outlawed are parties that foster or promote "racist or nationalist hatred." In a similar vein, the Penal Code of Poland declares "incitement" of hateful sentiments or violence against national, ethnic or religious minorities as punishable offences (excluded are hateful acts directed against people with minority sexual orientations, i.e. homosexuals).

Poland has been criticized by NGOs for the country's non-intervention in cases of politically oriented/prejudiced criminal offences. Openly anti-Semitic and homophobic sentiments are widespread, and even have been present in attitudes among those in political power. Between 2004 and 2009 a "National Program against Racist Discrimination, Xenophobia and Related Intolerance" was instituted. This project has allegedly led to research projects and administrative measures. Thus far, little has been revealed about any findings or effects.

In contrast to official crime statistics which talk about a total of 12 cases of hate crimes (2006), NGO sources like *Nigdy Wiecej* (Never Again), which investigate racist incidents and right-wing violence, documented about 130 cases of related crimes in 2007. Among such cases are grievous bodily assaults. Victims of right-wing and racist attacks are members of ethnic minorities (Roma), homosexuals (both male and female), trans- and bisexual persons, and members of leftist/alternative groupings or subcultures. Included are reports about incidents of an anti-Semitic nature, and the desecration of Jewish places, threats, and racist speech. The problem of the remarkable difference between the criminal justice data and such NGO statistics is a legacy of the police/criminal justice use of the term *hooliganism* (rowdiness) during the Stalinist/post-Stalinist era in the former Warsaw Pact. This category of the penal code still serves as a "one size fits all" container for violent attacks, conveniently trivializing crimes that are in fact acts of racism and anti-Semitism.

Since the early 1990s the *Nigdy Wiecej* organization has registered thousands of hate crimes, roughly 300 per year, and about 40 incidents with lethal outcomes. The actual figure of such crimes being not reported to the police is estimated to be close to 90 percent. Criminal justice authorities handed out 35 hate crime sentences in 2006, with a high rate of cases being dismissed or having proceedings closed. Denial of the Holocaust is featured frequently in the print journal *Szczerbiec* (The Sword of Coronation), often combined with antagonistic rhetoric: anti-immigration ("mixture of races"), anti-homosexual, anti-abortion, anti-privilege for national or ethnic minorities: "In Poland there is little protest against fascist or racist statements because there is a high level of acceptance of such slogans in society" (Weiß 2008: 110, trans. by the authors). In the public mind, corruption and unemployment are seen as more pressing problems than racism and right-wing extremism.

As far as survey results about anti-Semitism are concerned, between 1992 and 2002 "traditional" anti-Semitism ("Jews as Crucifiers") remained basically the same at 11 percent. In the same time period "modern" (secular) anti-Semitism increased from 17 percent to 27 percent. A major forum of anti-Semitism is the weekly journal *Teraz Poliska*, published by Leszek Bubel with its brutish offenses against Jews. Another influential media source for similar attitudes is *Radio Maryja*, founded by a Catholic priest in 1991. There appear to be links between this radio station and the fundamentalist Catholicism of political parties like *Liga Polskich Rodzin* (Polish Family League) with its closed right-wing extremist ideology. Jews are depicted as the enemies of the Polish nation. Other enemies are homosexuals and feminists (Hankel 2010: 84f).

An organization that openly condones violence is *Narodowe Odrodzenie Polski* (NOP, National Rebirth of Poland), particularly popular among skinheads (Wolf 2009). The denial of the Holocaust, anti-Semitism, xenophobia and homophobia are open elements of this political organization. It has links to the "Blood & Honour" neo-Nazi movement. As in Western and other Eastern European countries, young recruits have been drawn from the community of soccer fans and so-called soccer ultras. Loose style groupings are similar to their German counterparts (*Kameradschaften*). However, because of the nationalist (patriotic) sentiment at the base of such subcultures' norms and values, co-operation with the German *Neonazi-Szene* tends not to be very popular. The pronounced dislike of the neighboring nation can be understood as a common denominator of all nationalistic organizations in Poland. Only NOP is an exception. Soccer stadiums in Poland have experienced displays of symbols, slogans and chants of open neo-Nazism, anti-Semitism, xenophobia and homophobia. Some of these subcultures have similarities with the German *Kameradschaften*, who also operate in soccer stadiums and on the Internet, where they publish lists of "enemies of the white race" (Wolf 2009, cf. Kersten 2004, 2007; Hankel 2010: 88ff).

Parts of the Roman Catholic Church are traditionally not only seen as being supportive of the extreme right but also of anti-Semitism. There is also a link between the broader *Solidarnosc* movement and right-wing splinter parties. As mentioned above, Western European classification systems of right- and left-wing parties do not really sit very well with the gamut of political parties in Poland.

Ukraine (population 45.8 million)

The Ukraine is divided into a central, a southern, an eastern, and a western part. The east is the industrial region and mostly urbanized; 50 percent of its inhabitants speak Russian as their mother tongue. An emphasized and xenophobic nationalist sentiment is particularly noticeable in western Ukraine, which is the agrarian part of the country. Ukraine gained independence from Soviet Russia in 1991, and is presently assessed as a deficient democracy by political experts in Eastern European studies. Although legal provisions, similar to Russia and Poland, clearly rule out hate crimes, racism, xenophobia etc. (up to eight years of imprisonment for group assault and crimes with serious consequences), hate crimes and xenophobic attacks amount to roughly 100 cases per annum. Because of the quality of the data, the motivation for such crimes cannot be ascertained with accuracy.

The population of the Ukraine is described as suffering from anomie and the failure of the legal system, lacking normative orientation and not trusting the government. Alcoholism is nearly as grave a problem as in Russia, with similar consequences for the life expectancy of males (alcohol abuse/life expectancy of males: see below). The main deficiencies are seen in widespread corruption: in the economy, in the administration, in the court, health and education systems. Medical doctors, administrators, and teachers have very low salaries. Corruption seems necessary to keep the system running. Just below 50 percent of the population is living in poverty. The economic crisis had a strong effect on the country: unemployment stands at 9 percent.

The mass demonstrations of 2004 (the "Orange Revolution") have led to a change in the government. There was a new leadership, but the political mechanisms and the actual personnel of the functional elites remained the same, and continued similar undemocratic practices. Presently the country is run by the very man who was the main target of the 2004 Orange Revolution protest. Transformation thus is incomplete, and there appears to be a widespread desire to return to the old value system, to the old symbols of Ukrainian identity. For example, the hairstyle of Yulia Tymoshenko, the Ukrainian Prime Minister in 2005 and from 2007 to 2010, is an exaggerated symbol of Ukrainian traditionalism. Stepan Bandera (1909–59), who had co-operated with the Nazi occupation forces and who is supposed to have been involved in the killing of Jews, was declared the country's "national hero" in 2010 (against strong protests from the EU). A Ukrainian court later withdrew the award, and it has since been annulled because the new government takes a different stand on historical issues.

In the Ukraine, similar to Poland, a victim status defines the national identity. Catastrophes like the 1932/33 famine, caused by Stalin's Soviet Russia, and the 1986 Chernobyl nuclear plant disaster that left large regions uninhabitable, run deep in the collective memory. In contrast, the ambivalent role of the Ukraine during the time of Nazi occupation (Ukrainians volunteered for SS divisions and as concentration camp guards) remains in the collective subconscious. Peter Potichnyj has done extensive research on the differences between the Ukrainian Insurgent Army (UPA) and the Organization of Ukrainian Nationalists (OUN), with the latter being led by Bandera. In order to discredit the UPA, the post-war Soviet historiography conflated both organizations (cf. Canadian Institute of Ukrainian Studies 2007).

Across the vast country regional and clan influence often dominate over democratic rule, and the political parties do not function as players in a democratic system but consist of leaders surrounded by followers. Political programs of parties are virtually non-existent. During the parliamentary period 2002 to 2006, 262 (out of 450) members of parliament changed their party affiliation. There is no right–left scope in politics, but a center–right majority with populist radical elements. During election campaigns anti-Semitic slurs were used. In summary, nation building has not yet been finished, and the right-wing scenario consists of a peculiar mix of extreme "right" and "left" orientations and ideologies including xenophobic positions/representatives even around such figures as Tymoshenko and Wiktor Juschtschenko who included right-wing parties as part of their coalitions (Hankel 2010):

> The country's political culture, attitudes and values are still embedded in Soviet traditions. Politicians are not presenting good examples in that they constantly violate democratic norms and obviate the terms of the constitution … Informal procedures, personal networks, the commingling of the economy and politics, corruption, and the exclusive position of the oligarchs are contrary to Western concepts of democracy. Democracy and the rule of law are not consolidated.
>
> (Kappeler 2009: 302, trans. by the authors)

On the very right margin of the political spectrum the Freedom Union has been observed to use hate speech against Jews and Russians. Furthermore, the Union has organized racist demonstrations. The Ukrainian National Workers' Union maintains links to skinheads and to the country's subsidiary of England's "Blood & Honour" Nazi group. As in other Eastern European countries, the groups most likely to use violence have skinhead members, and they get their new recruits from among soccer fans. They frequently join right-wing rock concerts and participate in anti-immigration marches. The 2002 skinhead attack on the Kiev synagogue was one of the more infamous incidents by Ukraine's right wing. The number of neo-Nazi skinheads is estimated at 500.

Ukrainian anomie is rooted in a lack of a common value system, in the failure of the rule of law, and the prevailing mistrust directed against the government and the administration.

A commitment to Western democratic values may well be lip service by both the populace and the government, and the fertile soil for the lasting existence of intolerance, racism, and xenophobia in Ukraine could well be its widespread parochialism. As long as lawmakers in the Ukrainian parliament consist of oligarchs and businessmen who fend mostly for their own

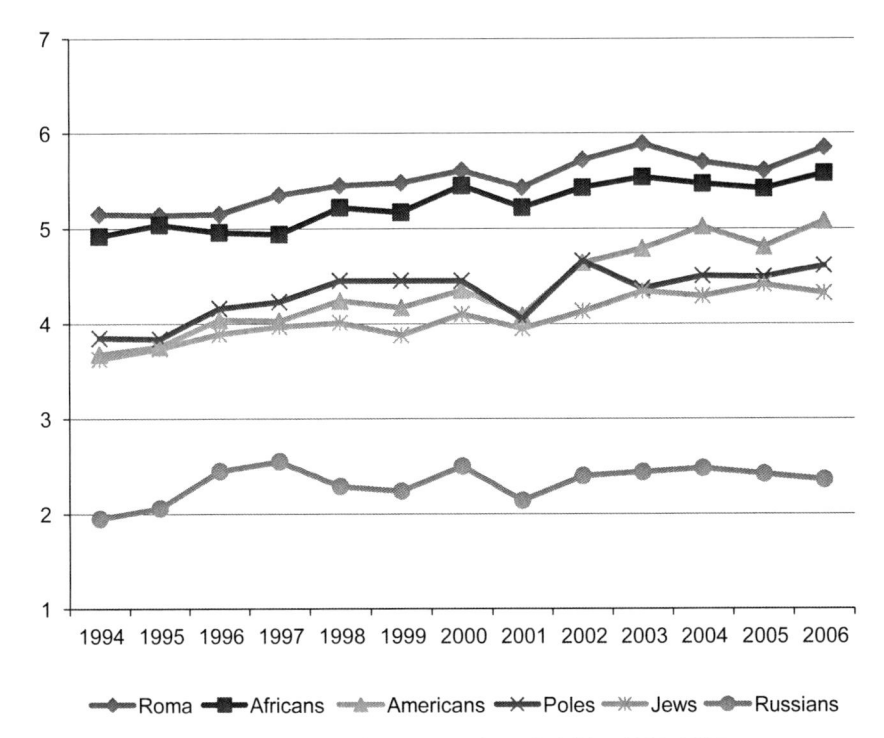

Figure 6.1 Social distance of Ukrainians to other ethnicities 1994–2006
Source: Kiev International Institute of Sociology
Note: 1 = lowest social distance; 7 = highest social distance.

corporations' interests and profit from their status of immunity from prosecution for offences, a reform of the democratic system does not appear to be very likely (Göls 2009: 5):

> The right-wing scenario in the Ukraine is a variegated mix of parties, movements and informal, partly violent groups. Organizational and ideological links and divisions between the groupings are mostly blurred. Many groups are clearly not "only" right-wing extremist, but also express left-wing extremist positions, in particular regarding social and economic issues.
> (Zimmer and van Praagh 2008: 2, trans. by the authors)

In comparison to other Eastern European countries, hate crimes had been less visible in the Ukraine until 2005. The increase since then appears to be caused by the amalgamation of informal youth groupings, in particular skinhead groupings that use Nazi symbols and attack persons with "non Slavic looks."

The criminal justice system tends to classify such acts as *hooliganism* (Hankel 2010: 65). Since 2008 there appears to be a more explicit response to such crimes by the police and the courts, which has led to a decrease of violent offences against "others" (Hankel 2010: 67). Also, the target groups of

94 *Joachim Kersten and Natalia Hankel*

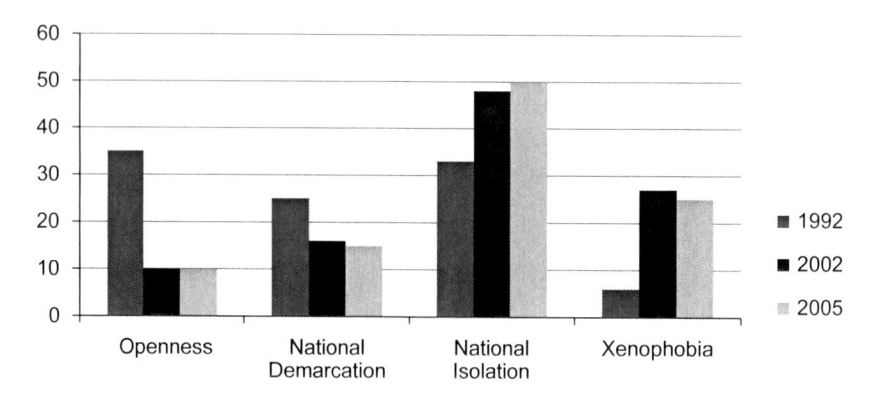

Figure 6.2 General indicators of national tolerance in Ukraine (% of population)

such attacks have been alarmed and tend to be more careful and avoid encounters with violent subcultures. However, the tendency to classify right-wing terrorism as *hooliganism* included a 2009 failed bomb attack on a Jewish Center (Hankel 2010). On average the yearly number of victims of attacks fluctuates at around eight, but was down in 2009. Neo-Nazi publications have been targeted by a National Commission and due to bans their number has been reduced. However, in the subcultures the basis for an expression of right-wing and Nazi ideologies and hate has remained.

> Important segments of the right-wing scenario are bands with racist songs. The dividing line between violent skinheads and parts of soccer hooliganism is hard to establish. On a routine basis, skinhead groupings organize public marches and concerts during which they chant fascist slogans.
> (Zimmer and van Praagh 2008: 3, trans. by the authors)

As an example, in February 2010 Kiev saw the "festival of German-Slavonic Brotherhood" with right-wing Ukrainian, Russian, and German bands. In contrast to similar subcultures in Poland, violent Ukrainian right-wing groupings are subdivisions of international neo-Nazi organizations like White Power, Blood & Honour and the World Church of the Creator Ruthena (Hankel 2010: 63). Furthermore, the Viktor Janokovic administration voted into office in 2010 has abolished all committees where civil society organizations and state institutions had established forms of co-operation after the Orange Revolution: "Even the best laws are useless when in reality there is no rule of law" (Ukrainian expert statement in Hankel 2010: 69, trans. by the authors).

Russia (population: 142 million)

In spite of its 160 different ethnicities, Russians make up 80 percent of the population of Russia, with other populations in percentages below 5 percent (Tatars 4 percent; Ukrainians 2 percent; Chechens 1 percent). Half of Russia is atheist, the other half mostly Russian Orthodox. Islamic, Catholic, Jewish, and Buddhist religious denominations are in the minority.

Although the country has abundant energy reservoirs of oil, natural gas, coal, and other natural resources, which make up 65 percent of its export industry, the infrastructure is still ailing. Due to the economic crisis unemployment has soared from 6 percent (2007) to more than 9 percent (2010), which means that nearly 7 million Russian citizens are out of work. Nearly one-quarter of the population is poverty stricken. This mostly concerns young persons who are easily convinced that this is caused by "enemies," and who therefore tend to share nationalist/extremist political orientations.

Alcoholism is an unsolved problem and has epidemic dimensions. It affects the demography since the mortality age for males is 59 years and the mortality age differential between the sexes is 14 years, and as such the highest of all industrialized countries. Some 80 percent of lethal crime offenders (50 percent of victims), half of the suicides, and 60 percent of traffic accident fatalities are alcohol related (Hankel 2010: 15f).

While Russian attitudes towards the former parts of the Soviet Union that have become separate states are claimed to be "brotherly" (an exception are relations to the Baltic countries), these feelings are rarely mutual. The Soviet system was experienced as a colonial dictatorship. Russia has used war to fight independence movements (two wars against Chechen rebels with more than 100,000 people killed). In the first stage of transformation (1990–2000) the country followed a course towards democratization, while the latter period has seen an increase of state control and cutbacks in democratic institutions, procedures and freedom of the press. The country under Putin and Medvedev is seen as being far from democratic standards and on its way into another autocratic dictatorship. Neither the Russian parliament nor the courts are independent, and the media are largely controlled by the state. On television, which is the main source of information for 85 percent of the population, Vladimir Putin is presented as a powerful leader in control of the fate of the nation (Rabitz 2007). The economic crisis of the late 1990s depleted public trust in the democratic system, and because of Putin's success in stopping the downfall, the Russian population appears to accept the country's bureaucratic authoritarianism and to waive its rights for political participation and democratic opposition. The broader spectrum of Russian political parties contains segments that amalgamate nationalism, communism, ethnocentrism and racism. Putin's anti-liberal and anti-Islam stance is popular and finds widespread support among the electorate.

In general, people in Russia appear to have few objections to political authoritarianism/dictatorship. A *Levada* survey (Analytisches Zentrum *Yury Levada* 2006) quotes Russian citizens' belief in a strong leader to solve the country's problems (51 percent) while only 30 percent see democracy as a solution. Some 54 percent prefer order over human rights (38 percent), and "Russia for the Russians" finds support by more than half of the respondents, while only 32 percent disagree with this slogan. More than 60 percent expect the government to restrict immigration into Russia (Analytisches Zentrum *Yury Levada* 2006: 145; Hankel 2010: 22).

The demise of the Soviet empire, as much as it led to independent nation states in Eastern Europe and ended the Cold War, is not perceived as an advantage by the Russians themselves, but as a painful loss of the great power status and a superior national identity. The country's military operations against Georgia are seen as a return to that status and its former grandeur.

Until 1999 the Russian Federation had an inefficient but pluralistic party system. Since Putin's presidency the party affiliation United Russia is the centre of power with Putin in control. Before 2007 Putin took over the party leadership (without being a member).

There are three political parties with right-wing elements. The Communist Party of the Russian Federation (KPRF) is the strongest opposition party with a combined socialist and nationalistic program. The Liberal Democratic Party of Russia (LDPR) with its charismatic populist leader Vladimir Chirinovsky is characterized as a "commercial structure." While officially still an opposition party, it cooperates on a continuous basis with Putin's ruling party, KPRF, LDPR and *Sprawedliwaja Rossija* (SR, Justice Russia):

> [Russians] ... base their contemporary ideologies [*Weltanschauungen*] on the ideas of Russian nationalism and Soviet communism, and by doing so they combine socialist with ethnocentric, respectively racist objectives of politics.
> (Thieme 2007b: 24, trans. by the authors)

The parliament of the Russian Federation has at least nine members who openly confess to radical nationalistic and xenophobic positions. The 2003 foundation of the *Rodina* (homeland) party has amalgamated with SR, joining parliament in 2007.

People from the Caucasus region (which are not Caucasians in the US census definition) tend to meet hostile reactions. Since the early 1990s persons from the Caucasus and from Central Asia are called "blacks." In a 2006 survey 41 percent of respondents expressed open anti-Semitism in that they demanded the restriction of the "influence of Jews" in politics, in the economy, in the justice system, in schools and universities, and in the entertainment sector (Analytisches Zentrum *Yury Levada* 2006; cf. Hankel 2010: 22).

The attraction of the radical right dates back to the aftermath of the Soviet collapse. Large parts of the Russian population experienced the fall of the Soviet empire as a personal catastrophe. The right wing offered the promise of ethnic solidarity, of Russian traditions and values, and they provided a plan for a rapid national rescue. Among the organizations is the Congress of Russian Communities (*Kongress russkich obschtschin*) centered on the protection of ethnic Russian in the post-Soviet area called "external Russia," an indication of the prevailing imperialist connotation of Russian nationalism. The movement received Putin's support and is now integrated into the *Rodina* parliament faction. Both opposition parties, KPRF and LDPR, nourish xenophobic sentiments. The "Movement against Illegal Immigration" (founded in 2002) has 20,000 members and operates in 30 regions against the non-Slavonic population whom they label "illegal migrants." They are at the core of the Russian right-wing network and on their initiative the "Russian Marches" have been carried out on November 4. These demonstrations are an expression of the political aim of the movement to achieve the unification of the Russian extreme right. The 2005 "march" in Moscow saw 3,000 participants, in 2006 marches took place in 15 cities; in 2007 another 3,000 marched in Moscow and in 19 other cities. In 2009 the Moscow march was down to 1,000 participants. There were reports of xenophobic chants and the destruction of a food stall.

Russian National Unity (RNE) existed from 1990 until 2000 and with its 15,000 members (an estimated 50,000 supporters) and its paramilitary outlook it was considered to be the most effective formation of Russian right-wing extremism. Four branches of the organization were banned and presently there are only splinter groups left. The National Socialist Party (founded in 2004) propagated a Russian National Socialism and the construction of concentration camps (for "aliens"); it was banned in 2008. Alexander Dugin who used to be in a marginal position, but is now thought to have connections to influential political circles and organizations, media and universities, has founded the "International Eurasian Movement," and is also located on the extreme right of the political spectrum.

Similar to the Polish constitution (see above) the Russian Federation outlaws the incitement of social, racially based, nationalistic, and religious hatred and the propagation of fascist ideologies. Although in indirect terms the denial of war crimes that aim at the total or partial extermination of ethnic, social, national or religious groups are the object of penal sanctions, these laws/ordinances are controversial because they are also used against the democratic opposition and critical journalists.

> In Russia extremism is not so much a category to check the relationship between democracy and extremism but rather a term used to combat political opponents and disagreeable attitudes ... Additionally, the term extremism ... has become an instrument of the administration and Kremlin-friendly media, to exclude political opponents from the democratic game rather than to judge their constitutional legitimacy.
> (Thieme 2007b: 26f., trans. by the authors)

Sanctions for individual persons using Nazi propaganda or symbols are at 500 to 1,000 Roubles or imprisonment of up to 15 days. If used by organizations (legal entities) fines can be between 20,000 and 100,000 Roubles. In the wording of penal sanctions there is an interchangeable use of the terms "fascism" and "nationalism." The category "extremism" (25.07.02/29.04.08) contains (among other offences): incitement of racial, national, social, and religious hate in combination with violence or invocation of violence; debasement of national honor; and human rights violations.

Equally, there is punishment for Nazi propaganda and the justification of war crimes that were aimed at the total or partial extermination of ethnic, social, national, or religious groups. In 2008 in Russia the foundation of a Department of the Prevention of Extremism took place with branches in all regional police departments. Since 2005 organizations like *Naschi* (aka "Putin Youth"), a Kremlin-supported youth organization, use the term "fascist" to brand persons as "anti-Russian," including critics and journalists. *Naschi* has a membership of 120,000 and directs its very blunt activities mainly against the political opposition and against "the West." Due to bans and law enforcement activities, right-wing extremism is presently keeping a more moderate profile. Openly racist and xenophobic propaganda is confined to closed meetings while officially the fight is against alcoholism and for healthy sport activities. Recruitment for the right-wing movement happens at "symbolic" events like the aforementioned "Russian marches" and concerts.

The Department of the Prevention of Extremism lists 150 right-wing extremist formations which propagate nationalistic and racist ideologies and are prepared to use violence and criminal activities to achieve their aims, in particular neo-Nazi and skinhead groupings in Moscow, St Petersburg and other larger Russian cities. Recruitment occurs among students, cliques and their members and soccer fans/hooligans. Officially the membership of right-wing extremist groupings is estimated at 10,000, but in civil rights groups/NGO reports the estimate is five times that number. Nazi skinheads, soccer ultras and hooligans also meet at private rock music concerts, either clandestine "private" activities with audiences between 150 and 250, or at "open" music events with audiences up to 800 persons. The right-wing groupings "play" with Nazi ideology and symbolism, they publicly use racist slogans, and they maintain links to European and Ukrainian right-wing groups.

> The situation is escalating, because in the eyes of the impoverished young people the newly rich behave "indecently." They tend to display their wealth in all kinds of ways. This antagonizes the young people because they anticipate that this [wealth] will never be accessible to them themselves.
> (Interview statement IP4RU: 3, in Hankel 2010: 29, trans. by the authors)

The skinhead subculture helps young men to overcome their inferiority complex. They experience feelings of solidarity and power:

> Present Russian society is radically split (into haves and have-nots). Officially the proportion is 1:24, i.e. there is a very tiny echelon of very rich Russians and a large majority of people who are on the verge of poverty. Accordingly, one should not underestimate the potential for extremism. Considering that the old systems of socialization were destroyed at the beginning of the 1990s, and that they have not yet been replaced by new ones, the age cohort of young people of the 1990s can be perceived as a lost generation. They do not abide by stable basic norms. Their altercations

amongst each other are very brutal. The use of violence poses no problem to them. In society in general and especially among young people violence is widespread.

(IP4RU: 4, in Hankel 2010: 29f., trans. by the authors)

Most Russian skinheads are extremely racist. Their aim is not only the annihilation of non-Russians but the "ethnic cleansing" of Russian territory, "the purification of Russian soil." In 2009 the reported case load of extremist offenses was a total of 548 (in 2008, 460) of which 430 were cleared. Among them were 19 homicides, 11 cases of threats of murder, and 142 cases of assault. In view of the total number of criminal offenses, however, these cases amount to less than 0.02 percent.

However, such data have to be handled with some skepticism. Sova statistics report 71 fatal incidences for the year 2009 (333 injured). In 2008 the number of people killed was 109 and 486 were injured. Victims tend to be of Central Asian descent (29 killed, 68 injured) or from the Caucasus region (Chechens), with 11 killed and 47 injured. Attacks occur in the cities and outskirts of Moscow (38 killed, 131 injured) and Saint Petersburg (60 killed, 47 injured).

Offenders come predominantly from youth groupings committed to a Russian nationalist denomination: skinheads, Vanguard of Red Youth, National Bolsheviks, Movement Against Illegal Immigrants, etc. Persons with "non-Slavic" looks become victims, among them South Korean students or tourists.

According to the Sova the number of sentenced extremist offenders has increased since 2004 from 20 to 140. In the course of 2009 there were a total of 46 court rulings related to hate crimes in 25 regions of the Russian Federation, with 135 persons sentenced, 21 percent of whom received parole. In Moscow alone 40 skinheads were sentenced because of hate crimes.

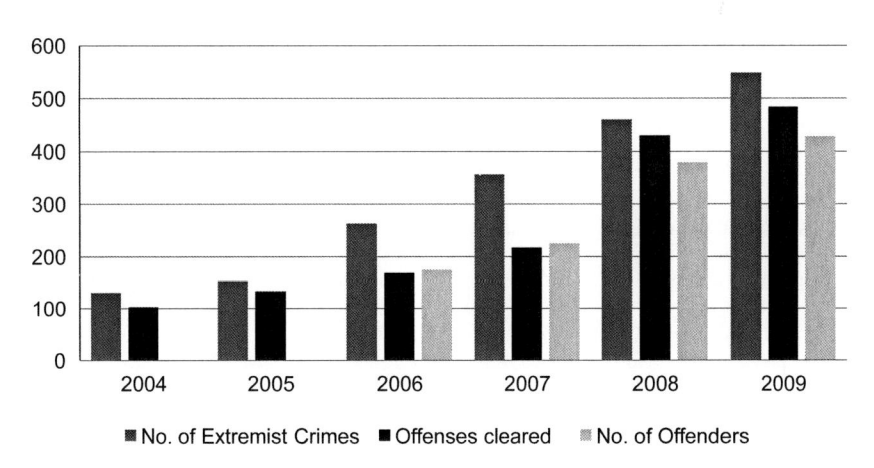

Figure 6.3 Number of xenophobic offenses 2004–09
Source: Ministry of the Interior (Russia) 2009b; Hankel 2010: 38

In 2008 the authorities had to prosecute a series of 20 homicides against "non-Slavic" persons (Central Asians, Caucasus) committed by a Moscow skinhead group. The offenders were 17 to 22 years of age and students at Moscow's universities. The leader of the group was a fine arts student who finally confessed to a total of 37 killings. The homicides were filmed by a female group member and put on the Internet.

Media attention first turned to extremism when in 2001 300 skinheads attacked the Moscow supermarket *Zarizinsky*, and four employees of Central Asian/Caucasus origin were killed and 80 seriously injured. In 2004 skinheads assaulted a family from Tajikistan, and a girl of nine years old was brutally knifed to death.

Most offenses of an anti-Semitic nature are directed against synagogues, Jewish cemeteries and memorials. Since 2006 such activities have been monitored. In 2009 four attacks on Jews were recorded. Five persons were injured. In prior years there had been on average seven or eight assaults. In 2008 60 persons were sentenced with an anti-Semitic context, and of those 20 received prison terms.

Since the 1990s right-wing terrorists have been using arson/explosive attacks against synagogues and Jewish congregations. 2009 saw more than 50 such attacks. Presently, such crimes are directed against state institutions, including police stations, and no longer only against the "enemies of Russia." The right-wing movement is also seen behind the bomb attacks on the Grozny-Moscow train (2005) and the attack on the *Tscherkisofsky* market in Moscow, with 14 dead and more than 50 injured.

Conclusion

The post-socialist societies of Eastern Europe appear to be manqué and "belated" nation states (Minkenberg 2002). The emergence of national identities happened

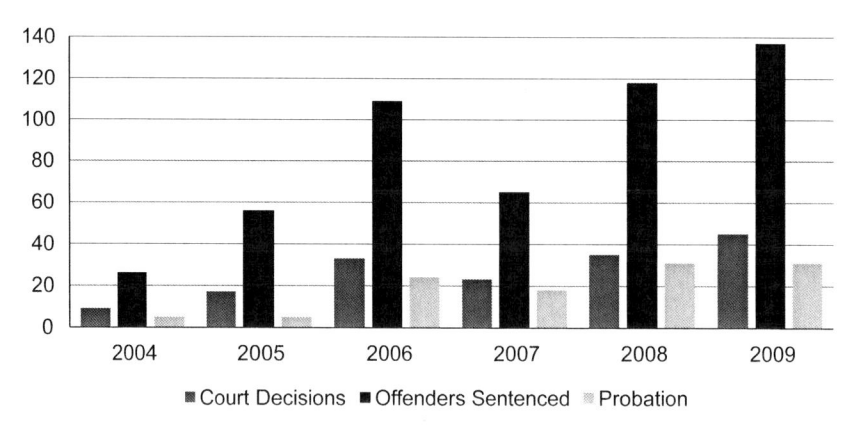

Figure 6.4 Sentenced offenders: right-wing extremist violence 2004–09
Source: Koschewnikowa 2010

without being based on an appropriate existing state. Accordingly, ethnic and cultural concepts of the state framed the idea of the nation. Culturally based nations are characterized by a perception of homogeneity without a political basis (Beichelt and Minkenberg 2002: 255f.). These forms of ethnic bonds are defined regularly by language, religion, history, and habits/cultural ways of life (Alter 1997: 36). Nation building is additionally complicated by the existence of national minorities and/or external national territories. This increases the risk of right-wing extremist activity (Beichelt and Minkenberg 2002: 256; Merkel 2010: 327). Right-wing extremism becomes apparent as related attitudes (covert extremism), and right-wing extremist behavior. Attitudes do not necessarily transform into respective behavior (voting, active membership in organizations, system protest, or violence) (Stöss 2010: 203; Minkenberg 2002: 21). Studies on extremism (Decker and Brähler 2008) differentiate between five right-wing extremist dimensions of attitudes:

- Support for right-wing autocratic systems or dictatorship
- Chauvinistic attitudes
- Anti-Semitism
- Social Darwinism
- Downplaying of National Socialism

We find milder or stronger expressions of these attitudes in all three countries under comparison with apparently stronger manifestations of all attitudes in Russia, with the exception of anti-Semitism which seems stronger in Poland.

Right-wing extremism and related xenophobia can be understood as a form of protest against modernization, activated in times of insecurity, of growing inequality between rich and poor, of increasingly widespread poverty, and *anomie*, plus a climate of societal antagonism. Ethnicity becomes a decisive marker of either inclusion or emphasized exclusion (Jaschke 2001: 20, 62ff.). Covert or explicit forms of the rejection of "foreigners," often aggressive, go hand in hand with the compartmentalization of life-worlds: "Xenophobia is always protest against the speed and the social faults of processes of modernization" (Jaschke 2001: 64).

Classical sociological theory (Durkheim, Merton) is a useful instrument to explain why and how right-wing concepts help to compensate for anomic situations. Dichotomous categories of "good" and "evil," "strong" and "weak," and "black" and "white," provide for easy-to-use tools of interpretation, to assign blame, and to favor populist "solutions."

A comparative perspective thus perceives right-wing hate activities and formations as closely related to problems of cultural and political transformations in Eastern Europe. When it comes to the role of anti-Semitism, all countries expose deep historical roots. While in Poland Roman Catholicism and its organization contribute to anti-Semitism, Ukrainian anomie resulting from culture clash, and Russian nationalism/chauvinism due to the loss of imperial status feed into a general atmosphere of antagonism and little respect for the rights of minorities. Anti-Semitism is an integral part of that.

In all countries economic crisis and subsistence difficulties of large parts of the working (or unemployed) population resulting from unrestricted predatory capitalism in weak states combined with a weak or non-consensual monopoly on the use of force increase the political instability and with it rather grim prospects for the immediate future of minority rights.

In large segments of the Russian population the breakdown of the Soviet rule coincided with a loss of identity. Right-wing extremist movements still seem to offer compensation: "Russia first!" ethnic identity and solidarity, old traditions and values and a foolproof rescue plan for the nation. The value system of Russian right-wing extremism sees the interests of the nation above those of the state, followed by rhetoric of a "white race." Patriotism, the fight against "enemies" like Jews, Americans, the oligarchy, the non-Russians, are in one line with "order," the national revolution, and the "leader" who will guide and save the nation. In light of this, the question has been posed whether or not Russia is a democracy. The fall of the Soviet empire continues to be experienced as a major defeat (and not as liberation from a bureaucratic dictatorship). There was and is no *Vergangenheitsbewältigung* (coming to terms with the past) as far as the crimes of the Stalinist system are concerned. Anti-Semitism remains a persistent component of xenophobia in Russian society to this day.

Note

[1] However, in this survey anti-migrant attitudes were more prevalent in Germany and particularly in Greece than in the East of Europe.

References

Alter, Peter (1997) "Kulturnation und Staatsnation—Das Ende einer langen Debatte?" in Gerd Langguth (ed.) *Die Intellektuellen und die nationale Frage*, Frankfurt am Main: Campus Verlag, 33–44.
Analytisches Zentrum *Yury Levada* (ed.) (2006) *Rossia dlja russkich ... ?* August 25, 2006, www.levada.ru/press/2006082500.html (accessed July 25, 2010).
Babbie, Earl (1999) *The Basics of Social Research*, Belmont, CA: Wadsworth.
Beichelt, Timm and Michael Minkenberg (2002) *Rechtsradikalismus in Transformationsgesellschaften – Entstehungsbedingungen und Erklärungsmodell. Europa-Universität Viadrina Frankfurt/Oder*, www.kuwi.europa-uni.de/de/lehrstuhl/vs/politik3/dokumente/publikationen/beicheltminkenberg2002rechtsradikalismus.pdf.
Canadian Institute of Ukrainian Studies (2007) *Dr. Peter Potichnyj Adresses Controversies Realted to the Ukranian Insurgent Army (UPA) in Forty-First Annual Shevchenko*, Lecture, University of Alberty, Edmonton, www.ualberta.ca/CIUS/announce/media/Media%202007/2007-04-25_Potichnyj%20Speaks%20on%20UPA%20(eng).pdf (accessed July 27, 2011).
Decker, Oliver and Elmar Brähler (2008) *Bewegung in der Mitte. Rechtsextreme Einstellungen in Deutschland 2008 mit einem Vergleich von 2002 bis 2008 und der Bundesländer*, Berlin: Friedrich-Ebert-Stiftung.
Douglas, Mary (2007 [1966]) *Purity and Danger*, Routledge: London and New York.
European Social Survey (2006) www.europeansocialsurvey.org.

Falter, Jürgen W., Hans-Gerd Jaschke and Jürgen R. Winkler (eds) (1996) *Rechtsextremismus. Ergebnisse und Perspektiven der Forschung*, Opladen: Westdeutscher Verlag.
Göls, Cornelia (2009) "Die politischen Parteien in der Ukraine – (wie) funktionieren sie wirklich?" *Ukraine-Analysen* 52: 2–7.
Hankel, Natalia (2010) *Rechtsextremismus, Nationalismus und Fremdenfeindlichkeit in Osteuropa: eine vergleichende Analyse am Beispiel der Länder Russland, Ukraine und Polen*, Master's thesis, German Police University, Münster.
Informationsanalytisches Zentrum Sova (ed.) (2008) *W Moskwe idet sledstwie po delu gruppirowki nazi-skinhedow, sowerschiwschich ubijstwa po motiwu nazionalnoj nenawisti*, xeno.sova-center.ru/45A2A1E/B705A18?pub_copy=on (accessed July 25, 2010).
——(2010a) *Ubitye i tjaschelo ranenye po motiwy nenawisti: predwaritelnaja statistika MWD*, www.sova-center.ru/racism-xenophobia/publications/2010/02/d17966/ (accessed July 25, 2010).
——(2010b) *Antiextremistskaja statistika MWD Rossii sa 2009 god*, xeno.sova-center.ru/29481C8/E5CFBE0 (accessed July 25, 2010).
Informationsgesetz der Ukraine (2005) *Sakon Ukrajiny Pro informaziju*, zakon.rada.gov.ua/cgi-bin/laws/main.cgi?nreg=2657-12 (accessed July 25, 2010).
Informburo.org (ed.) (2009a) *Ukrainu schdet koritschnewaja tschuma*, June 15, informburo.org/articles/pero/612-ukrainu-zhdet-korichnevaja-chuma.html (accessed July 25, 2010).
——(2009b) *Ukrainskie nationalisty skoro prijdut k wlasti*, September 11, informburo.org/articles/analitika/1882-ukrainskie-nacionalisty-vskore-pridut-k-vlasti.html (accessed July 25, 2010).
Jaschke, Hans-Gerd (2001) *Rechtsextremismus und Fremdenfeindlichkeit. Begriffe, Positionen, Praxisfelder*, second edn, Wiesbaden: Westdeutscher Verlag.
Jones, David W. (2008) *Understanding Criminal Behaviour—Psychosocial Approaches to Criminality*, Devon: Willan.
Juergensmeyer, Mark (2008) *Global Rebellion—Religious Challenges to the Secular State from Christian Militias to Al Qaeda*, Berkeley: University of California Press.
Kappeler, Andreas (2009) *Kleine Geschichte der Ukraine*, third edn, München: Verlag C.H. Beck.
Kiev International Institute of Sociology (ed.) (2006) *Dumky naselennja Ukrajiny pro golodomor 1932–1933 rokiw; dynamyka xenofobiji w Ukrajini 1994–2006*, September 11, www.kiis.com.ua (accessed July 25, 2010).
Koschewnikowa, Galina (2008) *Radikalnyj nationalism w Rossii i protiwodejstwie emu w 2007 godu*, July 1, www.sova-center.ru/racism-xenophobia/publications/2008/02/d12582/ (accessed July 25, 2010).
——(2008) *Osen 2007: Nazistskie rejdy, russkie marschi i Putin-Stirliz*, in polit.ru, www.polit.ru/analytics/2008/01/16/autumn2007.html (accessed July 25, 2010).
——(2010) *Pod snakom polititscheskogo terrora: Radikalnyj nazionalism w Rossii i protiwodejstwie emu w 2009 godu*, February 2, xeno.sova-center.ru/29481C8/E4FA706 (accessed July 25, 2010).
Kupferberg, Feiwel (1998) *The Break-Up of Communism in East Germany and East Europe*, Basingstoke: Palgrave Macmillan.
Merkel, Wolfgang (2009) "Gegen alle Theorie?—Die Konsolidierung der Demokratie in Ostmitteleuropa," in Uwe Backes, Tytus Jaskułowski and Abel Polese (eds) *Totalitarismus und Transformation: Defizite der Demokratiekonsolidierung in Mittel-und Osteuropa*, Göttingen: Vandenhoeck & Ruprecht, 27–48.

—— (2010) *Systemtransformation: Eine Einführung in die Theorie und Empirie der Transformationsforschung*, second edn, Wiesbaden: VS Verlag für Sozialwissenschaften.
Ministry of the Interior (Russia) (eds) (2009) *Interview Ministra wnutrennich del Rossijskoj Federazii generala armii Raschida Nurgaliewa*, May 22, www.mvd.ru/press/interview/6485/ (accessed July 25, 2010).
—— (2010a) *Interview natschalnika Departamenta po protiwodejstwiju extremismu MWD Rossii general-polkownika milizii Juria Kokowa*, January 25, www.mvd.ru/press/interview/7347/ (accessed July 25, 2010).
—— (2010b) *Sostojanie prestupnosti w Rossijskoj Federazii sa dekabr 2009*, accessed July 25, 2010.
Ministry of the Interior (Ukraine) (ed.) (2010) *Stan ta struktura slotschunnosti w Ukrajini 2009*, mvs.gov.ua/mvs/control/main/uk/publish/control/main/uk/publish/article/233004 (accessed July 25, 2010).
Minkenberg, Michael (2002) "Rechtsradikalismus in Mittel-und Osteuropa nach 1989," in Thomas Grumke and Bernd Wagner (eds) *Handbuch Rechtsradikalismus. Personen, Organisationen, Netzwerke vom Neonazismus bis in die Mitte der Gesellschaft*, Opladen: Leske, Budrich, 61–74.
Moskauer Büro für Menschenrechte (ed.) (2005) *Nationalism, xenofobia, antisemitism w Dume RF*, antirasizm.ru/index.php/publications?ff64eda6be7c8c0a513b4f753d39ad99=ef709bc1b8a1c1e8daeaecd05f42943d (accessed July 25, 2010).
—— (2006) *Rasism, xenofobia, antisemitism, etnitscheskaja diskriminazia w Rossijskoj Federazii w 2005 godu*, antirasizm.ru/index.php/publications?ff64eda6be7c8c0a513b4f753d39ad99=ef709bc1b8a1c1e8daeaecd05f42943d (accessed July 25, 2010).
—— (2008) *Kratkij obsor projawlenij agressiwnoj xenofobii na territorii Rossijskoj Federazii w 2007 godu*, antirasizm.ru/index.php/publications?ff64eda6be7c8c0a513b4f753d39ad99=ef709bc1b8a1c1e8daeaecd05f42943d (accessed July 25, 2010).
—— (2009) *Ultraprawyj terrorism. Wtoraja Wolna*, antirasizm.ru/index.php/publications?ff64eda6be7c8c0a513b4f753d39ad99=ef709bc1b8a1c1e8daeaecd05f42943d (accessed July 25, 2010).
Nigdy Więcej and Opferperspektive (eds) (n.d.) *Studie "Monitoring hate crimes and victim Assistance in Poland and Germany": Zusammenfassung* (unpublished report).
Panina, Natalia (2005) "Faktory nazionalnoj identitschnosti, tolerantnosti, xenofobii i antisemitisma w sowremennoj Ukraine," *Soziologia: teoria, metody, marketing* 4: 26–45.
Rabitz, Cornelia (2007) "Gelenkte Demokratie—gelenkte Medien. Beobachtungen im russischen Wahlkampf," *Russland-Analysen* 147: 2–4.
Ruchniewicz, Krzysztof (2005) "Die historische Erinnerung in Polen," *APuZ* 5–6: 18–26.
Steinberg, Guido (2005) *Der nahe und der ferne Feind – Die Netzwerke des islamistischen Terrorismus*, München: C.H. Beck.
Stöss, Richard (2010) *Rechtsextremismus im Wandel*, 2nd edn, Berlin: Friedrich Ebert Stiftung, library.fes.de/pdf-files/do/08223.pdf.
Thieme, Tom (2007a) *Hammer, Sichel, Hakenkreuz. Parteipolitischer Extremismus in Osteuropa: Entstehungsbedingungen und Erscheinungsformen*, Baden-Baden: Nomos.
—— (2007b) "Extremistische Parteien im postkommunistischen Osteuropa," *APuZ* 43: 21–26.
Vereinigung jüdischer Organisationen und Gemeinden der Ukraine (eds) (2009) *Antisemitskije akzii i puplikazii w periodistscheskich isdanijach Ukrainy 2008 goda*, www.vaadua.org/News/news2009/2009-02/public2008.html (accessed July 25, 2010).
Vetter, Reinbold (2009) "Polen fünf Jahre in der EU—wirtschaftlich ein großer Erfolg," *Polen-Analysen* 53: 2–11.

——(2010) "Der Vergangenheit näher als der Zukunft: Ein nüchterner Blick auf die Präsidentschaft von Lech Kaczyński," *Polen-Analysen* 69: 2–13.
Weiß, Wioletta (2008) "Attacke von Links. In: Netzwerk für Osteuropa-Berichterstattung," in n-ost e.V. (ed.) *Rechtsextremismus und Antisemitismus in Mittel-, Ost-und Südosteuropa*, Berlin, 107–11, www.n-ost.de/cms/images//n-ost-stipendien-doku.pdf (accessed July 25, 2010).
Winkler, Jürgen R. (2006) "Fremdenfeindlichkeit und Rechtsextremismus in der Bundesrepublik Deutschland. Die Perspektive der Politikwissenschaft," in Michael Minkenberg, Dagmar Sucker and Agnieszka Wenninger (eds) *Radikale Rechte und Fremdenfeindlichkeit in Deutschland und Polen: Nationale und europäische Perspektiven, Informationszentrum Sozialwissenschaften*, Bonn: Informationszentrum Sozialwissenschaften, 128–51.
Wolf, Joachim (2007) "Fußball und Rechtsextremismus in Europa," *Bundeszentrale für politische Bildung*, February 15, www.bpb.de/themen/4IFKR4,0,Fu%DFball_und_R echtsextremismus_in_Europa.html (accessed July 25, 2010).
——(2009) "Rechtsextremismus in Polen," *Netz-gegen-Nazis.de*, July 10, www.netz-ge gen-nazis.de/artikel/rechtsextremismus-polen-2919 (accessed July 25, 2010).
Zimmer, Kerstin and Femke van Praagh (2008) "Fremdenfeindlichkeit in der Ukraine," *Ukraine-Analysen* 41: 2–6.

7 Welfare chauvinism, ethnic heterogeneity and conditions for the electoral breakthrough of radical right parties
Evidence from Eastern Europe

Lenka Bustikova

Radical politics and the use of inflammatory political appeals are enduring features of post-communist politics, yet the causes, effects and dynamics of radical party politics in post-communist democracies are still poorly understood, especially when compared to the copious scholarship on the Western European extreme right, Latin American populism, and racial politics in the US.[1] Notable exceptions do exist, but many of the most fundamental research questions remain unanswered, including why radical parties are strong and persistent in some countries, but weak and short-lived in others.[2]

The strength of radical parties varies considerably across countries and over time. For example, the League of Polish Families and the Czech Republican Party (SPR-RSC) were making headline news not long ago in Central Europe, only to fade into oblivion. Bosnian, Croatian, Romanian, Russian, Serbian, Slovak and Slovenian radical parties were viable in the 1990s, but their electoral fates and degrees of radicalism have since varied greatly. By contrast, Albania, Georgia and Ukraine have never produced any significant radical parties, despite their turbulent economies and political instability. Cross-national differences in economic uncertainty, political volatility, levels of corruption and past experience with inter-war radicalism do not explain why radical parties are stronger in some countries and weaker in others. This article proposes an answer to this basic question that focuses on the interplay of ethnic politics, party competition and the political economy of redistribution. More specifically, I argue that certain policy configurations (of general and targeted redistribution) provide the most fertile political 'breeding ground' for radical right parties (Mudde 2007). The chapter unpacks this argument and tests it empirically.

Before we proceed further, defining radical parties, and distinguishing them from other party families, will prove beneficial. According to Kitschelt (2007), the grid-group theoretical framework developed by anthropologist Mary Douglas and adopted by Douglas and Wildavsky (1982) offers a parsimonious framework for classifying radical parties. Two ideological elements are key (radical nationalism and radical socio-cultural conservatism), and correspond to two modes of social control: *grid* and *group*.[3]

The grid dimension captures authoritarian social and cultural conservatism. In its pure form, it has no ethnic basis. A political party scoring high on the grid dimension might campaign against accommodating gay and lesbian couples (on Poland and Latvia see O'Dwyer and Schwartz 2010) or against abortion (League of Polish Families). Similarly, a party that promotes law and order, along with uncritical obedience to authority, whether religious or secular, would score high on the grid dimension.

The group dimension captures nationalism and is therefore associated with exclusionary ethnicity-based appeals. It conceptualizes identity in terms of "the ethnic other" and clearly distinguishes the in-group from the out-group (Ramet 1999). A party that propagates nationalism on behalf of the titular nationality scores high on the group dimension, whereas a party making cross-ethnic appeals would score low on the group dimension. Small economically and socially liberal parties, for example, generally score low both on the grid and on the group dimension, as do ethnic and green parties.[4] On the contrary, ethnocentric, from the perspective of a majority, and socially conservative radical parties are located in the high-grid, high-group quadrant. Based on this logic of classification, Table 7.1 provides a list of radical parties as well as mainstream parties.

Economically (populist) radical right parties support "a nativist economic model, i.e. an economy that (solely) benefits the 'natives' and that is protected against 'alien' influences" (Mudde 2007: 132). Such parties are therefore often called welfare chauvinistic. Welfare chauvinism—a preference for policies that

Table 7.1 Party names

		Party	Vote (t)	Vote (t-1)
Albania	PD	Democratic Party of Albania PD; (DPA)	44.1	36.8
	PS	Socialist Party of Albania PS; (SPA)	39.4	41.5
Bulgaria	BSP	Bulgarian Socialist Party	31	17.1
	NDSV	National Movement for Stability and Progress	19.9	42.7
	Ataka	National Union Attack	8.1	0
	MRF	The Movement for Rights and Freedoms (DPS)	12.8	7.4
Czech R.	ODS	Civic Democratic Party	35.4	24.5
	CSSD	Czech Social Democratic Party	32.3	30.2
	KSCM	Communist Party of Bohemia and Moravia	12.8	18.5
Croatia	HDZ	Croatian Democratic Union	36.6	33.9
	SDP	Social Democratic Party of Croatia	31.2	22.6
	HSP	Croatian Party of Rights	3.5	6.4
Estonia	ERP-Reform	Estonian Reform Party (Reform)—ERP	27.8	17.7
	CPE-Kesk	Centre Party of Estonia (Kesk)—CPE	26.1	25.4
	IRL	Union of Pro Patria and Res Publica (UPR)	17.9	31.9

(continued on next page)

Table 7.1 (continued)

		Party	Vote (t)	Vote (t-1)
Georgia	UNM	United National Movement	59.2	67
	NCP	New Rights (Conservative) Party of Georgia	17.7	7.6
Hungary	Fidesz	The Fidesz ñ Hungarian Civic Union	36.1	36.3
	MSZP	Hungarian Socialist Party	43.2	42
	Jobbik	Jobbik	–	–
	MIEP	The Hungarian Justice and Life Party	–	–
Latvia	TP	The People's Party	19.6	16.6
	JL	The New Era Party	16.4	23.9
	TB/LNNK	Fatherland and Freedom/LNNK	6.9	5.4
	UGF	Union of Greens and Farmers (ZZS)	16.7	9.4
Lithuania	DP	Labour Party	9.0	28.4
	TT	Order and Justice	12.3	11.4
	TS	Homeland Union – Christian Democrats (Lithuanian Conservatives)	19.7	14.6
Moldova	PCRM	Communist Party of Moldova	49.5	46.0
	PAMN	Party Alliance Our Moldova	9.8	18.4
	PL	Liberal Party of Moldova	13.1	0.0
Poland	PO	Civic Platform	41.5	24.1
	PiS	Law and Justice	32.1	27.0
	LPR	League of Polish Families	1.3	8.0
Romania	PSD	Social Democratic Party	31.9	31.5
	PDL	Democratic Liberal Party	32.4	13.5
	PRM	Greater Romanian Party	3.2	13.0
Russia	UR	United Russia	64.3	37.6
	CPRF	Communist Party of the Russian Federation	11.6	12.6
	LDPR	The Liberal Democratic Party of Russia	8.1	11.5
	SR	Fair Russia: Motherland/Pensioners/Life	7.7	12.1
Slovakia	SMER	Direction – Social Democracy	29.1	13.5
	SKDU-DS	Slovak Democratic and Christian Union – Democratic Party	18.4	15.1
	SNS	Slovak National Party	11.7	3.3
Slovenia	SD	Social Democrats	30.5	10.2
	SDS	Slovenian Democratic Party	29.3	29.1
	SNS	Slovenian National Party	5.4	6.3
	LDS	Liberal Democracy of Slovenia	5.2	22.8
Ukraine	BYU	Bloc Yuliya Tymoshenko	30.7	22.3
	PR	Party of Regions	34.4	32.1
	OU-PSD	Our Ukraine – People's Self-Defense Bloc	14.2	14.0
Macedonia	SDSM	Social Democratic Union of Macedonia	15.8	23.3
	VMRO-DPMNE	The Internal Macedonian Revolutionary Organization/ Democratic Party for Macedonian National Unity	48.8	32.5
Serbia	SRS	Serbian Radical Party	29.5	28.6
	DS	Democratic Party	24.2	22.7

Source: Democratic Accountability Project

transfer government resources exclusively towards the titular nationality—has long been recognized as a constitutive element of radical right party ideology (Betz 1994; Kitschelt, with McGann 1995; Mudde 2007). Welfare altruism, on the contrary, is a preference for governmental transfers that benefit ethnic minorities.

These economic and identity-based preferences relate to the structural preconditions under which radical parties succeed and draw away votes from a mainstream party. In theory, two large mainstream parties can be locked in one of two economic configurations: comprehensive or targeted. Comprehensive means that a party advocates an economic policy that is *the same* for all citizens, regardless of their ethnicity or minority status. As a consequence of this ethnically neutral position on redistribution, the accommodation of ethno-cultural minority demands does *not* become a salient feature of party competition.

Targeted redistribution means that a party advocates an economic policy that is different for different groups of citizens, usually one policy for the majority and one for the minority. Welfare chauvinism is an extreme form of targeted redistribution. In the literature, welfare chauvinistic preferences of radical parties have been studied in isolation from the redistributive preferences of mainstream parties. This approach, however, ignores the strategic interaction between the welfare chauvinism of the radicals and the targeted redistributive preferences of other parties. It would be more reasonable to stipulate that parties consider the policy positions of their competitors in formulating their own policies.[5]

If we believe that parties are strategic in this manner, then we are able to posit configurations of party positions that are conducive to the success of radical right parties. This paper hypothesizes that the existence of a mainstream party that embraces moderate welfare chauvinism counterbalanced by a party advocating moderate welfare altruism provides a political opportunity for the radical right. The reason is that the presence of a mainstream party with a moderate welfare chauvinistic agenda increases the issue salience of identity and ethnicity (Bélanger and Meguid 2008). The increased salience of identity benefits the radical right because it can claim issue ownership on certain identity issues since welfare chauvinism is an important ideological component of radical party programs.

Policies of comprehensive redistribution breed issue neutrality. Targeted distribution increases the salience of ethnicity and culture in party competition. When mainstream parties advocate policies of targeted redistribution, they create a permissive environment for radical right parties to highlight their niche issues, such as welfare chauvinism. Consider a left-wing mainstream party that advocates more state spending in general, but less spending on a minority group and a right-wing mainstream party that advocates tax cuts and fiscal austerity, but may be willing to guarantee subsidies to preserve the unique culture of a minority group. This configuration markedly increases the salience of the identity dimension of party competition on which radical parties possess a comparative advantage. By contrast, comprehensive distribution occurs when a mainstream party that supports redistribution in general also advocates spending on minorities; the other major mainstream party supports free markets and does *not* advocate state involvement in redressing minority issues. This configuration makes identity a non-issue, precluding the radical parties from exploiting identity issues. In this paper, I treat configurations of political parties as given and as structural conditions for the success of a radical party. I also show that targeted configuration occurs most commonly in countries with small ethnic minorities.

Unlike in Western Europe, welfare chauvinism in Eastern Europe is not a response to the economic threat posed by immigration, since this threat is minimal in Eastern Europe. Instead, welfare chauvinism is targeted against ethnic minorities that have been settled for centuries.[6] Moreover, unlike some neoliberal radical right parties in Western Europe, welfare chauvinists in Eastern Europe do not advocate dismantling the welfare state. On the contrary, post-communist constituencies, including radical party voters, expect the state to be their primary shelter against economic hardship. Advocates of welfare retrenchment seek to limit government transfers *only* to "unpopular" ethnic groups and socially liberal causes, e.g. state-sponsored campaigns against racism and institutions enforcing minority rights. Radical right parties in post-communist Europe by and large support *more* government spending in general (they are center-left on the economy), but radically *oppose* government spending on minorities and socially liberal issues.[7]

Importantly, the targeted redistributive preferences configuration, which I have argued increases the salience of identity, is related to the positions of both *mainstream* parties, not just to the position of the proximate radical right competitor. If the divergence between the direction of the general and ethnic economic preferences increases the salience of identity, then convergence has the opposite effect—it decreases the salience of identity because it subsumes the identity issue under the umbrella of comprehensive redistribution. Targeted redistribution disaggregates class-based and identity-based economic preferences, increasing the salience of ethnic issues. Class divisions under the comprehensive configuration subsume ethnicity and culture. If the mainstream parties embrace comprehensive redistribution (Figure 7.1)—one mainstream party supports more spending on minorities and more spending in general and the other major party opposes both— then spending on minorities does not stand out as a separate issue. Transfers to minority ethnic groups are part of a broad, class-based package of economic considerations, whereas particularism, which separates general and ethnic redistributive preferences, singles out an ethnic group, making transfers to ethnicities and socially liberal causes a special, separate and politically salient issue, distinct from general issues of taxation and spending (Figure 7.1). Removing an ethnic group from the context of general redistributive issues increases the salience of identity. Given the radical parties' comparative advantage, competence, and claims of ownership of identity issues, the presence of a targeted configuration affords them a rare opportunity to make genuine inroads into the electorate.

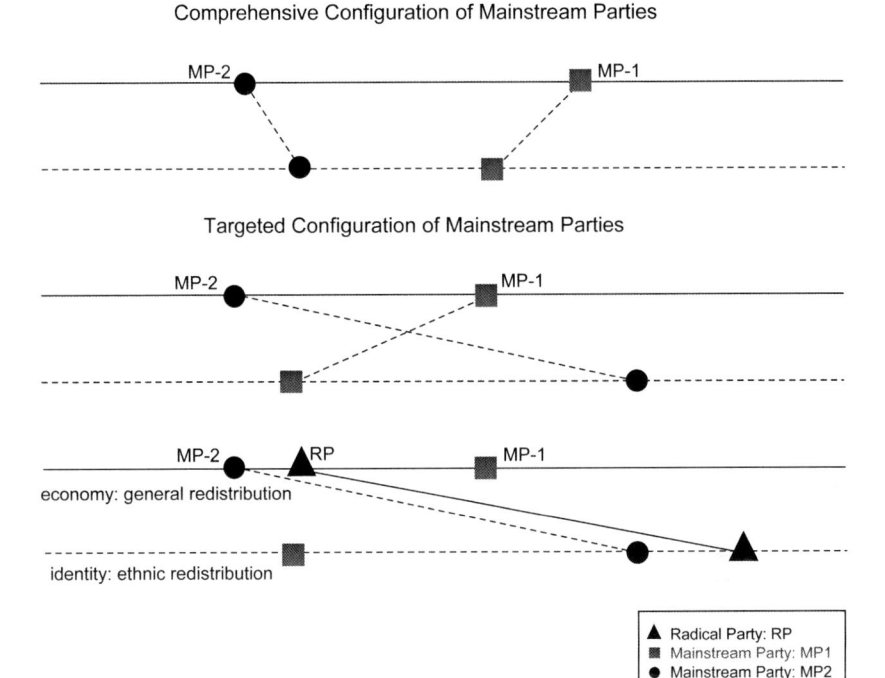

Figure 7.1 Ideal types of mainstream parties configurations

While ethnic parties are obvious candidates to campaign for targeted transfers to ethnic minorities, mainstream parties may advocate ethnic altruism as well when they need support from an ethnic party to form a coalition, or when the party seeks to distinguish itself from a welfare chauvinist mainstream party. When minorities demand government transfers to support schooling and culture or identity preservation, governments may oblige when ethnic votes are needed to form a governing coalition. If the party courts the ethnic vote in this manner, however, the resulting alliance of the mainstream party and the ethnic party may induce the formation of targeted redistributive positions because the mainstream party may need to advocate more minority accommodation than originally intended to satisfy its coalition partner or gain support in the parliament.

In the face of economic difficulties, however, it may be difficult to justify targeted redistribution for a small ethnic minority, so ethnic altruism tends to decline as economic uncertainty increases. Moreover, since identity politics is often used to divert attention from difficult economic issues that parties are unable to address, ethnic minorities are convenient scapegoats for fiscal troubles, unemployment, and economic crisis. Targeted government transfers to "undeserving" ethnicities and socially liberal causes are therefore red flags that stimulate bullish radical parties and their voters.

Radical parties offer an electorally appealing configuration of policies to their voters: center-left on the economy, but extreme opposition to targeted transfers for minorities. Just as mainstream parties can re-package ethnicity as a universal redistributive issue—to sanitize the ethnic component of their redistributive preferences and contain radical parties, so radical parties can also re-package redistribution as an ethnic issue in order to appeal to the radical welfare chauvinistic preferences of their voters. The best response strategy for the mainstream party is therefore to decrease the issue salience by maintaining comprehensive (that is, non-targeted) policy positions.

Once identity politics have become politically salient, the radical party and its competitors compete over issue ownership, which typically involves battling over historical narratives. Prominent recent examples of party competition over such narratives include whether to apologize to Germans and Hungarians that were expelled from some East European countries after World War II, whether to express regret over Jews murdered by domestic resistance movements fighting the invading Soviet army, and whether to award state medals to controversial historical figures who are deemed heroes by some groups but villains by others. Since radical parties are particularly competent on identity issues, they are well-positioned to present their version of these controversial historical narratives and to present themselves as defenders of national pride against the onslaught of accusations that include charges of collaboration with occupying forces, violence against civilians, and intolerance against out-groups.

This narrative resonates loudly and clearly with many voters, who are themselves or whose parents are the target of historical revisionism. Furthermore, anti-revisionist narratives are fully consistent with those propagated in the communist schooling system, which traditionally offered a narrow, straightforward version of state formation and nation building in Eastern Europe. The contemporary titular ethnicities were the victims of war atrocities and great power politics. The slain were brave fighters, defending national independence, ensuring the nation's survival and protecting its glory (Rothschild and Wingfield 2000).

The Polish Institute of National Remembrance, for example, challenged the historical narrative of the Jedwabne pogrom in 1941. It was long assumed that the murder of Jews was an act committed by Germans and not Poles, but the Institute demonstrated that this was not the case. The Institute's findings presaged the emergence of the League of Polish Families, which immediately sought to revise the historical record in favor of one in which Poles were victims not victimizers. Similarly, in 1991, then presidential candidate Vaclav Havel suggested that Czechs should apologize for the expulsion of Sudeten Germans in 1945–47. The radical Czech Republicans soon emerged to challenge the charge and successfully tapped into anti-German fears, garnering 6 percent of the vote and 14 seats in parliament. Radical parties offer a flattering historical narrative and a combative defense of national pride, an approach that gains appeal when mainstream parties increase the salience of identity by promoting policies that target non-core groups with selective benefits and by seeking to redress their historical discrimination and mistreatment by the state.

After the fall of communism, less flattering versions of history surfaced, both from within and from abroad. These changes were often related to the European Union (EU) accession process, particularly its emphasis on minority rights and the open exchange of ideas (Kelley 2004; Vachudova 2005). Many political parties in the EU accession countries that promoted economic reforms, privatization, and free markets also advocated tolerance and socially liberal positions, e.g. protection of minorities, gender equality and cosmopolitanism (Art and Brown 2007; Kitschelt et al. 1999; O'Dwyer and Schwartz 2010; Vachudova 2005).[8]

The focus on ethnic redistributive preferences provides a direct link between ethnicity and the economy, and explains why a mainstream party would adopt targeted policies. In an ethnically homogenous country, galvanizing voters around redistribution towards ethnic minorities provides fewer political payoffs to vote-maximizing parties.[9] It follows that radical party mobilization (and greater political contestation over targeted transfers) should occur more often in countries with large ethnic minorities, but the reverse is actually closer to the truth, and there are rational reasons to explain why.

Theories that associate larger minority groups (and large influxes of immigrants) with increased political mobilization along ethnic lines (Olzak 1992: 35) assume a linear relationship with ethnic group size. Instead, I show that there are much better reasons to expect radical party mobilization to be lowest in homogeneous societies and in polities with large minorities, but highest in countries with relatively small minority groups. A preliminary glance at the empirical evidence from post-communist Europe is consistent with the idea linking weak radical parties with large minorities (Macedonia, Moldova and Ukraine) and strong radical parties with small minorities (Bulgaria, Romania and Slovakia).

The theoretical underpinning of this non-linear expectation is based on two distinct mechanisms that drive radical party success: one mechanism that operates in peaceful democratic competition and one for violent political mobilization. All else equal, larger ethnic minorities pose a greater risk of violent mobilization than smaller ethnic groups. If aggressive mobilization against a very large minority is more likely to result in violence, then risk-averse politicians should avoid stirring ethnic hatred against large ethnic groups so much that it spirals out of control into violence. Mobilizing against small ethnic groups involves significantly less risk of large-scale violence, since the group cannot threaten to control the country and often cannot even exclusively claim a peripheral part of it.

Moderate politicians may therefore seek alliances with ethnic minority representatives to ensure the support of ethnic voters in peaceful democratic settings, especially when rival parties are engaged in intense competition. Paradoxically, when the major parties, which are dominated by the titular nationality, need small ethnic parties to form coalitions in government, this increases the salience of ethnic divides in party competition (Wilkinson 2004). Ethnic composition predisposes countries with small minorities to radical political appeals because the moderates from the ethnic majority need ethnic voters for coalition building—and when ethnicity becomes salient, radical parties prosper—so coalitions between mainstream and ethnic parties, which are intended to secure the ownership of the identity issue, may actually inadvertently enhance the radical party's chances of success by increasing the general salience of ethnicity in party competition.

In Eastern Europe, the duty to fund education, from primary schools to universities, rests primarily with central governments, and the extent to which governments provide such funding for minorities in practice is highly variable. For example, Romania and Slovakia extensively fund minority schooling for their Hungarian minority, while Estonia only provides language rights for minorities who are citizens, which excludes the disenfranchised Russians who have been settled in Estonia for decades (Rechel 2009). Mobilizing opposition against transfers to an ethnic minority, even as small as Roma, while preserving general levels of redistribution, is easier in countries with small minorities. In a country with two large ethnic groups, it is electorally unrealistic for a party to promote more transfers towards one large group, but not the other, since the redistributive preferences of the large minority are likely to be absorbed into mainstream party competition. Feuds over transfers to a large ethnic group, which necessarily involves significant resources, force the major parties to formulate comprehensive policies, transforming the dispute into a major political issue. This polarization on economic issues between two mainstream parties, coupled with universalism in their redistributive preferences, prevents small radical parties from emerging as strong challengers in the political arena.

The electoral success of radical parties can therefore be derived primarily from the behavior of the mainstream parties, yet neither containment nor engagement (Meguid 2005) serves as the key mechanism through which the mainstream parties matter. Instead, the central argument concerns the mainstream parties' redistributive policies, which are crafted to garner enough votes from ethnic minorities to win the election. The size of that minority influences whether those policies are universal or targeted because it determines the risk associated with pursuing targeted policies. In particular, it is riskier and more costly to promote targeted redistribution when the ethnic minority is large, making universal configurations more likely, and less risky and costly when the size of the minority is small, making targeted redistribution more likely, and providing the structural conditions for radical parties to emerge.[10]

Figure 7.2 depicts the configuration of mainstream parties on two issues—economic spending (economy) and minority accommodation (identity)—in five diverse countries: Albania, Czech Republic, Georgia, Lithuania and Ukraine.[11] Although these five countries differ in terms of their geography, history, economic growth, affluence, ethnic composition, levels of corruption and political volatility, they all possess party systems in which the mainstream parties are locked in a comprehensive, universal policy configuration.[12]

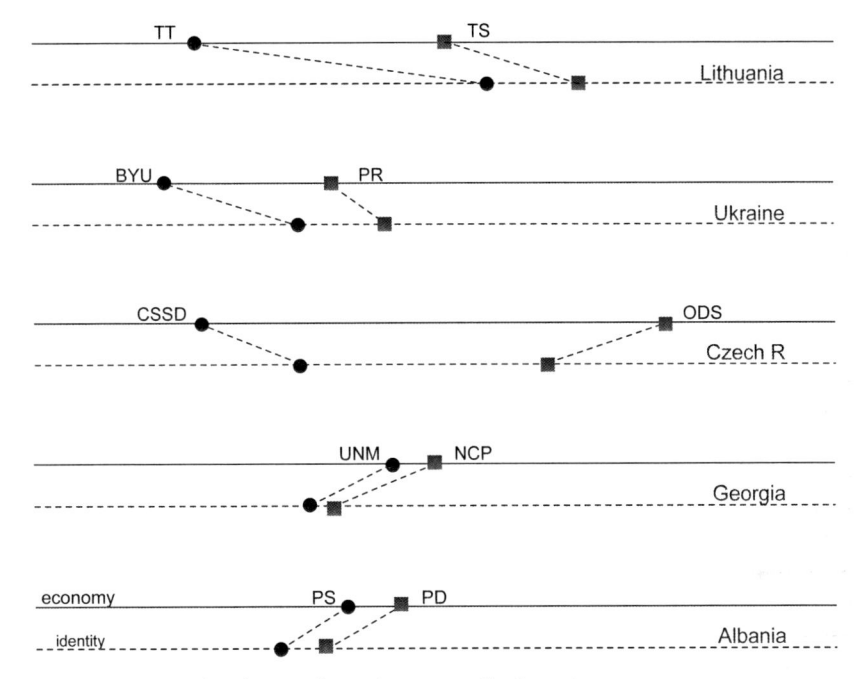

Figure 7.2 Comprehensive configuration, no radical parties

Despite fringe far-right movements in Lithuania (Racius 2010) and western Ukraine (Kuzio 2009; Mudde 2005), none of these countries has had a radical party since the late 1990s. This is because the Czech, Lithuanian and Ukrainian major mainstream parties are heavily polarized on economic issues and their position towards ethnic accommodation is consistent with their general economic positions: if they are in favor of more redistribution in general, they are also in favor of more targeted redistribution, and vice versa.

What matters is the party position vis-à-vis its primary mainstream competitor not in absolute terms. The policy positions of mainstream parties, for example in Albania and Georgia, are very close (signaling convergence). Theories of convergence (Carter 2002; Kitschelt, with McGann 1995; Norris 2005; van der Brug *et al.* 2005) lead us to expect radical parties in such systems, since the lack of differentiation between the mainstream parties should serve to increase the salience of ethnicity, but the issue involves more than just convergence and polarization.

Yet despite the contentious nature of ethnic politics in Albania's region and the troubling status of Albanians in neighboring countries, none of the two mainstream parties in Albania put ethnic issues either domestic or abroad on the agenda. Similarly, Georgia's explosive politics and violent strenuous relationship with Russia constrains any diversification on the ethnic dimension. A similar pattern can be observed in the Ukraine, and to some extent in Lithuania. Any aggressive move against the Russian minority would be met with Russia's political or economic retaliation, e.g. through gas price increases, an irksome issue of Ukrainian-Russian foreign policy, shutting down oil supplies (as in Lithuania in 2006), or cyber-attacks (as in Estonia in 2007). This suggests, consistent with the claim that radical politics thrives in countries with small—not large—minorities and that mainstream parties are able to bury identity politics, thus effectively eliminating its salience as an issue in party competition, when faced with large blocks of contentious ethnic minorities. None of the parties in these five countries advocates ethnic accommodation if they are against more redistribution in general, or ethnic exclusion if they are in favor of more redistribution in general.[13]

Targeted redistribution—when the mainstream parties are either welfare chauvinists or welfare altruists—creates a favorable environment for the success of radical parties due to the increased salience of identity in party competition. Figure 7.3 shows the policy positions of the major parties and the radical party in targeted configurations. Figure 7.3 shows that radical parties are present in a range of highly diverse countries with targeted configurations—Bulgaria, Hungary, Latvia, Poland, Romania, Serbia, Slovakia and Slovenia—and commonly cited competing explanations do not offer much explanatory leverage. While the economy in Hungary and Latvia underwent extremely

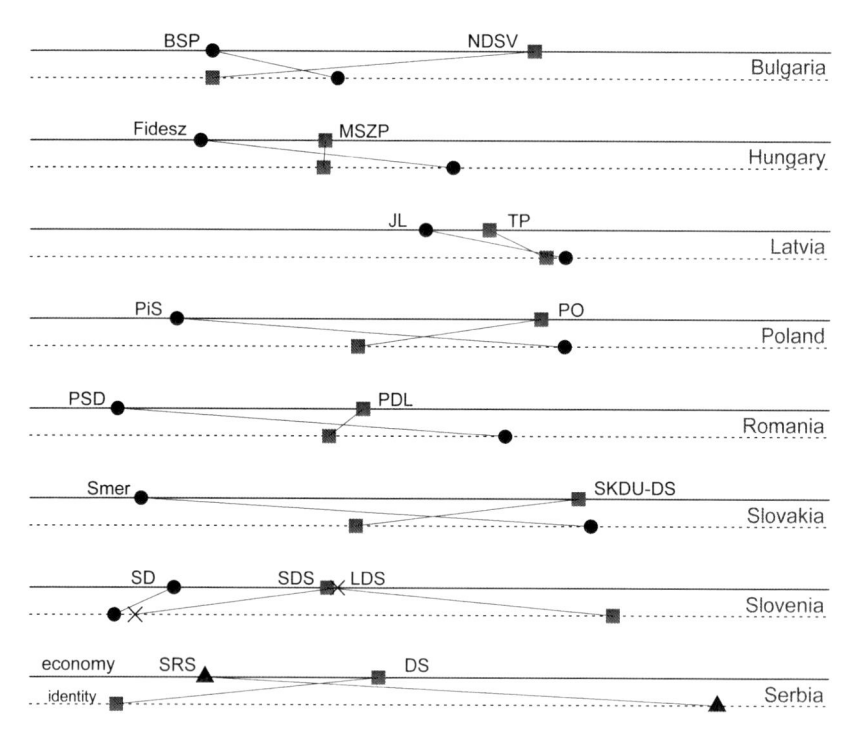

Figure 7.3 Policy positions of the major parties and the radical party in targeted configurations

Evidence from Eastern Europe 117

troubling economic contractions in recent years, the economy in Poland, Slovakia and Slovenia remains prosperous. Differences in electoral formulas cannot account for the variation in success of radical parties either (Carter 2002). While most East European countries fall under the broader umbrella of party systems with proportional representation, Hungary has a mixed electoral system that penalizes small parties. Yet Hungary has produced two radical right parties— the Hungarian Justice and Life Party (MIEP) in 1990s and Jobbik in the 2000s—which stunned political analysts by becoming the third largest party in the 2010 elections, acquiring 12 percent of the seats in the Hungarian parliament.

The presence of a small ethnic minority, matched with a political party that represents its preferences, is associated with targeted redistribution because the mainstream party will have to accommodate the ethnic party due to its coalition potential: see, for example, the Turkish party in Bulgaria, the Russian party in Latvia, the Hungarian parties in Romania and Slovakia, and the Hungarian, Croat and Bosniak parties in Serbia.

Ethnically homogeneous countries—such as Hungary, Poland and Slovenia— have the functional equivalents of ethnic parties: small economically and socially liberal parties. Ethnic and small liberal parties are two forms of extreme "welfare altruism" and represent counterpoints to radical parties.

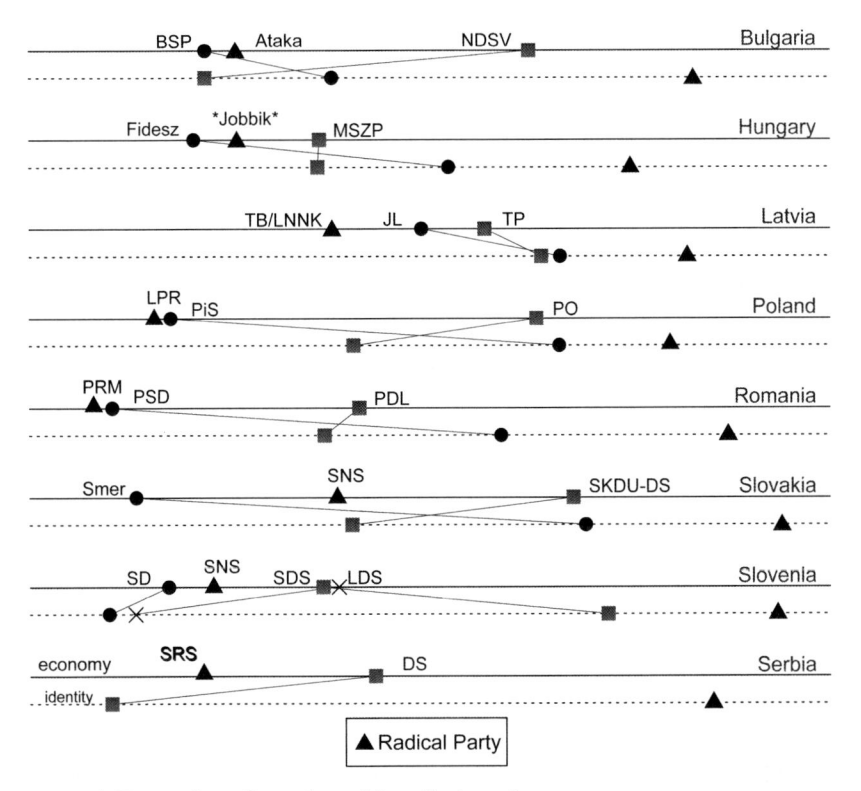

Figure 7.4 Targeted configuration with radical parties

118　*Lenka Bustikova*

When mainstream parties need small parties to form coalitions, their inclusion in a large coalition can reconfigure the policies of the mainstream parties, which must advocate one position on redistribution in general (against) and another (in favor) on targeted redistribution. The association between targeted redistribution and the existence of a radical party in the political system is abundantly clear in Figure 7.4 and cannot be explained by commonly cited structural factors and country characteristics.

Figure 7.5 depicts the party positions in countries with mixed prospects for radical right parties. Estonia, Macedonia and Moldova have no radical parties, which is attributable to the fact that the large proximate competitors are already heavily radicalized. The same applies to Croatia, which now has a very small radical party, but where the mainstream nearby competitor was formerly a radical party. Similarly, the dominant party in Russia is heavily radicalized: the position of the United Russia on identity issues is very close to the radical Liberal Democratic Party of Russia (LDPR), but this proximity does not diminish electoral gains for the LDPR.

The radicalization of the mainstream competitor has mixed effects on the prospects for a radical right. The effect of policy preferences on identity

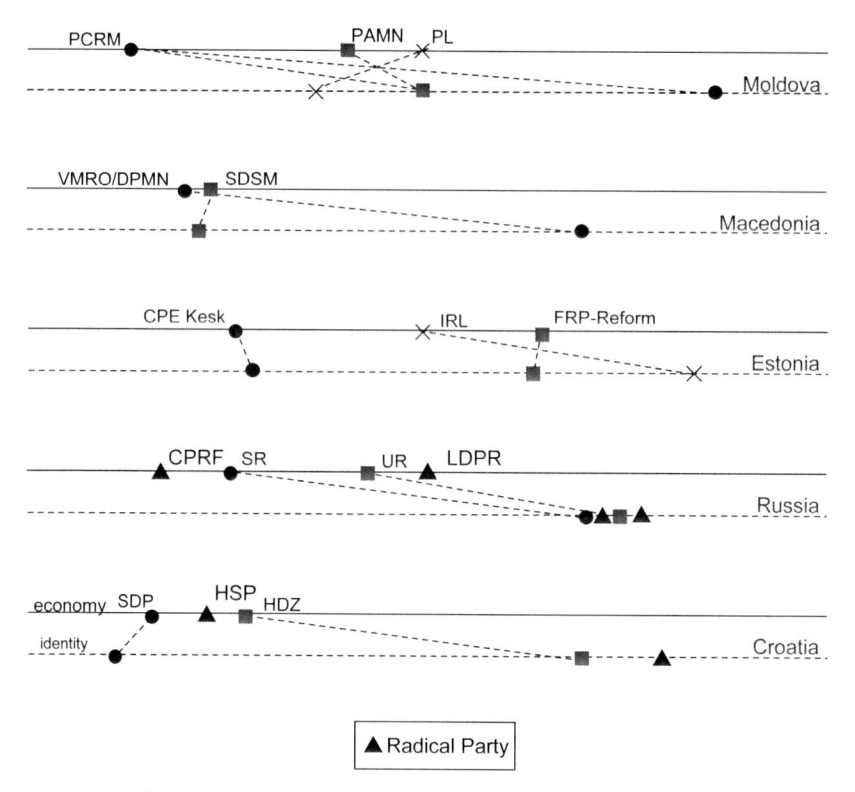

Figure 7.5 Radicalized large major parties

salience is mediated by the competitiveness of the electoral system. Dominant radicalized mainstream parties can push their small proximate competitors out of the electoral arena unless they decide to tolerate them or even cultivate a proximate radical right, in order to preserve an appearance of electoral choices to the voter.

In conclusion, the structural pre-conditions for the electoral success of radical right parties can be derived from the policy configurations of the mainstream parties and can be stated simply: small but mobilized ethnic minorities encourage mainstream parties interested in coalitions to pursue targeted redistribution, but targeted policies increase the salience of identity in party competition, where radical parties hold a comparative advantage, and thereby enhance the electoral prospects for radical parties.

A more nuanced account of the survival of radical parties would have taken into consideration the strategic interaction between the radical right and the mainstream parties. The goal of this chapter has been to outline the structural pre-conditions for the success of the radical right, and to demonstrate a remarkable empirical relationship between targeted policy configurations and the success of a radical political party. Commonly cited cultural, economic or institutional theories cannot explain why radical parties succeed in Eastern Europe. This chapter's main argument is that the variance in the success of radical parties is structurally determined by the redistributive policy configurations of the mainstream parties, which have the potential to raise or restrain the salience of ethnic issues, and thereby to open or close the door on radical parties.

Notes

1 I use the term radical, rather than extremist, to connote a party that does not challenge the democratic order of a given country, following Carter (2005).
2 Studies of the radical right in Eastern Europe focus on economic deprivation (Minkenberg 2002; Lewis 2009; Ost 2005), the ideological roots of radical parties dating back to the inter-war period and the role of legacies in party competition (Held 1996; Hockenos 1993; Minkenberg 2009; Mudde 2005; Ramet 1999), territorial disputes (Mareš 2009); European Union conditionality (Kelley 2004; Kopecký and Mudde 2002, 2003; Vachudova 2008) and the role of party systems (Art and Brown 2007; Ekiert 2006; Pop-Eleches 2010; Shafir 2008). For scholarship on unreformed former communist parties, see Bozoki and Ishiyama 2002; Ishiyama 1997; and Grzymala-Busse 2002.
3 In Mary Douglas's view: "variability of an individual's involvement in social life can be adequately captured by two dimensions of sociality: grid and group" (Thompson *et al.* 1990).
4 An ethnic party that primarily caters to its own nationality and seeks moderation and funds from the titular nationality would score low on the group dimension as well since it demands a multiethnic, altruistic approach to statehood from the titular ethnic majority.
5 Jenne (2007) analyzes variation in ethnic demands over time and finds that the intensity of minority demands can be explained by the intervention of a powerful actor that comes from abroad, and lobbies on behalf of the minority to the majority.

6 Some countries even experience ethnic dominance reversals, leading to status reversals: Turks, Hungarians or Russians are currently minority groups in states where they used to be dominant ethnic groups less than a century ago. Some radical agenda is fueled by discussions of the legitimacy of expulsion of German and Hungarian minorities after World War II (on anti-German sentiments in Central Europe see, for example, Cordell 2000).

7 Their natural coalition partners are nearby parties that are also pro-government spending parties. The key difference, of course, is that they are less radical on identity issues, such as minority spending (see Figure 7.4). Although the economic platforms of radical right parties are often underdeveloped, since they focus on identity issues and criticizing corrupt elites, closer examination reveals that both radical left and radical right parties in Eastern Europe support more government redistribution to the poor (Bustikova and Kitschelt 2009).

8 Despite ethnic diversity in Eastern Europe, all radicals universally hate Roma. Radical parties contest generous welfare benefits to fertile, often unemployed and impoverished Roma, funding schools or even universities with minority-language instruction or policies aiming at a de facto bilingual administration of a country. These may seem like petty political issues with marginal economic consequences, but limited domain of economic contestation may result in the disassociation of redistributive preferences and new configurations. Many radicals are anti-Semitic as well, but the intensity of hatred towards Jews varies. For example, one of the first acts of a newly established extremist paramilitary Czech National Guard was to offer a security protection against vandalism to the Holocaust memorial in Terezín (Zeman 2008).

9 Radical parties can mobilize around 'grid' issues as well, but the redistributive impact of socially liberal policies is less profound. Alternatively, a minority abroad (Albanians, Hungarians, Serbs, Russians) can substitute for the lack of an in-group against which to mobilize. For irredentism and influence of external actors in domestic minority rights see Jenne 2007; Mareš 2009; and Saideman 2001.

10 Exogenous changes in the country's economic conditions can have a large impact, since resource scarcity makes it more difficult for parties to justify both welfare retrenchment and minority accommodation. It follows that the electoral prospects for radical parties are remarkably bright when targeted redistribution combines with welfare retrenchment.

11 The policy positions of parties are based on an expert survey conducted in 2008 under the auspices of the Democratic Accountability Project (DAP 2008; Kitschelt *et al.* 2008; Kitschelt *et al.* 2009).

12 With the exception of the Czech Republic, none of these countries produced a viable radical right political party since the early 1990s.

13 The expert survey (DAP 2008) was conducted in 2008 and reflects party positions at that time. It cannot therefore account for the reasons why no radical parties emerged in these countries since the early 2000s, assuming temporal stability of party positions, but electoral prospects and policy positions of mainstream parties evolve over time. This explains why the comprehensive configuration of Czech parties in 2008 cannot account for the electoral success of Czech Republicans (SPR-RSC) who were present in two Czech parliaments in the early 1990s. SPR-RSC success can be attributed to the separation of the Czechoslovak federation, which the Republicans vocally opposed. Their political opposition to the separation was unique in the Czech Republic and so was their resistance towards the appeasement efforts of former dissident President Havel seeking accommodation with Germans expelled from Czechoslovakia after 1945. Moreover, Czech politics in the mid-1990s was dominated by an uncontested coalition of three economically liberal right-wing parties pursuing rapid, uncontested privatization, yet at the same time allowed for a costly separation of the Czechoslovak federation in

order to accommodate demands of Slovak nationalistic, secessionist forces. It was only later that the mainstream major right-wing party, the Civic Democratic Party (ODS), embraced more contentious identity issues, and even radical Euro-skepticism, incarnated in its extreme form in the ODS' former party leader and current Czech President Vaclav Klaus.

References

Art, David and Dana Brown (2007) *Making and Breaking the Radical Right in Central Eastern Europe*, manuscript.

Bélanger, Eric and Bonnie Meguid (2008) "Issue Salience, Issue Ownership, and Issue-Based Vote Choice," *Electoral Studies* 27: 477–91.

Betz, Hans-Georg (1994) *Radical Right-Wing Populism in Western Europe*, Basingstoke: Macmillan.

Bozoki, Andras and John T. Ishiyama (eds) (2002) *The Communist Successor Parties of Central and Eastern Europe*, New York: M.E. Sharpe.

Bustikova, Lenka and Herbert Kitschelt (2009) "The Radical Right in Post-Communist Europe. Comparative Perspectives on Legacies and Party Competition," *Communist and Post-Communist Studies* 42(4): 459–83.

Carter, Elisabeth (2002) "Proportional Representation and the Fortunes of Right-Wing Extremist Parties," *West European Politics* 45(3): 125–46.

——(2005) *The Extreme Right in Western Europe: Success or Failure?* Manchester: Manchester University Press.

Cordell, Karl (ed.) (2000) *The Politics of Ethnicity in Central Europe*, New York: St Martin's Press.

Democratic Accountability Project (DAP) (2008) *Herbert Kitschelt and Phil Keefer Dataset: Project on Democratic Accountability and Citizen-Politician Linkages around the World*, Duke University and the World Bank, www.duke.edu/web/democracy/.

Douglas, Mary and Aaron Wildavsky (1982) *Risk and Culture: An Essay on the Selection of Technological and Environmental Dangers*, Berkeley: University of California Press.

Ekiert, Grzegorz (2006) "L'instabilité du système partisan. Le maillon faible de la consolidation démocratique en Pologne," *Pouvoirs* 118: 37–58.

Grzymala-Busse, Anna (2002) *Redeeming the Communist Past*, Cambridge: Cambridge University Press.

Held, Joseph (ed.) (1996) *Populism in Eastern Europe. Racism, Nationalism, and Society*, Boulder, CO: East European Monographs, 163–96.

Hockenos, Paul (1993) *Free to Hate: The Rise of the Right in Post-Communist Eastern Europe*, New York: Routledge.

Ishiyama, John T. (1997) "The Sickle or the Rose?" *Comparative Political Studies* 30 (3): 299–330.

——(2009) "Historical Legacies and the Size of the Red Brown Vote in Post Communist Politics," *Communist and Post-Communist Studies* 42(4): 485–504.

Jenne, Erin (2007) *Ethnic Bargaining: The Paradox of Minority Empowerment*, Ithaca, NY: Cornell University Press.

Kelley, Judith (2004) *Ethnic Politics in Europe. The Power of Norms and Incentives*, Princeton University Press.

Kitschelt, Herbert (2007) "Growth and Persistence of the Radical Right in Post-industrial Democracies: Advances and Challenges in Comparative Research," *West European Politics* 30(5): 1176–206.

Kitschelt, Herbert, with Anthony McGann (1995) *The Radical Right in Western Europe: A Comparative Analysis*, Ann Arbor: University of Michigan Press.

Kitschelt, Herbert *et al.* (2008) *Democratic Accountability and Linkages Project*, Duke University, www.duke.edu/web/democracy/.

Kitschelt, Herbert, Kent Freeze, Kiril Kolev and Yi-Ting Wang (2009) "Measuring Democratic Accountability: An Initial Report on an Emerging Data Set," *Revista de Ciencia Politica* 29(3): 741–73.

Kitschelt, Herbert, Zdenka Mansfeldova, Radoslaw Markowski and Gábor Tóka (1999) *Post-communist Party Systems: Competition, Representation, and Inter-party Cooperation*, Cambridge: Cambridge University Press.

Kopecký, Petr and Cas Mudde (2002) "The Two Sides of Euroscepticism: Party Positions on European Integration in East Central Europe," *European Union Politics* 3 (3): 297–326.

——(eds) (2003) *Uncivil Society? Contentious Politics in Post-Communist Europe*, London: Routledge.

Kuzio, Taras (2009) *Populism in Ukraine in Comparative European Context*, Association for the Study of Nationalities Conference Paper, Columbia University, April 24.

Lewis, Paul G. (2009) *Party System Stabilisation in Central Europe: Records and Prospects in a Changing Socio-Economic Context*, ECPR General Conference, Potsdam, September 10–12.

Mareš, Miroslav (2009) "The Extreme Right in Eastern Europe and Territorial Issues," *Central European Political Studies Review* 11(2–3): 82–106.

Meguid, Bonnie (2005) "Competition between Unequals: The Role of Mainstream Party Strategy in Niche Party Success," *American Political Science Review* 99(3): 347–59.

Minkenberg, Michael (2002) "The Radical Right in Postsocialist Central and Eastern Europe: Comparative Observations and Interpretations," *East European Politics and Society* 16(2): 335–62.

——(2009) "Leninist Beneficiaries? Pre-1989 Legacies and the Radical Right in Post-1989 Central and Eastern Europe. Some Introductory Observations," *Communist and Post-Communist Studies* 42(4): 445–58.

Mudde, Cas (2005) *Racist Extremism in Central and Eastern Europe*, London: Routledge.

——(2007) *Populist Radical Right Parties in Europe*, Cambridge: Cambridge University Press.

Norris, Pippa (2005) *Radical Right. Voters and Parties in the Electoral Market*, Cambridge: Cambridge University Press.

O'Dwyer, Conor and Katrina Schwartz (2010) "Minority Rights After EU Enlargement: A Comparison of Antigay Politics in Poland and Latvia," *Comparative European Politics* 8(2): 220–43.

Olzak, Susan (1992) *The Dynamic of Ethnic Competition and Conflict*, Stanford University Press.

Ost, David (2005) *The Defeat of Solidarity. Anger and Politics in Postcommunist Europe*, Cornell University Press.

Pop-Eleches, Grigore (2010) "Throwing Out the Bums: Protest Voting and Anti-Establishment Parties after Communism," *World Politics* 62(2): 221–60.

Racius, Egdunas (2010) "The Place of Islamophobia among the Radical Lithuanian Nationalists—The Neglected Priority?" Conference *Far right networks in Northern and Eastern Europe*, Uppsala University, March 25–27.

Ramet, Sabrina (ed.) (1999) *The Radical Right in Central and Eastern Europe Since 1989*, Pennsylvania State University Press.

Rechel, Bernd (ed.) (2009) *Minority Rights in Central and Eastern Europe*, Taylor and Francis.

Rothschild, Joseph and Nancy M. Wingfield (2000) *Return to Diversity. A Political History of East Central Europe Since World War II*, third edn, Oxford: Oxford University Press.

Saideman, Stephen (2001) *The Ties that Divide: Ethnic Politics, Foreign Policy, and International Conflict*, New York: Columbia Press.

Shafir, Michael (2008) "Rotten Apples, Bitter Pears: An Updated Motivational Typology of Romania's Radical Right's Anti-Semitic Post-Communism," *Journal for the Study of Religions and Ideologies* 7(21).

Swank, Duane and Hans-Georg Betz (2003) "Globalization, the Welfare State and Right-Wing Populism in Western Europe," *Socio-Economic Review* 1(2): 215–45.

Thompson, Michael, Richard Ellis and Aaron Wildavsky (1990) *Cultural Theory*, Boulder, San Francisco and Oxford: Westview Press.

Vachudova, Milada Anna (2005) *Europe Undivided: Democracy, Leverage, and Integration after Communism*, Oxford: Oxford University Press.

——(2008) "Tempered by the EU? Political Parties and Party Systems before and after Accession," *Journal of European Public Policy* 15(6): 861–79.

van der Brug, Wouter, Fennema Meindert, and Jean Tillie (2005) "Why Some Anti-immigrant Parties Fail and Others Succeed: A Two-step Model of Aggregate Electoral Support," *Comparative Political Studies* 38(5): 537–73.

Wilkinson, Steven (2004) *Votes and Violence. Electoral Competition and Ethnic Riots in India*, Cambridge University Press.

Zeman, Václav (2008) "Kam míří česká ultrapravice," *MF DNES*, May 23, peopleinneed.cz/index2.php?id=143&idArt=815 (accessed March 1, 2010).

8 From Tea Parties to militias

Between the Republican Party and the insurgent ultra-right in the US[1]

Chip Berlet

Introduction

The rapid rise of the Tea Party movement in the US from 2008 to 2010 highlights the range of groups that exist between the core of the Republican Party and the militant ultra-right. The latter sector consists of neo-Nazis, the Ku Klux Klan and other formations of organized white supremacists, doctrinaire anti-Semites, and aggressive xenophobes. Martin Durham suggests that more attention be paid to the boundaries that separate all these groups on the political right (Durham 2000). In public discussions of mass dissent in the US, however, there is a tendency to picture an idealized political center periodically under attack by radicals and extremists of the left and right. In this model, subtle analysis and the complexity of boundaries are discarded.

Most social scientists have a more complicated view of the political spectrum in which a range of dissident reform-oriented social and political movements exist between the centrist political parties and the revolutionary ideologues of the insurgent ultra-left and ultra-right. The Tea Parties and the armed citizen militias active in the contemporary US are two examples of this type of dissident yet reform-oriented right-wing populist mass movement. Similar movements with a regressive restorationist frame have blossomed periodically since the Jacksonian period in the mid-1800s (Berlet and Lyons 2000). This paper explores current manifestations of dissident right-wing populism in the US as rooted in and prompted by a number of factors:

- economic fears, reflecting the harsh reality of downsizing, job loss, and mortgage foreclosures while financial institutions that propelled the recession hand out bonuses;
- the inflammation of legitimate fears and the identification of scapegoats by histrionic claims and convoluted conspiracy theories about betrayal by liberal elites, socialists, and Democrats;
- the election of Barack Obama as president;
- a backlash among many white people in the US worried about shifts in racial demographics; the changing faces of recent immigrants (especially Mexicans, Africans, Muslims, and Arabs); and

- gender anxiety exacerbated by portraying abortion and gay rights as threatening traditional hierarchical family structures interpreted as an integral element in preserving the "American way of life."

In Europe there are a number of dissident right-wing populist movements that overlap in parliamentary systems with a broad range of conservative and right-wing electoral political parties large and small. Hans-Georg Betz has shown that right-wing populists in Europe tend to draw from two constituencies: economic libertarians and xenophobes concerned with immigration (Betz 1994). The economic libertarians tend to be in the upper-middle class or small entrepreneurs who want less government regulation and taxation. The xenophobes tend to be in the lower-middle class or are wage workers, and according to Betz gravitate toward national "populist parties ... which espouse a radically xenophobic and authoritarian program" (Betz 1993: 663). Taras has studied the spread of this tendency across Europe, especially its form as Islamophobia (Taras 2009, 2012). In right-wing populism, we can see both libertarian, neoliberal, or laissez-faire ideologies as well as ethnocentric nationalism used by the middle class to justify attempts to protect their precarious relative class position (Disch 2010).

In the US these constituencies are involved in the Tea Parties and other contemporary examples of the right-wing populist backlash. Unlike Europe, however, there is also a very large sector of the Tea Parties composed of politically active Christian fundamentalists and evangelicals who are organized through a variety of Christian Right social movements and institutions.

Right-wing social movements

Sara Diamond states that to be right wing means to "support the state in its capacity as enforcer of order and to oppose the state as distributor of wealth and power downward and more equitably in society" (Diamond 1995: 9). Rory McVeigh extends this to argue that it is shifts in power dynamics that disrupt traditional hierarchies in economic, political, and social power relationships that launch the processes by which right-wing groups mobilize a mass base large enough to intrude into public debates in the larger society (McVeigh 2009).

Earlier social movement theories that were based on studying left-wing movements had much value in explaining the patterns and practices of right-wing movements, but some theories including Resource Mobilization and the Political Process Model are not sufficient for the study of right-wing movements. These theories worked best when studying left-wing liberation movements and movements in which relatively oppressed groups seek equality. Organizing in defense of power and privilege has limited appeal to a mass audience, so populist rhetoric can be used to mask the underlying (and perhaps unconscious) outcomes of certain policy decisions. Right-wing populist rhetoric spans the spectrum of the political right, and is a common feature of the dissident reform-oriented movements and groups that coalesce between the Republican

Party and the insurgent ultra right. The distinctions separating these movements and groups are important to observe and take into account in any analysis, but so are the dynamics that link them and allow for interactions, even when indirect, unacknowledged, or unconscious.

Conspiracist scapegoating and apocalyptic aggression

The formation of movements such as the Tea Parties and armed citizens' militias is facilitated in the US by the spadework done by previous right-wing movements that tell stories of elite conspiracies to subvert the nation. These conspiracist movements have spread across the US since the beginning of the republic. Periodically the conspiracy theories gain a major audience and produce religious and political witch hunts in a search for subversives. These subversion panics sometimes take center stage in US politics as right-wing counter-subversion movements expand. Subversion fears and panics can appear anywhere on the political spectrum, but in the US their emergence as major political motifs tends to have more significance when mobilizing right-wing constituencies (Berlet 2011).

Christian fundamentalism is a major source of support for right-wing populism in the US. For many Christian fundamentalists it is important to look at current events through the lens of a belief in biblical prophecies about the "End Times." For some this entails a search for subversive political and religious leaders seen as betraying Christianity and the country to agents of Satan (Fuller 1995). The basic apocalyptic frame of many fundamentalists, which helps write the script for the Tea Parties and militias, is that time is running out before the occurrence of a world-changing event that will change history and reveal hidden truths.

While apocalypticism in the US begins as part of a Christian colonial culture, it escaped into secular society in the form of novels such as *Moby Dick*, films such as *High Noon*, and TV shows including *Buffy the Vampire Slayer*. Between 20 percent and 40 percent of the population of the US believes in End Times biblical prophecies in some form or another. Many foresee a cataclysmic battle between Godly Christians and the evil Satanic forces. As this battle rages, some fundamentalists believe that Christians are duty bound to confront the Antichrist—Satan's chief agent on earth. This can create a form of apocalyptic aggression stemming from what Dick Anthony and Thomas Robbins have dubbed "exemplary dualism" (Anthony and Robbins 1996).

During the Cold War, this was linked to a liberal conspiracy to weaken America and pave the way for a Soviet communist invasion. During the 1970s and 1980s there were dozens of books published exploring the liberal conspiracy to promote secular humanism and take God out of America. Some argued that the very idea of public education was part of a plot to brainwash children to defy authority, disobey their parents, and reject religion. The idea of a vast and sinister secular humanist conspiracy has been circulated by a number of leading right-wing organizations, including the John Birch Society,

Christian Anti-Communism Crusade, Christian Coalition, the Eagle Forum, Concerned Women for America, and the American Coalition for Traditional Values. All of these groups allied with the Christian Right.

Christian Right activists Gary Bauer and James Dobson described the struggle between Christians and secular humanists as a "great Civil War of Values" (Martin 1996). Together they authored *Children at Risk: The Battle for the Hearts and Minds of Our Kids*, which suggested that public education had been distorted by secular humanists (Dobson and Bauer 1990). One of the most prolific authors in this area is Tim LaHaye, a leading Christian Right activist who wrote books about the secular humanist conspiracy prior to co-writing the best-selling *Left Behind* series of apocalyptic novels (LaHaye 1975, 1980, 1982, 1995). According to LaHaye, the secular humanist conspiracy gained headway with the election of Franklin D. Roosevelt, and now controls America and Europe (LaHaye 2003: 2, 1999).

During the 1970s and 1980s some Protestant fundamentalists were influenced by the work of Christian evangelical writer Hal Lindsey, who argued in a 1970 book, *The Late Great Planet Earth*, that contemporary world events revealed the signs of the prophesied End Times heralding the Apocalypse and the second coming of Christ (Lindsey and Carlson 1970). For many Christian fundamentalists in the US, there is an idiosyncratic way to read the prophecies in the book of Revelation in the New Testament as well as other books in the Christian *Bible*. This reading suggests that the End Times bring a conspiracy of leading political and religious leaders who join forces with Satan to build a one world government and create a new world order ruled by the Antichrist (Boyer 1992; Fuller 1995; Frykholm 2004; FitzGerald 1985). This tendency has been criticized by co-religionists in both mainline and even evangelical Protestant circles (Abanes 1998).

The discussion in fundamentalist circles was about whether the spread of secular humanism was just a symptom of liberal permissiveness, part of a long-standing secret communist conspiracy to spread Godlessness, or even part of the Satanic End Times conspiracy. When communism collapsed in Europe, anti-communism as the glue that held together various sectors of the political right began to dissolve. According to George Marsden, the new focus shifted to secular humanism, which "revitalized fundamentalist conspiracy theory." The threats of "Communism and socialism could, of course, be fit right into the humanist picture," wrote Marsden, "but so could all the moral and legal changes at home without implausible scenarios of Russian agents infiltrating American schools, government, reform movements, and mainline churches" (Marsden 1991: 109). When the Soviet Union collapsed, the belief in a conspiracy of secular humanists provided continuity, and allowed for a seamless shift in targets from the Red Menace to contemporary threats such as the feminist movement, abortion, and the gay rights movement. Apocalyptic ideas, whether religious or secular, play a significant role in shaping voter attitudes towards elections and legislation in the US, especially in forming specific argumentative patterns (Harding 1994).

Since the 1970s a "Dominionist" tendency has emerged among evangelicals who believe that they must make the US a "Christian Nation" (Diamond 1989; Barron 1992; Goldberg 2006; Berlet 2011). According to Diamond, the "concept that Christians are Biblically mandated to 'occupy' all secular institutions has become the *central unifying ideology* for the Christian Right" (Diamond 1989: 138). For some, especially in militias or insurgent right groups based on Christianity, this can include taking up arms in anticipation of secular state repression or the need for armed revolution. Most Dominionists, however, seek political power through the electoral system, playing a major role in the Republican Party (Diamond 1998).

Insurgent revolutionary right groups

The Tea Partiers and the more moderate wing of the militias seek to maintain their autonomy, yet since they are vocal, angry, mobilized, and energetic they are targeted as prime recruitment pools for both the Republican Party and a variety of white supremacist groups. The more aggressive militias are not just autonomous, but often underground, and are primarily recruited by white supremacist organizers. This intersection between the patriotic movements of Tea Partiers and militia adherents is denied by many movement members, while it is publicly discussed by white supremacists, including those with an ultimate agenda of overthrowing the government.

The best-known insurgent right group that challenged the authority of the federal government in the US was the original Ku Klux Klan of the late 1800s. The Klan used terror to suppress the newly emancipated black slaves. Since then there have been at least five other "eras" of Klan activity by the accounting of movement members, including the largest mass movement of its kind in the 1920s. In addition to the Klan, there have been a variety of relatively small pro-Nazi and neo-Nazi groups in the US.

White supremacists believe in genetic racial hierarchies, and in the US there is usually some form of anti-Semitism, a masculinist perspective, and antipathy towards gays and lesbians. As is typical of right-wing populism across the spectrum of the right, revolutionary right groups utilize dualism, demonization, scapegoating, apocalypticism, and a reliance on conspiracy theories. Stanislav Vysotsky argues that to understand how white supremacists operate in the public sphere, it helps to separate them into categories based on how they organize themselves as political, religious, or youth cultural movements such as racist skinheads (Berlet and Vysotsky 2006).

Armed citizens' militias

Spinning out of the broad patriot movement in the 1990s were the armed citizens' militias which gained headlines in the mid-1990s. Like today, this earlier militia activism was part of a right-wing populist surge that ran from the Republican Party on the reform side to organized white supremacist groups on the insurgent side (Levitas 2002). This is not one unified movement, but a series of overlapping ones—think of the Olympic symbol of five interlocking rings. It's quite plausible that sectors of the broad patriot movement can work together on a common project without all of them actually agreeing on anything but stopping the secular liberal conspiracy to enslave America.

The story embraced by the armed militias in the 1990s was that the government of the US was part of a secret plan to establish a one world government as part of building a new world order. The debate at the patriot and militia meetings I attended in the 1990s was whether or not the plot was controlled by the Freemasons, the Skull and Bones Society, the corporate elites, the "Bilderbergers," or the agents of Satan in the End Times. Occasionally, someone would pull me aside and whisper that it was actually the Jews.[2]

The 1990s militias are widely seen as part of a right-wing populist revolt against the Administration of Democrat Bill Clinton, but it actually began under the Administration of Republican George H.W. Bush (1989–93), who was seen as a cosmopolitan internationalist eager to build the nefarious and tyrannical new world order. Today's militia activism can be traced in part to the North American Union conspiracy theory that percolated up during the administration of George W. Bush (2001–09). Several scholars have studied the dynamic interactions between the revolutionary right and the citizens' militias of the 1990s, especially in terms of armed confrontations, murder, and terrorism (Dyer 1998; Hamm 1997, 2002; Nobel 1998). This dynamic poses a serious threat to public safety, since it is what led to the bombing of the Oklahoma City Federal Building in 1995.

While the convicted bombers Timothy McVeigh and Terry Nichols were both involved in the militia movement milieu, McVeigh had moved on to become involved in the neo-Nazi underground, and evidence suggests he chose to bomb the building during the day when it was occupied, without the knowledge of Nichols, who accordingly was spared the death sentence by the jury. McVeigh, then, was carrying out the act of terrorism as a form of "propaganda of the deed," in an effort to move the primarily reformist militia movement into a revolutionary insurgent stance. Like most such acts of terrorism on the political right and left, this tactic failed, yet the dynamic is worth noting (Dyer 1998; Hamm 1997, 2002).[3]

In March 2010, nine members of the Hutaree Militia were charged with, among other things, seditious conspiracy, which carries a maximum of a life imprisonment if convicted. The name "Hutaree" (pronounced hoo-TAR-ee) is said to mean "Christian warrior" in a secret language the group claims to have invented. The Hutaree were preparing "for the end time battles to keep the testimony of Jesus Christ alive." They formed an underground armed citizens' militia unit because they believed that "one day, as prophecy says, there will be an Antichrist. All Christians must know this and prepare, just as Christ commanded" (Berlet 2010).[4] Federal officials say the Hutaree began the planning in August 2008. A judge later dismissed the serious charges, stating the group lacked the ability to carry out an armed revolution. Nonetheless, the

Southern Poverty Law Center reports a dramatic increase in groups involved in spreading such "Rage on the Right" over the past several years (Potok 2010).

Tea Parties, Town Halls, and patriots

Before the Tea Party movement emerged, libertarian gadfly Ron Paul ran a presidential campaign based on tax protest themes, including an event held in Boston on December 16, 2007, "timed to coincide with the 234th anniversary of the Boston Tea Party." That event raised over US$5 million in one 24-hour period, and "smashed the one-day fund-raising record for a Republican presidential candidate." This surpassed the $4.2 million they raised on November 5, 2007, an event "timed to coincide with Guy Fawkes Day, which commemorates a British mercenary who tried unsuccessfully to kill King James I on Nov. 5, 1605" (Levenson 2007).

The US Tea Party movement was originally an idea conceived by several conservative and Republican political organizations in the hopes of creating opposition to health care and other policy proposals by the Democratic Obama Administration. Critics charged this was "astroturfing"—the practice of creating the appearance of a grassroots movement when none really exists (Mayer 2011; Good 2009; Berlet 2012a, 2012b).

Much to the surprise of some observers, an actual Tea Party movement was spread across the country by grassroots organizers linked together on the Internet and influenced by the exhortations of the elite propaganda machine and like-minded television and radio broadcasters (Berlet 2012a, 2012b). By late 2009 there were grassroots Tea Party chapters in most states. Almost immediately, state-based Tea Party activists began to meet with and struggle over political issues with leaders and elected officials from the Republican Party in their state.[5]

Like many newly created social movements, the Tea Party movement in 2010 was still in a process of developing its frames, narratives, and issue boundaries. Ideologically it was still in tension, with an awkward amalgam of ideological positions cobbled together from several pre-existing formations on the political right:

- economic libertarians who worry about big government meddling with the "free market";
- anti-taxation activists;
- Christian Right conservatives who oppose liberal government social policies;
- right-wing apocalyptic Christians who fear a Satanic new world order; and
- nebulous conspiracy theorists who fear a totalitarian new world order.

In addition, several other sectors began to gravitate towards the Tea Party and Town Hall movements:

- gun rights activists;
- nationalistic ultra-patriots concerned that US sovereignty is eroding;

- armed citizens militias;
- xenophobic anti-immigrant white nationalists who worry about preserving the "real" America; and
- recruiters from the insurgent white supremacist movement.

The original idea of pro-corporate Republican strategists was to harness popular anti-tax energy to free market policies as a way to block the Obama Administration's proposed economic reforms. The Tea Party quickly picked up this theme and welded it to pre-existing conspiracy theories about government tyranny popular on the political right. Town Hall protests began in early August 2009 (George 2009). Many Tea Party activists joined in the Town Hall protests, which were built around confronting elected representatives who supported the Obama Administration's plans for health care reform. Conspiracy claims were common at the Town Hall confrontations.

Two key themes emerged:

- Obama was a socialist whose policies would usher in fascistic totalitarian rule; and
- federal health care would lead to unplugging grandma and other forms of ruthless cost-effective euthanasia seen as paralleling the policies of Nazi Germany.

Both claims emerged as hyperbolic conspiracy theories, but were originally rooted in longstanding arguments favored by the political right (Berlet 2010). Even so, the startling graphic images depicting the face of President Obama morphed with the addition of a Hitler cowlick and mustache were originally produced by a cadre from the neo-fascist Lyndon LaRouche network (based in the US and Germany).

When the Town Hall and Tea Party activists warn that Obama's big government policies will lead to totalitarian rule (so that Obama is like both Hitler and Stalin), the most likely source is the work of free-market economic libertarian Friedrich August von Hayek, or those theories as transmogrified by the conspiracist John Birch Society. When right-wing populists warn that Obama's health care plan will pull the plug on grandma, they're likely drawing from the anti-abortion and anti-euthanasia writings of conservative Christian philosopher Francis Schaeffer, or those theories as refracted through the lens of apocalyptic Christian conspiracy theorists such as Tim LaHaye and Pat Robertson (Berlet 2010).

Both the Town Hall and Tea Party movements rearticulated conspiracy theories from the 1990s militia and patriot movements alongside more recent conspiracy claims about an alleged plan to dissolve US sovereignty and establish a North American Union. These claims were spread by right-wing ideologues including Jerome Corsi, Phyllis Schlafly, and Pat Buchanan, and were amplified by CNN reporter and commentator Lou Dobbs, before he was terminated in 2009 (Berlet 2009).

The John Birch Society, formed in 1959, is the apparent original source of much of the conspiracy mongering of demagogues such as Glenn Beck, formerly on the major television network Fox News. Fox News openly supports the Tea Party movement and is the source of false claims and histrionic reporting that demonizes the Obama Administration and critics of the Tea Party movement.[6]

Studies have shown that "most people who agree with the religious right also support the Tea Party," but that "support for the Tea Party is not synonymous with support for the religious right." Some 46 percent of Tea Party supporters "had not heard of or did not have an opinion about" the Christian Right. Yet 42 percent "said they agree with the conservative Christian movement." As has been true for roughly 30 years, some 16 percent of registered voters say they support the Christian Right; 27 percent of registered voters "expressed agreement" with the Tea Party movement. They also are "much more likely than registered voters as a whole to say that their religion is the most important factor in determining their opinions on these social issues. And they draw disproportionate support from the ranks of white evangelical Protestants" (Clement and Green 2011).

That same study found that Tea Party supporters "tend to have conservative opinions not just about economic matters, but also about social issues such as abortion and same-sex marriage" (Clement and Green 2011). Thomas J. Keil and Jacqueline M. Keil studied the websites of 137 "Tea Party backed candidates [who] stood for election to the US House of Representatives in the 2010 elections." They found that "[o]ne of the strongest areas of commonality amongst the Tea Party candidates was that they were all overwhelmingly Pro-Life; and they took great pains to present their overall opposition to abortion." Most also supported the "traditional family" and "traditional marriage" (Keil and Keil 2012: 43).

A study by Christopher Parker at the University of Washington shows that prejudice toward blacks and Latinos is significantly higher among Tea Party supporters than among those who oppose the Tea Party movement (Parker 2010). Another study asked "[is] racism still a major problem in America?" Some "75-percent of people questioned believe it is, but that belief drops to 61 percent among conservative voters and 58 percent among Tea Party supporters" (Gardner and Thompson 2010). In their study, Keil and Keil concluded through a statistical analysis of voter demographics that support for the Tea Party-backed candidates in the 2010 election was largely based on:

> ... racial anxieties of White voters who were reluctant to support a political agenda framed by and a political party led by a Black man. In some sense, then, the 2010 election was a racial referendum—a reaction by Whites who wanted "to take back" "their country" from the usurpers who had won the 2008 election. This drive to "take back" the country had little to do with class issues or with economic distress. Because of their racialist sentiments, White voters were willing to support radical

right-wing—some of whom frequently used words long associated with negative evaluations and treatment of Blacks—words such as "school choice", "States' rights", "personal responsibility", amongst others.

(Keil and Keil 2012: 46)

Conceptualizing populism and producerism

Two universal elements across populist movements were identified by Margaret Canovan (1981: 11): "some kind of exaltation of and appeal to 'the people,' and all are in one sense or another antielitist." Canovan divided forms of populism into agrarian and political (Canovan 1981: 13, 128–38). The agrarian forms included movements of commodity farmers with egalitarian economic demands including the People's Party of the late 1800s in the US; subsistence peasant movements with the East European Green Rising as an example; and farmers and peasants who built agrarian movements as did the Russian *narodniki*—often idealized and romanticized by intellectuals who had never planted a potato.

In the category of political populism, Canovan placed forms of populist participation in democracy and calls for popular referendums. She also identified the cynical use of populist rhetoric as "politicians' populism," which is marked by non-ideological appeals for "the people" to build an organic unified coalition. For "populist dictatorship" Canovan used the example of Juan Perón in Argentina. "Reactionary populism," the last of the seven forms identified by Canovan, is often associated with white backlash movements in the US.

According to Canovan, the various forms of political populism frequently overlap and share characteristics. Therefore forms of right-wing populism might include "a charismatic leader, using the tactics of politicians' populism to go past the politicians and intellectual elite and appeal to the reactionary sentiments of the populace" (Canovan 1981: 292). Examples include World War II figures Charles de Gaulle of France, Corneliu Codreanu of Romania, Adolf Hitler of Germany, and Father Coughlin of the US (Canovan 1981). Other US political activists who fit into the category of right-wing populism include George Wallace, Ross Perot, Pat Robertson, Pat Buchanan, and David Duke. After the Civil War in the US, white supremacists used producerist narratives to fuel the overtly racist attacks on the freed black former slaves in the US South (Kantrowitz 2000: 4–9, 109–14, 153). This contributed to the dissolution of the populist movements during this period.

Paul Taggart argues there are five common features to populism as an ideal type. First, according to Taggart, is that "populism is hostile to representative politics." Populists can be frustrated by the complexity of representative politics and may turn to charismatic leaders who pledge to improve government through processes of direct democracy. "The security offered by 'rights' (especially individual and minority rights) or the resort to complex judicial redress for injustices are anathema to populists" (Taggart 2004: 273).

Second, "populists tend to identify themselves with a 'heartland' that represents the idealized conception of the community they serve." From this they create an emotional and largely imaginary "people." Populism therefore "asserts that there was a good life before the corruptions and distortions of the present." That there is much ambiguity in these conceptions masks "divisions among its constituency" and aids the populists "who portray themselves as monolithic and untainted by internal conflict, even when the reality is that populism is particularly given to factionalism" (Taggart 2004: 274).

Third, a common "theme of populism is that it lacks core values" because the values are ascribed to the idealized past of the heartland. "The variety of versions of the heartland explains why populism is attached to some very different ideological positions from the left to the right" (Taggart 2004: 274)

Fourth, "populism is a reaction to a sense of extreme crisis." While some may see this crisis as due to "moral decay," it "always spills over onto a critique of politics and into the sense that politics as usual cannot deal with the unusual conditions of the crisis" (Taggart 2004: 275). The actual existence of a crisis of legitimacy is open to debate, but the crisis is clearly perceived by populists.

Fifth, "it becomes very difficult to sustain populist movements in the long term." As populist movements "become institutionalized into politics they inevitably lose a major part of their popular appeal." This and other factors make them self-limiting (Taggart 2004: 276).

In the US, populism is highly significant in mobilizing political and social movements. A frequent rhetorical frame of right-wing populism is to valorize the productive "common man" as being crushed by a viperous nest of corrupt politicians and wealthy plutocrats up above and a lazy, sinful, and subversive mob of parasites below the middle class on the socioeconomic ladder (Berlet and Lyons 2000).

In the classic right-wing conspiracist book *None Dare Call it Conspiracy*, conservative activists Gary Allen and Larry Abraham actually illustrated this idea with a graphic depicting the middle class being squeezed in a vise (Allen and Abraham 1972). Writing in 1972, Allen and Abraham claimed the "Communist tactic of pressure from above and pressure from below" was being used in the US (Allen and Abraham 1972: 124).

According to the authors, the "pressure from above comes from secret, ostensible respectable Comrades in the government and Establishment," including the Rockefeller and Rothschild families and the elites at the Council on Foreign Relations. From below the vise is squeezed by "radicalized [leftist] mobs in the streets" and community organizers including the Students for a Democratic Society, the Black Panthers, the Young Socialist Alliance, and Common Cause. People in these groups are described as "pawns, shills, puppets, and dupes for an oligarchy of elitist conspirators working above to turn America's limited government into an unlimited government with total control over our lives and property" (Allen and Abraham 1972: 124). Update the names of the villains, and in many ways this is a narrative popular in the Tea Party movement, which fears that President Obama is planning to collectivize the nation through Big Government and social programs that will lead to totalitarian rule.

Lisa Disch (2010) argues that the idea of a productive middle class being squeezed is similar to what scholars in Europe call the "Precariat." Their class position is precarious, as illustrated by Barbara Ehrenreich in *Fear of Falling: The Inner Life of the Middle Class* (Ehrenreich 1989).

Populism, especially right-wing populism, often has a majoritarian focus.[7] Michael Kazin sees populism in the US today as "a persistent yet mutable style of political rhetoric with roots deep in the nineteenth century" (Kazin 1995: 5). He also detects ethnocentric prejudice:

> … the romance of producerism had a cultural blind spot; it left unchallenged strong prejudices toward not just African-Americans but also toward recent immigrants who had not learned or would not employ the language and rituals of this variant of the civil religion … Even those native-born activists who reached out to immigrant laborers assumed that men of Anglo-Saxon origins had invented political democracy, prideful work habits, and well-governed communities of the middling classes.
>
> (Kazin 1995: 5)

Catherine McNicol Stock observes that ironically, with populism, "the roots of violence, racism, and hatred can be and have been nourished in the same soil and from the same experiences that generate … movements for democracy and equality" (McNicol Stock 1996: 148). Douglas R. Holmes looks at attempts by what he calls European "integralists" to exploit resentment and alienation. He highlights Jean-Marie Le Pen as skillfully mixing left and right elements from populism, expressionism, and pluralism (Holmes 2000: 6–9, 13, 58).

Mabel Berezin sees in new Europe forms of right-wing populism emerging to craft new stable identities which are themselves a reaction against immigration which brings strange people and foreign ideas—the very root of the term xenophobia (Berezin 2009). In the US similar anti-immigrant movements, which grew stronger in the 1990s, focused their antagonism primarily on Mexicans (Perea 1997; Knobel 1996). According to Doug Brugge:

> An important ingredient in the success of the Right's anti-immigrant campaign is its ability to deflect anger about any negative effects of the U.S. economic, environmental or cultural situation onto the scapegoat of immigrants. This tactic nests within a larger goal of capturing political gain by exploiting a popular issue.
>
> (Brugge 1995)

Ray Taras studies how "in Western Europe the rise of xenophobia is nearly synonymous with the anti-immigrant backlash," especially against non-Europeans and "people who are not racially Caucasian or religiously Judeo-Christian"

(Taras 2009: 93). Taras traces the development of "phobias" built around ethnic hierarchies in which prejudice against immigrants—especially asylum seekers—is notably high. He sees great anxiety produced by the transition from old Europe to new Europe (Taras 2009: 83–172).

In both Europe and the US antipathy towards Muslims remains high (Gottschalk and Greenberg 2007; Boyer 2003; Martin 1999). Fear of Muslims in the US predates the terrorist attacks of September 11, 2001, with a prime example being *The Clash of Civilizations* by Samuel P. Huntington (1997). Communitarian Amitai Etzioni criticized Huntington for being a "systematic and articulate advocate of nationalism, militaristic regimes, and an earlier America in which there was one homogenous creed and little tolerance for pluralism" (Etzioni 2005: 485). Others simply condemn the late Huntington as an Islamophobe. Anti-Muslim sentiments in the US are primarily produced by the neo-conservative intellectual movement and the Christian Right (Berlet 2008).

Roger Griffin, a leading scholar of fascism and neo-fascism, considers populist rhetoric to be a key element in his definition of generic fascism. According to Griffin:

> ... fascism is best defined as a revolutionary form of nationalism, one that sets out to be a political, social and ethical revolution, welding the "people" into a dynamic national community under new elites infused with heroic values. The core myth that inspires this project is that only a populist, trans-class movement of purifying, cathartic national rebirth (palingenesis) can stem the tide of decadence.
>
> (Griffin 1991: xi)

Producerist scapegoating of Jews helped the Nazis recruit an alienated mass base (Payne 1995).

Producerist storylines can weave together strands of integralism, organicism, and *völkish* nationalism (Berlet 2005). Both right-wing populism and fascism use the producerist narrative as a scapegoating mechanism (Berlet 2005). Few right-wing populist movements, however, become full-blown fascist movements, and it is rare for them to seize state power.

The role of palingenesis in populism and the Tea Parties was considered by John Cassidy, writing on *The New Yorker* website blog. Cassidy was critical of Michelle Bachmann, leader of the Tea Party Caucus in Congress which boasted 60 members in 2011 (Bachmann 2011). Cassidy observed that:

> From National Socialism to Poujadism to the Tea Party, the suggestion that the motherland needs reclaiming from alien forces has been central to populist right-wing movements. This was clearly what Bachmann was driving at when she commented in 2008 that President Obama "may have anti-American views," and, even though she's since expressed the wish she had expressed herself differently, her supporters get the message loud and clear.
>
> (Cassidy 2011)

Conclusions

The US Constitution is amended by a Bill of Rights which begins with the First Amendment guarantee of free speech and freedom to practice religion. It is legal to call for the overthrow of the US government by force of arms, so long as one is sufficiently vague, is not busy collecting arms, and does not set a date. In Germany, as Cas Mudde observes:

> ... the difference between radicalism and extremism is that the former is *verfassungswidrig* (opposed to the constitution), whereas the latter is *verfassungsfeindlich* (hostile to the constitution). This difference is of the utmost practical importance for the political parties involved, as extremist parties are extensively watched by the (federal and state) *Verfassungsschutz* and can even be banned, whereas radical political parties are free from this control.
>
> (Mudde 2000: 12)[8]

Yet in the US, banning a political partly is almost unthinkable, and absent evidence of criminal intent, law enforcement is supposed to refrain from continuous snooping on political organizing (although since the terrorist attacks on 9/11 surveillance authority has been expanded). According to Jérôme Jamin:

> The cordon sanitaire has given the [*Vlaams Blok* in Belgium], like the Austrian FPÖ [*Freiheitliche Partei Österreichs*] and the French Front National, the appearance of a democratic party; its members have been in public councils for twenty years without being able to implement a fascist program. Once again, the progressive community had to deal with an obvious contradiction between old, deep and strong words (fascism, Nazism, etc.) and daily life with a party which, whatever its rhetoric, lacked the opportunity to differentiate itself in practical terms from others. Even worse, it had to deal with a democracy that institutes a quarantine against an elected party to keep it out of power. Does it still deserve to be called a democracy? Focusing on the words of the extreme right might be useful for showing its historical links with the fascism of the 1930s, or to highlight the racist views of some of its leaders. But this understanding is not enough to convince the electorate that the extreme right is a threat to democracy and to democratic values.
>
> (Jamin 2005)[9]

European democracies based on a parliamentary model are very different from the US, which has a "winner takes all" two-party system. More research needs to be done on whether or not this makes a substantial difference in the way contemporary right-wing populist movements function in the political sphere.

138 Chip Berlet

Democrats and Republicans frequently claim the political high ground of the center, while denouncing each other as wing nuts on the far fringes of political life. This histrionic rhetoric apparently is successful in fundraising efforts, but it can create poisonous polarization in civil society, especially when amplified by opportunistic politicians and lazy or unscrupulous mass media demagogues.

Democracy is based on informed consent. Demonization and dismissal of dissident social movements with substantial grievances weakens the body politic and sets the stage for further counter-productive confrontations. This applies to all political and social movements.

This is not an indictment of all populist movements. Robert McMath has observed of the agrarian populist movements in Canada and the US that "conspiratorial thinking and scapegoating" were present, but that it is unfair to label them "fundamentally a conspiratorial, xenophobic, and reactionary movement" (McMath 1995). Kazin (1995: 284) suggests that "when a new breed of inclusive grassroots movements does arise, intellectuals should contribute their time, their money, and their passion for justice. They should work to stress the harmonious, hopeful, and pragmatic aspects of populist language and to disparage the meaner ones … "

The solution to periods of right-wing populism is government transparency, a full and open public debate over policies, and refraining from caricaturizing reform-oriented political opposition as stupid, crazy, or planning to rend the fabric of society and plunge the nation into the abyss of totalitarian rule. Most right-wing populist movements never become fascist, and most fascist movements never gain state power, but the turmoil created in these volatile periods of apocalyptic aggression can undermine civil society, and harm the individuals targeted as scapegoats (Cohn 1970, 1993; Northcott 2004).

Notes

1 Author's note: Some of the ideas and explanations in this paper appeared in previously published text or conference papers which are cited as appropriate in the footnotes. My research would not be possible without the support of Political Research Associates. A more detailed discussion examining the differences between right-wing movements in Europe and the US keyed to this chapter is at www.researchforprogress.us/sectors/euro-us/.
2 Portions of this section appeared in Berlet 2010, "'Christian Warriors': Who are the Hutaree Militia and Where Did they Come from?" *Religion Dispatches*, March 31, tinyurl.com/apocamil.
3 The author of this paper was subpoenaed as an expert analyst by the defense team for Terry Nichols, and believes the available evidence supports this thesis.
4 The quotes from the Hutaree are from their website, which is now offline. Copies in possession of the author. For some, the confrontation with the Antichrist is tied to the need to convert all nations to Christianity, based on an idiosyncratic interpretation of the "Great Commission" in 1 Matthew 28:18–20. In the King James translation it reads: "And Jesus came and spake unto them, saying, All power is given unto me in heaven and in earth. Go ye therefore, and teach all nations, baptizing them in the name of the Father, and of the Son, and of the Holy Ghost:

Teaching them to observe all things whatsoever I have commanded you: and, lo, I am with you always, even unto the end of the world. Amen." In the NIV version used by most conservative Protestant evangelicals in the US, a key passage reads: "make disciples of all nations, baptizing them ... and teaching them to obey everything I have commanded you." As early as the mid-1800s in the US, some read this passage to mean aggressively converting all non-believers. For example, see Charles G. Finney, 1845, "The Church Bound to Convert the World, (Concluded)," sermon, reported by J.N. Cook, *The Oberlin Evangelist*, April 23, www.gospeltruth.net/1845OE/450423_world_convertpt2.htm.
5 Portions of this section are adapted from Chip Berlet 2011a. A revised version appears as Berlet, "Collectivists, Communists, Labor Bosses, and Treason."
6 Fox News publicized false claims about the conference from which this chapter emerged. Fox claimed the conference and this paper were calling Tea Party members neo-Nazis. In fact, the main focus of the conference was examining neo-Nazis and other denizens of the ultra-right in Germany and the US. From the beginning the purpose of my paper was to show that while the Tea Parties drew from right-wing populism, they were not accurately classified as a form of neo-Nazism. See, for example, Fox News, www.foxnews.com/search-results/m/30482035/right-wingers-are-neo-nazis.htm. For me, the point of the conference and books like this is to ensure we have learned the horrible lessons of the Nazi genocide, and continuously explore it from a variety of perspectives. Despite a range of analytical views expressed at the conference, I ended my presentation by observing that all of us could agree on one point: never again.
7 Portions of this section are adapted from Berlet 2012b.
8 As Martin Durham has observed, in this area of research there is much terminology that is used differently by different authors. In Germany, as explained by Mudde, being "opposed to the constitution" makes "radicalism" less threatening to the health of the nation than "extremism," which is defined as being "hostile to the constitution." In the US context scholars might write that "radicals" challenge the constitution, while "extremists" and other insurgents seek to overturn it. Personal correspondence with Cas Mudde, July 5, 2012; Durham 2000.
9 This thesis was later expanded into a book, Jamin 2009.

References

Abanes, Richard (1998) *End Time Visions: The Road to Armageddon?* New York: Four Walls, Eight Windows.
Allen, Gary and Larry Abraham (1972 [1971]) *None Dare Call it Conspiracy*, Rossmoor: Concord Press.
Anthony, Dick and Thomas Robbins (1996) "Religious Totalism, Violence, an Exemplary Dualism: Beyond the Extrinsic Model," in Barkun (ed.) *Millennialism and Violence*, London: Frank Cass.
Aukerman, Dale (1993) *Reckoning with Apocalypse*, New York: Crossroad.
Bachmann, Michelle (2011) *Members of the Tea Party Caucus*, bachmann.house.gov/News/DocumentSingle.aspx?DocumentID=226594.
Barron, Bruce (1992) *Heaven on Earth? The Social and Political Agendas of Dominion Theology*, Grand Rapids: Zondervan.
Berezin, Mabel (2009) *Illiberal Politics in Neoliberal Times: Culture, Security and Populism in the New Europe*, Cambridge: Cambridge University Press.
Berlet, Chip (2005) "Christian Identity: The Apocalyptic Style, Political Religion, Palingenesis and Neo-Fascism," in Griffin (ed.) *Fascism, Totalitarianism, and Political Religion*, London: Routledge.

—— (2008) "The United States: Messianism, Apocalypticism, and Political Religion," in Griffin, Feldman, and Tortice (eds) *The Sacred in Twentieth Century Politics: Essays in Honour of Professor Stanley G. Payne*, Basingstoke: Palgrave Macmillan.

—— (2009) "Fears of Fédéralisme in the United States: The Case of the 'North American Union' Conspiracy Theory," *Fédéralisme Régionalisme* 9(1), popups.ulg. ac.be/federalisme/document.php?id = 786.

—— (2010) "The Roots of Anti-Obama Rhetoric," in Cunnigen and Bruce (eds) *Race in the Age of Obama* (*Research in Race and Ethnic Relations*, Vol. 16), Emerald Group Publishing Ltd, 301–19.

—— (2011a) "Taking Tea Parties Seriously: Corporate Globalization, Populism, and Resentment," in *Perspectives on Global Development and Technology*, Global Studies Association of North America, Vol. 10, No. 1: 11–29.

—— (2011b) "Protocols to the Left, Protocols to the Right: Conspiracism in American Political Discourse at the Turn of the Second Millennium," in Landes and Katz (eds) *The Paranoid Apocalypse: A Hundred Year Retrospective on the Elders of Zion*, New York: New York University Press.

—— (2011c) "How We Coined the Term 'Dominionism'," *Talk to Action*, talk2action. org/story/2011/8/31/17047/5683.

—— (2012a) "Collectivists, Communists, Labor Bosses, and Treason: The Tea Parties as Right-Wing Populist Counter-Subversion Panic," *Critical Sociology* (38)4: 1–23, in press.

—— (2012b) "Reframing Populist Resentments in the Tea Party Movement," in Rosenthal and Trost (eds) *Steep: The Precipitous Rise of the Tea Party*, Berkeley: University of California Press.

Berlet, Chip and Matthew Lyons (2000) *Right Wing Populism in America: Too Close for Comfort*, New York: Guilford Press.

Berlet, Chip and Stanislav Vystosky (2006) "Overview of White Supremacist Groups," *Journal of Political and Military Sociology* 34(1): 11–48.

Betz, Hans Georg (1993) "The Two Faces of Radical Right Wing Populism in Western Europe," *The Review of Politics* 55(4): 663–85.

—— (1994) *Radical Right Wing Populism in Western Europe*, New York: St Martins Press.

Boyer, Paul S. (1992) *When Time Shall Be No More: Prophecy Belief in Modern American Culture*, Cambridge: Harvard University Press.

—— (2003) "John Darby Meets Saddam Hussein: Foreign Policy and Bible Prophecy," *Chronicle of Higher Education*, February 14, B10–B11, chronicle.com/article/John-Darby-Meets-Saddam/18413.

Brent, Sandy D. (2002) *Plowshares and Pruning Hooks: Rethinking the Language of Biblical Prophecy and Apocalyptic*, Downers Grove: InterVarsity.

Brugge, Doug (1995) "Pulling Up the Ladder: The Anti-Immigrant Backlash," *The Public Eye* (Summer), www.publiceye.org/ark/immigrants/PullingLadder.html.

Camp, Gregory S. (1991) *Selling Fear: Conspiracy Theories and End Times Paranoia*, Grand Rapids: Baker Books.

Canovan, Margaret (1981) *Populism*, New York: Harcourt Brace Jovanovich.

Cassidy, John (2011) "Rational Irrationality," *The New Yorker*, June 28, www.newyorker. com/online/blogs/johncassidy/2011/06/bachmanns-bounce-the-view-from-brooklyn.html.

Clement, Scott and John C. Green (2011) *The Tea Party, Religion and Social Issues*, Pew Forum on Religion & Public Life, February 23, pewresearch.org/pubs/1903/tea-party-movement-religion-social-issues-conservative-christian.

Cohn, Norman (1970 [1957]) *The Pursuit of the Millennium: Revolutionary Millenarians and Mystical Anarchists of the Middle Ages*, New York: Oxford University Press.
——(1993) *Cosmos, Chaos and the World to Come: The Ancient Roots of Apocalyptic Faith*, New Haven: Yale University Press.
Diamond, Sara (1989) *Spiritual Warfare: The Politics of the Christian Right*, Boston: South End Press.
——(1995) *Roads to Dominion: Right Wing Political Movements and Political Power in the United States*, New York: Guildford.
——(1998) *Not By Politics Alone: The Enduring Influence of the Christian Right*, New York: Guilford Press.
Disch, Lisa (2010) *Tea Party Movement: The American "Precariat"?* Paper presented at Fractures, Alliances, and Mobilizations in the Age of Obama: Emerging Analyses of the "Tea Party Movement," UC Berkeley.
Dobson, James and Gary L. Bauer (1990) *Children at Risk: The Battle for the Hearts and Minds of Our Kids*, Dallas: Word Publishing.
Durham, Martin (2000) *The Christian Right, The Far Right, and the Boundaries of American Conservatism*, Manchester: Manchester University.
Dyer, Joel (1998) *Harvest of Rag: Why Oklahoma City is the Beginning*, Boulder: Westview.
Ehrenreich, Barbara (1989) *Fear of Falling: The Inner Life of the Middle Class*, New York: Harper Perennial.
Etzioni, Amitai (2005) "The Real Threat: An Essay on Samuel Huntington," *Contemporary Sociology* 34(5): 477–85.
FitzGerald, Frances (1985) "The American Millennium," *The New Yorker* (9/11): 105–96.
Frykholm, Amy Johnson (2004) *Rapture Culture: Left Behind in Evangelical America*, New York: Oxford University Press.
Fuller, Robert C. (1995) *Naming the Antichrist: The History of an American Obsession*, New York: Oxford University Press.
Gardner, Amy and Krissah Thompson (2010) "Tea Party Groups Battling Perceptions of Racism," *The Washington Post*, May 5, www.washingtonpost.com/wp-dyn/content/article/2010/05/04/AR2010050405168.html.
George, Patrick (2009) "Lloyd Doggett Faces Angry Crowd at Randalls," *Austin Statesman*, August 2, www.statesman.com/blogs/content/shared-gen/blogs/austin/austin/entries/2009/08/02/.
Goldberg, Michelle (2006) *Kingdom Coming: The Rise of Christian Nationalism*, New York: W.W. Norton.
Good, Chris (2009) "The Tea Party Movement: Who's In Charge?" *The Atlantic*, April 13, www.theatlantic.com/politics/archive/2009/04/the-tea-party-movement-whos-in-charge/13041/.
Gottschalk, Peter and Gabriel Greenberg (2007) *Islamophobia: Making Muslims the Enemy*, Lanham: Rowman & Littlefield.
Griffin, Roger (1991) *The Nature of Fascism*, New York: Routledge.
Hamm, Mark (2002) *In Bad Company: America's Terrorist Underground*, Boston: Northeastern University Press.
Harding, Susan (1994) "Imagining the Last Days: The Politics of Apocalyptic Language," in Marty and Appleby (eds) *Accounting for Fundamentalisms: The Fundamentalism Project*, Vol. 4, Chicago: University of Chicago Press, 57–78.
Holmes, Douglas R. (2000) *Integral Europe: Fast-Capitalism, Multiculturalism, Neofascism*, Princeton: Princeton University Press.

Huntington, Samuel P. (1997) *The Clash of Civilizations and the Remaking of World Order*, New York: Touchstone.

Jamin, Jérôme (2005) "The Extreme Right in Europe: Fascist or Mainstream?" *The Public Eye* 19(1), www.publiceye.org/magazine/v19n1/jamin_extreme.html.

——(2009) *L'Imaginaire du Complot: Discours d'extrême droite en France et aux Etats-Unis*, Amsterdam: University of Amsterdam.

Kantrowitz, Stephen (2000) *Ben Tillman & the Reconstruction of White Supremacy*, Chapel Hill: University of North Carolina.

Kazin, Michael (1995) *The Populist Persuasion: An American History*, New York: Basic Books.

Keil, Thomas J. and Jacqueline M. Keil (2012) "The Characteristics of the Congressional District and Tea Party Victories in 2010," *Ethnicity and Race in a Changing World: A Review Journal* Vol. 3, Issue 1: 43–46, www.manchesteruniversitypress.co.uk/data/ip/ip021/docs/Comment_Keil.pdf.

Knobel, Dale T. (1996) *"America for the Americans": The Nativist Movement in the United States*, New York: Twayne.

LaHaye, Tim (1975) *Revelation: Illustrated and Made Plain*, Grand Rapids: Zondervan.

——(1980) *The Battle for the Mind*, Old Tappan: Fleming H. Revell.

——(1982) *The Battle for the Family*, Old Tappan: Fleming H. Revell.

——(1999) "Antichrist Philosophy Already Controls America and Europe," *Pre Trib Perspectives*, timlahaye.com/about_minstry/pdf/sept.tim.pdf.

——(2003) "119 Million American Evangelicals in these Last Days," *Pre Trib Perspectives* 8(1): 1–3.

LaHaye, Tim and Jerry Jenkins (1995) *Left Behind: A Novel of the Earth's Last Days*, Wheaton: Tyndale House Publishers.

Levenson, Michael (2007) "Ron Paul Backers Stage Boston Tea Party, Raise Millions," *Boston Globe*, December 17, www.boston.com/news/nation/articles/2007/12/17/ron_paul_backers_stage_boston_tea_party_raise_millions.

Levitas, Daniel (2002) *The Terrorist Next Door: The Militia Movement and the Radical Right*, New York: St Martin's.

Lifton, Robert J. (2003) *Superpower Syndrome: America's Apocalyptic Confrontation with the World*, New York: Thunder's Mouth Books/Nation Books.

Lindsey, Hal and C.C. Carlson (1970) *The Late Great Planet Earth*, Grand Rapids: Zondervan.

Marsden, George M. (1991) *Understanding Fundamentalism and Evangelicalism*, Grand Rapids: William B. Eerdmans Publishing Co.

Martin, William (1996) *With God on Our Side: The Rise of the Religious Right in America*, New York: Broadway Books.

Mayer, Jane (30 Aug 2011) "Covert operations: The Billionaire Brothers Who are Waging War against Obama," *The New Yorker*, August 30, www.newyorker.com/reporting/2010/08/30/100830fa_fact_mayer.

Monbiot, George (2010) "The Tea Party Movement: Deluded and Inspired by Billionaires," *The Guardian* (UK), www.guardian.co.uk/commentisfree/cifamerica/2010/oct/25/tea-party-koch-brothers.

McMath, Robert C. Jr. (1995) "Populism in Two Countries: Agrarian Protest in the Great Plains and Prairie Provinces," *Agricultural History* 69(4): 517–47.

McNicol Stock, Catherine (1996) *Rural Radicals: Righteous Rage in the American Grain*, Ithaca: Cornell University Press.

McVeigh, Roy (2009) *The Rise of the Klu Klux Klan: Right Wing Movements and National Politics*, Minneapolis: University of Minnesota Press.

Mudde, Cas (2000) *The Ideology of the Extreme Right*, Manchester: Manchester University Press.

Nobel, Kerry (1998) *Tabernacle of Hate*, Prescott, Ontario: Voyager.

Northcott, Michael (2004) *An Angel Directs the Storm: Apocalyptic Religion & American Empire*, London: I.B. Tauris.

O'Leary, Stephen (1994) *Arguing the Apocalypse: A Theory of Millennial Rhetoric*, New York: Oxford University Press.

Parker, Christopher (2010) *2010 Multi-state Survey on Race & Politics*, University of Washington, Institute for the Study of Ethnicity, Race and Sexuality, Seattle, depts.washington.edu/uwiser/racepolitics.html.

Payne, Stanley G. (1995) *A History of Fascism, 1914–45*, Madison: University of Wisconsin Press.

Perea, Juan F. (1997) *Immigrants Out! The New Nativism and the Anti-Immigrant Impulse in the United States*, New York: New York University Press.

Postone, Moishe (1986) "Anti-Semitism and National Socialism," in Rabinbach and Zipes (eds) *Germans & Jews Since the Holocaust: The Changing Situation in West Germany*, New York: Homes & Meier.

Potek, Mark (2010) *Rage on the Right: The Year in Hate and Extremism*, Intelligence Report, Southern Poverty Law Center, splcenter.org/get-informed/intelligence-report/browse-all-issues/2010/spring/rage-on-the-right.

Taggart, Paul (2004) "Populism and Representative Politics in Contemporary Europe," *Journal of Political Ideologies* 9(3): 273.

Taras, Ray (2009) *Europe Old and New: Transnationalism, Belonging, and Xenophobia*, Lanham: Rowan & Littlefield.

——(2012) *Xenophobia and Islamaphobia in Europe*, Edinburgh: Edinburgh University Press.

Zeskind, Leonard (2009) *Blood and Politics: The History of the White Nationalist Movement, From the Margins to the Mainstream*, New York: Farrar, Straus, & Giroux.

9 Cycles of right-wing terror in the US

Pete Simi

Violent fundamentalist insurgency is growing worldwide (Almond *et al.* 2003; Barber 1995; Brouwer *et al.* 1996) and right-wing extremists are part of this global phenomenon. Russia, in particular, has experienced a rapid growth of neo-Nazis since the fall of the Soviet Union. In the early 1990s, Russia had fewer than 100 neo-Nazi skinheads, but by 2005, more than 50,000 roamed Russia's streets (Liss 2010; Osborn 2005). Since reunification, Germany has also witnessed a troubling increase in right-wing extremism. A recent study found that one in 20 West German and one in eight former East German male 15 year olds claimed membership in a neo-Nazi faction (Pfeiffer 2009). In the US, the resurgence of right-wing extremist groups has been equally dramatic. The Southern Poverty Law Center estimates that hate groups are currently at record levels, with almost 1,000 arrayed across the US:

> Anti-immigrant vigilante groups soared by nearly 80%, adding some 136 new groups during 2009. And ... so-called 'Patriot' groups—militias and other organizations that see the federal government as part of a plot to impose 'one-world government' on liberty-loving Americans—came roaring back after years out of the limelight.
>
> (Potok 2010)

Despite a significant international and national presence of right-wing extremism (RWE), in the post-9/11 era (since the terrorist attacks on the US on September 11, 2001), terrorism has become synonymous with Islamic extremism (Vohryzek-Bolden *et al.* 2001). Narrowly focusing on Islamic fundamentalism, however, neglects the threat posed by other types of extremists and thus has dangerous implications. In particular, right-wing terrorism (RWT) in the US has been neglected, with relatively few studies examining the dynamics influencing episodes of domestic right-wing terrorism (for exceptions see Blee 2005; Smith 1994; Simi and Futrell 2010; Wright 2007; Freilich *et al.* 2009; Hamm 2001; Blazak 2001; Kaplan 1995; Sprinzak 1995).

The goal of this chapter is twofold. The current obsession with Islamic jihadi terrorism has a blinding effect on the conception of terrorism, including, ultimately, how society responds to terrorism. This chapter is intended to add to the dialogue about other types of terrorist threats by focusing on right-wing extremism. The focus on right-wing extremism challenges the tendency among academics, government officials, and the general public narrowly to define "real" terrorism. Second, this chapter is an effort to assess empirically the dynamics and patterns of US right-wing terrorism by comparing two recent waves as well as examining the current status of right-wing terrorism.

Perceiving right-wing terror

Most observers agree that a "perfect storm" of political conditions is fueling a current surge of US right-wing extremism (Potok 2010; Berlet and Lyons 2000; Simi 2010; Simi and Futrell 2010). By now the culprits have been widely noted and include: fear of illegal immigration, the depressed economy, and the election of Barack Obama, the nation's first African American president. A difficulty remains, however, in perceiving the link between right wing extremism and terrorism. The response to the Department of Homeland Security's (2009) report regarding the threat of right-wing terrorism is evidence of this resistance. For example, some observers criticized the report suggesting that terrorism is not part of the repertoire of the right-wing (Thompson 2009). In addition, leading terrorism experts tell us that right-wing extremists pose little threat in terms of an ongoing organized capacity to commit large-scale acts of terrorism (Hoffman 2006).

The characterization of right-wing extremism as a bizarre but ultimately impotent underground world of "misfits" is misguided and stems, in part, from notable incidents of domestic terrorism like the Oklahoma City and the Olympic Park bombings being divorced from the extremist ideology and relational links that helped produce them (Chermak 2002; Wright 2007). Although both incidents received substantial media coverage (Chermak and Gruenewald 2006), neither was connected to a larger campaign of right-wing terror. For example, an internal study conducted by the Federal Bureau of Investigation (FBI) (Turchie and Puckett 2007) erroneously classified Timothy McVeigh as a "lone wolf" offender despite substantial evidence that McVeigh was deeply integrated into a potent culture of paranoia, conspiracy, and violence. His journey from learning extremist views to taking radical action was guided by involvement in a persistent network of right-wing extremists (Wright 2007; Hamm 2001). More specifically, there is evidence that links McVeigh to Elohim City, a white separatist community near Muldrow, Oklahoma, members of the Aryan Republican Army (ARA), a neo-Nazi terror cell active in the mid-1990s, and White Aryan Resistance (WAR) (Arena and Arrigo 2000; Hamm 2001; Wright 2007). In terms of beliefs, McVeigh was inspired by the late neo-Nazi leader William Pierce's *The Turner Diaries* (1978), which he sold at gun shows across the country and reportedly used as a blueprint for the bombing (Arena and Arrigo 2000; Hamm 2001; Wright 2007).

Another example of RWE divorced from a larger political campaign is Eric Rudolph's violence—which killed two and injured 119 people—included setting off bombs at the 1996 Olympic Games in Atlanta, abortion clinics in Atlanta and Birmingham, Alabama, and a lesbian nightclub in Atlanta. Rudolph is vehemently anti-abortion, anti-gay, anti-feminist, anti-Semitic and feels that American culture is rapidly deteriorating (e.g. see Rudolph's writing on ArmyofGod.com). Rudolph's beliefs reflect his adherence to Christian Identity theology, a racist religious doctrine that preaches that Jews are the literal descendants of Satan and non-whites are subhuman (Barkun 1994). In addition to his beliefs, Rudolph has a history of associations with Christian Identity adherents. For example, when Rudolph was 18 he lived for six months at Pastor Dan Gayman's Christian Identity community, the Church of Israel, in Schell City, Missouri. While Rudolph lived there, Gayman served as his mentor and considered Rudolph as a potential spouse for one of his daughters (Vollers 2006). Despite Rudolph's clear ideological and associational ties to right-wing extremist groups, his activity is often described as "single-issue, anti-abortion" terrorism, or he is more generically referred to as a "radical Christian."

Part of the failure to connect incidents like the Oklahoma City bombing to a larger strategy of right-wing terror is related to the decentralized nature of right-wing extremist networks. For instance, Buford Furrow's "lone wolf" shooting spree in a Jewish community center in 1999 was not simply an individual act of violence and hatred but represented the ideological tenets of the Aryan Nations, a group with which Furrow was affiliated prior to the killings. In addition, Furrow considered himself a "front-line warrior" in an effort to "save the white race from genocide." According to Furrow, he intended to ignite a "race war" by providing " ... a wake-up call to America to kill Jews" (Gibney 1999). Likewise, in 1999, former World Church of the Creator (WCOTC) member Ben Smith launched a three-day, one-man ethnic-cleansing campaign that killed two people and wounded seven. Smith's actions were lauded by Matt Hale, the WCOTC's leader at the time: "Maybe he lost his life to make us a household name ... I have nothing but good things to say about Ben Smith ... " (www.g21.net, no date).

When small groups and even single individuals commit acts of violence on behalf of a larger cause, these incidents should be viewed as part of a larger strategy of violence and not simply as random acts of isolated violence by deranged individuals. In this respect, while Turk's (2004) claim that domestic extremists have shifted from organizational to individual terrorism is accurate, the use of the term "individual" is highly misleading. Turk's example of the Oklahoma City bombing as an individual act of terrorism is a case in point. Because right-wing extremist violence is often attributed to isolated individuals, specific incidents are not seen as part of a larger campaign which inevitably discourages observers from viewing right-wing extremist violence as terrorism. Some observers may counter that these incidents were not coordinated and thus lumping them together distorts the nature of right-wing violence. My point, however, is terror violence does not need to be completely coordinated to be part of a larger wave. The decentralized nature of right-wing extremist networks creates a "camouflage" of sorts that leads some astute observers to mistake decentralization for disorganization and thus irrelevance (e.g. Hoffman 2006; Gardell 2003).

This chapter is concerned with documenting and examining the incidence of right-wing terrorism in the US. I use the terms "waves" and "episodes" interchangeably to avoid redundancy and because both terms suggest a period of time of intensified and heightened activity that eventually diminishes. Two waves were chosen for comparative analysis (the mid-1980s and mid-1990s) because previous research has highlighted each one as a significant wave of right-wing terrorism (Smith 1994; Simi 2008). The chapter concludes with a discussion of the current phase of right-wing extremism including the most recent episodes of RWE violence. The two episodes share important similarities in terms of close proximity in time and space, yet distinctive features also characterize each episode. The wave of terror during the 1980s was part of a wider political backlash against the social change and unrest prominent during the 1960s (Bennett 1995; Gibson 1994). The second episode coincided with the election of a Democratic president, major international transformations such as the fall of the Soviet Union, and globalizing trends affecting economic markets, culture, and technology (Zeskind 2009). As part of the effort to understand these episodes, this chapter uses a social movement perspective to focus on the internal dynamics that shape RWT.

Defining terrorism in relation to political mobilization

Before proceeding with a comparison between the two episodes, some definitional issues about the nature of extremism and terrorism are in order. Defining terrorism remains a contentious issue (Schmid and Jongman 2005). In this chapter, terrorism is defined as acts or threats of violence committed by an individual or group intended to generate fear beyond the immediate victim(s) and motivated, at least in part, by politics (Schmid and Jongman 2005; Blee 2005). By default, all terrorists are also extremists. Most extremists, however, do not explicitly plan or participate in acts of terrorism, therefore most extremists are not terrorists (Bjorgo 1995; Sprinzak 1995). Terrorism, by definition, involves action. Extremism, on the other hand, can be defined more in terms of adherents' beliefs and involves a broader range of behavior than terrorism. In terms of right-wing extremism, this can be defined as a constellation of individuals, informal groups, and formal organizations that espouse a combination of anti-government, racist, anti-Semitic, homophobic, anti-abortion, and anti-immigrant beliefs (Blee 2002; Hamm 2001; Kaplan 1995). Right-wing extremists utilize a variety of legal tactics including forming political parties, organizing public marches and rallies, creating and distributing extremist literature, developing separatist communities and illegal activities such as bombing abortion clinics, violent attacks on "out-group" members, bank robbery, drug distribution, identity theft, counterfeiting, and tax evasion (see Berlet and Lyons 2000; Blazak 2001; Diamond 1995; Freilich and Chermak 2009;

Freilich *et al.* 2001; Futrell and Simi 2004; Hamm 2001; Kaplan 1995; McCurrie 1998; Simi and Futrell 2010; Simi *et al.* 2008; Smith 1994; Sprinzak 1995; Weinberg 1998).

Although terrorism is widely recognized as one type of political violence, most terrorism scholars do not adequately address the extent to which terrorism is part of a larger social movement (Tilly 2004). Recently, however, several observers have begun utilizing the field of social movements as a framework for understanding terrorism (Borum and Gelles 2005; Oberschall 2004; Sageman 2004). One of the conceptual tools from the social movement field that may be especially useful for understanding the ebb and flow of terrorist violence is the cycle of contention which refers to a rise and fall of social movement activity including periods of time characterized by heightened levels of conflict (Tarrow 1994, 1989; della Porta 1995; della Porta and Tarrow 1986). Tarrow's (1989) and della Porta's (1995) research in Italy shows that political violence including terrorism is present from the beginning of a protest cycle but varies in relation to the level of mass mobilization. In Italy political violence increased as organized protest weakened. Cycles of contentious politics influence a movement's "repertoire" of political tactics including decisions among movement groups/members to use terror violence (Tilly 1995; Gamson 1975). Using the cycle of contention concept, this chapter focuses on two episodes of right-wing terror.

Setting the stage for terror

Compared to the 1950s and 1960s when the Ku Klux Klan routinely initiated violent terrorist attacks against civil rights targets (McAdam 1999; Newton and Newton 1991) and Roger DePugh's Minutemen were organizing themselves into small cells, stockpiling weapons, and preparing for a communist invasion, the 1970s witnessed relatively little RWT (Ross and Gurr 1989). By the late 1970s, however, that began to change as groups affiliated with various branches of the Ku Klux Klan were on the rise corresponding with a larger growth of American paramilitary culture (Gibson 1994). According to Gibson (1994), losing the Vietnam War along with changes in traditional gender and racial hierarchies led to a "backlash" (see also Faludi 1991), which in the most extreme forms manifested itself in a growth in racist, paramilitary groups trying to defend themselves against a government overrun by various racial enemies. The seeds for a resurgence of RWE during the 1980s were certainly planted in the broader political culture, yet external conditions are often ripe for generating mobilization (Snow *et al.* 1980). There were significant internal dynamics that were also present and helped facilitate the resurgence of right-wing extremism during the 1980s. As part of this resurgence of RWE, a wave of RWT began in the mid-1980s lasting several years.

The historian Phillip Jenkins (2008) finds that over the 20th century, an historical pattern suggests waves of RWT typically coincide with the election of a Democratic president when the election follows at least two Republican presidential terms (Jenkins 2008). While Jenkins does not assume the pattern is perfect, his neglect of the wave of RWT that occurred in the mid-1980s is significant in that this wave does not follow the pattern Jenkins identified, suggesting that presidential politics alone are not sufficient for generating waves of terrorism. So why did a segment of RWE turn to terror tactics at a time when the larger society was already moving in a right-wing direction? Unlike other waves of RWT that Jenkins notes, RWT during the mid-1980s was not a response to an immediate shift in political culture in a liberal direction.

One might explain the RWT of the 1980s as a response to the liberal movements of the 1960s, or alternatively one might explain this wave of violence as an extension of the conservative movement that gained momentum during the same time. In either case, the explanation assumes that external conditions are, in fact, the chief motivator of terrorist behavior. Internal dynamics, however, are also important in terms of explaining when a group decides to adopt terror tactics. In this sense, extremists may have such firmly established mindsets and worldviews that only the most immediate external conditions are relevant. External conditions that are further removed such as shifts in political culture may be largely irrelevant to the "true believer" (Hoffer 1951). An RWE is likely to perceive either a Republican or Democratic president as a "puppet" of the fabricated enemy "Zionist occupational government" (ZOG). What really matters is whether the group experiences the internal processes necessary for the planning and the implementation of terror violence. The process of radicalization involves to a large extent social settings where adherents cultivate autonomy from dominant groups and nurture oppositional movement identities (Simi and Futrell 2010). These social settings or "free spaces" provide extremist groups secrecy and control in terms of planning and experimenting with radical action (both violent and nonviolent). Without access to certain types of social settings, the level of radicalization necessary for terroristic violence may not be achieved by the members of the extremist group.

Right-wing terror during the 1980s

Although the contemporary image of terrorism is largely shaped by 9/11, the empirical reality is very different (Jenkins 2003; Smith 1994). A general overview of American terrorism during the 1980s reveals that right-wing extremists constituted two-thirds of the individuals indicted for federal terrorism-related charges. Two right-wing terror groups, in particular—the Silent Brotherhood and the Covenant, the Sword, and the Arm of the Lord (CSA)—generated a substantial portion of these federal indictments.

The Silent Brotherhood

Robert Jay Mathews founded the Bruder Schweigen/Silent Brotherhood (also known as the Order), a terror cell formed in 1983 and active for less than two years. At first, the group consisted of a small inner circle of members mostly recruited from a variety of existing right-wing extremist groups (e.g. Aryan Nations, National Alliance, and Ku Klux Klan). Eventually, however, the group grew to more than 30 members and was in the process of forming multiple cells across the country when a federal investigation resulted in a series of arrests that led to the group's downfall (Flynn and Gerhardt 1995). While 28 members of the Silent Brotherhood were indicted under the Racketeer Influenced and Corrupt Organization Act (RICO), Mathews was unwilling to surrender and ultimately killed during a two-day standoff with federal authorities on Whidbey Island, WA (Flynn and Gerhardt 1995). Prior to the group's demise, the Silent Brotherhood was responsible for multiple murders, bombings, weapons violations, and two armored truck robberies that generated approximately US$4 million for the group and other right-wing extremist organizations (Flynn and Gerhardt 1995; Smith, 1994).

The Covenant, Sword, and Arm of the Lord (CSA)

Minister James Ellison formed the CSA in 1971 as a Christian evangelical retreatist commune, but the group grew increasingly radical by the late-1970s after Ellison claimed to have a vision of a coming race war (Noble 1998). CSA members also created paramilitary training areas that included a mock village called "Silhouette City ... complete with pop-up targets of blacks, Jews, and police officers wearing Star of David badges" (Smith 1994: 64). In 1982, the FBI suspected that the CSA had over 100 active members living on or in close proximity to their compound on the Arkansas–Missouri border (Noble 1998), while others estimated the number at closer to 200 (Wright 2007). CSA members prepared for the coming race war by attending gun shows, where they formed alliances with members of other radical groups including Aryan Nations, Silent Brotherhood, Posse Comitatus, local Ku Klux Klan chapters, Elohim City, and the Christian Patriot Defense League (Wright 2007).

By the early 1980s the CSA declared the compound "an arms depot and paramilitary training ground for Aryan warriors" (Smith 1994: 64). Following their declaration, the CSA planned the assassinations of a local FBI agent and a US district judge, and plotted arsons, bombings, and the poisoning of municipal water supplies. The original plan to destroy the Alfred P. Murrah Federal Building in Oklahoma City was hatched by CSA members nearly 12 years before Timothy McVeigh and his accomplices completed the act (Noble 1998). Although the CSA failed to execute most of their terrorist plans, community members and their associates did bomb a Missouri community church known to support homosexuality and an Indiana Jewish community center. CSA members also detonated explosives near a natural gas pipeline in Arkansas, robbed and murdered a pawnshop owner they thought was Jewish, and murdered an African American Arkansas state trooper (Smith 1994).

The CSA's spree of violence ended in April 1985 after Ellison and others surrendered at their compound following a four-day standoff with federal agents (Noble 1998). The FBI's search of the CSA compound uncovered nearly 200 firearms, including land mines, machine guns, assault rifles, thousands of rounds of ammunition, anti-tank rockets, and a large supply of cyanide (Noble 1998). The raid led to the federal indictment of 17 CSA members and in September 1985 CSA leaders James Ellison and Kerry Noble and four other CSA activists were sentenced to lengthy federal prison terms on racketeering and weapons charges, which effectively destroyed the group and the settlement.[1]

In addition to the Silent Brotherhood and CSA, several other right-wing terror groups were active during the 1980s. For example, the Order II, a small seven-person terror cell that committed five bombings in 1986 alone. The group was inspired by the Silent Brotherhood and members were either current or former members of Aryan Nations (Smith 1994). The group's leader David Dorr was responsible for at least six of the bombings and at least two murders (Smith 1994). By 1988, the group's remaining members were convicted for various crimes. Other right-wing terror groups active during the 1980s included the Arizona Patriots and the White Patriots Party (Smith 1994).

Framing threat, triggering events, and the cult of martyrdom

Social movement activists frequently use diagnostic techniques to frame social issues (Snow and Benford 1992; Snow *et al.* 1986) as a means to push for broad-scale change, garner organizational resources (e.g. fundraising), and recruit new members. However, the identification of new "hot-button" issues may affect adherents as well as "sympathetic bystanders" at a social-psychological and psychological level (Opp 1988). Individuals and groups may experience these new problems as "strains" (Smelser 1962) by developing heightened perceptions of imbalance, deprivation, power loss, conflict, and ambiguity; all are potential catalysts for political mobilization (Smelser 1962; Useem 1997). These strains, in turn, may lead individual activists or groups of activists to reach a threshold or tipping point (Granovetter 1973). When this occurs, activists may find existing tactics unsuitable for these "new" problems.

In particular, right-wing extremists may be especially responsive to a sense of threat as these catalysts seem to play a significant role in generating RWT (Sprinzak 1995; Wright 2007). Triggering events are specific incidents that are likely to be perceived as threatening because of the events' high intensity and close proximal relationship to the aggrieved party. For example, the threat of federal authority diminishing individual liberty may be evoked by new legislation but until the legislation results in specific incidents the perceived threat is likely to remain distant. Alternatively, a federal siege of an anti-government community that results in one or more fatalities is likely to be perceived as an immediate, direct threat—even an attack. The exposure to conditions such as economic depression, demographic change, and political/cultural change may threaten an individual's or group's status but these events may not provide the same type of clear threat to the existence of the individuals and/or groups. Hot button issues that evoke a sense of mortality are especially likely to generate a heightened level of violence (Greenberg *et al.* 1997).

The wave of RWT during the 1980s was spurred by the death of Gordon Kahl. In 1983 Gordon Kahl, a North Dakota farmer, tax resister, and Christian Identity minister was killed by law enforcement in a shootout. Prior to his death, Kahl had been a fugitive and wanted for tax evasion and resisting arrest. Although members of the CSA provided him with refuge, Kahl was killed during a shootout in Smithville, Arkansas, and his death galvanized right-wing extremists across the country. Kahl's death inspired the declaration of "WAR in 84," a credo that involved a loose confederation of groups committed to implementing a multi-pronged strategy to overthrow the US government (Smith 1994). Kahl's martyrdom was strengthened, in part, by his personal characteristics (i.e. he was a war veteran, father and small farmer).

Splinter factions and organizational resources

In any social movement very few groups ever come to use terror tactics (Sprinzak 1995). Groups that do often have overlapping relationships with other political organizations that do not use this type of violence. In some cases, terror groups use these more moderate groups for the purpose of recruitment and generating resources (Sprinzak 1995; Smith 1994). During the 1980s, many right-wing terror groups were splinters from above-ground extremist groups. Unlike terror groups, above-ground extremist groups are primarily oriented toward conventional political action such as marches, rallies, and propaganda production and distribution. Although most of these extremist groups do not engage in terror tactics, these groups provide violent factions with an important source of personnel, resources, and social-psychological support (della Porta 1995).

Factionalization is the process by which a new group forms as a splinter from one or more existing groups. Factionalization requires the existence of an organizational base. New splinter groups may themselves splinter in subsequent years resulting in a more complex maze of partly overlapping but partly distinct groups. Movements split and fragment for a variety of reasons including differences regarding the use of radical violent strategies (McCauley and Moskalenko 2011; McAdam et al. 2001; Haines 1984; Gamson 1975). Laqueur (1977) notes that most terror groups emerge from existing political organizations and that such splits may generate conflict among the competing groups including increased radicalization among both factions.

The Silent Brotherhood drew members from the National Alliance, the Aryan Nations, the Ku Klux Klan, and another terror cell, the CSA (Smith 1994; Flynn and Gerhardt 1995). The Order II was composed entirely of Aryan Nations members who were interested in carrying on the work of the Silent Brotherhood/the Order (Smith 1994). An organizational base is important for several reasons. First, a violent faction is able to recruit new members from the base. The larger base is also more likely to have greater resources at its disposal. In addition to recruiting members from Aryan Nations, the Silent Brotherhood also covertly used the Aryan Nation's printing press as part of a counterfeiting scheme to fund the development of their terror cell. Second, the existence of an organizational base is also important in that members of the terror cell are able to position themselves in relation to the more conventional tactics of the base. Terror cell members are able to tell themselves and each other that while all extremists agree about what should be done, they are part of a "select few" (i.e. the vanguard) willing to sacrifice everything for the cause. The organizational base provides terrorists with a "stepping stone" to more intense involvement but also a point of dissatisfaction and distinction. The radical talk in which extremists engage is critical to developing and sustaining a collective identity (Simi and Futrell 2010; Futrell and Simi 2004), but at some point terrorists come to see talk as insufficient. This perceptual fissure is a significant part of the radicalization process (McCauley and Moskalenko 2011).

Right-wing terror in the 1990s

During the 1990s 44 percent of terrorism-related federal indictments involved right-wing extremists (Simi 2008). Aside from 9/11, the Oklahoma City bombing is the most serious act of terrorism to occur on American soil. However, RWT during the 1990s neither began nor ended with McVeigh and his conspirators. The Southern Poverty Law Center reports that in the five years following the Oklahoma City bombing, more than 36 terrorist plots were planned or carried out by right-wing extremists (Blejwas *et al.* 2005: 1). The list includes plans to bomb or burn government buildings, banks, refineries, utilities, clinics, synagogues, mosques, memorials and bridges; to assassinate police officers, judges, politicians, civil rights figures and others; to rob banks, armored cars and other criminals; and to amass illegal machine guns, missiles, explosives, and biological and chemical weapons.

Prior to the Oklahoma City bombing, the Aryan Republican Army (ARA) began a spree of 22 bank robberies across the Midwest lasting from 1994 until 1996. According to some reports (Hamm 2001; Wright 2007), the ARA was linked to Timothy McVeigh and the Oklahoma City bombing. In the months following the Oklahoma City bombing, the "Sons of Gestapo" derailed an Amtrak train near Hyder, Arizona, killing one passenger and injuring scores of others. The perpetrators were never apprehended (Blejwas *et al.* 2005). In November 1995, four members of the Oklahoma Constitutional Militia were indicted on federal charges related to plans of bombing abortion clinics, gay bars, and the Southern Poverty Law Center office in Montgomery, Alabama (Blejwas *et al.* 2005).

Triggering events during the 1990s

Similar to the 1980s, two major triggering events occurred in the early 1990s that catalyzed RWEs across the country: Ruby Ridge and Waco. In August of 1992 Randy Weaver, a white separatist, Christian Identity family that included

Weaver's spouse and three children living in the rugged wilderness of northern Idaho were involved in a standoff with federal authorities. Weaver was wanted on firearms charges and failure to appear, and had been holed up in his remote cabin when a team of federal law enforcement keeping his whereabouts under surveillance led to a series of events that resulted in the shooting deaths of Weaver's 14 year-old son Sammy and his wife Vicky. Immediately following the incident and in the years since it occurred, the official version of events has changed and has been widely disputed (Walter 1996; Dobratz and Shanks-Meile 2000). Sammy was shot in the back while running away from several US Marshals and Vicky was shot in the head by an FBI sniper while standing behind her cabin's front door and holding her 10 month-old baby. The impact of Ruby Ridge on the far right was potent and served as the catalyst for the 1992 Estes Park, Colorado meeting where a virtual "who's who" of the far right converged to discuss the prospects of an armed insurrection to combat government despotism demonstrated by the federal siege in Ruby Ridge (Walter 1996; Dobratz and Shanks-Meile 2000). During the Estes Park meeting, Louis Beam advocated for a change in organizational strategy among RWEs. Beam called for "leaderless resistance," an organizational philosophy where individuals form phantom cell structures, non-hierarchical in nature and designed to combat an established adversary such as a government (Beam 1992).

A year later, in 1993, just outside of Waco, Texas, a 50-day standoff between the Bureau of Alcohol, Tobacco, and Firearms (ATF) and David Koresh's Branch Davidians ended when a fire of unknown origins engulfed the Davidian compound killing more than 76 people including 20 children. Americans were horrified at the devastating loss of life but some Americans, like Timothy McVeigh, stood by watching, convinced that Waco was a clear sign the federal government had declared war on its own citizens (Berlet and Lyons 2000).

Comparing the 1980s and 1990s

Important differences distinguish the waves of terrorism during the 1980s and 1990s. Unlike the 1980s, the 1990s followed the pattern Jenkins (2008) identified. Compared to the 1980s, the 1990s reveal much less explicit convergence between above-ground political organizations and terror cells. The terror groups in the 1990s were smaller than the groups in the 1980s and less tied to widely known above-ground extremist groups (Smith 1994). Although McVeigh was involved in a larger subculture of extremism, he was not a formal member of any particular group. Even groups like the ARA, during the 1990s, were smaller and less formalized than CSA and the Silent Brotherhood. The organizational convergence between violent and conventional factions during the 1980s created more of a unifying nucleus as compared to the RWT during the 1990s. One reason that accounts for decreasing organizational convergence is the advocacy of leaderless resistance strategies stemming from the 1992 Estes Park meeting in Colorado (Smith 1994).

In terms of similarities, each wave ended primarily as a result of large-scale arrests initiated by federal law enforcement. Neither wave experienced any significant broader public support. Most importantly, each episode was characterized by significant triggering events demonstrating immediate and direct threat to the mortality of RWEs.

The contemporary context

Now, I turn to the current phase of right-wing extremism. In this section, I discuss the current conditions and the resurgence of RWE that has reportedly been occurring over the past several years. According to Chip Berlet, noted political analyst:

> We are in the midst of one of the most significant right-wing populist rebellions in United States history ... We see around us a series of overlapping social and political movements populated by people [who are] angry, resentful, and full of anxiety. They are raging against the machinery of the federal bureaucracy and liberal government programs and policies including health care, reform of immigration and labor laws, abortion, and gay marriage.
>
> (quoted in Potok 2010)

The resurgence of RWE, however, is more accurately a resurfacing of individuals and groups that have been cultivating their extremism in relatively hidden but vibrant free spaces (Simi and Futrell 2010; Futrell and Simi 2004). These frees spaces are where extremists gather in order to nurture their radical beliefs. The current resurgence is possible because individuals and groups have been quietly maintaining themselves in these spaces which afford them opportunities for networking. Social contact is an essential component of the radicalization process.

One of the most significant developments since the 1990s is the trend toward individual terrorism (Turk 2004). Individual terrorism, more widely known as "lone wolf" violence, has been promoted by several leading RWE ideologues since at least the 1980s. The concept was popularized by white supremacists Alex Curtis and Tom Metzger (whose resist.com website features a snarling wolf on the front page) in the 1990s. Louis Beam, a leading Klan and Aryan Nations representative, however, proposed a "point system" that awarded scores to would-be assassins based on the importance of their targets in the early 1980s (Anti-Defamation League 2009). Other prominent white supremacist leaders such as William Pierce (now deceased), founder of the National Alliance and author of *Hunter* (a book that celebrated a fictional lone wolf but which the author dedicated to Joseph Paul Franklin, a real lone wolf) have also advocated lone wolf violence as a useful strategy at a time when white supremacists are greatly outnumbered and do not have the resources to wage a "full frontal attack."

During 2009 lone wolf radicals killed at least 10 people in incidents that ranged from the neo-Nazi James von Brunn's attempted massacre at the Holocaust Museum in Washington, DC; to Scott Roeder's shooting and killing of a Kansas doctor known for performing late-term abortions; to alleged neo-Nazi Richard Poplawski who was arrested for shooting and killing three Pittsburgh police officers, in part because he feared losing his gun rights; to Joe Stack, the anti-tax activist who hoped to ignite a war against the federal government by flying his twin airplane into an IRS building in Austin, Texas, killing one person and himself.

The characteristics of lone wolves are currently unclear (Simi et al. 2010). In some cases, lone wolves' connections to extremist groups may be indirect. Ironically, it is possible that lone wolves' social connections may approximate those described by Granovetter's (1973) classic research regarding the "strength of weak ties." Decisions among extremists to innovate by carrying out lone wolf operations may, in part, reflect the influence of information dissemination that seems to occur with loose connections as opposed to strong ones.

Conclusion

The current tendency toward individual terrorism (Turk 2004) reinforces our perception that RWE does not pose a significant threat. This chapter's focus on RWT invites the question of why observers remain reluctant to define this type of violence as terrorism. The consensus suggests that RWEs are not "real terrorists" and thus the violence these groups produce poses relatively little threat. However, perceptions are often flawed and, in this case, the insistence to minimize RWE threat may reflect the tendency to perceive "outsiders" as inherently more threatening and "insiders" as "one of us" (Erikson 1966).

This chapter emphasizes the role of internal dynamics in relation to cycles of right-wing terrorism. Observers typically focus on right-wing extremism as reactionary movements that are simply responding to external conditions. Less attention has been given to issues of organizational dynamics including group linkages, leadership, and more immediate triggering events. Although studies of liberal progressive movements pay careful attention to internal movement characteristics, the study of right-wing extremism is dominated by a focus on external factors such as economic conditions, political alignments, and demographic change. While current conditions appear "ripe" in terms of producing another wave of RWT, one notable difference between these earlier waves and today is the lack of a triggering event evoking a high level of mortality salience such as the Gordon Kahl shootout, Ruby Ridge and Waco. Unless a similar triggering event occurs, I expect RWT to remain more individualized. While these types of triggering events may not be necessary for wider mobilization, these incidents may be necessary as a "tipping point" toward a broader scale of terror violence involving a collective or group campaign.

Notes

1 Kerry Noble, James Ellison's right-hand man, testified against Ellison, rejected Aryan ideology, and now writes and speaks publicly about the threat of domestic terrorism from extremist white power groups.

References

Almond, Gabriel A., R. Scott Appleby, and Emmanuel Sivan (2003) *Strong Religion: the Rise of Fundamentalisms Around the World*, Chicago: University of Chicago Press.

Anti-Defamation League (2009) *Extremism in America—Louis Beam*, www.adl.org/learn/ext_us/beam.asp?LEARN_Cat=Extremism&LEARN_SubCat=Extremism_in_America&xpicked=2&item=beam (accessed 20 October, 2009).

Arena, Michael and Bruce Arrigo (2000) "White Supremacist Behavior: Toward an Integrated Social Psychological Model," *Deviant Behavior* 21(3): 213–44.

Barber, Benjamin (1995) *Jihad vs. McWorld*, New York: Times Books.

Barkun, Michael (1994) *Religion and the Racist Right: the Origins of the Christian Identity Movement*, Chapel Hill, NC: University of North Carolina Press.

Beam, Louis (1992) "Leaderless Resistance," *The Seditionist* 12 (February), www.louisbeam.com/leaderless.htm.

Bennett, David H. (1995) *The Party of Fear: From Nativist Movements to the New Right in American History*, Chapel Hill, NC: University of North Carolina Press.

Berlet, Chip and Mathew Lyons (2000) *Right-wing Populism in America: Too Close for Comfort*, New York: Guilford Press.

Bjorgo, Tore (1995) *Terror from the Extreme Right*, London: Frank Cass.

Blazak, Randy (2001) "White Boys to Terrorist Men: Target Recruitment of Nazi Skinheads," *The American Behavioral Scientist* 44(6): 982–1000.

Blee, Kathleen (2002) *Inside Organized Racism: Women in the Hate Movement*, Berkeley: University of California Press.

——(2005) "Racial Violence in the United States," *Ethnic and Racial Studies* 28: 599–619.

Blejwas, Andrew, Anthony Griggs, and Mark Potok (2005) "Terror from the Right," Southern Poverty Law Center *Intelligence Report* No. 118, summer.

Borum, Randy and Michael Gelles (2005) "Al-Qaeda's Operational Evolution: Behavioral and Organizational Perspectives," *Behavioral Sciences and the Law* 23: 467–83.

Brouwer, Steve, Paul Gifford, and Susan D. Rose (1996) *Exporting the American Gospel: Global Christian Fundamentalism*, New York: Routledge.

Chermak, Steven (2002) *Searching for a Demon: the Media Construction of the Militia Movement*, Boston, MA: Northeastern University Press.

Chermak, Steven and Jeff Gruenewald (2006) "The Media's Coverage of Domestic Terrorism," *Justice Quarterly* 23: 428–61.

della Porta, Donatella (1995) *Social Movements, Political Violence, and the State: A Comparative Analysis of Italy and Germany*, Cambridge, UK: Cambridge University Press.

della Porta, Donatella and Sidney Tarrow (1986) "Unwanted Children: Political Violence and the Cycle of Protest in Italy, 1966–73," *European Journal of Political Research* 14(5–6): 607–32.

Department of Homeland Security (2009) *Right-Wing Extremism: Current Economic and Political Climate Fueling Resurgence of Recruitment and Radicalization*, unclassified report, Office of Intelligence and Analysis.

Diamond, Sara (1995) *Roads to Dominion: Right-wing Movements and Political Power in the United States*, New York: Guilford Press.

Dobratz, Betty and Stephanie Shanks-Meile (2000) *White Power! White Pride!: the White Separatist Movement in the United States*, New York: Twayne Publishers.

Erikson, Kai (1966) *Wayward Puritans: A Study in the Sociology of Deviance*, New York: John Wiley & Sons.

Faludi, Susan (1991) *Backlash: the Undeclared War Against Women*, New York: Three Rivers Press.

Flynn, Kevin, and Gary Gerhardt (1995) *Silent Brotherhood: The Chilling Inside Story of America's Violent, Anti-Government Militia Movement*, New York: Signet.

Freilich, Joshua and Steven Chermak (2009) "Preventing Deadly Encounters Between Law Enforcement and American Far-Rightists," *Crime Prevention Studies* 25: 141–72.

Freilich, J.D., S.M. Chermak and D. Caspi (2009) "Critical Events in the Life Trajectories of Domestic Extremist White Supremacist Groups: A Case Study Analysis of Four Violent Organizations," *Criminology and Public Policy* 8(3): 497–530.

Freilich, Joshua D., Jeremy A. Pienik and Gregory J. Howard (2001) "Toward Comparative Studies of the U.S. Militia Movement," *International Journal of Comparative Sociology* 42: 163–210.

Futrell, Robert and Pete Simi (2004) "Free Spaces, Collective Identity, and the Persistence of U.S. White Power Activism," *Social Problems* 51(1): 16–42.

Gamson, William (1975) *The Strategy of Social Protest*, Hollywood, IL: Dorsey Press.

Gardell, Mattias (2003) *Gods of the Blood: the Pagan Revival and White Separatism*, Durham, NC: Duke University Press.

Gibney, Frank Jr. (1999) "The Kids Got in the Way," *Time Magazine*, The Nation Volume 154, #8.

Gibson, William (1994) *Warrior Dreams: Violence and Manhood in Post-Vietnam America*, New York: Hill & Wang Publisher.

Granovetter, Mark (1973) "The Strength of Weak Ties," *American Journal of Sociology* 78: 1360–80.

Greenberg, J., S. Solomon, T. Pyszczynski, T. (1997) "Terror Management Theory of Self-esteem and Cultural Worldviews: Empirical Assessments," *Advances in experimental social psychology* 29: 139.

Haines, Herbert (1984) "Black Radicalization and the Funding of Civil Rights: 1957–70," *Social Problems* 32(1): 31–43.

Hamm, Mark S. (2001) *In Bad Company: America's Terrorist Underground*, Boston, MA: Northeastern University Press.

Hoffer, Eric (1951) *The True Believer: Thoughts on the Nature of Mass Movements*, New York: Harper Perennial.

Hoffman, Bruce (2006) *Inside Terrorism*, second edn, New York: Columbia University Press.

Jenkins, Philip (2003) *Images of Terror: What We Can and Can't Know About Terrorism*, Edison, NJ: Aldine Transaction.

——(2008) "Home-Grown Terror: Think the Oklahoma City bombing in 1995 was a Fluke? Think Again," *Los Angeles Times*, articles.latimes.com/2008/mar/10/opinion/oe-jenkins10.

Kaplan, Jeffrey (1995) "Right-Wing Violence in North America," in Tore Bjorgo (ed.) *Terror from the Extreme Right*, London: Frank Cass.

Laqueur, Walter (1977) *Terrorism*, Boston: Little, Brown Publishers.

Liss, Artyom (2010) "Russia Jails Neo-Nazi Murderers," BBC News, Moscow, newsvote. bbc.co.uk/mpapps/pagetools/print/news.bbc.co.uk/2/hi/europe/8537861.

McAdam, D. (1999 [1982]) *Political Process and the Development of Black Insurgency*, Chicago: University of Chicago Press.

McAdam, Doug, Sidney Tarrow, and Charles Tilly (2001) *Dynamics of Contention*, Cambridge University Press.

McCurrie, Thomas (1998) "White Racist Extremist Gang Members: A Behavioral Profile," *Journal of Gang Research* 5: 51–60.

McCauley, Clark and Sophia Moskalenko (2011) *Friction: How Radicalization Happens to Them and Us*, Oxford University Press.

McDonald, Andrew [William Pierce] (1989 [1978]) *The Turner Diaries*, Hillsboro, WV: National Vanguard Books.

Newton, Michael and Judy Ann Newton (1991) *Racial and Religious Violence in America: A Chronology*, New York: Garland Publishers.

Noble, Kerry (1998) *Tabernacle of Hate: Why They Bombed Oklahoma City*, Prescott, ON: Voyageur Publications.

Oberschall, Anthony (2004) "Explaining Terrorism: the Contribution of Collective Action Theory," *Sociological Theory* 22: 26–37.

Opp, Karl-Dieter (1988) "Grievances and Participation in Social Movements," *American Sociological Review* 53: 853–64.

Osborn, Andrew (2005) "Violence and Hatred in Russia's New Skinhead Playground," *The Independent*, January 25, www.independent.co.uk/news/world/europe/violence-and-hatred-in-russias-new-skinhead-playground-488154.html.

Pfeiffer, Christian (2009) *Young People in Germany as Victims and Perpetrators of Violence*, Lower Saxony Criminological Research Institute.

Potok, Mark (2010) *Rage on the Right: the Year in Hate and Extremism*, Intelligence Report, Spring 137.

Ross, Jeffrey and Ted Gurr (1989) "Why Terrorism Subsides: A Comparative Study of Canada and the United States," *Comparative Politics* 21(4): 405–26.

Sageman, Marc (2004) *Understanding Terror Networks*, Philadelphia, PA: University of Pennsylvania Press.

Schmid, Alex P. and A.J. Jongman (2005) *Political Terrorism: A New Guide to Actors, Authors, Concepts, Data Bases, Theories, and Literature*, Transaction Publishers.

Simi, Pete (2008) *Recruitment among Right-Wing Terrorist Groups*, National Institute of Justice, Final Report (2006-IJ-CX-0027).

——(2010) "Why Study White Supremacist Terror?: A Research Note," *Deviant Behavior: An Interdisciplinary Journal* 31: 251–73.

Simi, Pete *et al.* (2010) "Defining Lone Wolf Terrorism: A Research Note," in *Terrorism, Research, and Analysis Protocol (TRAP): A Collection of Thoughts, Ideas, and Perspectives*, Department of Justice, Federal Bureau of Investigation, Washington, DC.

Simi, P. and R. Futrell (2010) *American Swastika: Inside the White Power Movement's Hidden Spaces of Hate*, Lanham, MD: Rowman & Littlefield.

Simi, Pete, Lowell Smith, and Ann Reeser Stacey (2008) "From Punk Kids to Public Enemy Number One, *Deviant Behavior* 29: 1–22.

Smelser, Neil J. (1962) *Theory of Collective Behavior*, New York: Free Press of Glencoe.

Smith, Brent (1994) *Terrorism in America: Pipe Bombs and Pipe Dreams*, Albany, NY: New York University Press.

Snow, David A. and Robert D. Benford (1992) "Master Frames and Cycles of Protest," in Aldon D. Morris and Carol McClurg Mueller (eds) *Frontiers of Social Movement Theory*, New Haven: Yale University Press, 133–55.

Snow, David A., E. Burke Rochford, Steven K. Worden and Robert D. Benford (1986) "Frame Alignment Processes, Micromobilization, and Movement Participation," *American Sociological Review* 51: 464–81.

Snow, David, Louis Zurcher Jr., and Sheldon Ekland-Olson (1980) "Social Networks and Social Movements: A Microstructural Approach to Differential Recruitment," *American Sociological Review* 45: 787–801.

Sprinzak, Ehud (1995) "Right-wing Terrorism in a Comparative Perspective: the Case of Split Delegitimation," in Tore Bjorgo (ed.) *Terror from the Extreme Right*, London: Frank Cass.

Tarrow, Sidney (1989) *Democracy and Disorder: Protest and Politics in Italy 1965–1975*, Oxford: Clarendon Press.

——(1994) *Power in Movement: Social Movements and Contentious Politics*, Cambridge: Cambridge University Press.

Thompson, Bennie (2009) *Letter to Department of Homeland Security*, 24ahead.com/bennie-thompson-dumbfounded-dhs-rightwing-extremist-report.

Tilly, Charles (1995) *Popular Contention in Great Britain, 1758–1834*, Cambridge, MA: Harvard University Press.

——(2004) "Terror, Terrorism, Terrorists," *Sociological Theory* 22 (1): 5–13.

Turchie, Terry and Kathleen Puckett (2007) *Hunting the American Terrorist: The FBI's War on Homegrown Terror*, Palisades, NY: History Publishing Company.

Turk, Austin (2004) "Sociology of Terrorism," *Annual Review of Sociology* 30: 271–86.

Useem, Bert (1997) "Disorganization and the New Mexico Prison Riot of 1980," *American Sociological Review* 50: 667–88.

Vohryzek-Bolden, M., G. Olson-Raymer, and J. Whamond (2001) *Domestic Terrorism and Incident Management*, Springfield, IL: Charles C. Thomas.

Vollers, Maryanne (2006) *Lone Wolf*, New York: HarperCollins.

Walter, Jess (1996) *Every Knee Shall Bow*, New York: HarperCollins.

Weinberg, Leonard (1998) "An Overview of Right-Wing Extremism in the Western World: A Study of Convergence, Linkage, and Identity," in Jeffrey Kaplan and Tore Bjorgo (eds) *Nation and Race: the Developing Euro-American Racist Subculture*, Boston, MA: Northeastern University, 3–33.

Wright, Stuart (2007) *Patriots, Politics, and the Oklahoma City Bombing*, Cambridge: Cambridge University Press.

Zeskind, Leonard (2009) *Blood and Politics: The History of the White Nationalist Movement from the Margins to the Mainstream*, New York: Farrar, Straus and Giroux.

10 Adolf Hitler's *Mein Kampf*
A book of the past in the present

Othmar Plöckinger

Introduction

To discuss the importance of Hitler's book *Mein Kampf* for right-wing extremist circles today means to discuss not just a text, but a powerful symbol—a symbol of the Nazi ideology, the Nazi regime, Nazi crimes and the long shadow National Socialism continues to cast on European history to the present day. First drafted over 85 years ago by a little-known radical Bavarian agitator who had just failed to overthrow the German government in Berlin, the book's pathetic style and its right-wing, nationalist, anti-democratic, anti-Bolshevist, and anti-Semitic ramblings mirror the attitudes found in many publications of the 1920s. While most publications were forgotten only a few years after their release, *Mein Kampf* is still known today not thanks to its originality—a great deal of its content was neither new nor special—but because it was written by Adolf Hitler. The author's subsequent rise to power and the Nazis' atrocities lend the text an aura of power that cannot be explained by its content alone. It is that aura with which historians are confronted when undertaking a critical edition of the text. The publication of such an edition requires careful consideration of its historical, political, and ethical context.

In German libraries, *Mein Kampf* continues to be available only to historians with special permission to access the restricted sections dubbed "poison closet" (*Giftschrank*). By focusing on the book's ideological and historical context, a team of scholars at the *Institut für Zeitgeschichte* (Institute of Contemporary History) in Munich aims to debunk the myths surrounding *Mein Kampf* in a first critical edition.

Origins and contemporary reception

Immediately after World War II a number of widespread myths and legends surrounded *Mein Kampf*, some of which are still circulating today: for example, the notion that Hitler did not actually write the book himself or that nobody really read it when it first came out. Post-war German society was grateful for this kind of revisionism, as it fit well with the idea of Hitler as the solely responsible evil-doer who had come from somewhere outside to mislead his first victims, the German people.

Such mythmaking has long been debunked by historians of the period. The main phases of the inception of *Mein Kampf* are well known and uncontested among historians today. After the failed *coup d'état* of Munich in November 1923, Adolf Hitler started to work on his manuscript in prison in December of that year. Initially his goal was to justify his attempt to overthrow the Bavarian and German governments, and to accuse his political enemies of betraying him and his political aims. In mid-1924, his purpose changed. He withdrew himself from all political activities and began to write a book aimed at founding a National Socialist ideology (Plöckinger 2006: 29–56), and at presenting his own life as that of the ideal Nazi (Plöckinger 2009: 112–14). This stage in the writing process is now particularly well documented, thanks to the discovery of parts of the manuscript in Munich in 2006. The documents show the development of Hitler's ideology during these important months. They prove, for example, that he integrated his anti-Semitic agenda into a broader racist ideology relatively late in the writing process, and that he did not use the key term *Lebensraum* (living space) before 1924 (Beierl and Plöckinger 2009: 290–94).

After his release from prison in December 1924 Hitler was eager to publish his book. However, since he was forbidden to speak in public in Bavaria and

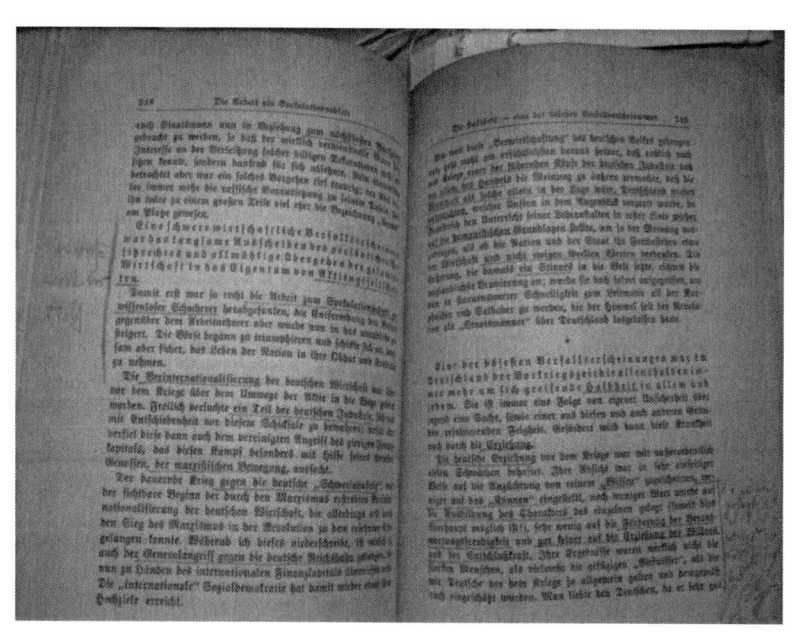

Figure 10.1 Heinrich Himmler's personal copy of *Mein Kampf* Vol. 2 by Adolf Hitler, 1927
Source: Anonymous donation in special honor of the girl in the red coat, Museum of Jewish Heritage—A Living Memorial to the Holocaust, New York.

since the question of his citizenship was still open, it was decided in spring 1925 that the book would not be published in its existing form. Instead, it was divided into two parts, and all critical passages about recent Bavarian and German politics were removed. After these major changes, a rather purified version was published as Volume One in July of 1925 (Plöckinger 2006: 67–68, 76–78). Since this first volume was a big success, a second edition was published only a few months later. Nevertheless, although many newspapers and magazines reviewed the book, the second volume, released after several postponements at the end of 1926, was not able to attract as much interest as the

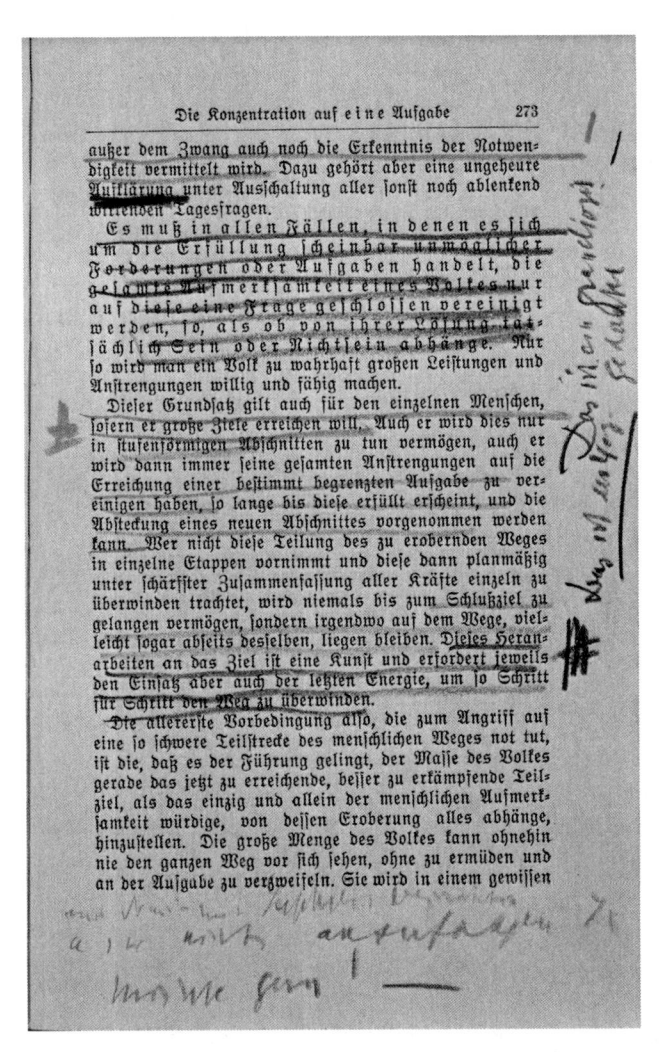

Figure 10.2 Gerhard Hauptmann's personal copy of *Mein Kampf*
Source: Staatsbibliothek zu Berlin—Preußischer Kulturbesitz, Berlin; © bpk—Bildagentur für Kunst, Kultur, und Geschichte

first one did. This may have been due to the fact that Hitler did not yet play a significant role in German politics at that time. That changed after 1929, however, and interest in his book immediately increased, as can be seen from the examples of a number of influential readers: Heinrich Himmler, later the notorious chief of the SS and the German police, studied *Mein Kampf* very carefully after the release of the two volumes, as his copy which is now held at the Museum of Jewish Heritage in New York, clearly shows. Even Himmler's father Gebhard, headmaster of a *Gymnasium* in Munich and the former educator of the princes of Wittelsbach (the family of the kings of Bavaria until 1918), borrowed the book from his son to read it in the early 1930s. Judging by his comments in the margins, this representative of the national-conservative elite in Bavaria seems to have been quite taken by the book and its author (Plöckinger 2009: 177). Another interesting example is Gerhard Hauptmann, the well-known author and winner of the Nobel Prize for literature in 1912.

Hauptmann also read the book with great interest in 1933, as can be seen by the numerous remarks and comments he made on several pages of his copy, now held at the *Staatsbibliothek* in Berlin. Not only private individuals, but also public authorities seem to have given a great deal of attention to Hitler's book during those years. Numerous state institutions from the Foreign Ministry to the police headquarters in Berlin wrote reports and memoranda about Hitler and the Nazis, wherein they analyzed *Mein Kampf* from different points of view. The last one, written by the Prussian Ministry of the Interior in spring 1932, ran more than 200 pages and issued a strong warning about the Nazi party in general and Hitler in particular (Plöckinger 2006: 214–24).

Thus, contrary to the widely published notion that *Mein Kampf* received little attention when it first came out, we must conclude that Hitler's book was read widely and his dangerous ideology was recognized to a remarkable extent long before he held any position of power. Until the beginning of 1933, about 241,000 copies were sold in Germany, starting with a leap in sales in the spring of 1930—months before the Nazi party celebrated its first big electoral successes.

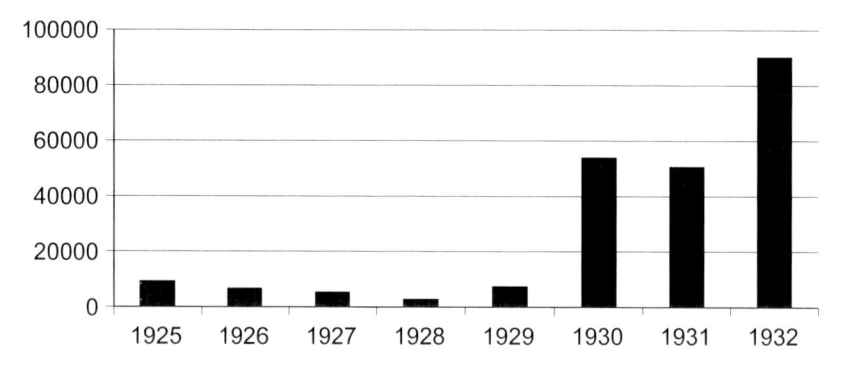

Figure 10.3 Number of copies sold of *Mein Kampf* in Germany 1925–32

In 1933 the interest in the book increased extraordinarily, but already the following year showed almost as significant a decline. The most surprising finding is that during the war years sales figures ended up being highest: about two-thirds of all copies of the book were sold between 1939 and 1944 (Plöckinger 2006: 173–88).

The book's success spread to foreign countries, too, for example to the US, where a license for a translation of the book was sold to the Boston publishing house Houghton Mifflin in 1933 (Plöckinger 2006: 461–64), which is why copies of *Mein Kampf* can be bought legally in English-speaking countries today. Indeed, the English translation received a significant amount of attention in the US in spite of, or perhaps thanks to, its abridged form. Reviews and excerpts were published in several newspapers, as for example in *The New York Times* in October of 1933 (*The New York Times* 1933).

However, in the US there was also a great deal of criticism, even protests against the publication of the book, mainly from Jewish organizations, as a letter from Houghton Mifflin to President Roosevelt indicates:

> In confidence I may add that we have had no end of trouble over the book—protests from the Jews by the hundred, and not all of them from the common run of shad. Such prominent citizens as Louis Kirstein and Samuel Untermeyer and others have added their protest, although I am glad to say that a number of intellectual Jews have also written complimenting us upon the stand we have taken.
>
> (Houghton Mifflin 1933)

The President himself seems to have had reservations vis-à-vis the translated version of the book, and was clearly aware of its significance. He noted in his copy, available today at the Franklin D. Roosevelt Library in New York: "This translation is so expurgated as to give a wholly false view of what Hitler really is or says—the German original would make a different story."

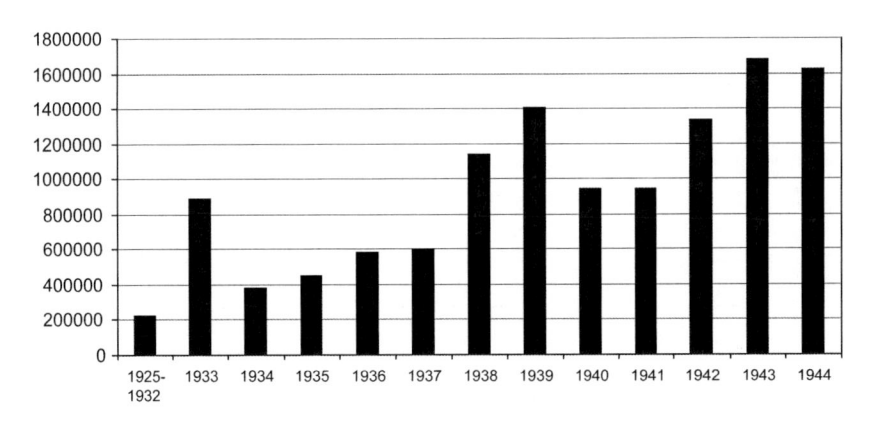

Figure 10.4 Number of copies sold of *Mein Kampf* in Germany 1925–44

Discussions about *Mein Kampf* after 1945

After the war the American authorities transferred ownership of the Nazi party's central publishing house Franz-Eher & Nachfolger to the state of Bavaria. The Bavarian state also became the administrator of Adolf Hitler's estate and therefore owner of the copyright for *Mein Kampf*. Up to the present day that has been the legal instrument of the Bavarian Ministry of Finance to prevent and prosecute new editions of the book all around the world. Two main motivations support these efforts: in the first place, the authorities wish to respect the feelings of victims of Nazi terror who might be offended if *Mein Kampf* were to be republished with official German approval; in turn, this would very likely hurt the country's international reputation. Officials have also striven to prevent individual publishing houses or specific political groups from profiting financially or politically from the book. However, since the 1990s the efforts of the Bavarian Ministry of Finance to restrict access to the text have become more and more ineffective due in large part to the Internet.

It was the myths and legends that mainly motivated the first post-war German President Theodor Heuss to demand a new edition of *Mein Kampf* in 1959. As a young member of the *Reichstag* in Berlin (the parliament of the Weimar Republic), he had written a very successful book about Hitler in 1932 entitled *Hitlers Weg* (Hitler's Path), in which he presented a careful critical analysis of *Mein Kampf*. As president after 1945 he continued to be dedicated to the idea of full disclosure about the origins and the history of National Socialism. Thus he believed the engagement with Hitler's book would have an educational effect on German post-war society by demonstrating the fact that Hitler had formulated his political and ideological attitudes quite openly in his book for everyone to see. However, Heuss failed to convince other institutions, particularly the Bavarian Ministry of Finance and the Foreign Ministry in Bonn. In addition to the reasons mentioned above they were also afraid of the propagandistic benefits the communist regime in the German Democratic Republic (GDR) could have derived from seeing a new edition of the foundational work of Nazi ideology officially published in what was in their eyes the "fascist" enemy in Western Germany.

Heuss's was the first of several failed attempts at preventing the book from growing into a powerful Nazi symbol. Instead the book became more and more coveted for ideological reasons, proven by the fact that in German library collections, which had kept copies of the book in the first years after the war, there are only a few copies left today. For example, the City Library of Munich had owned around 80 copies in 1950, 74 of which have since been stolen, the large majority of them in recent decades.

Mein Kampf and the extreme right today

Many of the stolen copies have likely found their way into the hands of old and new right-wing extremists. In 1979 the *Bundesgerichtshof* (the German equivalent to the US Supreme Court) ruled that the possession and sale of copies of *Mein Kampf* that were produced before 1945 was not illegal. From this time forward old copies of *Mein Kampf* began to surface openly in second-hand bookstores and were treated as sacred relics among neo-Nazis. In the 1970s the first and largest militant right-wing organization, the *Wehrsportgruppe Hoffmann*, was quite influential in the neo-Nazi scene, but links to Hitler and *Mein Kampf* were rare in the group (Fromm 1998: 489–90).[1] This remained unchanged in the successor organizations in the 1980s (*Wehrsportgruppe Hoffmann* was banned in 1980) (Fromm 1998: 470). Even in the early 1990s Hitler's book had only little relevance for small radical groups. It was the ideological basis for the *Gesinnungsgemeinschaft der Neuen Front* (Mecklenburg 1996: 270) and its leader Michael Kühnen, as well as for the US-based *Nationalsozialistische Deutsche Arbeiterpartei/Auslands-und Aufbauorganisation* (NSDAP/AO) led by Garry Lauck (Mecklenburg 1996: 298). The most important legal right-wing extremist party in Germany today, however, the *Nationaldemokratische Partei Deutschlands* (NPD), carefully avoids any connection to Hitler and his book. The party's lawyers know that any association with Hitler memorabilia would risk an official ban. Instead, the party platform focuses on contemporary issues such as anti-foreigner and anti-European Union (EU) sentiments (Hoffmann 1999: 276). The NPD learned from its predecessor *Sozialistische Reichspartei* (SRP), which openly presented itself as the heir to the old Nazi party and was outlawed in 1952 (Hansen 2007: 9, 112–15). Since the mid-1990s many members of outlawed neo-Nazi organizations have joined the NPD and criticized its approach, but the NPD maintains its strategy to protect its legal status (Botsch and Kopke 2009: 39–42). Open references to *Mein Kampf* are therefore quite rare in the political spectrum. The book continues to play a role, however, among neo-Nazis and other right-wing extremist groups such as, for example, the *Reichsbürgerbewegung* of Horst Mahler or the so-called *Freie Kameradschaften* (free comradeships), which are loosely connected autonomous groups. For the members of these groups to possess a copy of *Mein Kampf* is of symbolic significance. For this reason a so-called "jubilee edition" or "resistance edition" of the text illegally produced in Denmark for the German market in 1989, the centenary of Hitler, became popular among neo-Nazis. Ironically, there is serious doubt among experts about whether the book is actually read by its new owners. Historical and educational institutions in Germany and Austria dealing with the organization and subculture of neo-Nazi groups report that the book is seldom mentioned or discussed in these circles. It seems fair to conclude that the importance of *Mein Kampf* for extreme right-wing groups is indeed limited to the symbolic realm.[2] This does not mean, however, that it is not influential. The symbolic significance of the book becomes noticeable in the linkage of *Mein Kampf* with the *Koran* since the terrorist attacks on September 11, 2001.[3] In demonstrations as well as in political discussions the linkage between the two books nowadays is used either to call for the legalization of Hitler's book or for the ban of the *Koran*, as for instance by the right-wing populist Geert Wilders in the Netherlands.

Wilders's spectacular statements in 2007 led to court proceedings and brought him much notoriety.[4] They also found widespread resonance in the right-wing Internet community as far away as in the US, for example, on the pages of such organizations as *Militant Islam Monitor* or *Prophet of Doom*.[5] However, it would be too simple to equate the ideological impact of the use of these books, because the extreme right is divided (not only) in its attitude towards Islam and Arab nationalism—for example there are supporters of Arabs fighting Israel and there are supporters of Israel as an enemy of Islam. It is for these reasons that *Mein Kampf* has become quite popular in other European countries.[6] Since the end of the communist regimes in Eastern Europe, editions of *Mein Kampf* can be found in almost every country of that region, mostly printed and sold illegally. The rebirth of nationalism gave way to its extremist shape in racist movements which directly or implicitly link to fascist traditions of the 1930s and 1940s. Not only the ideological content of *Mein Kampf* but also the authoritarian structure of politics and government with a "Führer" as central figure presented in the book seem to be of interest. That is why even in Russia an edition was published in 1992, and it took until March 2010 to ban it.[7] In Turkey several publishing houses jointly published *Mein Kampf* illegally in 2004—and the book even made it onto the Turkish best-seller list.[8] It was banned two years later in response to legal action on the part of the Bavarian state, which used its copyright to try to control the spread of new editions.[9]

Problems of the scholarly edition

All those recent publications show how difficult it has become for the Bavarian state to control the circulation of *Mein Kampf*, not to speak of the several Internet platforms where the book can be downloaded in numerous languages. That is why the discussion about how best to deal with the text has become more and more intense during the last 10 years, especially in light of the upcoming end of the copyright in 2015—70 years after Hitler's suicide in his bunker in Berlin. There is the danger that after 2015 publishing houses will try to re-publish the book for financial or even ideological gains in Germany itself and abroad. That is why historians are demanding a scholarly edition now. Most agree that *Mein Kampf* is an important source for the analysis of both National Socialism and Hitler's ideology. A minority claims that there are more than enough sources on Hitler and National Socialism, and that it would make no significant difference whether *Mein Kampf* was to see a critical edition or not. In Germany not only most historians but also (especially younger) members of the Jewish community speak in favor of a scholarly edition, as for example Stefan Kramer, general secretary of the *Zentralrat der Juden in Deutschland* (Central Council of the Jews in Germany), in 2008. Even the Bavarian Minister of Science Wolfgang Heubisch said in 2009 that he would support such a project.[10] However, the Bavarian Ministry of Finance, which has to make the ultimate decision, continues to be against a scholarly edition for the same reasons mentioned above (protecting Nazi victims and

Nach Jahrzehnten im Giftschrank:

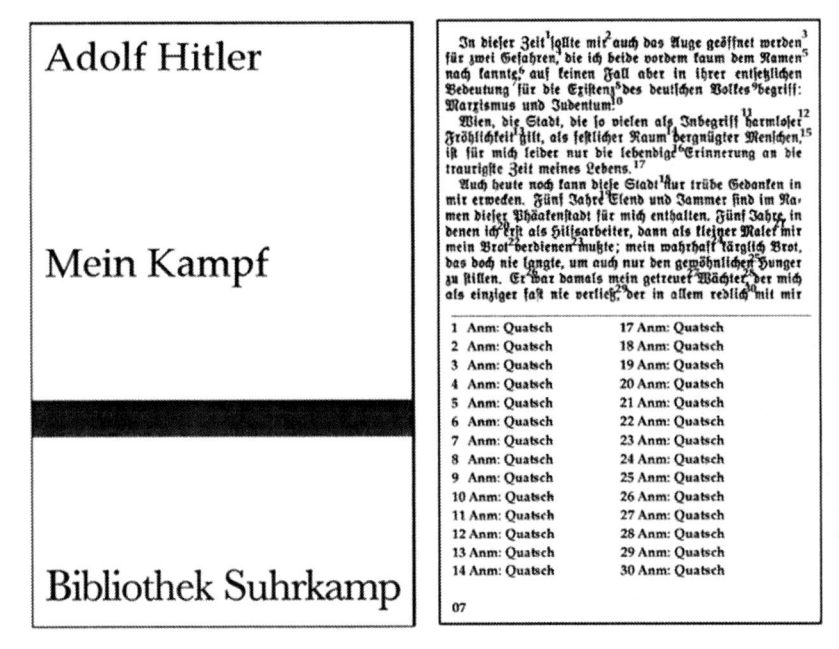

Adolf Hitler Mein Kampf Bibliothek Suhrkamp	In dieser Zeit sollte mir auch das Auge geöffnet werden für zwei Gefahren, die ich beide vordem kaum dem Namen nach kannte, auf keinen Fall aber in ihrer entsetzlichen Bedeutung für die Existenz des deutschen Volkes begriff: Marxismus und Judentum. Wien, die Stadt, die so vielen als Inbegriff harmloser Fröhlichkeit gilt, als festlicher Raum vergnügter Menschen, ist für mich leider nur die lebendige Erinnerung an die traurigste Zeit meines Lebens. Auch heute noch kann diese Stadt nur trübe Gedanken in mir erwecken. Fünf Jahre Elend und Jammer sind im Namen dieser Phäakenstadt für mich enthalten. Fünf Jahre, in denen ich erst als Hilfsarbeiter, dann als kleiner Maler mir mein Brot verdienen mußte; mein wahrhaft kärglich Brot, das doch nie langte, um auch nur den gewöhnlichen Hunger zu stillen. Er war damals mein getreuer Wächter, der mich als einziger fast nie verließ, der in allem redlich mit mir
	1 Anm: Quatsch 17 Anm: Quatsch 2 Anm: Quatsch 18 Anm: Quatsch 3 Anm: Quatsch 19 Anm: Quatsch 4 Anm: Quatsch 20 Anm: Quatsch 5 Anm: Quatsch 21 Anm: Quatsch 6 Anm: Quatsch 22 Anm: Quatsch 7 Anm: Quatsch 23 Anm: Quatsch 8 Anm: Quatsch 24 Anm: Quatsch 9 Anm: Quatsch 25 Anm: Quatsch 10 Anm: Quatsch 26 Anm: Quatsch 11 Anm: Quatsch 27 Anm: Quatsch 12 Anm: Quatsch 28 Anm: Quatsch 13 Anm: Quatsch 29 Anm: Quatsch 14 Anm: Quatsch 30 Anm: Quatsch 07

Die historisch-kritische Ausgabe kommt!

Figure 10.5 Satirical proposal for comments on *Mein Kampf* in a scholarly edition
Source: © TITANIC-online, September 8, 2009
Note: *Quatsch* = nonsense.

Germany's image abroad). Of course it does make a difference if Hitler's book is sold in bookshops in England or the US, where it has been available for the last decades, or in Germany, where it contributed to the atrocities of the Third Reich and was subsequently outlawed for decades. That is one of the main problems facing the scholarly edition project, which finally started at the *Institut für Zeitgeschichte* in Munich in the fall of 2009. The historians involved will also have to figure out how to deal with the book's content: it is practically impossible to try to correct all the lies and distortions we can find in *Mein Kampf*, as a German satire magazine noted (see Figure 10.5).[11] The edition will have to make clear that Hitler's book and its ideology belong to the past, and only by treating it this way can the symbolic relevance the book has achieved in right-wing groups in recent years be eliminated.

Notes

1 The founder of this group, Karl-Heinz Hoffmann, was referring mainly to military organizations of the pre-war time such as the *Stahlhelm* and not necessarily to Hitler's *Sturmabteilung* (SA).

2 Supporting evidence was provided by the *Dokumentationsarchiv des Österreichischen Widerstandes* (Vienna), the *Dokumentationszentrum Reichsparteitagsgelände* (Nuremberg), the *Institut für interdisziplinäre Konflikt-und Gewaltforschung* (Bielefeld), the *Mauthausen Komitee* (Vienna), as well as the *Moses Mendelsohn Zentrum* (Potsdam).
3 This comparison had already been made in the 1930s, but at that time the focus was on the importance of the book for the German people and not on its content. Several contemporaries thought that *Mein Kampf* would have the same inspiring effect on the Nazis as the *Koran* had for the Arabs centuries ago. See Plöckinger 2006: 479, 504, 553.
4 *Spiegel* Online, August 8, 2007; tagesspiegel.de, November 6, 2010. In June 2011 Wilders was acquitted. See FAZ.net, June 23, 2011.
5 See the article "Enough is Enough" from August 14, 2007 on www.militantislammonitor.org/article/id/3094 (accessed February 3, 2011), or the exuberant text on prophetofdoom.net/Prophet_of_Doom_16_Mein_Kampf.Islam (accessed February 3, 2011).
6 This is true about editions in India and Pakistan as well, where Hitler is seen as a main contributor to the independence from Great Britain and therefore has quite a positive image. In the Arab world much more attention is paid to the *Protocols of the Elders of Zion*. While in Europe only some small groups of esoterically inspired anti-Semites refer to that book, in the Arab world it is still widely viewed as an historical document for a worldwide Jewish conspiracy. That is how it found its way into the Charta of Hamas in the Gaza Strip, see avalon.law.yale.edu/20th_century/hamas.asp (accessed February 3, 2011).
7 *Spiegel* Online, March 26, 2010.
8 *The Guardian*, March 29, 2005.
9 *Die Welt*, August 23, 2007. An English edition of Hitler's book has become quite popular in India, but in contrast to non-English editions the Bavarian state has no chance to take legal action against it: Telegraph.co.uk, April 20, 2009.
10 *Die Welt*, June 30, 2009.
11 Titanic-online, August 9, 2009.

References

Beierl, Florian and Othmar Plöckinger (2009) "Neue Dokumente zu Hitlers Buch *Mein Kampf*," *Vierteljahrshefte für Zeitgeschichte* 57(2): 261–318.

Botsch, Gideon and Christoph Kopke (2009) *Die NPD und ihr Millieu. Studien und Berichte*, Münster and Ulm: Klemm & Oelschläger.

Fromm, Rainer (1998) *Die "Wehrsportgruppe Hoffmann": Darstellung, Analyse und Einordnung. Ein Beitrag zur Geschichte des deutschen und europäischen Rechtsextremismus*, Frankfurt: Peter Lang.

Hansen, Henning (2007) *Die Sozialistische Reichspartei (SRP). Aufstieg und Scheitern einer rechtsextremen Partei*, Düsseldorf: Droste.

Hoffmann, Uwe (1999) *Die NPD. Entwicklung, Ideologie und Struktur*, Frankfurt: Peter Lang.

Houghton Mifflin (1933) Letter from Houghton Mifflin publishing executive to president Roosevelt, written October 13, held in Franklin D. Roosevelt Library, New York (unidentified signature).

Kröger, Christine, Stefan Schölermann and Andrea Suhn (2008) *Rechtsabbieger. Die unterschätzte Gefahr: Neonazis in Niedersachsen*, Bremen.

Mecklenburg, Jens (ed.) (1996) *Handbuch Deutscher Rechtsextremismus*, Berlin: Elefanten Press.

The New York Times (1933) Excerpts from *Mein Kampf*, published from October 11 (The former American Ambassador to Germany James W. Gerard published a detailed review of the book in *The New York Times* on October 15, 1933, in conjunction with his review of *The Brown Book of the Hitler Terror and the Burning Reichstag*).

Plöckinger, Othmar (2006) *Geschichte eines Buches. Adolf Hitlers "Mein Kampf" 1922–1945*, München: Oldenbourg.

——(2009) "Heinrich Himmlers Privatexemplar von 'Mein Kampf' als zeitgeschichtliche Quelle," *Zeitschrift für Religions-und Geistesgeschichte* 61(2): 171–78.

Afterword

Kathleen Blee

During the 1980s and 1990s, Gary "Gerhard" Lauck, founder of the neo-Nazi *Nationalsozialistische Deutsche Arbeiterpartei/Auslands-und Aufbauorganisation* (NSDAP/AO—overseas division), produced millions of pieces of Nazi propaganda in 10 languages at his Lincoln, Nebraska headquarters. He then exported these materials to 30 countries, including Germany and other nations in which such materials were banned and difficult to access. His distribution network propelled the "Farm Belt Fuhrer" to a central role in the resurgence of neo-Nazism in late 20th-century Europe until the advent of the Internet made neo-Nazi propaganda easier to acquire across borders and undermined his business.[1] Eventually, Lauck was arrested in Denmark and extradited to Germany where he was sentenced to four years in prison. After his prison term, Lauck returned to the US and set up a web-hosting company for Germans who wanted to avoid what he termed the "political repression" and "censorship" of that nation's anti-Nazi laws.

Lauck's peculiar trajectory from small town American Nazi to a central supplier for a sprawling network of European neo-Nazis illustrates the complex international dimensions of right-wing radicalism. Far-right groups and activists in North America and Europe are linked through networks of personal ties, communications, and, in some cases, money. As the essays of this volume demonstrate, these networks shape a transatlantic far right with a surprising and troubling ideological and strategic coherence. These extremists are committed to virulent anti-Semitism, broad hatred of ethnic and racial minorities, fierce opposition to entry and citizenship rights for immigrant people of color in Europe and North America, and, for some, a belief that violence is an acceptable means to accomplish their goals. Extremists on both sides of the Atlantic also share the contradictions of modern right-wing extremism. These include a desire both to distance themselves from a Nazi past of defeat and embrace World War II-era Nazi symbols, and, for many, a simultaneous distaste for national governments and aspiration to seize state power.

Scholars increasingly see right-wing radicalism as a multi-layered enterprise and this volume moves us further in this effort. At its core, the transatlantic far right is composed of individuals and groups of true believers. To enact its extremist ideas and agendas, however, the far right must engage with mainstream populations and institutions. It thus takes advantage of political opportunities in the wider society, such as electoral openings created by economic crises, high levels of global migration, and persistent ethnic and national hostilities. The far right also depends on an influx of new recruits converted from the political mainstream who become energized by its propaganda and willing to take risks to further its goals. It relies on the organizations of standard political life, such as rightist parties, alliances, and coalitions that operate alongside more loosely affiliated groups like neo-Nazi gangs and violent racist skinheads. As this volume demonstrates, a rich understanding of right-wing radicalism requires attention to each of these distinct yet intersecting layers.

Comparison across the Atlantic provides many lessons. As the chapters in the volume show, there is an enormous variety in the organizations and types of far-right groups in Europe and the US. In some nations, the far-right emerged as a xenophobic response to immigration, especially the influx of racial, ethnic, or religious minority groups. Yet in Russia and other parts of Eastern Europe, right-wing radicalism exploded in the virtual absence of immigration. Some movements of the far right operate primarily through action, not talk, like racist skinheads who are only loosely guided by ideology and political strategy. Other parts of the far right draw from an intellectual tradition and are more deeply entrenched in ideological debates. Some are virulently nationalist; for others, the sense of the nation rests on loyalty to race rather than place.

This volume underscores the need for studies of right-wing extremism that attend to its increasingly transnational and even global nature and that explore how the far right can become integrated into mainstream populations. Effective strategies against rightist radicalism depend on understanding its broad reach within society and across national borders.

Notes

1 www.splcenter.org/get-informed/intelligence-files/profiles/gary-gerhard-lauck (accessed July 12, 2011).

Bibliography

Abanes, Richard (1998) *End-Time Visions: The Road to Armageddon?* New York, NY: Four Walls, Eight Windows.
Ahlheim, Klaus and Bardo Heger (2008) *Nation und Exklusion. Der Stolz der Deutschen und seine Nebenwirkungen*, Schwalbach/Ts.
Allen, Gary and Larry Abraham (1972 [1971]) *None Dare Call it Conspiracy*, Rossmoor, CA/Seal Beach, CA: Concord Press.
Almeida, Dimitri (2010) "Europeanized Eurosceptics? Radical Right Parties and European Integration," *Perspectives on European Politics and Society* 2(3): 237–53.
Almond, Gabriel A., R. Scott Appleby, and Emmanuel Sivan (2003) *Strong Religion: the Rise of Fundamentalisms Around the World*, Chicago: University of Chicago Press.
Alter, Peter (1997) "Kulturnation und Staatsnation—Das Ende einer langen Debatte?" in *Die Intellektuellen und die nationale Frage*, Gerd Langguth (ed.) Frankfurt am Main: Campus Verlag, 33–44.
Analytisches Zentrum Yury Levada (ed.) (2006) "Rossia dlja russkich … ?" Аналитический Центр Юрия Левады: "Россия для русских…?" [Russia to the Russians?], August 25, www.levada.ru/press/2006082500.html.
Andrews, Molly (1991) *Lifetimes of Commitment. Aging, Politics, Psychology*, Cambridge: Cambridge University Press.
Anthony, Dick and Thomas Robbins (1996) "Religious Totalism, Violence and Exemplary Dualism: Beyond the Extrinsic Model," in Michael Barkun (ed.) *Millennialism and Violence*, Cass Series on Political Violence, London: Frank Cass, 10–50.
Anti-Defamation League (2009) *Extremism in America—Louis Beam*, www.adl.org/learn/ext_us/beam.asp?LEARN_Cat=Extremism&LEARN_SubCat=Extremism_in_America&xpicked=2&item=beam.
Arena, Michael and Bruce Arrigo (2000) "White Supremacist Behavior: Toward an Integrated Social Psychological Model," *Deviant Behavior* 21(3): 213–44.
Art, David (2011) *Inside the Radical Right: The Development of Anti-Immigrant Parties in Western Europe*, Cambridge University Press.
Art, David and Dana Brown (2007) *Making and Breaking the Radical Right in Central Eastern Europe*, unpublished manuscript.
Arzheimer, Kai (2008) *Die Wähler der extremen Rechten 1980–2002*, Wiesbaden.
Aukerman, Dale (1993) *Reckoning with Apocalypse*, New York, NY: Crossroad.
Babbie, Earl (1999) *The Basics of Social Research*, Belmont CA: Wadsworth.
Backes, Uwe and Henrik Steglich (eds) (2007) *Die NPD. Erfolgsbedingungen einer rechtsextremistischen Partei*, Baden-Baden: Nomos Verlag.

Barber, Benjamin (1995) *Jihad vs. McWorld*, New York: Times Books.

Barkun, Michael (1994) *Religion and the Racist Right: the Origins of the Christian Identity Movement*, Chapel Hill, NC: University of North Carolina Press.

Barron, Bruce (1992) *Heaven on Earth? The Social & Political Agendas of Dominion Theology*, Grand Rapids, MI: Zondervan.

Beierl, Florian and Othmar Plöckinger (2009) "Neue Dokumente zu Hitlers Buch," *Mein Kampf. Vierteljahrshefte für Zeitgeschichte* 57(2): 261–318.

Bélanger, Eric and Bonnie Meguid (2008) "Issue Salience, Issue Ownership, and Issue-Based Vote Choice," *Electoral Studies* 27: 477–91.

Bennett, David H. (1995) *The Party of Fear: From Nativist Movements to the New Right in American History*, Chapel Hill, NC: University of North Carolina Press.

Berbrier, Mitch (1998) "White Supremacists and the (Pan-)Ethnic Imperative: On 'European-Americans' and 'White Student Unions'," *Sociological Inquiry* 68: 498–516.

Berezin, Mabel (2009) *Illiberal Politics in Neoliberal Times: Culture, Security and Populism in the New Europe*, Cambridge University Press.

Berlet, Chip (2005) "Christian Identity: The Apocalyptic Style, Political Religion, Palingenesis and Neo-Fascism," in Roger Griffin (ed.) *Fascism, Totalitarianism, and Political Religion*, London: Routledge, 175–210.

——(2008) "The United States: Messianism, Apocalypticism, and Political Religion," in Griffin, Feldman, and Tortice (eds) *The Sacred in Twentieth Century Politics: Essays in Honour of Professor Stanley G. Payne*, Basingstoke, UK: Palgrave Macmillan, 2008.

——(2009) "Fears of Fédéralisme in the United States: The Case of the 'North American Union' Conspiracy Theory," *Fédéralisme Régionalisme Le fédéralisme américain* 9(1), popups.ulg.ac.be/federalisme/document.php?id=786.

——(2010a) "The Roots of Anti-Obama Rhetoric," in Bruce Cunnigen (eds) *Race in the Age of Obama* (*Research in Race and Ethnic Relations*), Vol. 16, Emerald Group Publishing Ltd, 301–19.

——(2010b) "'Christian Warriors': Who are the Hutaree Militia and Where Did they Come From?" *Religion Dispatches*, tinyurl.com/apocamil.

——(2011a) "Taking Tea Parties Seriously: Corporate Globalization, Populism, and Resentment," *Perspectives on Global Development and Technology* 10(1): 11–29.

——(2011b) "How We Coined the Term 'Dominionism'," *Talk to Action*, www.talk2action.org/story/2011/8/31/17047/5683.

——(2012a) "Collectivists, Communists, Labor Bosses, and Treason: The Tea Parties as Right-Wing Populist Counter-Subversion Panic," in *Critical Sociology* 38(4): 565–87.

——(2012b) "Reframing Populist Resentments in the Tea Party," in Rosenthal and Trost (eds) *Steep: The Precipitous Rise of the Tea Party*, Berkeley: University of California Press, 47–66.

Berlet, Chip and Matthew N. Lyons (2000) *Right-Wing Populism in America: Too Close for Comfort*, New York, NY: Guilford Press.

Berlet, Chip and Stanislav Vysotsky (2006) "Overview of U.S. White Supremacist Groups," *Journal of Political and Military Sociology* 34(1): 11–48.

Betz, Hans-Georg (1994) *Radical Right-wing Populism in Western Europe*, New York, NY: St Martin's Press.

Bizeul, Daniel (2003) *Avec ceux de FN: Un sociologue au Front National*, Paris: La Découverte.

Bjorgo, Tore (ed.) (1995) *Terror from the Extreme Right*, London: Frank Cass.

Blazak, Randy (2001) "White Boys to Terrorist Men: Target Recruitment of Nazi Skinheads," *The American Behavioral Scientist* 44(6): 982–1000.

Blee, Kathleen (1992) *Women of the Klan: Racism and Gender in the 1920s*, University of California Press.
—— (2002) *Inside Organized Racism. Women in the Hate Movement*, Berkeley: University of California Press.
—— (2005) "Racial Violence in the United States," *Ethnic and Racial Studies* 28: 599–619.
Blejwas, Andrew, Anthony Griggs, and Mark Potok (2005) "Terror from the Right," *Southern Poverty Law Center. Intelligence Report* 118.
Boorstein, Michelle (2010) "For Critics of Islam, 'Sharia' Becomes Shorthand for Extremism," *The Washington Post*, August 26, www.washingtonpost.com/wp-dyn/content/article/2010/08/25/AR2010082504298.html.
Borum, Randy and Michael Gelles (2005) "Al-Qaeda's Operational Evolution: Behavioral and Organizational Perspectives," *Behavioral Sciences and the Law* 23: 467–83.
Botsch, Gideon (2011) "Die extreme Rechte als 'nationales Lager.' 'Versäulung' im lebensweltlichen Milieu oder Marsch in die Mitte der Gesellschaft?" in Christoph Kopke (ed.) *Die Grenzen der Toleranz. Rechtsextremes Milieu und demokratische Gesellschaft in Brandenburg. Bilanz und Perspektiven*, Potsdam: Universitätsverlag, 57–81.
—— (2011) "Parteipolitische Kontinuitäten der 'Nationalen Opposition.' Von der Deutschen Reichspartei zur Nationaldemokratischen Partei Deutschlands," in *Zeitschrift für Geschichtswissenschaft (ZfG)* 59: 113–37.
—— (2012) *Die extreme Rechte in der Bundesrepublik 1949 bis heute*, Darmstadt: Wissenschaftliche Buchgesellschaft.
Botsch, Gideon and Christoph Kopke (2008) "'Raumorientierte Volkswirtschaft' und 'Nationale Solidarität.' Zur wirtschafts-und sozialpolitischen Programmatik und Propaganda der NPD und ihres neo-nationalsozialistischen Umfeld," in *Bulletin für Faschismus-und Weltkriegsforschung* 31/32: 50–71.
—— (2009) *Die NPD und ihr Millieu. Studien und Berichte*, Münster/Ulm: Klemm & Oelschläger.
Boyer, Paul S. (1992) *When Time Shall Be No More: Prophecy Belief in Modern American Culture*, Cambridge, Mass.: Belknap/Harvard University Press.
—— (2003) "John Darby Meets Saddam Hussein: Foreign Policy and Bible Prophecy," *Chronicle of Higher Education*, Supplement, B10–B11 (February 14), chronicle.com/article/John-Darby-Meets-Saddam/18413.
Bozoki, Andras and John T. Ishiyama (eds) (2002) *The Communist Successor Parties of Central and Eastern Europe*, New York: M.E. Sharpe.
Brandstetter, Marc (2006) *Die NPD im 21. Jahrhundert. Eine Analyse ihrer aktuellen Situation, ihrer Erfolgsbedingungen und Aussichten*, Marburg: Tectum Verlag.
Braun, Stephan, Alexander Geisler, and Martin Gerster (eds) (2009) *Strategien der extremen Rechten. Hintergründe—Analysen—Antworten*, Wiesbaden: VS-Verlag für Sozialwissenschaften.
Brent, Sandy D. (2002) *Plowshares & Pruning Hooks: Rethinking the Language of Biblical Prophecy and Apocalyptic*, Downers Grove, IL: InterVarsity.
Breuer, Stefan (2010) *Die radikale Rechte in Deutschland 1871–1945: Eine politische Ideengeschichte*, Stuttgart: Reclam.
Brouwer, Steve, Paul Gifford, and Susan D. Rose (1996) *Exporting the American Gospel: Global Christian Fundamentalism*, New York: Routledge.
Brugge, Doug (2001 [1995]) "Pulling Up the Ladder: The Anti-Immigrant Backlash," *The Public Eye*, www.publiceye.org/ark/immigrants/PullingLadder.html.
Bundesamt für Verfassungsschutz (2009) *"Autonome Nationalisten"—Rechtsextremistische Militanz*, Cologne, www.verfassungsschutz.de.

Buruma, Ian (2011) "Europe's Turn to the Right," *The Nation*, August 29–September 5, www.thenation.com/article/162698/europes-turn-right.

Bustikova, Lenka and Herbert Kitschelt (2009) "The Radical Right in Post-Communist Europe. Comparative Perspectives on Legacies and Party Competition," *Communist and Post-Communist Studies* 42(4): 459–83.

Butterwegge, Christoph (2011) "Finanzmarktkrise, Armut und rechtsextreme Politik," in Christoph Kopke (ed.) *Die Grenzen der Toleranz. Rechtsextremes Milieu und demokratische Gesellschaft in Brandenburg. Bilanz und Perspektiven*, Potsdam: Universitätsverlag, 41–55.

Camp, Gregory S. (1997) *Selling Fear: Conspiracy Theories and End-Times Paranoia*, Grand Rapids, MI: Baker Books.

Canovan, Margaret (1981) *Populism*, New York, NY: Harcourt Brace Jovanovich.

Carter, Elisabeth (2002) "Proportional Representation and the Fortunes of Right-Wing Extremist Parties," *West European Politics* 45(3): 125–46.

Cassidy, John (2011) "Rational Irrationality," *The New Yorker* website blogs, June 28, www.newyorker.com/online/blogs/johncassidy/2011/06/bachmanns-bounce-the-view-from-brooklyn.html.

Chermak, Steven (2002) *Searching for a Demon: the Media Construction of the Militia Movement*, Boston, MA: Northeastern University Press.

Chermak, Steven and Jeff Gruenewald (2006) "The Media's Coverage of Domestic Terrorism," *Justice Quarterly* 23: 428–61.

Clemens, Dominik (2009) "Die NPD: Eine 'neue' Arbeiterpartei von rechts?" in Gebhardt and Clemens (eds) *Volksgemeinschaft statt Kapitalismus? Zur sozialen Demagogie der Neonazis*, Köln: Papyrossa Verlag.

Clement, Scott and John C. Green (2011) "The Tea Party, Religion and Social Issues," *Pew Forum on Religion & Public Life*, February 23, pewresearch.org/pubs/1903/tea-party-movement-religion-social-issues-conservative-christian.

Cohn, Norman (1970 [1957]) *The Pursuit of the Millennium: Revolutionary Millenarians and Mystical Anarchists of the Middle Ages*, revised and expanded, New York, NY: Oxford University Press.

——(1993) *Cosmos, Chaos and the World to Come: The Ancient Roots of Apocalyptic Faith*, New Haven: Yale University Press.

Cordell, Karl (ed.) (2000) *The Politics of Ethnicity in Central Europe*, New York: St Martin's Press.

Decker, Frank (ed.) (2006) *Populismus. Gefahr für die Demokratie oder nützliches Korrektiv?* Wiesbaden: Verlag für Sozialwissenschaften.

Decker, Oliver and Elmar Brähler (2008) *Bewegung in der Mitte. Rechtsextreme Einstellungen in Deutschland 2008 mit einem Vergleich von 2002 bis 2008 und der Bundesländer*, Berlin: Friedrich-Ebert-Stiftung.

Della Porta, Donatella (1995) *Social Movements, Political Violence, and the State: A Comparative Analysis of Italy and Germany*, Cambridge, UK: Cambridge University Press.

Della Porta, Donatella and Sidney Tarrow (1986) "Unwanted Children: Political Violence and the Cycle of Protest in Italy, 1966–73," *European Journal of Political Research* 14(5–6): 607–32.

Democratic Accountability Project (DAP) (2008) *Herbert Kitschelt and Phil Keefer Dataset: Project on Democratic Accountability and Citizen-Politician Linkages around the World*, Duke University and the World Bank, www.duke.edu/web/democracy.

Department of Homeland Security (2009) "Right-Wing Extremism: Current Economic and Political Climate Fueling Resurgence of Recruitment and Radicalization," unclassified report, Office of Intelligence and Analysis.

Deutsche Stimme-Verlag (ed.) (2006) *Taschenkalender des Nationalen Widerstandes 2006*, Riesa, www.ds-versand.de.

de Witte, Hans (1996) "On the 'Two Faces' of Rightwing Extremism in Belgium. Confronting the Ideology of the Extreme Rightwing Parties in Belgium with the Attitudes and Motives of their Voters," *Res Publica. Belgian Journal of Political Science* 38: 397–411.

Diamond, Sara (1989) *Spiritual Warfare: The Politics of the Christian Right*, Boston: South End Press.

——(1995) *Roads to Dominion: Right-Wing Movements and Political Power in the United States*, New York, NY: Guilford Press.

——(1998) *Not by Politics Alone: The Enduring Influence of the Christian Right*, New York, NY: Guilford Press.

Disch, Lisa (2010) "Tea Party Movement: The American 'Precariat'?" *Conference on Fractures, Alliances and Mobilizations in the Age of Obama: Emerging Analyses of the 'Tea Party Movement*, University of California at Berkeley, October 22, ccsrwm. berkeley.edu/sites/default/files/shared/docs/Disch%20paper.pdf.

Dobratz, Betty and Stephanie Shanks-Meile (2000) *White Power! White Pride!: The White Separatist Movement in the United States*, New York: Twayne Publishers.

Dobson, James and Gary L. Bauer (1990) *Children at Risk: The Battle for the Hearts and Minds of Our Kids*, Dallas: Word Publishing.

Doosje, Bertjan, Nyla R. Branscombe, Russell Spears and Antony S.R. Manstead (1998) "Guilty by Association: When One's Group Has a Negative History," *Journal of Personality and Social Psychology* 75: 872–86.

Döring, Uta (2006) "'National befreite Zonen.' Zur Entstehung und Karriere eines Kampfbegriffs," in Klärner and Kohlstruck (eds) *Moderner Rechtsextremismus in Deutschland*, 177–206.

Douglas, Mary (2007 [1966]) *Purity and Danger*, London and New York: Routledge.

Douglas, Mary and Wildavsky Aaron (1982) *Risk and Culture: An Essay on the Selection of Technological and Environmental Dangers*, University of California Press.

Dudek, Peter and Hans-Gerd Jaschke (1984) *Entstehung und Entwicklung des Rechtsextremismus in der Bundesrepublik. Zur Tradition einer besonderen politischen Kultur*, Opladen: Westdeutscher Verlag.

Duke, David (1998) *My Awakening*, Covington, LA: Free Speech Press.

Durham, Martin (2000) *The Christian Right, the Far Right, and the Boundaries of American Conservatism*, Manchester: Manchester University.

Dyer, Joel (1998) *Harvest of Rage: Why Oklahoma City is Only the Beginning*, revised, Boulder: Westview.

Eatwell, Roger (2004) "The Extreme Right in Britain: The Long Road to 'Modernization'," in Eatwell and Mudde (eds) *Western Democracies and the New Extreme Right Challenge*, London and New York, 62–80.

Ehrenreich, Barbara (1989) *Fear of Falling: The Inner Life of the Middle Class*, New York, NY: Harper Perennial.

Ekiert, Grzegorz (2006) "L'instabilité du système partisan. Le maillon faible de la consolidation démocratique en Pologne," *Pouvoirs* 118: 37–58.

Erikson, Kai (1966) *Wayward Puritans: A Study in the Sociology of Deviance*, New York: John Wiley & Sons.

Etzioni, Amitai (2005) "The Real Threat: An Essay on Samuel Huntington," *Contemporary Sociology* 34(5): 477–85.
European Network Against Racism (ENAR) (ed.) (2008) *Shadow Report 2008: Racism in Germany*.
Falter, Jürgen W., Hans-Gerd Jaschke and Jürgen R. Winkler (eds) (1996) *Rechtsextremismus. Ergebnisse und Perspektiven der Forschung*, Opladen: Westdeutscher Verlag.
Faludi, Susan (1991) *Backlash: The Undeclared War Against Women*, New York: Three Rivers Press.
Fichte, Johann Gottlieb (1979) *Der geschloßne Handelsstaat. Ein philosophischer Entwurf als Anhang zur Rechtslehre, und Probe einer künftig zu liefernden Politik, mit einem bisher unbekannten Manuskript Fichtes "Ueber StaatsWirthschaft,"* ed. Hamburg: Hans Hirsch.
Finney, Charles G. (1845) "The Church Bound to Convert the World (Concluded). Sermon," reported by J.N. Cook, *The Oberlin Evangelist*, April 23, www.gospeltruth.net/1845OE/450423_world_convertpt2.htm.
FitzGerald, Frances (1985) "The American Millennium," *The New Yorker*, 11 November, 105–96.
Flemming, Lars (2005) *Das NPD-Verbotsverfahren*, Baden-Baden.
Flynn, Kevin and Gary Gerhardt (1990) *Silent Brotherhood: The Chilling Inside Story of America's Violent, Anti-Government Militia Movement*, New York: Signet.
Freilich, Joshua D. and Steven M. Chermak (2009) "Preventing Deadly Encounters Between Law Enforcement and American Far-Rightists," *Crime Prevention Studies* 25: 141–72.
Freilich, Joshua D., Steven M. Chermak and David Caspi (2009) "Critical Events in the Life Trajectories of Domestic Extremist White Supremacist Groups: A Case Study Analysis of Four Violent Organizations," *Criminology and Public Policy* 8(3): 497–530.
Freilich, Joshua D., Jeremy A. Pienik and Gregory J. Howard (2001) "Toward Comparative Studies of the U.S. Militia Movement," *International Journal of Comparative Sociology* 42: 163–210.
Friedrich-Ebert-Stiftung (ed.) (2006) *Neue Entwicklungen des Rechtsextremismus. Internationalisierung und Entdeckung der sozialen Frage*, Berlin.
Fromm, Rainer (1998) *Die "Wehrsportgruppe Hoffmann": Darstellung, Analyse und Einordnung. Ein Beitrag zur Geschichte des deutschen und europäischen Rechtsextremismus*, Frankfurt: Peter Lang.
Frykholm, Amy Johnson (2004) *Rapture Culture: Left Behind in Evangelical America*, New York, NY: Oxford University Press.
Fuller, Robert C. (1995) *Naming the Antichrist: The History of an American Obsession*, New York, NY: Oxford University Press.
Futrell, Robert and Pete Simi (2004) "Free Spaces, Collective Identity, and the Persistence of U.S. White Power Activism," *Social Problems* 51(1): 16–42.
Gamper, Markus and Helmut Willems (2006) "Rechtsextreme Gewalt—Hintergründe, Täter und Opfer," in Heitmeyer and Schröttle (eds) *Gewalt. Beschreibungen, Analysen, Prävention*, Bonn, 439–61.
Gamson, William (1975) *The Strategy of Social Protest*, Hollywood, IL: Dorsey Press.
Gardell, Mattias (2003) *Gods of the Blood: The Pagan Revival and White Separatism*, Durham, NC: Duke University Press.
Gardner, Amy and Krissah Thompson (2010) "Tea Party Groups Battling Perceptions of Racism," *The Washington Post*, May 5.

George, Patrick (2009) "Lloyd Doggett Faces Angry Crowd at Randalls," *Austin Statesman*, August 2, www.statesman.com/blogs/content/shared-gen/blogs/austin/austin/entries/2009/08/02.

Gibney, Frank Jr. (1999) "The Kids Got in the Way," *Time Magazine, The Nation* 154(8).

Gibson, William (1994) *Warrior Dreams: Violence and Manhood in Post-Vietnam America*, New York: Hill & Wang Publisher.

Gnad, Oliver (2005) *Handbuch zur Statistik der Parlamente und Parteien in den westlichen Besatzungszonen und in der Bundesrepublik Deutschland, Vol. III: FDP sowie kleinere bürgerliche und rechte Parteien. Mitgliedschaft und Sozialstruktur 1945–1990*, Düsseldorf.

Göls, Cornelia (2009) "Die politischen Parteien in der Ukraine—(wie) funktionieren sie wirklich?" in *Ukraine-Analysen* 52: 2–7.

Goldberg, Jonah (2008) *Liberal Fascism: The Secret History of the American Left: From Mussolini to the Politics of Meaning*, New York: Doubleday.

Goldberg, Michelle (2006) *Kingdom Coming: The Rise of Christian Nationalism*, New York: W.W. Norton.

Goodwyn, Laurence B. (1978) *The Populist Moment*, Oxford, London, New York: Oxford University Press.

Gottschalk, Peter and Gabriel Greenberg (2007) *Islamophobia: Making Muslims the Enemy*, Lanham: Rowman & Littlefield.

Granovetter, Mark (1973) "The Strength of Weak Ties," *American Journal of Sociology* 78: 1360–80.

Greenberg, Jeff, Sheldon Solomon, and Tom Pyszczynski (1997) "Terror Management Theory of Self-Esteem and Cultural Worldviews: Empirical Assessments," *Advances in Experimental Social Psychology* 29: 139.

Greven, Thomas and Thomas Grumke (eds) (2006) *Globalisierter Rechtsextremismus? Die extremistische Rechte in der Ära der Globalisierung*, Wiesbaden, VS-Verlag.

Griffin, Roger (1991) *The Nature of Fascism*, New York, NY: Routledge.

Grumke, Thomas (2006) "Die transnationale Infrastruktur der extremistischen Rechten," in Greven and Grumke (eds) *Globalisierter Rechtsextremismus? Die extremistische Rechte in der Ära der Globalisierung*, Wiesbaden: VS-Verlag, 130–59.

——(2008) "Die rechtsextremistische Bewegung," in Roth and Rucht (eds) *Die Sozialen Bewegungen in Deutschland seit 1945. Ein Handbuch*, Frankfurt/M., 475–92.

——(2009) "'Sozialismus ist braun': Rechtsextremismus, die soziale Frage und Globalisierungskritik," in *Strategien der extremen Rechten. Hintergründe—Analysen—Antworten*, Wiesbaden: VS-Verlag für Sozialwissenschaften, 148–62.

Grumke, Thomas and Andreas Klärner (2006) *Rechtsextremismus, die soziale Frage und Globalisierungskritik. Eine vergleichende Studie zu Deutschland und Großbritannien seit 1990*, Berlin: Friedrich Ebert Stiftung Forum Berlin.

Grzymala-Busse, Anna (2002) *Redeeming the Communist Past*, Cambridge: Cambridge University Press.

Haines, Herbert (1984) "Black Radicalization and the Funding of Civil Rights: 1957–70," *Social Problems* 32(1): 31–43.

Hamm, Mark S. (1997) *Apocalypse in Oklahoma: Waco and Ruby Ridge Revenged*, Boston: Northeastern University Press.

——(2002) *In Bad Company: America's Terrorist Underground*, Boston: Northeastern University Press.

Hankel, Natalia, *Rechtsextremismus, Nationalismus und Fremdenfeindlichkeit in Osteuropa: Eine Vergleichende Analyse am Beispiel der Länder Russland, Ukraine*

und Polen, unpublished Master's thesis, German Police University Münster/ Germany, 2010.
Hansen, Henning (2007) *Die Sozialistische Reichspartei (SRP). Aufstieg und Scheitern einer rechtsextremen Partei*, Düsseldorf: Droste.
Harding, Susan (2004) "Imagining the Last Days: The Politics of Apocalyptic Language," in Marty and Appleby (eds) *Accounting for Fundamentalisms, The Fundamentalism Project Vol. 4*, Chicago: University of Chicago Press, 57–78.
Hartleb, Florian (2009) "Gegen Globalisierung und Demokratie. Die NPD als eine Neue Soziale Bewegung im Europäischen Kontext?" *Zeitschrift für Parlamentsfragen* 1: 96–108.
Häusler, Alexander (ed.) (2008) *Rechtspopulismus als Bürgerbewegung. Kampagnen gegen Islam und Moscheebau und kommunale Gegenstrategien*, Wiesbaden: Verlag für Sozialwissenschaften.
Heiler, Kurt (2009) "'Linke Leute von rechts.' Anmerkungen zur Karriere eines politischen Kampfbegriffs," in Gebhardt and Clemens (eds) *Volksgemeinschaft statt Kapitalismus? Zur sozialen Demagogie der Neonazis*, Köln: Papyrossa Verlag, 17–40.
Held, Joseph (ed.) (1996) *Populism in Eastern Europe. Racism, Nationalism, and Society*, Boulder, CO: East European Monographs.
Hentges, Gudrun (2004) "Das Janusgesicht der Aufklärung. Antijudaismus und Antisemitismus in der Philosophie von Kant, Fichte und Hegel," in Samuel Salzborn (ed.) *Antisemitismus—Geschichte und Gegenwart*, Giessen: Verlag für politische Bildung, Kultur, und Kommunikation, 11–32.
Hockenos, Paul (1993) *Free to Hate: The Rise of the Right in Post-Communist Eastern Europe*, New York: Routledge.
Hoffer, Eric (1951) *The True Believer: Thoughts on the Nature of Mass Movements*, NY: Harper Perennial.
Hoffman, Bruce (2006) *Inside Terrorism. Revised and Expanded Edition*, New York: Columbia University Press.
Hoffmann, Uwe (1999) *Die NPD. Entwicklung, Ideologie und Struktur*, Frankfurt am Main/New York: Peter Lang.
Informationsanalytisches Zentrum Sova (ed.) (2008) "W Moskwe idet sledstwie po delu gruppirowki nazi-skinhedow, sowerschiwschich ubijstwa po motiwu nazionalnoj nenawisti" [Investigations of a Nazi skinhead group in Moscow which has committed murders considered hate crimes], July 24, xeno.sova-center.ru/45A2A1E/ B705A18?pub_copy=on.
——(2010a) *Ubitye i tjaschelo ranenye po motiwy nenawisti: predwaritelnaja statistika MWD* [Number of victims killed and injured in hate crimes: preliminary statistic of the interior ministry], November 2, www.sova-center.ru/racism-xenophobia/publications/ 2010/02/d17966.
——(2010b) *Antiextremistskaja statistika MWD Rossii sa 2009 god* [Anti-extremist statistics from the Russian Ministry of the Interior for the year 2009], December 2, xeno.sova-center.ru/29481C8/E5CFBE0.
Ishiyama, John T. (1997) "The Sickle or the Rose?" *Comparative Political Studies* 30 (3): 299–330.
——(2009) "Historical Legacies and the Size of the Red Brown Vote in Post-Communist Politics," *Communist and Post-Communist Studies* 42(4): 485–504.
Jamin, Jérôme (2005) "The Extreme Right in Europe: Fascist or Mainstream?" *The Public Eye* 19(1), www.publiceye.org/magazine/v19n1/jamin_extreme.html.

——(2009) *L'Imaginaire du Complot: Discours d'extrême droite en France et aux Etats-Unis*, Amsterdam: University of Amsterdam.
Jaschke, Hans-Gerd (1993) "Sub-Cultural Aspects of Right-Wing Extremism," in Berg-Schlosser and Rytlweski (eds) *Political Culture in Germany*, Houndmills: Basingstoke and London, 126–36.
——(2001) *Rechtsextremismus und Fremdenfeindlichkeit. Begriffe, Positionen, Praxisfelder*, second edn, Wiesbaden: Westdeutscher Verlag.
——(2006) *Politischer Extremismus*, Wiesbaden.
Jenkins, Philip (2003) *Images of Terror: What We Can and Can't Know About Terrorism*, Edison, NJ: Aldine Transaction.
——(2008) "Home-Grown Terror: Think the Oklahoma City Bombing in 1995 was a Fluke? Think Again," *Los Angeles Times*, March 10, articles.latimes.com/2008/mar/10/opinion/oe-jenkins10.
Jenne, Erin (2007) *Ethnic Bargaining: The Paradox of Minority Empowerment*, Ithaca, NY: Cornell University Press.
Jones, David W. (2008) *Understanding Criminal Behaviour—Psychosocial Approaches to Criminality*, Devon: Willan.
Juergensmeyer, Mark (2008) *Global Rebellion—Religious Challenges to the Secular State from Christian Militias to Al Qaeda*, Berkeley: University of California Press.
Hobsbawm, Eric (1994) *The Age of Extremes. The Short Twentieth Century 1914–1991*, London.
Hoffmann, Uwe (1999) *Die NPD. Entwicklung, Ideologie und Struktur*, Frankfurt: Peter Lang.
Huntington, Samuel P. (1997) *The Clash of Civilizations and the Remaking of World Order*, New York, NY: Touchstone.
Kahrs, Horst (1992) "Von der 'Großraumwirtschaft' zur 'Neuen Ordnung'," in Götz Aly (ed.) *Modelle für ein deutsches Europa. Ökonomie und Herrschaft im Großwirtschaftsraum*, Berlin: Rotbuch Verlag, 9–28.
Kailitz, Steffen (2007a) "Das nationalsozialistische Vertreibungs-und Nationalisierungsprogramm der NPD," *Politische Studien, Themenheft* 1: 44–53.
——(2007b) "Die nationalsozialistische Ideologie der NPD," in Backes and Steglich (eds) *Die NPD. Erfolgsbedingungen einer rechtsextremistischen Partei*, Baden-Baden: Nomos Verlag, 339–53.
Kaindl, Christina (2006) "Antikapitalismus und Globalisierungskritik von rechts—Erfolgskonzepte für die extreme Rechte?" in Bathke and Spindler (eds) *Neoliberalismus und Rechtsextremismus in Europa. Zusammenhänge—Widersprüche—Gegenstrategien*, Berlin: Dietz Verlag, 60–75.
Kantrowitz, Stephen (2000) *Ben Tillman & the Reconstruction of White Supremacy*, Chapel Hill: University of North Carolina.
Kaplan, Jeffrey (1995) "Right Wing Violence in North America," in Tore Bjorgo (ed.) *Terror from the Extreme Right*, London: Frank Cass, 44–95.
Kappeler, Andreas (2009) *Kleine Geschichte der Ukraine*, third edn, München: Verlag C.H. Beck.
Kazin, Michael (1995) *The Populist Persuasion: An American History*, New York, NY: Basic Books.
Keil, Thomas J. and Jaqueline M. Keil (2011) "The Characteristics of the Congressional District and Tea Party Victories in 2010," *Ethnicity and Race in a Changing World. Review Journal*: 43–46, www.manchesteruniversitypress.co.uk/data/ip/ip021/docs/Comment_Keil.pdf.

Kelley, Judith (2004) *Ethnic Politics in Europe. The Power of Norms and Incentives*, Princeton University Press.
Kiev International Institute of Sociology (ed.) (2006) *Dumky naselennja Ukrajiny pro golodomor 1932–1933 rokiw; dynamyka xenofobiji w Ukrajini 1994–2006* [Public Opinion in Ukraine about the Famine of the years 1932–33; Development of Xenophobia in Ukraine 1994–2006], November 9, www.kiis.com.ua.
Kirchheimer, Otto (1967) "Wandlungen der politischen Opposition," in Kurt Kluxen Köln (ed.) *Parlamentarismus*, Berlin: Kiepenheuer & Witsch, 410–24.
Kissenkoetter, Udo, *Gregor Straßer und die NSDAP*, Stuttgart: Deutsche Verlags-Anstalt, 1978.
Kitschelt, Herbert (2007) "Growth and Persistence of the Radical Right in Postindustrial Democracies: Advances and Challenges in Comparative Research," *West European Politics* 30(5): 1176–206.
Kitschelt, Herbert, with Anthony McGann (1995) *The Radical Right in Western Europe: A Comparative Analysis*, Ann Arbor: University of Michigan Press.
Kitschelt, Herbert *et al.* (2008) *Democratic Accountability and Linkages Project*, Duke University, www.duke.edu/web/democracy/.
Kitschelt, Herbert, Kent Freeze, Kiril Kolev and Yi-Ting Wang (2009) "Measuring Democratic Accountability: An Initial Report on an Emerging Data Set," *Revista de Ciencia Politica* 29(3): 741–73.
Kitschelt, Herbert, Zdenka Mansfeldova, Radoslaw Markowski and Gábor Tóka (1999) *Post-communist Party Systems: Competition, Representation, and Inter-party Cooperation*, Cambridge: Cambridge University Press.
Klärner, Andreas and Michael Kohlstruck (2006) *Moderner Rechtsextremismus in Deutschland*, Hamburg.
Klandermans, Bert (1997) *The Social Psychology of Protest*, Oxford: Blackwell.
——(2003) "Collective Political Action," in Sears, Huddy, and Jervis (eds) *Oxford Handbook of Political Psychology*, Oxford: Oxford University Press, 670–709.
Klandermans, Bert and Nonna Mayer (2009) *Extreme Right Activists in Europe: Through the Magnifying Glass*, Routledge Studies in Extremism and Democracy, Amsterdam: Free University, findarticles.com/p/articles/mi_qa3719/is_200607/ai_n16855770.
Klandermans, Bert, M. Werner, and M. van Doorn (2008) "Redeeming Apartheid's Legacy: Collective Guilt, Political Ideology, and Compensation," *Political Psychology* 29: 331–50.
Klarmann, Michael (2009) "Nationalsozialismus extrem modern: Die Autonomen Nationalisten," in Gebhardt and Clemens (eds) *Volksgemeinschaft statt Kapitalismus? Zur sozialen Demagogie der Neonazis*, Köln: Papyrossa Verlag, 90–113.
Klausen, Jytte (2008) *The Islamic Challenge: Politics and Religion in Western Europe*, Oxford University Press.
Knobel, Dale T. (1996) *"America for the Americans": The Nativist Movement in the United States*, New York, NY: Twayne.
Kopecky, Petr and Cas Mudde (eds) (2002) "The Two Sides of Euroscepticism: Party Positions on European Integration in East Central Europe," *European Union Politics* 3(3): 297–326.
——(2003) *Uncivil Society? Contentious Politics in Post-Communist Europe*, London: Routledge.
Koschewnikowa, Galina (2008a) *Osen 2007: Nazistskie rejdy, russkie marschi i Putin-Stirliz* [Fall 2007: Nazi enterprises, Russian parades, and Putin-Stirliz], January 16, www.polit.ru/analytics/2008/01/16/autumn2007.html.

―― (2008b) *Radikalnyj nationalism w Rossii i protiwodejstwie emu w 2007 godu* [Radical Nationalism in Russia and the fight against it in 2007], February 7, www.sova-center.ru/racism-xenophobia/publications/2008/02/d12582.

―― (2010) *Pod snakom polititscheskogo terrora: Radikalnyj nazionalism w Rossii i protiwodejstwie emu w 2009 godu* [Under the Sign of Political Terror: Radical Nationalism and the fight against it in 2009], February 2, xeno.sova-center.ru/29481C8/E4FA706.

Kriskofski, Torsten (2009) "Intellektualisierungsbemühungen im Rechtsextremismus", in Armin Pfahl-Traughber (ed.) *Jahrbuch für Extremismus-und Terrorismusforschung*, Bonn, 125–50.

Kröger, Christine, Stefan Schölermann, and Andrea Suhn (2008) *Rechtsabbieger. Die unterschätzte Gefahr: Neonazis in Niedersachsen*, Bremen: Bremer Tageszeitung AG.

Kühnl, Reinhard (1966) *Die nationalsozialistische Linke. 1925–1930*, Meisenheim am Glan: Hain.

Kühnl, Reinhard, Rainer Rilling and Christine Sager (1969) *Die NPD. Struktur, Ideologie und Funktion einer neofaschistischen Partei*, Frankfurt a.M.: Suhrkamp.

Kupferberg, Feiwel (1998) *The Break-Up of Communism in East Germany and East Europe*, Basingstoke: Palgrave Macmillan.

Kurth, James (2011) "A Tale of Four Crises: The Politics of Great Depressions and Recessions," *Orbis*: 500–23, www.fpri.org/orbis/5503/kurth.fourcrises.pdf.

Kuzio, Taras (2009) "Populism in Ukraine in Comparative European Context," *Association for the Study of Nationalities Conference*, Columbia University, April 24.

Lagrou, P. (2000) *The Legacy of Nazi Occupation. Patriotic Memory and National Recovery in Western Europe, 1945–1965*, Cambridge: Cambridge University Press.

LaHaye, Tim (1975) *Revelation: Illustrated and Made Plain*, Grand Rapids, MI: Zondervan.

―― (1980) *The Battle for the Mind*, Old Tappan, NJ: Fleming H. Revell.

―― (1982) *The Battle for the Family*, Old Tappan, NJ: Fleming H. Revell.

―― (2003) "119 Million American Evangelicals in these Last Days?" *Pre-Trib Perspectives* 8(1): 3.

―― (2007) "Anti-Christ Philosophy Already Controls America and Europe," *Pre-Trib Perspectives*, February 2.

LaHaye, Tim and Jerry B. Jenkins (1995) *Left Behind: A Novel of the Earth's Last Day Vol. 1*, Wheaton, IL: Tyndale House Publishers.

Laqueur, Walter (1977) *Terrorism*, Boston: Little, Brown Publishers.

Lausberg, Michael (2010) *Die PRO-Bewegung. Geschichte, Inhalte, Strategie der "Bürgerbewegung Pro Köln" und der "Bürgerbewegung Pro NRW."* Münster: Unrast Verlag.

Levenson, Michael (2007) "Ron Paul Backers Stage Boston Tea Party, Raise Millions," *Boston Globe*, December 17, www.boston.com/news/nation/articles/2007/12/17/ron_paul_backers_stage_boston_tea_party_raise_millions.

Levitas, Daniel (2002) *The Terrorist Next Door: The Militia Movement and the Radical Right*, New York, NY: St Martin's.

Lewis, Paul G. (2009) "Party System Stabilisation in Central Europe: Records and Prospects in a Changing Socio-Economic Context," *ECPR General Conference*, Potsdam, September 10–12.

Lifton, Robert J. (2003) *Superpower Syndrome: America's Apocalyptic Confrontation with the World*, New York, NY: Thunder's Mouth Books/Nation Books.

Lindsey, Hal and C.C. Carlson (1970) *The Late Great Planet Earth*, Grand Rapids, MI: Zondervan.

Lubbers, Marcel (2001) *Exclusionistic Electorates: Extreme Right-Wing Voting in Western Europe*, PhD dissertation, Catholic University, Nijmegen.

Madloch, Norbert (1994) "Zur Rezeption der Strasser-Ideologie im deutschen Neonazismus," in Kurt Gossweiler (ed.) *Die Strasser-Legende. Auseinandersetzung mit einem Kapitel des deutschen Faschismus*, Berlin: Edition Ost, 128–43.

Macgerle, Anton (2004) *Globalisierung aus Sicht der extremen Rechten*, Braunschweig: Bildungsvereinigung Arbeit und Leben Niedersachsen Ost.

——(2006) *Rechte und Rechtsextreme im Hartz IV-Protest*, Braunschweig: Bildungsvereinigung Arbeit und Leben Niedersachsen Ost.

Maier, Hans and Hermann Bott (2006) *Die NPD. Struktur und Ideologie einer "nationalen Rechtspartei,"* München: R. Piper & Co.

Mareš, Miroslav (2009) "The Extreme Right in Eastern Europe and Territorial Issues," *Central European Political Studies Review* 11(2–3): 82–106.

Marsden, George M. (1991) *Understanding Fundamentalism and Evangelicalism*, Grand Rapids, MI: William B. Eerdmans Publishing Co.

Martin, William (1996) *With God on Our Side: The Rise of the Religious Right in America*, New York: Broadway Books.

——(1999) "The Christian Right and American Foreign Policy," *Foreign Policy* 114: 219–22.

McAdam, Doug (1999 [1982]) *Political Process and the Development of Black Insurgency*, Chicago: University of Chicago Press.

McAdam, Doug, Sidney Tarrow, and Charles Tilly (2001) *Dynamics of Contention*, Cambridge University Press.

McCauley, Clark and Sophia Moskalenko (2011) *Friction: How Radicalization Happens to Them and Us*, Oxford University Press.

McCurrie, Thomas (1998) "White Racist Extremist Gang Members: A Behavioral Profile," *Journal of Gang Research* 5: 51–60.

McDonald, Andrew (William Pierce) (1989 [1978]) *The Turner Diaries*, Hillsboro, WV: National Vanguard Books.

McMath, Robert C. Jr. (1995) "Populism in Two Countries: Agrarian Protest in the Great Plains and Prairie Provinces," *Agricultural History* 69(4): 517–47.

McNicol Stock, Catherine (1996) *Rural Radicals: Righteous Rage in the American Grain*, Ithaca, NY: Cornell University Press.

McVeigh, Rory (2009) *The Rise of the Ku Klux Klan. Right-Wing Movements and National Politics*, Minneapolis: University of Minnesota Press.

Mecklenburg, Jens (ed.) (1996) *Handbuch Deutscher Rechtsextremismus*, Berlin: Elefanten Press.

Meguid, Bonnie (2005) "Competition between Unequals: The Role of Mainstream Party Strategy in Niche Party Success," *American Political Science Review* 99(3): 347–59.

Menhorn, Christian (2009/2010) "Dic Erosion der Skinhead-Bewegung als eigenständiger Subkultur," in Armin Pfahl-Traughber (ed.) *Jahrbuch für Extremismus-und Terrorismusforschung*, Bonn, 125–50.

Merkel, Wolfgang (2009) "Gegen alle Theorie?—Die Konsolidierung der Demokratie in Ostmitteleuropa," in Backes, Jaskulowski and Polses (eds) *Totalitarismus und Transformation: Defizite der Demokratiekonsolidierung in Mittel- und Osteuropa*, Göttingen: Vandenhoeck & Ruprecht, 27–48.

——(2010) *Systemtransformation: Eine Einführung in die Theorie und Empirie der Transformationsforschung*, second edn, Wiesbaden: VS Verlag für Sozialwissenschaften.

Bibliography

Michael, George (2003) *Confronting Right-Wing Extremism and Terrorism in the USA*, London and New York: Routledge.

Miller-Idriss, Cynthia (2009) *Blood and Culture. Youth, Right-Wing Extremism, and National Belonging in Contemporary Germany*, Duke University Press.

Ministry of the Interior (Germany) (ed.) (2009) *Annual Report on the Protection of the Constitution*, Berlin.

Ministry of the Interior (Russia) (ed.) (2009a) *Interview Ministra wnutrennich del Rossijskoj Federazii generala armii Raschida Nurgaliewa* [Interview with the Minister of the Interior of the Russian Federation Army General Raschid Nurgaliew], May 22, www.mvd.ru/press/interview/6485.

——*Sostojanie prestupnosti w Rossijskoj Federazii sa dekabr 2009* [Crime Statistics for December 2009b], www.mvd.ru/files/AauTOcPxyhbg2fK.pdf.

——(2010) *Interview natschalnika Departamenta po protiwodejstwiju extremismu MWD Rossii general-polkownika milizii Juria Kokowa* [Interview with the Head of the Department for the fight against extremism at the Interior Ministry of Russia, General Lieutenant of the Militia Jurij Kokow], January 25, www.mvd.ru/press/interview/7347.

Ministry of the Interior (Ukraine) (ed.) (2010) *Stan ta struktura slotschunnosti w Ukrajini 2009* [Crime Statistic 2009], mvs.gov.ua/mvs/control/main/uk/publish/control/main/uk/publish/article/233004.

Minkenberg, Michael (1998) *Die neue radikale Rechte im Vergleich. USA, Frankreich, Deutschland*, Opladen: Westdeutscher Verlag.

——(2002a) "Rechtsradikalismus in Mittel-und Osteuropa nach 1989," in Grumke and Wagner (eds) *Handbuch Rechtsradikalismus. Personen, Organisationen, Netzwerke vom Neonazismus bis in die Mitte der Gesellschaft*, Opladen: Leske + Budrich, 61–74.

——(2002b) "The Radical Right in Postsocialist Central and Eastern Europe: Comparative Observations and Interpretations," *East European Politics and Society* 16 (2): 335–62.

——(2009) "Leninist Beneficiaries? Pre-1989 Legacies and the Radical Right in Post-1989 Central and Eastern Europe. Some Introductory Observations," *Communist and Post-Communist Studies* 42(4): 445–58.

Moscow Office for Human Rights (ed.) (2002) *Ultraprawyj terrorism. Wtoraja Wolna* [Ultra-right Terrorism Second Wave], antirasizm.ru/index.php/publications?ff64eda6be7c8c0a513b4f753d39ad99=ef709bc1b8a1c1e8daeaecd05f42943d.

——(2006) *Rasism, xenofobia, antisemitism, etnitscheskaja diskriminazia w Rossijskoj Federazii w 2005 godu* [Racism, Xenophobia, Antisemitism, ethnic Discrimination in the Russian Federation in the year 2005], antirasizm.ru/index.php/publications?ff64eda6be7c8c0a513b4f753d39ad99=ef709bc1b8a1c1e8daeaecd05f42943d.

——(2008) *Kratkij obsor projawlenij agressiwnoj xenofobii na territorii Rossijskoj Federazii w 2007 godu* [Short Description of the Phenomenon of Aggressive Xenophobia on the Territory of the Russian Federation in the year 2007], antirasizm.ru/index.php/publications?ff64eda6be7c8c0a513b4f753d39ad99=ef709bc1b8a1c1e8daeaecd05f42943d.

Mudde, Cas (2000) *The Ideology of the Extreme Right*, Manchester, UK: Manchester University Press.

——(2005) *Racist Extremism in Central and Eastern Europe*, London: Routledge.

——(2007) *Populist Radical Right Parties in Europe*, Cambridge, UK: Cambridge University Press.

Newton, Michael and Judy Ann Newton (1991) *Racial and Religious Violence in America: A Chronology*, New York: Garland Publishers.
Noble, Kerry (1998) *Tabernacle of Hate*, Prescott, Ontario, Canada: Voyageur.
Norris, Pippa (2005) *Radical Right. Voters and Parties in the Electoral Market*, Cambridge: Cambridge University Press.
Northcott, Michael (2004) *An Angel Directs The Storm: Apocalyptic Religion & American Empire*, London: I.B. Tauris.
NPD (ed.) (2006) *Argumente für Kandidaten & Funktionsträger. Eine Handreichung für die öffentliche Auseinandersetzung*, Berlin.
Oberschall, Anthony (2004) "Explaining Terrorism: The Contribution of Collective Action Theory," *Sociological Theory* 22: 26–37.
O'Dwyer, Conor and Katrina Schwartz (2010) "Minority Rights After EU Enlargement: A Comparison of Antigay Politics in Poland and Latvia," *Comparative European Politics* 8(2): 220–43.
Ohlemacher, Thomas (1994) "Schmerzhafte Episoden. Wider die Rede von einer rechten Bewegung im wiedervereinigten Deutschland," *Forschungsjournal Neue Soziale Bewegungen* 4(7): 16–25.
O'Leary, Stephen D. (1994) *Arguing the Apocalypse: A Theory of Millennial Rhetoric*, New York, NY: Oxford University Press.
Olzak, Susan (1992) *The Dynamic of Ethnic Competition and Conflict*, Stanford University Press.
Opp, Karl-Dieter (1988) "Grievances and Participation in Social Movements," *American Sociological Review* 53: 853–64.
Osborn, Andrew (2005) "Violence and Hatred in Russia's New Skinhead Playground," *The Independent*, January 25, www.independent.co.uk/news/world/europe/violence-and-hatred-in-russias-new-skinhead-playground-488154.html.
Ost, David (2005) *The Defeat of Solidarity. Anger and Politics in Postcommunist Europe*, Cornell University Press.
Panina, Natalia (2005) "Faktory nazionalnoj identitschnosti, tolerantnosti, xenofobii i antisemitisma w sowremennoj Ukraine" [Factors of National Identity, Tolerance, Xenophobia, and Antisemitism], in *Soziologia: Teoria, Metody, Marketing* 4: 26–45.
Parker, Christopher (2010) *Multi-State Survey on Race & Politics*, Seattle, WA: University of Washington, Institute for the Study of Ethnicity, Race and Sexuality, depts.washington.edu/uwiser/racepolitics.html.
Payne, Stanley G. (1996) *A History of Fascism, 1914–45*, London/New York: Routledge.
Perea, Juan F. (1997) *Immigrants Out! The New Nativism and the Anti-Immigrant Impulse in the United States*, New York, NY: New York University Press.
Peters, Jürgen and Christoph Schulze (eds) (2009) *"Autonome Nationalisten." Die Modernisierung neofaschistischer Jugendkultur*, Münster: Unrast.
Pfahl-Traughber, Armin (2001) "Aufklärung und Antisemitismus. Kants, Lessings und Fichtes Auffassungen zu den Juden," *Tribüne. Zeitschrift zum Verständnis des Judentums* 40: 168–81.
——(2006) "Globalisierung als Agitationsthema des organisierten Rechtsextremismus in Deutschland," in Greven and Grumke (eds) *Globalisierter Rechtsextremismus? Die extremistische Rechte in der Ära der Globalisierung*, Wiesbaden: VS-Verlag, 30–51.
Pfeiffer, Christian (2009) *Young People in Germany as Victims and Perpetrators of Violence*, Lower Saxony Criminological Research Institute.
Philippsberg, Robert (2009) *Die Strategie der NPD. Regionale Umsetzung in Ost-und Westdeutschland*, Baden-Baden: Nomos Verlag.

188 Bibliography

Plöckinger, Othmar (2006) *Geschichte eines Buches. Adolf Hitlers "Mein Kampf" 1922–1945*, München: Oldenbourg.

——(2009) "Heinrich Himmlers Privatexemplar von *Mein Kampf* als zeitgeschichtliche Quelle," *Zeitschrift für Religions-und Geistesgeschichte* 61(2): 171–78.

Pop-Eleches, Grigore (2010) "Throwing Out the Bums: Protest Voting and Anti-Establishment Parties after Communism," *World Politics* 62(2): 221–60.

Postone, Moishe (1986) "Anti-Semitism and National Socialism," in Rabinbach and Zipes (eds) *Germans & Jews Since the Holocaust: The Changing Situation in West Germany*, New York, NY: Homes & Meier.

Potok, Mark (2004) "The American Radical Right: The 1990s and Beyond," in Eatwell and Mudde (eds) *Western Democracies and the New Extreme Right Challenge*, London and New York: Routledge, 41–61.

——(2010) "Rage on the Right: The Year in Hate and Extremism," *Intelligence Report, Southern Poverty Law Center* 137, www.splcenter.org/get-informed/intelligence-report/browse-all-issues/2010/spring/rage-on-the-right.

Rabitz, Cornelia (2007) "Gelenkte Demokratie—gelenkte Medien. Beobachtungen im russischen Wahlkampf," *Russland-Analysen* 147: 2–4.

Racius, Egdunas (2010) "The Place of Islamophobia among the Radical Lithuanian Nationalists—The Neglected Priority?" Paper presented at the Conference *Far Right Networks in Northern and Eastern Europe*, Uppsala University, March 25–27.

Ramet, Sabrina (ed.) (1999) *The Radical Right in Central and Eastern Europe Since 1989*, Pennsylvania State University Press.

Rechel, Bernd (ed.) (2009) *Minority Rights in Central and Eastern Europe*, Oxford: Taylor and Francis.

Rehse, Sebastian (2008) *Die Oppositionsrolle rechtsextremer Protestparteien. Zwischen Anpassung und Konfrontation in Brandenburg und Sachsen*, Baden-Baden: Nomos.

Richter, Karl (2002) "Der Chaoskanzler," *Opposition* 1(5): 1.

Röhr, Werner and Brigitte Berlekamp (eds) (1996) *"Neuordnung Europas." Vorträge vor der Berliner Gesellschaft für Faschismus-und Weltkriegsforschung 1992–1996*, Berlin: Edition Organon.

Ross, Jeffrey and Ted Gurr (1989) "Why Terrorism Subsides: A Comparative Study of Canada and the United States," *Comparative Politics* 21(4): 405–26.

Roth, S. (2003) *Building Movement Bridges. The Coalition of Labor Union Women*, Westport: Praeger.

Rothschild, Joseph and Nancy M. Wingfield (2000) *Return to Diversity. A Political History of East Central Europe Since World War II*, third edn, Oxford: Oxford University Press.

Ruchniewicz, Krzysztof (2005) "Die historische Erinnerung in Polen," *APuZ* 5–6: 18–26.

Rydgren, Jens (2005) "Is Extreme Right-Wing Populism Contagious? Explaining the Emergence of a New Party Family," *European Journal of Political Research* 44(3): 413–37.

Sageman, Marc (2004) *Understanding Terror Networks*, Philadelphia, PA: University of Pennsylvania Press.

Saideman, Stephen (2001) *The Ties that Divide: Ethnic Politics, Foreign Policy, and International Conflict*, New York: Columbia Press.

Scharenberg, Albert (2003) "Plädoyer für eine Mehrebenenanalyse des Rechtsextremismus," *Deutschland Archiv* 4: 659–72.

Schedler, Jan (2009) "Übernahme von Ästhetik und Aktionsformen der radikalen Linken. Zur Verortung der 'Autonomen Nationalisten' im extrem rechten Strategiespektrum," in Stephan Braun, Alexander Geisler and Martin Gerster (eds) *Strategien der extremen Rechten. Hintergründe—Analysen—Antworten*, Wiesbaden: VS-Verlag für Sozialwissenschaften, 332–57.

Schedler, Jan and Alexander Häusler (eds) (2011) *Autonome Nationalisten. Neonazismus in Bewegung*, Wiesbaden.

Scheuch, Erwin K. and Hans-Dieter Klingemann (1967) "Theorie des Rechtsradikalismus in westlichen Industriegesellschaften," in *Hamburger Jahrbuch für Wirtschafts-und Gesellschaftspolitik* 12: 11–29.

Schmid, Alex P. and A.J. Jongman (2005) *Political Terrorism: A New Guide to Actors, Authors, Concepts, Data Bases, Theories, and Literature*, Transaction Publishers.

Schmollinger, Horst W. (1986) "Nationaldemokratische Partei Deutschlands," in Richard Stöss (ed.) *Parteien Handbuch. Die Parteien der Bundesrepublik Deutschland 1945–1980*, Opladen, Vol. 4: NDP-WAV, 1922–94.

Schulze, Christoph (2009) "Das Viersäulenkonzept der NPD," in Stephan Braun, Alexander Geisler, and Martin Gerster (eds) *Strategien der extremen Rechten. Hintergründe—Analysen—Antworten*, Wiesbaden: VS-Verlag für Sozialwissenschaften, 92–108.

Shafir, Michael (2008) "Rotten Apples, Bitter Pears: An Updated Motivational Typology of Romania's Radical Right's Anti-Semitic Post-Communism," *Journal for the Study of Religions and Ideologies* 7, no. 21 (Winter): 149–87.

Simi, Pete (2008) "Recruitment among Right-Wing Terrorist Groups," *National Institute of Justice. Final Report. (2006-IJ-CX-0027)*.

——(2010) "Why Study White Supremacist Terror? A Research Note," *Deviant Behavior: An Interdisciplinary Journal* 31: 251–73.

Simi, Pete, Andy Bringuel, Steven Chermak, Joshua Freilich, and Gary LaFree (2010) "Defining Lone Wolf Terrorism: A Research Note," in *Terrorism, Research, and Analysis Protocol (TRAP): A Collection of Thoughts, Ideas, and Perspectives*, Washington, DC: Department of Justice, Federal Bureau of Investigation.

Simi, Pete and Robert Futrell (2010) *American Swastika: Inside the White Power Movement's Hidden Spaces of Hate*, Lanham, MD: Rowman & Littlefield.

Simi, Pete, Lowell Smith and Ann Reeser Stacey (2008) "From Punk Kids to Public Enemy Number One," *Deviant Behavior* 29: 1–22.

Simon, Bernd and Bert Klandermans (2001) "Toward a Social Psychological Analysis of Politicized Collective Identity: Conceptualization, Antecedents, and Consequences," *American Psychologist* 56: 319–31.

Smelser, Neil J. (1962) *Theory of Collective Behavior*, New York: Free Press of Glencoe.

Smith, Brent (1994) *Terrorism in America: Pipe Bombs and Pipe Dreams*, Albany, NY: New York University Press.

Snow, David, Burke Rochford, Steven Worden, and Robert Benford (1986) "Frame Alignment Processes, Micromobilization, and Movement Participation," *American Sociological Review* 51: 464–81.

Snow, David, Louis Zurcher Jr. and Sheldon Ekland-Olson (1980) "Social Networks and Social Movements: A Microstructural Approach to Differential Recruitment," *American Sociological Review* 45: 787–801.

Sprinzak, Ehud (1995) "Right-wing Terrorism in a Comparative Perspective: The Case of Split Delegitimation," in Tore Bjorgo (ed.) *Terror from the Extreme Right*, London: Frank Cass, 1–43.

Stegbauer, Andreas (2007) "The Ban of Right-Wing Extremist Symbols According to Section 86a of the German Criminal Code," *German Law Journal* 8(2): 173–84.

Steglich, Henrik (2006) *Die NPD in Sachsen. Organisatorische Voraussetzungen ihres Wahlerfolges 2004*, Göttingen.

Steinberg, Guido (2005) *Der nahe und der ferne Feind—Die Netzwerke des islamistischen Terrorismus*, München: C.H. Beck.
Stöss, Richard (2001) "Zur Vernetzung der extremen Rechten in Europa," *Arbeitshefte aus dem Otto-Stammer-Zentrum* 5: 1–34.
——(2004) "Globalisierung und rechtsextreme Einstellungen," in Bundesministerium des Innern (ed.) *Extremismus in Deutschland*, Berlin, 82–97.
——(2010) *Rechtsextremismus im Wandel*, Berlin, www.fes-gegen-rechtsextremismus.de.
Swank, Duane and Hans-Georg Betz (2003) "Globalization, the Welfare State and Right-Wing Populism in Western Europe," *Socio-Economic Review* 1(2): 215–45.
Taggart, Paul (2004) "Populism and Representative Politics in Contemporary Europe," *Journal of Political Ideologies* 9(3): 273.
Taras, Ray (2009) *Europe Old and New: Transnationalism, Belonging, Xenophobia*, Lanham: Rowman & Littlefield.
——(2012) *Xenophobia and Islamaphobia in Europe*, Edinburgh: Edinburgh University Press.
Tarrow, Sidne (1989) *Democracy and Disorder: Protest and Politics in Italy 1965–1975*, Oxford: Clarendon Press.
——(1994) *Power in Movement: Social Movements and Contentious Politics*, Cambridge: Cambridge University Press.
Teske, Nathan (1997) *Political Activists in America. The Identity Construction Model of Political Participation*, Cambridge: Cambridge University Press.
Thieme, Tom (2007a) "Extremistische Parteien im postkommunistischen Osteuropa," *APuZ* 43: 21–26.
——(2007b) *Hammer, Sichel, Hakenkreuz. Parteipolitischer Extremismus in Osteuropa: Entstehungsbedingungen und Erscheinungsformen*, Baden-Baden: Nomos.
Thompson, Bennie (2009) *Letter to Department of Homeland Security*, 24ahead.com/bennie-thompson-dumbfounded-dhs-rightwing-extremist-report.
Thompson, Michael, Richard Ellis and Aaron Wildavsky (1990) *Cultural Theory*, Boulder, San Francisco and Oxford: Westview Press.
Tilly, Charles (1995) *Popular Contention in Great Britain, 1758–1834*, Cambridge, MA: Harvard University Press.
——(2004) "Terror, Terrorism, Terrorists," *Sociological Theory* 22(1): 5–13.
Tristan, A. (1987) *Au Front*, Paris: Gallimard.
Turchie, Terry and Kathleen Puckett (2007) *Hunting the American Terrorist: The FBI's War on Homegrown Terror*, Palisades, New York: History Publishing Company.
Turk, Austin (2004) "Sociology of Terrorism," *Annual Review of Sociology* 30: 271–86.
Vachudova, Milada Anna (2005) *Europe Undivided: Democracy, Leverage, and Integration after Communism*, Oxford: Oxford University Press.
——(2008) "Tempered by the EU? Political Parties and Party Systems before and after Accession," *Journal of European Public Policy* 15(6): 861–79.
van der Brug, Wouter, Fennema Meindert, and Jean Tillie (2005) "Why Some Anti-immigrant Parties Fail and Others Succeed: A Two-step Model of Aggregate Electoral Support," *Comparative Political Studies* 38(5): 537–73.
Vereinigung jüdischer Organisationen und Gemeinden der Ukraine (ed.) (2009) "Antisemitskije akzii i puplikazii w perioditscheskich isdanijach Ukrainy 2008 goda" [Antisemitic Actions and Publications in the Periodicals of the Ukraine in the year 2008], www.vaadua.org/News/news2009/2009-02/public2008.html.
Vetter, Reinbold (2009) "Polen fünf Jahre in der EU—wirtschaftlich ein großer Erfolg," *Polen-Analysen* 53: 2–11.

Bibliography 191

——(2010) "Der Vergangenheit näher als der Zukunft: Ein nüchterner Blick auf die Präsidentschaft von Lech Kaczyński," *Polen-Analysen* 69: 2–13.

Virchow, Fabian (2006) "Dimensionen der 'Demonstrationspolitik' der extremen Rechten in der Bundesrepublik Deutschland," in Klärner and Kohlstruck (eds) *Moderner Rechtsextremismus in Deutschland*, Hamburg: Hamburger Edition, 68–101.

——(2007a) "Volks-statt Klassenbewegung. Weltanschauung und Praxeologie der extremen Rechten in der Bundesrepublik Deutschland seit 1990 am Beispiel der 'sozialen Frage'," in Hofmann and Schneider (eds) *ArbeiterInnenbewegung und Rechtsextremismus*, Wien: Akademische Verlagsanstalt, 165–85.

——(2007b) "Von der 'antikapitalistischen Sehnsucht des deutschen Volkes' zur Selbstinszenierung des Neofaschismus als Anwalt der 'kleinen Leute'," *UTOPIE kreativ* 198: 352–60.

Virchow, Fabian and Christian Dornbusch (eds) (2008) *88 Fragen und Antworten zur NPD*, Schwalbach/Ts: Wochenschau-Verlag.

Virtanen, Simo V. and Leonie Huddy (1996) "Old-Fashioned Racism and New Forms of Racial Prejudice," *The Journal of Politics* 60(2): 311–32.

Volkmann, Hans-Erich (1991) "Die NS-Wirtschaft in Vorbereitung des Krieges," in Desit, Messerschmidt, Volkmann, and Wette (eds) *Ursachen und Voraussetzungen des Zweiten Weltkrieges*, Frankfurt/M.: Fischer Taschenbuchverlag, 211–437.

Wagner, Bernd and Dierk Borstel (2009) "Der Rechtsextremismus und sein gesteigertes Bedrohungspotential," in Wilhelm Heitmeyer (ed.) *Deutsch-deutsche Zustände*, Bonn: Bundeszentrale für politische Bildung, 284–98.

Walter, Jess (1996) *Every Knee Shall Bow*, New York: HarperCollins.

Wamper, Regina (2009) "Gefühlter Antikapitalismus. Der Globalisierungsdiskurs in der Deutschen Stimme," in Gebhardt and Clemens (eds) *Volksgemeinschaft statt Kapitalismus? Zur sozialen Demagogie der Neonazis*, Köln: Papyrossa Verlag, 66–89.

Weinberg, Leonard (1998) "An Overview of Right-Wing Extremism in the Western World: A Study of Convergence, Linkage, and Identity," in Kaplan and Bjorgo (eds) *Nation and Race: the Developing Euro-American Racist Subculture*, Boston, MA: Northeastern University, 3–33.

Weiß, Wioletta (2008) "Attacke von Links," in Netzwerk für Osteuropa-Berichterstattung n-ost e.V (eds) *Rechtsextremismus und Antisemitismus in Mittel-, Ost-und Südosteuropa*, Berlin: 15 Grad, 107–11, www.n-ost.de/cms/images//n-ost-stipendien-doku.pdf.

Welzk, Stefan (1998) "Globalisierung und Neofaschismus," *Kursbuch* 134: 37–47.

Wilkinson, Steven (2004) *Votes and Violence. Electoral Competition and Ethnic Riots in India*, Cambridge University Press.

Winkler, Jürgen R. (2006) "Fremdenfeindlichkeit und Rechtsextremismus in der Bundesrepublik Deutschland. Die Perspektive der Politikwissenschaft," in Minkenberg, Sucker and Wenninger (eds) *Radikale Rechte und Fremdenfeindlichkeit in Deutschland und Polen: Nationale und europäische Perspektiven*, Bonn: Informationszentrum Sozialwissenschaften, 128–51.

Wolf, Joachim (2007) "Fußball und Rechtsextremismus in Europa," in *Bundeszentrale für Politische Bildung*, February 15, www.bpb.de/themen/4IFKR4,0,Fu%DFball_und_Rechtsextremismus_in_Europa.html.

——(2009) "Rechtsextremismus in Polen," *Netz-gegen-Nazis.de*, October 7, www.netz-gegen-nazis.de/artikel/rechtsextremismus-polen-2919.

Wright, Stuart (2007) *Patriots, Politics, and the Oklahoma City Bombing*, Cambridge: Cambridge University Press.

Zeskind, Leonard (2009) *Blood and Politics: The History of the White Nationalist Movement from the Margins to the Mainstream*, New York, NY: Farrar, Straus & Giroux.

Zeuner, Bodo *et al.* (2007) *Gewerkschaften und Rechtsextremismus*, Münster: Westfälisches Dampfboot.

Zimmer, Kerstin and Femke van Praagh (2008) "Fremdenfeindlichkeit in der Ukraine," in *Ukraine-Analysen* 41: 2–6.

Zuquete, Jose Pedro (2008) "The European Extreme-Right and Islam: New Directions?" *Journal of Political Ideologies* 13(3): 321–44.

Index

Aae, Per Lennart 43, 53n37
Abanes, Richard 127
Abraham, Larry 134
Action Française 66
activism: demands for 61; supply of 62
agrarian populist movements in US 138
Ahlheim, K. and Heger, B. 55n73
Akesson, Jimmie 32
Albania 106, 107; Democratic Party of Albania (DPA) 107; mainstream parties, configuration of 114–15; Socialist Party of Albania (SPA) 107
Alcohol, Tobacco, and Firearms (ATF), US Bureau of 154
Alleanza Nazionale (AN) in Italy 61, 62, 72, 73, 75, 76
Allen, Gary 134
Alles Große steht im Sturm (NPD publication) 14, 16
Almeida, Dimitri 4
Almond, G.A., Scott Appleby, R. and Sivan, E. 12n14, 144
Alter, Peter 101
Aly, Götz 53n39
Amaudruz, Gaston Armand 16
American Swastika: Inside the White Power Movement's Hidden Spaces of Hate (Simi, P. and Futrell, R.) 10
Analytisches Zentrum *Yury Levada* 95–96
Andrews, M. 64
Anthony, D. and Robbins, T. 126
anti-constitutionalism 35, 37
Anti-Defamation League 155
"anti-fascist protection wall" (*Antifaschistischer Schutzwall*) 1
anti-globalization 18, 39, 41, 50
anti-immigrant vigilante groups 144
anti-Semitism 1, 9, 11n8, 14, 16, 73, 161, 162, 170n6, 172; in Eastern Europe 85–86, 89–90, 92, 96, 100, 101; in Germany and Western Europe 22, 24–25, 44–45, 50, 161, 162, 170n6
anti-tax energies, harnessing to free market policies 131
"*Antikap-Kampagne*" (anti-capitalist campaign) 41
Apfel, Holger 13, 14, 16
apocalyptic aggression 126–28
Arena, M. and Arrigo, B. 145
Argumentationshilfe (argumentation help) 45–46
Arguments for Candidates and Officials: A Handout for Public Debate (NPD brochure) 17–18
Arizona Patriots 151
armed citizens' militias 128–30
ArmyofGod.com 146
Art, D. and Brown, D. 113, 119n2
Art, David 2
Aryan Nations 146, 150, 151, 152–53, 155; *Aryan Nations Liberty Net* 7
Aryan Republican Army (ARA) 145, 153, 154
Arzheimer, Kai 32, 34
"astroturfing" 130
Ataka in Bulgaria 107
Austria: *Bündnis Zukunft Österreich* 31, 32; *Freiheitliche Partei Österreichs* (FPÖ) 2, 3, 32, 137
Autonome (radical left-wing anarchist youth organizations) 40

Bachmann, Michelle 136
Backes, U. and Steglich, H. 50–51n2, 51–52n11, 53n36
Backes, Uwe 20n1

Index

Bakunin, Mikhail 2–3
Bandera, Stepan 91
banning, effects of policy of 30–31
Barber, Benjamin 144
Barkun, Michael 146
Barron, Bruce 128
Bathke, P. and Spindler, S. 51–52n11
Bauer, Gary 127
BBC News 5
Beam, Louis 154, 155
Beck, Glenn 11n7, 132
Beichelt, T. and Minkenberg, M. 101
Beierl, F. and Plöckinger, O. 162
Bélanger, E. and Meguid, B. 109
Belgium: *'t Pallieterke* (Flemish-national weekly) 65; *Vlaams Belang* 31, 32; *Vlaams Blok* 2, 62, 64–65, 72–73, 137; *Vlaams Nationaal Verbond* (VNV, National Flemish League) 65, 73, 83n5; *Volksunie* (VU, People's Union) in Belgium 65, 83n6
Bennett, David H. 147
Berbrier, Mitch 4
Berezin, Mabel 135
Berlet, C. and Lyons, M. 124, 134, 145, 147, 154
Berlet, C. and Vysotsky, S. 128
Berlet, Chip x, 9, 124–43, 155
Berlusconi, Silvio 35
Betriebsgemeinschaft, idea of 48
Betz, Hans-Georg 109, 125
Bible 127, 138–39n4
Big Government, concerns about 130, 131, 134–35
Bill of Rights in US 137
Bischoff, Reiner 45, 54n47
Bismarck, Otto von 45
Bitzan, Renate 12n16
Bizeul, D. 62
Bjorgo, Tore 147
Black Panthers 134
Blazak, Randy 144, 147
Blee, Kathleen x, 10, 12n15, 71, 144, 147, 172–73
Blejwas, A., Griggs, A. and Potok, M. 153
Bloc Yuliya Tymoshenko (BYU) in Ukraine 108
Blocher, Christoph 32
Blood & Honour (B&H) with *White Youth* in Germany 31, 90, 92, 94
Boorstein, Michelle 6
Borum, R. and Gelles, M. 148
Botsch, G. and Kopke, C. 167
Botsch, Gideon x, 8, 10, 37–59

Boyer, Paul S. 127, 136
Bozoki, A. and Ishiyama, J.T. 119n2
Brandstetter, Marc 50–51n2
Braun, S., Geisler, A. and Gerster, M. 51–52n11, 52n20, 52n22
Breivik, Anders Behring 3, 5, 10
Breuer, Stefan 54n43, 55n80
Britain: British National Party (BNP) 16, 18, 32–33; British Union of Fascists 31; modernization of right-wing extremism 32–33
Brookman, Henry 71
Brouwer, S., Gifford, P. and Rose, S.D. 144
Brugge, Doug 135
Bubel, Leszek 90
Buchanan, Pat 131, 133
Bulgaria 107, 113; Movement for Rights and Freedoms (DPS) 107; National Movement for Stability and Progress (NDSV) in Bulgaria 107; policy positions of major parties, radical party in targeted configurations 116–17; targeted configuration with radical parties 117–18
Bulgarian Socialist Party (BSP) 107
Bundesamt für Verfassungsschutz in Germany 35n2
Bundesgerichtshof (German Supreme Court) 166–67
Bundesrat (representatives of the states) in Germany 25
Bündnis Zukunft Österreich 31, 32
Buruma, Ian 6
Bush, George H.W. 129
Bush, George W. 129
Bustikova, L. and Kitschelt, H. 120n7
Bustikova, Lenka x–xi, 9, 106–23
Butterwegge, Christoph 50, 55n85

Cameron, David 5
Canadian Institute of Ukrainian Studies 92
Canovan, Margaret 133
Carter, Elisabeth 115, 117, 119n1
Cassidy, John 136
central themes of right-wing extremism 14–15
Centre Party of Estonia (CPE-Kesk) 107
Centrumdemocraten (CD) in Netherlands 62, 71–72, 78, 79–80
Centrumpartij '86 (CP '86) in Netherlands 70, 78, 80

charisma, leadership and 32
Chermak, S. and Gruenewald, J. 145
Chermak, Steven 145
Children at Risk: The Battle for the Hearts and Minds of Our Kids (Dobson, J. and Bauer, G.) 127
Chirinovsky, Vladimir 96
Christian Democratic Union (CDU) in Germany 24, 62, 69
Christian Patriot Defense League 150
Christian Social Union of Bavaria (CSU) 26, 62
Chrysi Avgi (Golden Dawn) in Greece 13
Civic Democratic Party (ODS) in Czech Republic 107, 120–21n13
Civic Platform (PO) in Poland 108
The Clash of Civilizations (Huntington, S.P.) 136
Clemens, Dominik 51n3, 53n28, 54n53
Clement, S. and Green, J.C. 132
Clinton, Bill 129
The Closed Trade State (Fichte, J.G.) 43–44
Codreanu, Corneliu 133
Cohn, Norman 138
Collegium Humanum (CH) with *Bauernhilfe e.V* in Germany 31
Common Cause 134
Communist Party of Bohemia and Moravia (KSCM) 107
Communist Party of Moldova (PCRM) 108
Communist Party of the Russian Federation (KPRF) 96–97, 108
Congress of Russian Communities (*Kongress russkich obschtschin*) 96
conspiracist scapegoating 126–28, 131
Cook, J.N. 138–39n4
Cordell, Karl 120n6
Corsi, Jerome 131
Coughlin, Father Charles E. 133
Council on Foreign Relations in US 134
Coutela, Jacques 5
Covenant, Sword, and Arm of the Lord (CSA) 149, 150–51, 152, 154
covert extremism 101
Croatia 106, 107, 118; radicalized large major parties 118–19; Social Democratic Party of Croatia (SDP) 107
Croatian Democratic Union (HDZ) 107
Croatian Party of Rights (HSP) 107
Curtis, Alex 155

Czech Republic 106, 112, 120–21n13, 120n12; Civic Democratic Party (ODS) 107, 120–21n13; Communist Party of Bohemia and Moravia (KSCM) 107; mainstream parties, configuration of 114–15
Czech Republican Party (SPR-RSC) 106, 120–21n13
Czech Social Democratic Party (CSSD) 107

Danish People's Party 32
Daudet, Léon 66
de Benoit, Alain 27
de Gaulle, Charles 67, 133
Decker, Frank 23
Decker, O. and Brähler, E. 101
Deist, W. *et al.* 53n39
Dekker, P. and van Praag, C. 61
della Porta, D. and Tarrow, S. 148
della Porta, Donatella 148, 152
democracies: differences between US and European models 137–38; modernization and democratization, reaction to speed of 35, 101
Democratic Accountability Project (DAP) 107–8, 120–21n13, 120n11
Democratic Liberal Party (PDL) in Romania 108
Democratic Party (DS) in Serbia 108
Democratic Party of Albania (DPA) 107
DePugh, Roger 148
Deutsche Alternative (DA) 31
Deutsche Reichs-Partei (DRP) 22
Deutsche Stimme (NPD paper) 18, 48
Deutsche Stimme-Verlag 16–17
Deutsche Volks-Union (DVU) 24, 25, 37
Deutscher Sozialismus (Sombart, W.) 43
Diamond, Sara 125, 128, 147
Little Dictionary of Basic Political Concepts (Deutsche Stimme-Verlag) 16, 17
Direction-Social Democracy (SMER) in Slovakia 108
Disch, Lisa 125, 135
Dobbs, Lou 131
Dobratz, B. and Shanks-Meile, S. 154
Dobson, James 127
Doctrine of Free Economy (Gesell, S.) 44
Doosje, B. *et al.* 61
Döring, Uta 29
Dorr, David 151
Douglas, M. and Wildavsky, A. 106–7
Douglas, Mary 85, 106–7, 119n3

196 *Index*

Drumont, Édouard 66
Drygalla, Nadja 12n16
Dudek, P. and Jaschke, H.-G. 50–51n2
Dugin, Alexander 97
Duke, David 7, 15, 133
Dupont, Henri 66
Durham, Martin 124, 139n8
Durkheim, Emile 86, 101
Dyer, Joel 129

Eastern Europe 173; anti-Semitism in 85–86, 89–90, 92, 96, 100, 101; comparative work on right-wing extremism in 86–87; xenophobia and violence in 89–90, 92, 97–99, 100, 101, 112, 113; *see also* Poland; radical right, conditions for breakthrough of; Russia; Ukraine
Eatwell, Roger 33
economic and sociopolitical platform (NPD) 37–55
economic libertarians 125, 130, 131
Edgers, Geoff 10
education, funding of 114
Ehrenreich, Barbara 135
Ekiert, Grzegorz 119n2
Ellison, James 150–51, 157n1
ENAR (European Network Against Racism) 27
Erhard, Ludwig 48
Erikson, Kai 156
Ernst, Karl 42
Estes Park meeting of far right groups 154
Estonia 87, 107, 114, 116; Centre Party of Estonia (CPE-Kesk) 107; radicalized large major parties 118–19; Union of Pro Patria and Res Publica (UPR) 108
Estonian Reform Party (ERP) 107
ethnic redistributive preferences 113
Etzioni, Amitai 136
Eucken, Walter 43
Europe 173; democracies in, differences from US model 137–38; economic libertarians in 125; Muslims in, antipathy towards 136; neo-Nazi networks in 172; radicalism and extremism, difference between 137; right-wing parties in Western Europe 31–33, 37; right-wing populism, emergence of 135–36; rise in Europe of right-wing extremism 80–81
European Parliament 4, 11n4, 18, 19, 33, 40

European Social Survey 85–86
European Union (EU) 19, 33, 34, 40, 45, 89, 91, 113, 119n2
Extremism, Russian Department of the Prevention of 98; *see also* right-wing extremism

factionalization 152–53
Fair Russia: Motherland/Pensioners/Life (SR) 108
Falter, J., Jasche, H.-G., and Winkler, J.R. 87
Faludi, Susan 148
Fatherland and Freedom/LNNK Party in Latvia 108
FBI (Federal Bureau of Investigation, US) 15–16, 145, 150–51, 154
Fear of Falling: The Inner Life of the Middle Class (Ehrenreich, B.) 135
Feder, Gottfried 44–45
Federal Criminal Police Office (BKA) in Germany 29
Fichte, Johann Gottlieb 43–44, 54n44
Fidesz ñ Hungarian Civic Union 108
Finney, Charles G. 138–39n4
First Internationale 3
FitzGerald, Frances 127
Flanders: Flemish National Song Festival (*Vlaams Nationaal Zangfeest*) 83n4; recruitment in 64–65; stigmatization in 73–74; *see also* Belgium
Flemming, Lars 25
Flynn, K. and Gerhardt, G. 150, 152
Ford, Henry 1
Fortuyn, Pim 82n2
Forza Nuova in Italy 18
Fox News 132, 139n6
France: *Action Française* 66; *Front National* 2, 5, 18, 27–28, 31, 32, 62, 66, 73, 74, 137; *Mouvement National Republicain* (MNR) 67, 74; *Nouvelle Droite* 27, 33; recruitment in 66–67; stigmatization in 74
Franklin, Joseph Paul 155
Freedom Union in Ukraine 92
Freie Demokratische Partie (FDP) in Germany 69
Freie Kameradschaften (free comradeships) 30–31, 167; *see also* Kameradschaften
Freie Kräfte Südthüringen (Free Forces of Southern Thuringia) 43
Die Freiheit (citizens' movement) 26–27

Index 197

Freiheitliche Deutsche Arbeiterpartei (FAP) 31, 41
Freiheitliche Partei Österreichs (FPÖ) 2, 3, 32, 137
Freilich, J. and Chermak, S. 147
Freilich, J.D. *et al.* 144, 148
Friedrich-Ebert-Stiftung 51–52n11
Fromm, Rainer 28, 167
Front National in France 2, 5, 18, 27–28, 31, 32, 62, 66, 73, 74, 137
Fronte della Gioventù (Youth Front) in Italy 75
Frykholm, Amy Johnson 127
Fuerza Nueva in Spain 31
Fuller, Robert C. 126, 127
Furrow, Buford 146
Futrell, R. and Simi, P. 148, 153, 155
Futrell, Robert 10

Gamper, M. and Willems, H. 30
Gamson, William 148, 152
Gansel, Jürgen 53n35, 54n40, 55n72, 55n82
Gardell, Mattias 147
Gardner, A. and Thompson, K. 132
Gayman, Pastor Dan 146
Gebhardt, R. and Clemens, D. 51–52n11, 52n22, 53n34, 53n41
Gemeinschaft see Volksgemeinschaft
George, Patrick 131
Georgia 96, 106, 108; mainstream parties, configuration of 114–15; New Rights (Conservative) Party (NCP) 108; United National Movement (UNM) 108
Germany: "anti-fascist protection wall" (*Antifaschistischer Schutzwall*) 1; *Betriebsgemeinschaft,* idea of 48; *Blood & Honour* (B&H) with *White Youth* 31, 90, 92, 94; *Bundesamt für Verfassungsschutz* 35n2; *Bundesgerichtshof* (Supreme Court) 166–67; *Bundesrat* (representatives of the states) 25; Christian Democratic Union (CDU) 24, 62, 69; *Christian Social Union of Bavaria* (CSU) 26, 62; *Collegium Humanum* (CH) with *Bauernhilfe e.V* 31; crimes with background of right-wing extremism in 29–30; *Deutsche Alternative* (DA) 31; *Deutsche Reichs-Partei* (DRP) 22; *Deutsche Stimme* (NPD paper) 18, 48; Deutsche Stimme-Verlag 16–17; *Deutsche Volks-Union* (DVU) 24, 25, 37; domestic *Lebensraum* (living space) 47, 162; far-right populism and right-wing extremism 22–35; Federal Criminal Police Office (BKA) 29; *Freie Demokratische Partie* (FDP) 69; *Freie Kameradschaften* (free comradeships) 30–31, 167; *Freie Kräfte Südthüringen* (Free Forces of Southern Thuringia) 43; *Die Freiheit* (citizens' movement) 26–27; *Freiheitliche Deutsche Arbeiterpartei* (FAP) 31, 41; *Gesellschaft* (society), concept of 48; *Gesinnungsgemeinschaft der Neuen Front* 167; *Grundgesetz* (basic law) 22; *Heimattreue Deutsche Jugend* (HDJ) 31; *Institut für Zeitgeschichte* (Institute of Contemporary History, Munich) 161, 169; Interior Ministry 25, 30; internationalization of right-wing extremism 19; *Junge Freiheit* (JF) 68; *Junge Nationaldemokraten* (JN) 14, 38, 40, 41–42; *Kameradschaften* 30–31, 40–42, 43, 47, 90; *Kommunistische Partei Deutschlands* (KPD) 30; *Die Linke* 38; *Nationaldemokratischer Hochschulbund* (NHB) 17; *Nationale Offensive* (NO) 31; *Nationale und soziale Aktivisten Mitteldeutschland* (NSAM) 40; *Nationalistische Front* (NF) 31; *Nationalsozialistische Deutsche Arbeiterpartei/Auslands-und Aufbauorganisation* (NSDAP/AO) 167, 172; *Nationalsozialistische Deutsche Arbeiterpartei* (NSDAP) 30, 34, 42, 44–45; *Partei des demokratischen Sozialismus* (PDS) 38; *Pro Deutschland* (citizens' movement) 26–27; recruitment in 68–70; *Die Republikaner* (REP) party 24, 26, 27, 62, 69–70, 76–77; *Ring Nationaler Frauen* (RNF) 46; Social Democratic Party (SPD) 27, 69; *Sozialistische Reichspartei* (SRP) 22, 30, 167; *Staatsbibliothek* in Berlin 163, 164; stigmatization in 76–77; transformation of right-wing extremism today in 23–28; *Wehrsportgruppe Hoffmann* in West Germany 28, 167; Weimar Republic 34, 35, 48, 166; *Zweckverbände* (organizations with shared goals) 48; *see also Nationaldemokratische Partei Deutschlands* (NPD)

198 Index

Germany Does Away with Itself. How we are Gambling with Our Country (Sarrazin, T.) 5, 27
Gesell, Silvio 44
Gesellschaft (society), concept of 48
Gesinnungsgemeinschaft der Neuen Front 167
Gibson, William 147, 148
globalism 3, 17, 20, 38
12 Theses on Globalism (*Nationaldemokratischer Hochschulbund,* NHB) 17
globalization 1, 3–4, 7–8, 22, 23, 33–34, 35; anti-globalization 18, 39, 41, 50; in context of right-wing extremism 18; globalized anti-globalists and 13, 16–17, 20; national solidarity and 'no' to 41–42, 45, 48–49; spread of right-wing extremism and 10, 13; *Volksgemeinschaft versus* 38–40
globalized anti-globalists, globalization and 13, 16–17, 20
Gnad, Oliver 50–51n2
Goldberg, Jonah 11n7
Goldberg, Michelle 128
Göls, Cornelia 93
Good, Chris 130
Goodwyn, Laurence B. 35
Gorbachev, Mikhail 85
Gossweiler, Kurt 53n34
Gottschalk, P. and Greenberg, G. 136
Granovetter, Mark 151, 156
Greater Romanian Party (PRM) 108
Greenberg, J.S., Solomon, T. and Pyszczynski, T. 151
Greven, T. and Grumke, T. 20
Griffin, Nick 18, 33
Griffin, Roger 136
Grumke, T. and Klärner, A. 51–52n11, 52n21
Grumke, Thomas xi, 3, 8, 13–21, 51–52n11
Grundgedanken (basic ideas of NPD) 47–48
Grundgesetz (basic law) in Germany 22
Grzymala-Busse, Anna 119n2

Haagsche Courant 71
Haider, Jörg 26, 32
Haines, Herbert 152
Hale, Matt 146
Hamm, Mark S. 129, 144, 145, 147, 148, 153
Hankel, Natalia xi, 8–9, 85–105
Hansen, Henning 167

Harding, Susan 127
Hartleb, Florian 34
Hauptmann, Gerhard 163, 164
Häusler, Alexander 26, 51n5
Havel, Vaclav 112, 120–21n13
Hayek, Friedrich August von 131
"heartland," populist identification with 134
Heiler, Kurt 53n34
Heimattreue Deutsche Jugend (HDJ) 31
Held, Joseph 119n2
Hentges, Gudrun 54n45
Heubisch, Wolfgang 168
Heuss, Theodor 166
Himmler, Heinrich 162, 164
historical narratives, competition over 112–13
Hitler, Adolf 9, 30, 42, 45, 86, 131, 133, 161–69
Hitler's Path (Heuss, T.) 166
Hobsbawm, Eric 31
Hockenos, Paul 119n2
Hoffer, Eric 149
Hoffman, Bruce 145, 147
Hoffmann, Karl-Heinz 167, 169n1
Hoffmann, Uwe 50–51n2
Hofmann, J. and Schneider, M. 51–52n11
Holmes, Douglas R. 135
Homeland Security, US Department of 145
Homeland Union-Christian Democrats (TS) in Lithuania 108
Huddy, Leonie 11n5
Hungarian Justice and Life Party (MIEP) 108, 117
Hungarian Socialist Party (MSZP) 108
Hungarian *Szeged* fascism 31
Hungary 2, 13, 108; Fidesz ñ Hungarian Civic Union 108; *Jobbik* party 13, 108, 117; policy positions of major parties, radical party in targeted configurations 116–17; targeted configuration with radical parties 117–18
Hunter (Pierce, W.L.) 155
Huntington, Samuel P. 136
Hutaree Militia 129, 138–39n4, 138n2

identity politics 111, 112, 116
IJzer pilgrimage 82–83n3
immigration 4, 5, 8, 15, 28–29, 31, 39, 48, 96, 110, 125, 135, 145, 155, 173; anti-immigration 27, 34, 48, 90, 92; "Movement against Illegal Immigration" 97

individual in logic of right-wing extremism 17
individual terrorism, trend towards 155–56
Inside the Radical Right: The Development of Anti-Immigrant Parties in Western Europe (Art, D.) 2
Institut für Zeitgeschichte (Institute of Contemporary History, Munich) 161, 169
insurgent revolutionary right groups in US 128
intellectual far-right, right-wing extremism and 27–28
interest slavery, NPD agitation against 44–45
Internal Macedonian Revolutionary Organization-Democratic Party for Macedonian National Unity (VMRO-DPMNE) 108
International Eurasian Movement 97
The International Jew (Ford, H.) 1
internationalization of right-wing extremism 1, 2–3, 6–7; ideological basis of 13–21; transnationalization 19–20
Internet 1, 3, 6–7, 11n12, 26, 90, 100, 130, 166, 168, 172
Ishiyama, John T. 119n2
Islamic extremism 5, 10, 144–45
Islamophobia 1, 4–6, 11n8, 31–32, 34, 51n5, 125
Italy: *Alleanza Nazionale* (AN) 61, 62, 72, 73, 75, 76; *Forza Nuova* 18; *Fronte della Gioventù* (Youth Front) 75; *Lega Nord* 18, 32; *Movimento Italiano Femminile* (Italian Movement of Women) 67–68; *Movimento Sociale-Fiamma Tricolore* (MS-FT) 67, 75, 76; *Movimento Sociale Italiana* (MSI) 31, 61, 67–68, 75, 76; recruitment in 67–68; stigmatization in 75–76

James I, King of Great Britain 130
Jamin, Jérôme 137
Janmaat, Hans 71
Janokovic, Viktor 94
Jaschke, Hans-Gerd xi, 8, 22–36, 86, 101
Jedwabne pogrom in Poland 112
Jenkins, Phillip 148–49
Jenne, Erin 119n5, 120n9
Jobbik party in Hungary 13, 108, 117
John Birch Society 126, 131, 132
Juenger, Ernst 27

Juergensmeyer, Mark 85
Junge Freiheit (JF) in Germany 68
Junge Nationaldemokraten (JN) 14, 38, 40, 41–42
Juschtschenko, Wiktor 92

Kacynski, Jaroslav and Lech 88
Kaczynski, Ted 3
Kahl, Gordon 152, 156
Kahrs, Horst 53n39
Kailitz, Steffen 48, 53n36, 55n74, 55n78
Kaindl, Christina 51–52n11
Kameradschaften 30–31, 40–42, 43, 47, 90
Kantrowitz, Stephen 133
Kaplan, Jeffrey 144, 147, 148
Kappeler, Andreas 92
Kazin, Michael 135, 138
Keil, T.J. and Keil, J.M. 132–33
Kelley, Judith 113, 119n2
Kersten, Joachim xi, 8–9, 85–105
Kirchheimer, Otto 55n84
Kirstein, Louis 165
Kissenkoetter, Udo 53n34
Kitschelt, H. et al. 113, 120n11
Kitschelt, H., with McGann, A. 109, 115
Kitschelt, Herbert 106
Klandermans, B., Werner, M. and van Doorn, M. 61
Klandermans, Bert xi–xii, 3, 8, 10, 60–84
Klarmann, Michael 52n22
Klärner, A. and Kohlstruck, M. 34, 52n21
Klaus, Vaclav 120–21n13
Klausen, Jytte 11n10
Knobel, Dale T. 135
Kohl, Helmut 28
Kommunistische Partei Deutschlands (KPD) 30
Kopeck, P. and Mudde, C. 119n2
Kopke, Christoph xii, 8, 10, 37–59
Koran 167–68, 170n3
Koresh, David 154
Koschewnikowa, Galina 100
Kramer, Stefan 168
Kriskofski, Torsten 28
Ku Klux Klan (KKK) 124, 128, 148, 150, 152, 155
Kühnen, Michael 14, 167
Kühnl, R., Rilling, R. and Sager, C. 51n6
Kühnl, Reinhard 53n34
Kupferberg, Feiwel 88
Kurth, James 11n2
Kuzio, Taras 115

200 *Index*

Labour Party (DP) in Lithuania 108
Lagrou, P. 61
LaHaye, T. and Jenkins, J.B. 127
LaHaye, Tim 127, 131
Lane, David 15, 19
Laqueur, Walter 152
The Late Great Planet Earth (Lindsey, H. and Carlson, C.C.) 127
Latvia 87, 107, 108; Fatherland and Freedom/LNNK Party 108; New Era Party (JL) 108; People's Party (TP) 108; policy positions of major parties, radical party in targeted configurations 116–17; targeted configuration with radical parties 117–18; Union of Greens and Farmers (ZZS) 108
Lauck, Garry "Gerhard" 167, 172
Law and Justice Party (PiS) in Poland 108
Le Pen, Jean-Marie 18, 26, 32, 62, 135
Le Pen, Marine 5, 11n4
Lebensraum (living space) 47, 162
Left Behind (LaHaye, T. and Jenkins, J.B.) 127
Lega Nord in Italy 18, 32
Leonardo da Vinci 75
Levenson, Michael 130
Levitas, Daniel 129
Lewis, Paul G. 119n2
Liberal Democracy of Slovenia (LDS) 108
Liberal Democratic Party of Russia (LDPR) 96–97, 108, 118
Liberal Party (PL) of Moldova 108
Liga Polskich Rodzin (Polish Family League) 90, 106, 107, 108, 112
Lijst Pim Fortuyn (LPF) in Netherlands 82n2
Lindsey, H. and Carlson, C.C. 127
Lindsey, Hal 127
Die Linke in Germany 38
Liss, Artyom 144
List, Friedrich 43
List, Peter 54n69
Lithuania 87, 88, 108, 116; Homeland Union-Christian Democrats (TS) 108; Labour Party (DP) 108; mainstream parties, configuration of 114–15; Order and Justice Party (TT) 108
loan capital, NPD agitation against 44–45
lone wolf radicals 155–56
Lubbers, M. 61

McAdam, D., Tarrow, S. and Tilly, C. 152
McAdam, Douglas 148
McCarty, Timothy Wyman xii, 1–12
McCauley, C. and Moskalenko, S. 152, 153
McCurrie, Thomas 148
Macedonia 108, 113; Internal Macedonian Revolutionary Organization-Democratic Party for Macedonian National Unity (VMRO-DPMNE) 108; radicalized large major parties 118–19; Social Democratic Union of Macedonia (SDSM) 108
McMath, Robert 138
McNicol Stock, Catherine 135
McVeigh, Rory 125
McVeigh, Timothy 129, 145, 150, 153, 154
Madloch, Norbert 53n34
Maegerle, Anton 52n12, 52n21, 52n25
Mahler, Horst 167
Maier, H. and Bott, H. 51n6
mainstream parties: behaviour of, success for right and 114–15; configurations of, ideal types of 110–11; radicalization of mainstream competitors, effects of 118–19
Mareš, Miroslav 119n2, 120n9
Marsden, George 127
Martin, William 127, 136
martyrdom, cult of 151–52
Marx, Karl 2–3
Mathews, Robert Jay 149–50
Maurras, Charles 66
Mayer, Jane 130
Mecklenburg, Jens 167
Medvedev, Dmitry 94
Meguid, Bonnie 114
Mein Kampf (Hitler, A.) 9, 161–69; discussions post-1945 about 166–69; early readership, widespread nature of 164–65; extreme right today and 166–68; importance for right-wing extremists 161; mythmaking about 161–62, 166; origins of 161–65; reception when published originally 161–65; satirical proposal for comments on 169; scholarly edition, problems of 168–69
Menhorn, Christian 26
Merkel, Angela 5
Merkel, Wolfgang 101

Merton, Robert K. 86, 101
Metzger, Tom 155
Michael, George 7
Mifflin, Houghton 165
migrants and foreign minorities, campaigns against 28
Militant Islam Monitor 168
Miller-Idriss, Cynthia 10
Minkenberg, Michael 20, 85, 100, 101, 119n2
Minutemen 148
Moelzer, Andreas 27
Mohler, Armin 27
Moldova 108, 113; Communist Party of Moldova (PCRM) 108; Liberal Party (PL) of Moldova 108; Party Alliance Our Moldova (PAMN) 108; radicalized large major parties 118–19
Möller, Einhart 53n27
Mosley, Oswald 31
Mouvement National Republicain (MNR) in France 67, 74
Movement against Illegal Immigration in Russia 97
Movement for Rights and Freedoms (DPS) in Bulgaria 107
Movimento Italiano Femminile (Italian Movement of Women) 67–68
Movimento Sociale-Fiamma Tricolore (MS-FT) in Italy 67, 75, 76
Movimento Sociale Italiana (MSI) 31, 61, 67–68, 75, 76
Mudde, Cas 31, 106, 107, 109, 115, 119n2, 137, 139n8
multi-layered nature of radicalism 172–73
Muslims, antipathy towards 136; *see also* Islamophobia
Mussolini, Alessandra 18–19
Mussolini, Benito 31
Mut Verlag 27

Narodowe Odrodzenie Polski (NOP, National Rebirth of Poland) 90
Naschi (aka "Putin Youth") 98
Nation Europa 27
National Alliance 14, 150, 152, 155; *National Alliance Bulletin* 15, 16
National Movement for Stability and Progress (NDSV) in Bulgaria 107
National Socialism (NS) in Germany 31, 40–42; ideology of 15; "National Socialist Underground" (*Nationalsozialistischer Untergrund*) 11n9

national solidarity and "no" to globalization 41–42, 45, 48–49
Nationaldemokratische Partei Deutschlands (NPD) 8, 13–14, 16–18, 18–19, 23–26, 28–29, 32, 34, 35n1, 68–69, 167; "*Antikap-Kampagne*" (anti-capitalist campaign) 41; *Argumentationshilfe* (argumentation help) 45–46; *The Closed Trade State* (Fichte, J.G.) and 43–44; crash and *angst* scenarios 49–50; domestic *Lebensraum* (living space) 47, 162; economic and sociopolitical platform 37–55; globalization, *Volksgemeinschaft versus* 38–40; *Grundgedanken* (basic ideas) 47–48; interest slavery, agitation against 44–45; internal crisis within 46; loan capital, agitation against 44–45; National Socialism 40–42; national solidarity platform 45–49; *Raumorientierte Volkswirtschaft* (spatially oriented national economy) 42–44; social Darwinist performance-oriented agenda 37–38; *Volksgemeinschaft*, notion of 39–40, 44, 48, 51–52n11, 51n3, 52n22, 53n34, 53n41; *Work-Family-Fatherland* slogan 37
Nationaldemokratischer Hochschulbund (NHB) 17
Nationale Offensive (NO) in Germany 31
Nationale und soziale Aktivisten Mitteldeutschland (NSAM) 40
Nationalistische Front (NF) in Germany 31
Nationalsozialistische Deutsche Arbeiterpartei (NSDAP) 30, 34, 42, 44–45
Nationalsozialistische Deutsche Arbeiterpartei/Auslands-und Aufbauorganisation (NSDAP/AO) 167, 172
Nederlands Blok (NB) 78–79
neo-Nazi networks in Europe 26, 37, 41, 43, 45, 48, 90, 92, 94, 98, 167–68, 172–73
Netherlands: *Centrumdemocraten* (CD) 62, 71–72, 78, 79–80; *Centrumpartij '86* (CP '86) 70, 78, 80; Lijst Pim Fortuyn (LPF) 82n2; *Nederlands Blok* (NB) 78–79; *Partij voor de Vrijheid* (PVV) 2, 5, 32, 82n2; recruitment in 70–72; *Social Democratic Party* (PvdA) 71; stigmatization in 77–80; *Voorpost* 73, 78, 79, 80; *Vrij Nederland* 71

New Era Party (JL) in Latvia 108
New Rights (Conservative) Party (NCP) in Georgia 108
New World Order (NWO) 17
New York Times 165
New Yorker 136
Newton, M. and Newton, J.A. 148
Nichols, Terry 129, 138n3
Nigdy Wiecej (Never Again) 89–90
Noble, Kerry 129, 150, 151, 157n1
None Dare Call it Conspiracy (Allen, G. and Abraham, L.) 134–35
Norris, Pippa 115
Northcott, Michael 138
Nouvelle Droite in France 27, 33

Obama, Barack (and administration of) 124, 130, 131, 135, 136, 145
Obermayr, Franz 11n4
Oberschall, Anthony 148
O'Dwyer, C. and Schwartz, K. 107, 113
Ohlemacher, Thomas 20
Olzak, Susan 113
Opp, Karl-Dieter 151
Order and Justice Party (TT) in Lithuania 108
Order II 151, 152
Orfali, B. 67
Organization of Ukrainian Nationalists (OUN) 92
organizational resources, splinter factions and 152–53
Osborn, Andrew 144
Ost, David 119n2
Our Ukraine-People's Self-Defense Bloc (OU-PSD) 108

palingenesis, role in populism 136
't Pallieterke (Flemish-national weekly) 65
pan-Aryan ideology (and identity) 4, 8, 15, 16, 19
pan-Aryan *Weltanschauung* 15
Parker, Christopher 132
Partei des demokratischen Sozialismus (PDS) in Germany 38
Partij voor de Vrijheid (PVV) in Netherlands 2, 5, 32, 82n2
Party Alliance Our Moldova (PAMN) 108
Party of Regions (PR) in Ukraine 108
past legacies 60–61
Paterson, Tony 3
Paul, Ron 130

Payne, Stanley G. 136
People's Party (TP) in Latvia 108
perceptions of right-wing terror 145–47
Perea, Juan F. 135
Perón, Juan 133
Perot, Ross 133
Peters, J. and Schulze, C. 52n22, 52n23
Pfahl-Traughber, Armin 17, 54n45
Pfeiffer, Christian 144
phenomena of right-wing extremism, definition of 86
Philippsberg, Robert 52n19
Pierce, Dr William L. 14, 15, 21n4, 145, 155
Plöckinger, Othmar xii, 9, 161–71
Poland 9, 107, 108; Civic Platform (PO) 108; extremism and hate crimes in 85, 87–89, 90, 91, 94, 101; Jedwabne pogrom 112; Law and Justice Party (PiS) 108; *Liga Polskich Rodzin* (Polish Family League) 90, 106, 107, 108, 112; *Narodowe Odrodzenie Polski* (NOP, National Rebirth of Poland) 90; policy positions of major parties, radical party in targeted configurations 116–17; *Solidarnosc* movement 88, 90; *Szczerbiec* (The Sword of Coronation) 90; targeted configuration with radical parties 117–18; *Teraz Polska* 90
policy configurations 109, 110–11, 112, 119
Polish Institute of National Remembrance 112
political challenge of right-wing extremism 22
political mobilization in US 147–48
political style of right-wing extremism 26
Pop-Eleches, Grigore 119n2
Poplawski, Richard 156
populism: concept of 133–36; features of 133–34; populist economics 107, 109, 112; right-wing extremism and, boundary between 33; right-wing populism, emergence of 135–36; right-wing populism in US, factors influencing 124–25
Posse Comitatus 150
post-communist politics 106
Potichnyj, Peter 92
Potok, Mark 7, 130, 144, 145, 155
prejudice 30, 34, 72, 75, 76, 89, 132, 135–36

Pro Deutschland (citizens' movement) 26–27
producerism 135, 136
Progress Party in Norway 32
Prophet of Doom 168, 170n5
The Protocols of the Elders of Zion 1, 170n6
Pühse, Jens 53n29
Putin, Vladimir 94, 96

Rabitz, Cornelia 94
racism 11n5, 86, 89–90, 91, 92–93, 95, 110; cultural racism 4; pan-Aryan racism 16; racial anxieties in US 132–33, 135; right-wing extremism and 22, 24, 26
Racius, Egdunas 115
Racketeer Influenced and Corrupt Organization Act (RICO, US) 150
radical parties, classification of 106–9
radical right, conditions for breakthrough of 106–21; education, funding of 114; ethnic redistributive preferences 113; historical narratives, party competition over 112–13; identity politics 112; mainstream parties' behaviour, success for right and 114–15; mainstream party configurations, ideal types of 110–11; policy configurations 109, 110–11, 112, 119; populist economics 107, 109, 112; post-communist politics 106; radical parties, classification of 106–9; radicalization of mainstream competitors, effects of 118–19; success mechanisms 113–14; targeted redistribution 109–11, 116–17; welfare altruism, counterpoint of 117–18; welfare chauvinism 107, 109, 110
radicalism 10, 10n1, 86, 106, 137, 139n8, 173; extremism and, difference between 137; *see also* right-wing extremism
radicalization of mainstream competitors, effects of 118–19
Radio Maryja 90
Ramet, Sabrina 107, 119n2
Raumorientierte Volkswirtschaft (spatially oriented national economy) 42–44
Rechel, Bernd 114
recruitment to right-wing extremism 64–72
Rehse, Sebastian 52n19
Reichsbürgerbewegung 167
religious right in US 132

Die Republikaner (REP) party in Germany 24, 26, 27, 62, 69–70, 76–77
Richter, Karl 17
Rieger, Jürgen 48, 54n67
right-wing extremism 1, 2, 4, 8–9, 60–61, 144–45, 145–46, 147; anti-constitutionalism and 35, 37; banning, effects of policy of 30–31; Britain and modernization of 32–33; central themes of 14–15; characterization in US of 145; charisma, leadership and 32; contradictions of modern extremism 172; cooperation across borders 16; covert extremism and 101; crimes in Germany with background of 29–30; demands for activism 61; democratization and modernization, reaction to speed of 35, 101; Eastern Europe, xenophobia and violence in 89–90, 92, 97–99, 100, 101, 112, 113; economic and social programs 44; external factors, scholarly focus on 156; Flanders, recruitment in 64–65; Flanders, stigmatization in 73–74; France, recruitment in 66–67; France, stigmatization in 74; Germany, recruitment in 68–70; Germany, stigmatization in 76–77; Germany and internationalization of 19; Germany and Western Europe, far-right populism and 22–35; globalism in 17; globalization and spread of 10, 13; globalization in context of 18; ideological counter-world of 20; individual in logic of 17; intellectual far-right and 27–28; Internet and 6–7; Italy, recruitment in 67–68; Italy, stigmatization in 75–76; *Mein Kampf* (Hitler, A.) and right today 161–62, 166–68; migrants and foreign minorities, campaigns against 28; mobilization of 63; multifaceted phenomenon 20; "National Socialism now!", call for 42; Netherlands, recruitment in 70–72; Netherlands, stigmatization in 77–80; parties in Western Europe 31–33, 37; past legacies and 60–61; phenomena of, definition of 86; political challenge of 22; political mobilization in US and 147–48; political style of 26; populism and, boundary between 33; racism and 26; recruitment to 64–72;

rise in Europe of 80–81; rise in US of 4, 144–45, 148–49, 155–56; rise of 5; role of 85; Russian extremism, nationalism and 102; Russian extremism, roots of 97–98; as social movement 34; stigmatization of 72–80; strategic alliances within 8; supply of activism 62; terror in US, cycles of 145, 146–47, 148–49, 150–51, 151–52, 155–56; transatlantic discourse on 10, 172–73; in transformation, Germay today and 23–28; transnationalization of 19–20; violence and 2, 4, 9, 15–16, 28–31, 49, 73, 135, 172; women as partners in 12n16; youth cultures, sub-cultures and 25–26; *see also* internationalization of right-wing extremism

right-wing populism, emergence of 135–36

right-wing social movements in US 125–26

right-wing terror, cycles in US of: Alcohol, Tobacco, and Firearms (ATF), Bureau of 154; Anti-Defamation League 155; anti-immigrant vigilante groups 144; Arizona Patriots 151; ArmyofGod.com 146; Aryan Nations 146, 150, 151, 152–53, 155; Aryan Republican Army (ARA) 145, 153, 154; Christian Patriot Defense League 150; comparison between 1980s and 1990s 154–55; Covenant, Sword, and Arm of the Lord (CSA) 149, 150–51, 152, 154; factionalization 152–53; Homeland Security, US Department of 145; individual terrorism, trend towards 155–56; internal dynamics of 156; lone wolf radicals 155–56; martyrdom, cult of 151–52; Minutemen 148; organizational resources, splinter factions and 152–53; perceptions of right-wing terror 145–47; Posse Comitatus 150; resurgence 155; right-wing terror during 1980s 149–51; right-wing terror during 1990s 153; setting stage for terror 148–49; Silent Brotherhood 149–50, 151, 152–53, 154; Southern Poverty Law Center 144, 153; terrorism, definition in relation to political mobilization 147–48; threat, framing of 151–52; triggers for events 151–52, 153–54; violent fundamentalist insurgency, growth of 144; Waco, Texas 153–54, 156; White Aryan Resistance (WAR) 145; White Patriots Party 151; World Church of the Creator (WCOTC) 146

Ring Nationaler Frauen (RNF) 46

Robertson, Pat 131, 133

Rodina (Homeland) party in Russia 96–97

Roeder, Scott 156

Röhm, Ernst 42

Röhr, W. and Berlekamp, B. 53n39

Romania 87, 106, 108, 113, 114, 133; Democratic Liberal Party (PDL) 108; Greater Romanian Party (PRM) 108; policy positions of major parties, radical party in targeted configurations 116–17; Social Democrat Party (PSD) 108; targeted configuration with radical parties 117–18

Romanian iron guards 31

Roosevelt, Franklin D. 127, 165

Ross, J. and Gurr, T. 148

Roth, S. 64

Rothschild, J. and Wingfield, N.M. 112

Ruby Ridge 153–54, 156

Ruchniewicz, Krzysztof 88

Rudolf Hess Memorial (May 1) 19

Rudolph, Eric 145–46

Russia 9, 15, 65, 106, 108, 114, 115–16, 133, 144, 168, 173; Analytisches Zentrum *Yury Levada* 95–96; Communist Party of the Russian Federation (KPRF) 96–97, 108; Congress of Russian Communities (*Kongress russkich obschtschin*) 96; extremism and hate crimes in 85, 87, 91, 92, 94–100, 101, 102; extremism in, nationalism and 102; extremism in, roots of 97–98; Fair Russia: Motherland/Pensioners/Life (SR) 108; Interior Ministry in 99; Liberal Democratic Party of Russia (LDPR) 96–97, 108, 118; Movement against Illegal Immigration 97; *Naschi* (aka "Putin Youth") 98; radicalized large major parties 118–19; *Rodina* (Homeland) party 96–97; *Sprawedliwaja Rossija* (SR, Justice Russia) 96; United Russia (UR) 108

Russian Marches 97

Russian National Socialist Party 97

Russian National Unity (RNE) 97

Rydgren, Jens 4

Sageman, Marc 148
Saideman, Stephen 120n9
Salzborn, Samuel 54n45
Sarkozy, Nicolas 35
Sarrazin, Thilo 5, 27
Schaeffer, Francis 131
Scharenberg, Albert 20
Schedler, Jan 52n22
Scheuch, E.K. and Klingemann, H.-D. 20
Schimmer, Arne 43
Schlafly, Phyllis 131
Schmid, A.P. and Jongman, A.J. 147
Schmitt, Carl 27
Schmollinger, Horst W. 50–51n2
Schoenhuber, Franz 26
scholarship 106, 119n2; comparative work on right-wing extremism in Eastern Europe 86–87; external factors, scholarly focus on effects on right-wing extremism 156; extreme right activists, recruitment and experiences of, study method 81–82; extreme right activists, study on recruitment and experiences of 60–82; global perspectives, need for 10; interdisciplinarity 7–8; new directions in 7–10; right-wing radicalism as multi-layered enterprise, focus on 172–73
Schulze, Christoph 52n20
Schweizer Volkspartei 31, 32
Serbia 2, 106, 108; Democratic Party (DS) 108; policy positions of major parties, radical party in targeted configurations 116–17; targeted configuration with radical parties 117–18
Serbian Radical Party (SRS) 108
Shafir, Michael 119n2
Shane, Scott 5
Shore, Raphael 11n11
Silent Brotherhood 149–50, 151, 152–53, 154
Simi, P. and Futrell, R. 144, 145, 148, 149, 153, 155
Simi, P. et al. 148, 156
Simi, Pete xii, 9, 10, 144–60
Simon, B. and Klandermans, B. 62
Slovak Democratic and Christian Union (SKDU-DS) 108
Slovak National Party (SNS) 108
Slovakia 108, 113, 114; Direction-Social Democracy (SMER) 108; policy positions of major parties, radical party in targeted configurations 116–17; targeted configuration with radical parties 117–18
Slovenia 106, 108; Liberal Democracy of Slovenia (LDS) 108; policy positions of major parties, radical party in targeted configurations 116–17; Social Democrats (SD) 108; targeted configuration with radical parties 117–18
Slovenian Democratic Party (SDS) 108
Slovenian National Party (SNS) 108
Smelser, Neil J. 151
Smith, Ben 146
Smith, Brent 144, 147, 148, 149, 150–51, 152, 154
Snow, D.A. and Benford, R.D. 151
Snow, D.A. et al. 148, 151
social Darwinism 37–38
Social Democratic Party (PSD) in Romania 108
Social Democratic Party of Croatia (SDP) 107
Social Democratic Party (PvdA) in Netherlands 71
Social Democratic Party (SPD) in Germany 27, 69
Social Democratic Union of Macedonia (SDSM) 108
Social Democrats (SD) in Slovenia 108
Socialist Party of Albania (SPA) 107
Solidarnosc movement in Poland 88, 90
Sombart, Werner 42, 43, 49, 53n33
Soros, George 45
Southern Poverty Law Center in US 144, 153
Sozialistische Reichspartei (SRP) 22, 30, 167
Spanish falangism 31
Spann, Othmar 43
Spengler, Oswald 42, 53n33
Der Spiegel 27, 31, 170n4
Sprawedliwaja Rossija (SR, Justice Russia) 96
Sprinzak, Ehud 144, 147, 148, 151, 152
Staatsbibliothek in Berlin 163, 164
Stack, Joe 156
Stalin, Josef 91, 131
Stegbauer, Andreas 30
Steglich, Henrik 52n19
Sternhell, Zeev 66
stigmatization of right-wing extremism 72–80

Stormfront 7
Stöss, Richard 13, 18, 25, 31, 50–51n2, 101
Strache, Heinz-Christian 3
Straßer, Gregor 42
strategic alliances 8
Students for a Democratic Society 134
Swank, D. and Betz, H.-G. 34
Szczerbiec (The Sword of Coronation) 90

Taggart, Paul 133–34
Taras, Ray 125, 135–36
targeted redistribution 109–11, 116–17
Tarrow, Sidney 148
Tea Party movement in US 9, 11–12n13, 124, 130–32, 134, 136, 139n6
Teraz Polska 90
terrorism 9, 94, 129, 144–45; definition in relation to political mobilization 147–48; individual terrorism, trend towards 155–56; perceptions of right-wing terror 145–47; *see also* right-wing terror in US, cycles of
Teske, N. 63, 64
Thieme, Tom 85, 87, 96, 97
Thompson, Bennie 145
Thompson, M., Ellis, R. and Wildavsky, A. 119n3
threat, framing of 151–52
Tilly, Charles 148
Times Mirror 87
Tixier-Vignancour, Jean-Louis 66
Town Hall movements in US 130–31
transnationalism 1, 3–4, 6, 13, 18–19, 85, 173
transnationalization of right-wing extremism 19–20
triggers for events 151–52, 153–54
True Finns 32
Turchie, T. and Puckett, K. 145
Turk, Austin 146, 155, 156
The Turner Diaries (Pierce, W.L.) 15, 145
Tymoshenko, Yulia 91, 92
Tyndall, John 16, 33

Überfremdungspolitik (inundation policy) in Germany 15, 49
Ukraine 9, 106, 108, 113; Bloc Yuliya Tymoshenko (BYU) 108; extremism and hate crimes in 85, 87, 91–94; Freedom Union 92; mainstream parties, configuration of 114–15; Organization of Ukrainian Nationalists (OUN) 92; Our Ukraine-People's Self-Defense Bloc (OU-PSD) 108; Party of Regions (PR) 108
Ukrainian Insurgent Army (UPA) 92
Ukrainian National Workers' Union 92
ultranationalism 13
Union of Greens and Farmers (ZZS) in Latvia 108
Union of Pro Patria and Res Publica (UPR) in Estonia 108
United National Movement (UNM) in Georgia 108
United Nations (UN) 3, 17
United Russia (UR) 108
United States 172, 173; agrarian populist movements 138; anti-tax energies, harnessing to free market policies 131; apocalyptic aggression 126–28; armed citizens' militias 128–30; "astroturfing" 130; Big Government, concerns about 130, 131, 134–35; Bill of Rights 137; Black Panthers 134; characterization of right-wing extremism in 145; Christian Patriot Defense League 150; Common Cause 134; conservatism 132; conspiracist scapegoating 126–28, 131; Council on Foreign Relations 134; democracy in, differences from European model 137–38; *Fear of Falling: The Inner Life of the Middle Class* (Ehrenreich, B.) 135; "heartland," populist identification with 134; ideological position of Tea Party 130; insurgent revolutionary right groups 128; John Birch Society 126, 131, 132; Ku Klux Klan (KKK) 124, 128, 148, 150, 152, 155; Muslims in, antipathy towards 136; *None Dare Call it Conspiracy* (Allen, G. and Abraham, L.) 134–35; palingenesis, role in populism 136; populism, concept of 133–36; populism, features of 133–34; prejudice 132; producerism 135, 136; racial anxieties 132–33; Racketeer Influenced and Corrupt Organization Act (RICO) 150; religious right in 132; right-wing extremists in 4; right-wing populism in, factors influencing 124–25; right-wing social movements in 125–26; rise in US of right-wing extremism 144–45, 148–49, 155–56; Students for a Democratic Society 134;

Town Hall movements 130–31; Young Socialist Alliance 134; *see also* right-wing terror, cycles in US of
Untermeyer, Samuel 165
Useem, Bert 151

Vachudova, Milada Anna 113, 119n2
van den Bruck, Moeller 27
van der Brug, W., Meindert, F. and Tillie, J. 115
Vergangenheitsbewältigung (coming to terms with the past) 102
Vetter, Reinbold 88
violence: Eastern Europe, xenophobia and violence in 89–90, 92, 97–99, 100, 101, 112, 113; right-wing extremism and 2, 4, 9, 15–16, 28–31, 49, 73, 135, 172; terror in US, cycles of 145, 146–47, 148–49, 150–51, 151–52, 155–56; violent fundamentalist insurgency, growth of 144
Virchow, F. and Dornbusch, C. 28, 29
Virchow, Fabian 51–52n11, 52n21, 53n31, 55n70
Virtanen, Simo V. 11n5
Vlaams Belang in Belgium 31, 32
Vlaams Blok in Belgium 2, 62, 64–65, 72–73, 137
Vlaams Nationaal Verbond (VNV, National Flemish League) 65, 73, 83n5
Vohryzek-Bolden, M., Olson-Raymer, G. and Whamond, J. 144
Voigt, Udo 13, 18, 37, 38, 39–41, 47
Volkmann, Hans-Erich 53n39
Volksgemeinschaft (community of the people) 14, 39–40, 44, 48, 51–52n11, 51n3, 52n22, 53n34, 53n41, 86
Volksunie (VU, People's Union) in Belgium 65, 83n6
Vollers, Maryanne 146
von Brunn, James 156
von Mering, Sabine xii–xiii, 1–12, 50n1
Voorpost (Netherlands) 73, 78, 79, 80
Vrij Nederland 71

Waco, Texas 153–54, 156
Wagner, B. and Borstel, D. 28
Wallace, George 133

Walter, Jess 154
Weaver, Randy 153–54
Wehrsportgruppe Hoffmann in West Germany 28, 167
Weimar Republic 34, 35, 48, 166
Weinberg, Leonard 148
Weiß, Wioletta 90
welfare altruism, counterpoint of 117–18
welfare chauvinism 107, 109, 110
Die Welt 170n9
Welzk, Stefan 13
White Aryan Resistance (WAR) 145
White Patriots Party 151
White Power 94
Wiking-Jugend (WJ) in Germany 31
Wilders, Geert 5, 6, 11n11, 82n2, 167–68, 170n4
Wilkinson, Steven 114
Williams, Michelle Hale 11n8
Willig, Angelika 53n33
Winkler, Jürgen R. 86
Wolf, Joachim 90
women as partners in right-wing extremism 12n16
Work-Family-Fatherland slogan (NPD) 37
World Church of the Creator (WCOTC) 94, 146
Wright, Stuart 144, 145, 150, 151, 153

xenophobia 44, 61, 85, 86, 89, 90, 91, 92–93, 101–2, 135

Young Socialist Alliance in US 134
youth cultures, sub-cultures and right-wing extremism 25–26

Zeman, Václav 120n8
Zentralrat der Juden in Deutschland (Central Council of the Jews in Germany) 168
Zeskind, Leonard 147
Zeuner, B. *et al.* 55n71
Zimmer, K. and van Praagh, F. 93, 94
ZOG ("Zionist occupied government") 15, 16, 17, 19, 149
Zuquete, Jose Pedro 5, 6
Zweckverbände (organizations with shared goals) 48

Taylor & Francis
eBooks
FOR LIBRARIES

ORDER YOUR FREE 30 DAY INSTITUTIONAL TRIAL TODAY!

Over 23,000 eBook titles in the Humanities, Social Sciences, STM and Law from some of the world's leading imprints.

Choose from a range of subject packages or create your own!

Benefits for you
- Free MARC records
- COUNTER-compliant usage statistics
- Flexible purchase and pricing options

Benefits for your user
- Off-site, anytime access via Athens or referring URL
- Print or copy pages or chapters
- Full content search
- Bookmark, highlight and annotate text
- Access to thousands of pages of quality research at the click of a button

For more information, pricing enquiries or to order a free trial, contact your local online sales team.

UK and Rest of World: online.sales@tandf.co.uk
US, Canada and Latin America:
e-reference@taylorandfrancis.com

www.ebooksubscriptions.com

ALPSP Award for BEST eBOOK PUBLISHER 2009 Finalist

Taylor & Francis eBooks
Taylor & Francis Group

A flexible and dynamic resource for teaching, learning and research.